Lecture Notes in Computer Science 8495

Commenced Publication in 1973
Founding and Former Series Editors:
Gerhard Goos, Juris Hartmanis, and Jan van L

Lecture Notes in Computer Science

José Francisco Martínez-Trinidad
Jesús Ariel Carrasco-Ochoa
José Arturo Olvera-López
Joaquín Salas-Rodríguez
Ching Y. Suen (Eds.)

Pattern Recognition

6th Mexican Conference, MCPR 2014
Cancun, Mexico, June 25-28, 2014
Proceedings

 Springer

Volume Editors

José Francisco Martínez-Trinidad
Jesús Ariel Carrasco-Ochoa
National Institute of Astrophysics, Optics and Electronics (INAOE)
Sta. Maria Tonantzintla, Mexico
E-mail: {fmartine; ariel}@inaoep.mx

José Arturo Olvera-López
Autonomous University of Puebla (BUAP)
Puebla, Mexico
E-mail: aolvera@solarium.cs.buap.mx

Joaquín Salas-Rodríguez
Instituto Politécnico Nacional (IPN)
Querétaro, Mexico
E-mail: jsalasr@ipn.mx

Ching Y. Suen
Concordia University
Montreal, QC, Canada
E-mail: parmidir@encs.concordia.ca

ISSN 0302-9743   e-ISSN 1611-3349
ISBN 978-3-319-07490-0   e-ISBN 978-3-319-07491-7
DOI 10.1007/978-3-319-07491-7
Springer Cham Heidelberg New York Dordrecht London

Library of Congress Control Number: 2014939232

LNCS Sublibrary: SL 6 – Image Processing, Computer Vision, Pattern Recognition, and Graphics

Typesetting: Camera-ready by author, data conversion by Scientific Publishing Services, Chennai, India

Printed on acid-free paper

Springer is part of Springer Science+Business Media (www.springer.com)

Preface

The 2014 Mexican Conference on Pattern Recognition (MCPR 2014) was the sixth MCPR conference jointly organized by the Computer Science Department of the National Institute for Astrophysics Optics and Electronics (INAOE) of Mexico and the Autonomous University of Puebla, under the auspices of the Mexican Association for Computer Vision, Neurocomputing, and Robotics (MACVNR), which is a member society of the International Association for Pattern Recognition (IAPR) This year, MCPR was held in Cancun, Mexico, during June 25-28, 2014.

As its name suggests, the conference attracts Mexican researchers and the broader international community in the area of pattern recognition. MCPR provides a forum for the exchange of scientific results, practice, and recently acquired knowledge, and also promotes cooperation among research groups in pattern recognition and related areas in Mexico and the rest of the world.

A total of 68 manuscripts, from 19 countries were received, resulting in 39 accepted papers. Each of these submissions was strictly peer-reviewed by at least two reviewers of the Program Committee, which consisted of 193 outstanding researchers, all of whom are specialists of pattern recognition.

The technical program of the conference included lectures of the following distinguished keynote speakers: Professor Ching Y. Suen, Centre for Pattern Recognition and Machine Intelligence, Concordia University, Canada; Professor Carlo Tomasi, Department of Computer Science, Duke University, USA; and Professor Fazel Famili, School of Electrical Engineering and Computer Science, University of Ottawa, Canada. They also presented enlightening tutorials during the conference. To all of them, we express our sincere gratitude for these presentations.

The selection of papers was extremely rigorous in order to maintain the high quality of the conference. We would like to thank the members of the Program Committee for their hard work in the reviewing process. This process is essential to the creation of a conference of high standard.We are also grateful to all of the authors who submitted papers to the conference, MCPR would not exist without their contributions.

For this edition of MCPR, the authors of accepted papers were invited to submit expanded versions of their papers for possible publication in a special issue titled "Advances in Pattern Recognition Methodologies and Applications" that will be published in Elsevier´s Neurocomputing.

Finally, our thanks go to IAPR (International Association for Pattern Recognition), for sponsoring one IAPR invited speaker at MCPR 2014, and also to the National Council of Science and Technology (CONACYT) and the Secretariat of Public Education (SEP) of Mexico for providing a key support to this event.

The next edition of MCPR will be held in the Center for Computing Research of the Nathional Politechique Institute of Mexico in 2015.

June 2014

José Francisco Martínez-Trinidad
Jesús Ariel Carrasco-Ochoa
José Arturo Olvera-López
Joaquín Salas-Rodríguez
Ching Y. Suen

Organization

MCPR 2014 was sponsored by the Computer Science Department of the National Institute of Astrophysics, Optics and Electronics (INAOE) and the Autonomous University of Puebla, Mexico.

General Conference Co-chairs

Ching Y. Suen	Centre for Pattern Recognition and Machine Intelligence, Concordia University, Montreal, Canada
José Francisco Martínez-Trinidad	Computer Science Department, National Institute of Astrophysics, Optics and Electronics (INAOE), Mexico
Jesús Ariel Carrasco-Ochoa	Computer Science Department, National Institute of Astrophysics, Optics and Electronics (INAOE), Mexico
José Arturo Olvera-López	Autonomous University of Puebla (BUAP), Mexico
Joaquín Salas-Rodríguez	Research Center on Applied Science and Advanced Technology (CICATA) of National Polytechnic Institute (IPN) of Mexico, Mexico

Local Arrangement Committee

Cerón Benítez Gorgonio	López Lucio Gabriela
Cervantes Cuahuey Brenda Alicia	Meza Tlalpan Carmen

Scientific Committee

Asano, A.	Kansai University, Japan
Ayala-Raggi, S.	BUAP, Mexico
Batyrshin, I.	Mexican Petroleum Institute, Mexico
Benedi, J.M.	Universidad Politécnica de Valencia, Spain
Bigun, J.	Halmstad University, Sweden
Borges, D.L.	Universidade de Brasília, Brazil

Chang-Fernández, L.	CENATAV, Cuba
Chen, Chia-Yen	National University of Kaohsiung, Taiwan
Chollet, G.	ENST, France
Dickinson, S.	University of Toronto, Canada
Escalante-Balderas, H.J.	INAOE, Mexico
Facon, J.	Pontifícia Universidade Católica do Paraná, Brazil
Ferri, F.J.	Universitat de Valencia, Spain
Gatica, D.	Idiap Research Institute, Switzerland
Gelbukh, A.	CIC-IPN, Mexico
Goldfarb, L.	University of New Brunswick, Canada
Gomez-Gil, M.P.	INAOE, Mexico
González, J.	Universitat Autònoma de Barcelona, Spain
González-Barbosa, J.J.	CICATA-IPN, Mexico
González-Bernal, J.A.	INAOE, Mexico
Graña, M.	University of the Basque Country, Spain
Grau, A.	Universitat Politécnica de Catalunya, Spain
Heutte, L.	Université de Rouen, France
Igual, L.	University of Barcelona, Spain
Jiang, X.	University of Munter, Germany
Kampel, M.	Vienna University of Technology, Austria
Klette, R.	University of Auckland, New Zealand
Kober, V.	CICESE, Mexico
Koster, W.	Universiteit Leiden, The Netherlands
Laurendeau, D.	Université Laval, Canada
Lazo-Cortés, M.S.	Universidad de las Ciencias Informaticas, Cuba
Lopez-de-Ipiña-Peña, M.K.	Universidad del País Vasco, Spain
Lorenzo-Ginori, J.V.	Universidad Central de Las Villas, Cuba
Mascarenhas, N.D.	University of São Paulo, Brazil
Mayol-Cuevas, W.	University of Bristol, UK
Medina, M.A.	INAOE, Mexico
Menezes, P.	University of Coimbra-Polo II, Brazil
Mihailidis, A.	University of Toronto, Canada
Montes Y Gómez, M.	INAOE, Mexico
Mora, M.	Catholic University of Maule, Chile
Morales, E.	INAOE, Mexico
Morales-Reyes, A.	INAOE, Mexico
Nolazco, J.A.	ITESM-Monterrey, Mexico
Pardo, A.	Universidad Católica del Uruguay, Uruguay
Pina, P.	Instituto Superior Técnico, Portugal
Pinho, A.	University of Aveiro, Portugal
Pinto, J.	Instituto Superior Técnico, Portugal
Pistori, H.	Dom Bosco Catholic University, Brazil

Raposo-Sanchez, J.M.	Instituto Superior Técnico, Portugal
Real, P.	University of Seville, Spain
Reyes-García, C.A.	INAOE, Mexico
Roman-Rangel, E.F.	University of Geneva, Switzerland
Ross, A.	West Virginia University, USA
Rueda, L.	University of Windsor, Canada
Ruiz-Shulcloper, J.	CENATAV, Cuba
Joaquín Salas	CICATA-IPN, Mexico
Sanchez-Cortes, D.	Idiap Research Institute, Switzerland
Sanniti di Baja, G.	Istituto di Cibernetica, CNR, Italy
Sansone, C.	Università di Napoli, Italy
Santana, R.	Universidad Politécnica de Madrid, Spain
Sappa, A.	Universitat Autònoma de Barcelona, Spain
Schizas, C.	University of Cyprus, Cyprus
Sossa-Azuela, J.H.	CIC-IPN, Mexico
Sousa-Santos, B.	Universidade de Aveiro, Portugal
Spyridonos, P.	University of Loannina, Grece
Stathaki, T.	Imperial College London, UK
Sucar, L.E.	INAOE, Mexico
Valev, V.	University of North Florida, USA
Vitria, J.	University of Barcelona, Spain
Zagoruiko, N.G.	Russian Academy of Sciences, Russia
Zhi-Hua, Z.	Nanjing University, China

Additional Referees

Da, Q.	Nunes Gonçalves, W.
Dias, P.	Padovani De Souza, K.
Huang, S.J.	Tao, J.
Lang, E.	Wang, Z.
Madeira, J.	Xu, Z.

Sponsoring Institutions

National Institute of Astrophysics, Optics and Electronics (INAOE)
Mexican Association for Computer Vision, Neurocomputing and Robotics (MACVNR)
International Association for Pattern Recognition (IAPR)
National Council of Science and Technology of Mexico (CONACYT)
Secretariat of Public Education of Mexico (SEP)

Table of Contents

Pattern Recognition and Artificial Intelligence

Computer Vision

Image Processing and Analysis

Animal Biometric Recognition

Applications of Pattern Recognition

Reduced Data Based Improved MEB/L2-SVM Equivalence

Lachachi Nour-Eddine and Adla Abdelkader

Computer Science Department, Oran University, Algeria
{Lach_Nour,AekAdla}@Yahoo.fr

Abstract. As a powerful tool in machine learning, support vector machine (SVM) suffers from expensive computational cost in the training phase due to the large number of original training samples. In addition, Minimal Enclosing Ball (MEB) has a limitation with a large dataset, and the training computational increases as data size becomes large. This paper presents an improved two approaches based SVMs reduced to Minimal Enclosing Ball (MEB) problems. These approaches find the concentric balls with minimum volume of data description to reduce the chance of accepting abnormal data that contain most of the training samples. Our study is experimented on speech information to eliminate all noise data and reducing time training. Numerical experiments on some real-world datasets verify the usefulness of our approaches for data mining.

Keywords: Support Vector Machines (SVMs), Minimal Enclosing Ball (MEB), Core-set.

1   Introduction

The theory of Support Vector Machines was introduced by Vapnik and was developed from the theory of Structural Risk Minimization [1]. SVMs learn the boundary regions between samples belonging to two classes by mapping the input samples into a high dimensional space, and seeking a separating hyperplane in this space. The separating hyperplane is chosen in such a way as to maximize its distance from the closest training samples (a quantity referred to as the margin).

Training a SVM involves solving a constrained quadratic programming problem, which requires large memory and enormous amounts of training time for large-scale problems. Goal is to find a separation hyperplane which implicates a $N \times N$ matrix density, where N is the number of points in the dataset. This needs more computational time and memory for large datasets, so the training complexity of SVM is highly dependent on the size of a dataset. Then, we partition the data in several data sources and we train them by Support Vector Machines (SVMs) using Fuzzy C-Mean Clustering Algorithm.

Here, we improve a technique cited in [2]. The improvement has based from an entropy algorithm that consider both Lagrangian duality and the Jaynes' maximum

J.F. Martínez-Trinidad et al. (Eds.): MCPR 2014, LNCS 8495, pp. 1–10, 2014.

entropy principle. The idea is to use information entropy and maximum entropy formalism in the solution of nonlinear programming problems [3].

Computation of such SVMs lead to find a Core-Set for the image of the data in a feature space. Thus, an alternative method is presented based on an equivalence between SVMs and Minimal Enclosing Ball (MEB) problems from which important improvements on training efficiency has been reported [4,5] for large-scale datasets. The study focus on multi-class problems where two methods explored to extend binary SVMs to the multi-category setting, which preserve the equivalence between the model and MEBs.

Algorithms to compute SVMs based on the MEB equivalence are based on the greedy computation of a core-set, a typically small subset of the data which provides the same MEB as the full dataset. Then, we formulate new multiclass SVM problem using core-sets for reduce large datasets which can be considered optimally matched to the input demands of different background architectures of speaker verification or Language Identification systems. The core idea of these two approaches cited above is to adopt multiclass SVMs formulation and Minimal Enclosing Ball to reduce dataset without influence data noise.

Along the whole paper, we define the variables as follows:

— f: Index of feature; F: number of features.
— n: Index of feature dimension; N: dimensionality of feature.
— l: Index of Classe; L: number of Classes.

2   L2-Support Vector Machines (L2-SVMs)

In [2] it is shown that for a binary classification, the L2-SVM build a separating hyperplane $f(z)$ by solving the following quadratic program:

$$
\min_{w,b,\rho,\xi} \frac{1}{2}\left(\|w\|^2 + b^2 + C\sum_{f=1}^{F}\xi_t^2\right) - \rho \\
st: y_f f(z_f) \geq \rho - \xi_f \quad f = 1,\dots,F
\tag{1}
$$

And for a given training task having L classes, these label vectors are chosen out of the definite set of vectors $\{y_1, y_2, \dots, y_F\}$. Hence, we can define the primal for the learning problem for the L2-SVM Multi-class classification as

$$
\min_{w,b,\rho,\xi} \frac{1}{2}\left(\|W\|^2 + \|b\|^2 + C\sum_{f=1}^{F}\xi_f^2\right) - \rho \\
st: y_f^T\left(W^T z_f + b\right) \geq \rho - \xi_f^2 \geq 0 \quad f = 1,\dots,F
\tag{2}
$$

where $z_f = \phi(x_f)$

After introducing Lagrange multipliers, for the both problem, we conduct to solve

$$
\min_{\alpha} \sum_{f=1}^{F}\sum_{f'}^{F} \alpha_f \alpha_{f'} K_{ff'} \\
st: \alpha_f \geq 0, \ \sum_{f=1}^{F}\alpha_f = 1
\tag{3}
$$

where $K_{ff'} = y_f y_{f'} k(x_f, x_{f'}) + y_f y_{f'} + \frac{\delta_{ff'}}{c}$ for binary classification and $K_{ff'} = y_f^T y_{f'} k(x_f, x_{f'}) + y_f^T y_{f'} + \frac{\delta_{ff'}}{c}$ for multi-class classification. $\delta_{ff'}$ is the Kronecker delta function $(\delta_{ff'} = 1 \; if \; f = f' \; otherwise \; 0)$ and $k(x_f, x_{f'})$ implements the dot-product $z_f^T z_{f'}$.

We note that there are two types of extensions to build Multi-Class SVMs [6,7]. The first is One-Versus-One approach (OVO) that use several binary classifiers, separately trained and joined into a multi-category decision function. The second is One-Versus-All approach (OVA), where a different binary SVM is used to separate each class from the All.

3   Minimal Enclosing Balls (MEB)

MEB has originally introduced to estimate the support of a high dimensional distribution [8]. Suppose we have a set of F independent and identically distributed observations $\{x_f\}_{f=1}^F$ from an unknown distribution function P. The MEB algorithm seeks to find a minimal region R, which surrounds almost all the data points. This approximated region lead to enclose with high probability the test examples presuming that they are drawn from the same probability distribution P.

Denoting training data set as $S = \{\tilde{z}_f = \phi(x_f)\}_{f=1}^F$. Let $\tilde{Z}$ a space equipped with a dot product $\tilde{z}_f^T \tilde{z}_{f'}$ that corresponding to norm $\|\tilde{z}\|^2 = \tilde{z}^T \tilde{z}$. We define the ball $\mathcal{B}(c, R)$ of center $c \in \tilde{Z}$ and radius R in $\mathbb{R}$ as the subset of points $\tilde{z} \in \tilde{Z}$ for which $\|\tilde{z} - c\|^2 \leq R^2$. The minimal-enclosing ball of a set of points $S = \{\tilde{z}_f\}_{f=1}^F$ in $\tilde{Z}$ is in turn the ball $\mathcal{B}^*(S, c^*, R^*)$ of smallest radius that contains S, that is, the solution to the following optimization problem.

$$\min_{R,c} R^2$$
$$st: \|\tilde{z} - c\|^2 \leq R^2 \quad \forall \tilde{z} \in S \tag{4}$$

After introducing Lagrange multipliers, we obtain from the optimality conditions the following dual problem

$$\min_\alpha \sum_{f=1}^T \sum_{f'=1}^F \alpha_f \alpha_{f'} \tilde{z}_f^T \tilde{z}_{f'} - \sum_{f=1}^F \alpha_f \tilde{z}_f^T \tilde{z}_f$$
$$st: \alpha_f \geq 0, \; \sum_{f=1}^F \alpha_f = 1 \tag{5}$$

if we consider that $\sum_{f=1}^F \alpha_f \tilde{z}_f^T \tilde{z}_f = \kappa$ a, we can drop it from the dual objective in Eq. (1), we obtain a simpler QP problem

$$\min_\alpha \sum_{f=1}^F \sum_{f'=1}^F \alpha_f \alpha_{f'} \tilde{z}_f^T \tilde{z}_{f'} = \min_\alpha \sum_{f=1}^F \sum_{f'=1}^F \alpha_f \alpha_{f'} \tilde{K}_{ff'}$$
$$st: \alpha_f \geq 0, \; \sum_{f=1}^F \alpha_f = 1 \tag{6}$$

In [9] it is shown that the primal variables c and R can be recovered from the optimal α as $c = \sum_{f=1}^{F} \alpha_f \tilde{z}_f$, $R = \sqrt{\sum_{f=1}^{F} \sum_{f'=1}^{F} \alpha_f \alpha_{f'} \tilde{z}_f^T \tilde{z}_{f'}}$ and the main appeal of the L2-SVM implementation Eq. (3) is that it supports a convenient equivalence to a Minimal Enclosing Ball (MEB) problem Eq. (6) when the kernel used in the SVM is normalized, that is $k(x,x) = \kappa \; \forall \, x \in X$, where κ is a constant. The advantage of this equivalence is that the Bǎdoiu and Clarkson algorithm [10] can efficiently approximate the solution of a MEB problem with any degree of accuracy.

Core-Set

Bǎdoiu and Clarkson [10] define the Core-Set of S as a set $C_S \subset S$ if the Minimal Enclosing Ball computed over C_S is equivalent to the Minimal Enclosing Ball considering all the points in S. A ball $\mathcal{B}(c,R)$ is said an ϵ-approximation to the Minimal Enclosing Ball $\mathcal{B}^*(S, c^*, R^*)$ of S if $R \leq R^*$ and it contains S up to precision ϵ, that is $S \subset \mathcal{B}(c, (1 + \epsilon)R)$. Consequently, a set $C_{S,\epsilon}$ is called a ϵ-core-set if the Minimal Enclosing Ball of $C_{S,\epsilon}$ is a ϵ-approximation to $\mathcal{B}^*(S, c^*, R^*)$.

In [10] the most usual version of the algorithm is presented.

4   Improved MEB/L2-SVM Equivalence Algorithm

Calculating the Lagrange multipliers leads to a simpler QP problem Eq. (3) or Eq. (6) with non-negative constraints and one normality condition, which is one of the difficulties in the original MEB algorithm. The improved MEB algorithm present a simple and efficient algorithm, which takes advantage of the features of problem Eq. (6). We derive an entropy-based algorithm for the considered problem by means of Lagrangian duality and the Jaynes' maximum entropy principle. The idea is to use the information entropy and maximum entropy formalism in the solution of nonlinear programming problems [3].

Consider that the MEB QP problem Eq. (6) written as the following form:

$$\min_\alpha L(\alpha) = \sum_{f=1}^{F} \sum_{f'=1}^{F} \alpha_f \alpha_{f'} \widetilde{K}_{ff'}$$
$$st: \alpha_{f'} \geq 0, \; \sum_{f'=1}^{F} \alpha_{f'} = 1 \text{ and } \tilde{z}_f^T \tilde{z}_{f'} = \widetilde{K}_{ff'} \tag{7}$$

From the constraints of optimization problem Eq. (7), we know that the dual variables go into the range $[0, 1]$ and sum to one, so they meet the definition of probability. Our approach to the solution of Eq. (7) based on a probabilistic interpretation show that the center of the ball represents the mean vector of the images of all data points and the Lagrange multiplier α_f represents the probability that x_f is a support vector SV. Hence, we may consider searching for the MEB as a procedure of probability assignments, which should follow the Jaynes' maximum entropy principle [3]. Thus instead of QP problem Eq. (7), we construct a composite minimization problem:

$$\min L_{\mathcal{P}}(\alpha) = L(\alpha) + H(\alpha)/\mathcal{P}$$
$$st: \alpha_{f'} \geq 0, \ \Sigma_{f'=1}^{F} \alpha_{f'} = 1 \tag{8}$$

Where $\mathcal{P}$ is a non-negative parameter, and

$$H(\alpha) = \Sigma_{f'=1}^{F} \alpha_{f'} \ln \alpha_{f'} \tag{9}$$

From information theory perspectives, $H(\alpha)$ represents an information entropy of the multipliers $\alpha_{f'}$. The additional term $H(\alpha)/\mathcal{P}$ is commensurate with the application of an extra criterion of minimizing the multipliers entropy to the original MEB QP problem Eq. (7). It is intuitively obvious that the entropy term on the solution of Eq. (8) will diminish as p approaches infinity.

To solve this problem we introduce the Lagrangian

$$L_{\mathcal{P}}(\alpha, \beta) = L(\alpha) + \frac{H(\alpha)}{\mathcal{P}} + \beta\left(\Sigma_{f'=1}^{F} \alpha_{f'} - 1\right) \tag{10}$$

where β is a Lagrange multiplier. Setting to zero the derivative of $L_{\mathcal{P}}(\alpha, \beta)$ with respect to α and β, respectively, leads to

$$\frac{\partial L}{\partial \alpha_{f'}} - \frac{1}{\mathcal{P}}(1 + \ln \alpha_{f'}) + \beta = 0 \tag{11}$$

and

$$\Sigma_{f'=1}^{F} \alpha_{f'} = 1 \tag{12}$$

Solving Eq. (11) for $\alpha_{f'}$, $f' = 1,2, \dots, F$

$$\alpha_{f'} = e^{\left(\mathcal{P}\left(\frac{\partial L}{\partial \alpha_{f'}} + \beta\right) - 1\right)} \tag{13}$$

Substituting α from Eq. (13) into Eq. (12), we obtain

$$e^{(\mathcal{P}\beta - 1)} \Sigma_{f'=1}^{F} e^{\left(\mathcal{P}\frac{\partial L}{\partial \alpha_{f'}}\right)} = 1 \tag{14}$$

Between Eq. (13) and Eq. (12), we eliminate the term $e^{(\mathcal{P}\beta - 1)}$ to give

$$\alpha_{f'} = \frac{e^{\left(\mathcal{P}\frac{\partial L}{\partial \alpha_{f'}}\right)}}{\Sigma_{f'=1}^{F} e^{\left(\mathcal{P}\frac{\partial L}{\partial \alpha_{f'}}\right)}} \tag{15}$$

By optimization problem Eq. (7), we have

$$L_{\alpha_{f'}}(\alpha) \equiv \frac{\partial L}{\partial \alpha_{f'}} = 2\Sigma_{f=1}^{F} \alpha_f K_{ff'} \tag{16}$$

Thus, we obtain the iterative formula

$$\alpha_{f'}^{(k+1)} = \frac{e^{\left(\mathcal{P}^{(k)}L_{\alpha_{f'}}(\alpha^{(k)})\right)}}{\Sigma_{f'=1}^{F}\, e^{\left(\mathcal{P}^{(k)}L_{\alpha_{f'}}(\alpha^{(k)})\right)}} \tag{17}$$

Based on formulas Eq(s) (8) – (11), we obtain the entropy-based iterative algorithm for the solution of optimization problem Eq. (7) as follows:

Algorithm 1 Entropy-based iterative algorithm

1: Let $\mathcal{P}^{(0)} = 0$; from Eq. (15) we get $\alpha_{f'}^{(0)} = 1/F$;
$f' = 1,2,...,F$;
let $\Delta \mathcal{P} \in (0,+\infty)$ and set $k = 0$

2: Based on formulas Eq. (16) and Eq. (17),
compute $\alpha_{f'}^{(k+1)}$, $f' = 1,2,...,F$; let $\mathcal{P}^{(k+1)} = \mathcal{P}^{(k)} + \Delta \mathcal{P}$

3: if Stop criteria satisfied, the stop; otherwise,
we set $k = k + 1$, then return to step **2**

In short, we start with rough estimates of Lagrange multipliers, calculate improved estimates by iterative formula Eq. (17), and repeat until some convergence criterion has met.

Here, we note an important deduction that through the improved estimation of Lagrange multipliers, the Bădoiu and Clarkson algorithm [10] is improved.

5   Reduced Data Approaches

The key idea of our method is to cast a L2-SVM as a MEB problem reduced in a Core-Set by using a feature space $\tilde{Z} = \phi(X)$ where the training examples are embedded via a mapping ϕ. Hence, we first formulate an algorithm to compute the MEB of the images $\tilde{S}$ of S in $\tilde{Z}$ when S is decomposed in a collection of subsets S_p. Then we will instantiate the solution for classifiers supporting the reduction to MEB problems. The algorithm is based on the idea of computing Core-Sets C_p for each set $\tilde{S}_p = \phi(S_p)$ and taking its union $C = \cup_p C_p$ as an approximation to a Core-Set for $\tilde{S} = \cup_p S_p$. In a first step the algorithm extracts a Core-Set for each subset S_p. In the second step, the MEB of the union of the Core-Sets is computed.

The decomposition of S in a collection of subsets S_p by Fuzzy C-Means (FCM) method clustering which allows one piece of data to belong to two or more clusters [11,12].

From the section 2 the kernel $\tilde{k}(x_f, x_{f'}) = y_f y_{f'} k(x_f, x_{f'}) + y_f y_{f'} + \frac{\delta_{ff'}}{c}$ for the binary case (OVO approach) and the kernel $\tilde{k}(x_f, x_{f'}) = y_f^T y_{f'} k(x_f, x_{f'}) + y_f^T y_{f'} + \frac{\delta_{ff'}}{c}$ in the multi-category case (OVA approach). In addition, for the both binary (OVO) and multi-category (OVA) Multi-Class case, we depict algorithm 2 and algorithm 3 respectively.

Algorithm 2 Computation of the MEB using OVO approach

1: **for** Each subset S_p , $p = 1, ..., P$ **do**
2:    **for** Each Class $l = 1, ..., L - 1$ **do**
3:      **for** Each Class $l' = l + 1, ..., L$ **do**
4:        Let $S_p^{ll'}$ the subset of S_p corresponding to class l and l'.
5:        Label $S_p^{ll'}$ using the standard binary codes $+1$ and -1 for class l and l' respectively
6:        Compute a core-set $C_p^{ll'}$ of $S_p^{ll'}$ [10] using the Kernel $\tilde{k}(x_f, x_{f'}) = y_f y_{f'} k(x_f, x_{f'}) + y_f y_{f'} + \frac{\delta_{ff'}}{C}$
7:      **end for**
8:    **end for**
9:    Take the union of the core-set inferred for each pair of classes $C_p = C_p^{ll'} \cup ... \cup C_p^{ll'}$
10: **end for**
11: Join core-set $C_S = C_1 \cup ... \cup C_P$.
12: Compute the minimal enclosing ball of C_S using the same kernel $\tilde{k}$

Algorithm 3 Computation of the MEB using OVA approach

1: **for** Each subset S_p , $p = 1, ..., P$ **do**
2:    Label each example $x_f \in S_p$ with the code y_{fl} assigned to the class of x_f and let y_f such label
3:    Compute a core-set C_p of S_p [10] using the kernel
$$\tilde{k}(x_f, x_{f'}) = y_f^T y_{f'} k(x_f, x_{f'}) + y_f^T y_{f'} + \frac{\delta_{ff'}}{C}$$
4: **end for**
5: Join the core-sets $C_S = C_1 \cup ... \cup C_P$.
6: Compute the minimal enclosing ball of C_S using the same kernel $\tilde{k}$

6   Experiments

This section presents the performance of text-independent speaker verification task based on the Gaussian Mixture Model – Universal Background Model (GMM-UBM) system described in [13]. As in [2], we compare the performance of speaker verification system with three UBMs, the first one was created directly from the Speaker Recognition corpus [14], consists of telephone speech. The two last later is the reduced first one from the application of our two algorithms developed above. The kernel used for the two algorithms is the Gaussian Radial Basis Function with a fixed value of σ with 0.50. We have trained a 512-mixture gender-independent from each UBM with diagonal covariance matrices. Speaker GMMs has trained by adapting only the mean vectors from the UBM using a relevance factor r of 16. The experiment based on the improved estimation of Lagrange multipliers cited previously is compared with the result in [2] where we used the same corpus.

The two figures below shows the detection error tradeoff (DET) curves for the three systems. The (A) represent the result issue from our previous study for the same corpus in [2] and (B) represent our experiences for the improved system enounced in this paper. In (A) we see that the system based reduced GMM-UBM2 from One-Versus-All multiclass L2-SVM outperforms the GMM-UBM with an equal-error-rate (EER) of 8.55 %, compared to 10,13 % of the GMM-UBM. The system based reduced GMM-UBM1 from One-Versus-One multiclass L2-SVMs exhibits the best performance with an EER of 7.60 %. On the other hand, in (B), the same system give an improved rate with an equal-error-rate (EER) of 6.15 %, compared to 10.13 % of the GMM-UBM. However, the system based reduced GMM-UBM2 from One-Versus-All L2-SVMs had given an EER of 7.80 %, that is also give a performance from the result issued in [2] for the same approach.

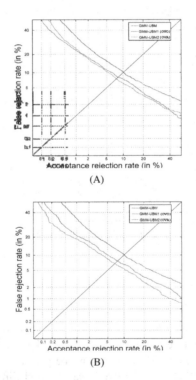

(A)

(B)

Fig. 1. Detection error tradeoff (DET) curves for the speaker verification system using three UBMs

In comparison from the two curves, we note that the best result given is for the system based reduced GMM-UBM1 from One-Versus-One in the order of 1.45 %.

7   Conclusion

In this paper, we proposed two algorithms that compute an approximation to the minimum enclosing ball of a given finite set of vectors based Core-Set for reducing huge dataset. Both algorithms is especially well-suited for large-scale instances of the Minimal Enclosing Ball (MEB) problem and can compute a small core set whose size depends only on the approximation parameter.

We have explored two improved methods based on the computation of Core-Sets to train multi-category SVM models when the set of examples is fragmented. The main contribution has been shown through our experiments, that the improved methods proposed give the best performance with a reproduction of high solution accuracy where the noisy sample in huge data set are eliminated, without complex and costly computation. SVMs based on Core-Sets have shown however important advantages in large-scale applications, which can hence be extended to distributed data-mining problems. A real contribution of this work has been an improved direct implementation of multi-category SVMs based Core-Sets supporting a reduction to a Minimal-Enclosing Ball (MEB) problem. Although the Core-Sets method exhibits always better prediction accuracy used with the OVO scheme, the direct implementation shows a lower complexity and it is better than the previous direct implementation proposed for MEB based SVMs.

References

1. Schölkopf, B., Smola, A.J.: Learning with Kernels: Support Vector Machines, Regularization, Optimization, and Beyond. MIT Press, Cambridge (2001)
2. Nour-Eddine, L., Abdelkader, A.: Reduced universal background model for speech recognition and identification system. In: Carrasco-Ochoa, J.A., Martínez-Trinidad, J.F., Olvera López, J.A., Boyer, K.L. (eds.) MCPR 2012. LNCS, vol. 7329, pp. 303–312. Springer, Heidelberg (2012)
3. Templeman, A.B., Li, X.S.: A maximum entropy approach to constrained nonlinear programming. Engineering Optimization 12, 191–205 (1987)
4. Kocsor, A., Kwork, J., Tsang, I.: Simpler core vector machines with enclosing balls. In: ICML 2007, pp. 911–918. ACM (2007)
5. Cheung, P.M., Kwok, J., Tsang, I.: Core vector machines: Fast SVM training on very large datasets. Journal of Machine Learning Research (6), 363–392 (2005)
6. Nour-Eddine, L., Abdelkader, A.: Multi-class Support Vector Machines Methodology. In: 1er Congrès International sur les Modèles, Optimisation et Sécurité des Systèmes, ICMOSS 2010, Tiaret, Algérie, pp. 325–329 (2010)
7. Hsu, C., Lin, C.: A comparison of methods for multiclass support vector machines. IEEE Transactions on Neural Networks 13(2), 415–425 (2002)
8. Scholkopf, B., Platt, J.C., Shawe-Taylor, J., Smola, A.J., Williamson, R.C.: Estimating the support of a high-dimensional distribution. Neural Computation 13, 1443–1471 (2001)

9. Tsang, I., Kwok, J., Cheung, P.M.: Core vector machines: Fast SVM training on very large data sets. Journal of Machine Learning Research 6, 363–392 (2005)
10. Bădoiu, M., Clarkson, K.L.: Optimal core-sets for balls. Computer Geometry Theory Application 40(1), 14–22 (2008)
11. Dunn, J.C.: A Fuzzy Relative of the ISODATA Process and Its Use in Detecting Compact Well-Separated Clusters. Journal of Cybernetics 3(3), 32–57 (1973)
12. Bezdek, J.C.: Pattern Recognition with Fuzzy Objective Function Algorithms. Plenum Press, New York (1981)
13. Alkanhal, M., Alghamdi, M., Muzaffar, Z.: Speaker Verification based on Saudi Acceted Arabic Database. In: 9th International Symposium on Signal Processing and its Applications, ISSPA 2007, Sharjah, United Arab Emirate, pp. 1–4 (February 2007)
14. Speaker corpus in,
    http://www.ll.mit.edu/mission/communication/ist/corpora/
    SpeechCorpora.html

Weighted Maximum Variance Dimensionality Reduction

Turki Turki[1,2] and Usman Roshan[2]

[1] Computer Science Department, King Abdulaziz University
P.O. Box 80221, Jeddah 21589, Saudi Arabia
tturki@kau.edu.sa
[2] Department of Computer Science, New Jersey Institute of Technology
University Heights, Newark, NJ 07102
usman@cs.njit.edu

Abstract. Dimensionality reduction procedures such as principal component analysis and the maximum margin criterion discriminant are special cases of a weighted maximum variance (WMV) approach. We present a simple two parameter version of WMV that we call 2P-WMV. We study the classification error given by the 1-nearest neighbor algorithm on features extracted by our and other dimensionality reduction methods on several real datasets. Our results show that our method yields the lowest average error across the datasets with statistical significance.

Keywords: dimensionality reduction, principal component analysis, maximum margin criterion.

1 Introduction

The problem of dimensionality reduction arises in many data mining and machine learning tasks. Among many such algorithms the principal component analysis [1] (PCA) is a very popular choice. PCA seeks a vector $w \in R^d$ that solves

$$\arg\max_{w} \frac{1}{2n} \sum_{i,j} \frac{1}{n} (w^T(x_i - x_j))^2 \qquad (1)$$

where $x_i \in R^d$ for $i = 0...n - 1$. In other words it maximizes the variance of the projected data without taking class labels into consideration. The maximum margin criterion (MMC) [2] is a supervised dimensionality reduction method that overcomes limitations of the Fisher linear discriminant and has also shown to achieve higher classification accuracy [2]. It is given by w that maximizes $trace(w^T(S_b - S_w)w)$ subject to $w^T w = I$. Using Lagrange multipliers one can show that w is given by the largest eigenvectors of $S_b - S_w$.

In this paper we consider a general version of Equation 1 that we call the maximum weighted variance given by

$$\arg\max_{w} \frac{1}{2n} \sum_{i,j} C_{ij}(w^T(x_i - x_j))^2 \qquad (2)$$

J.F. Martínez-Trinidad et al. (Eds.): MCPR 2014, LNCS 8495, pp. 11–20, 2014.
© Springer International Publishing Switzerland 2014

The above equation gives us both PCA and MMC for specific settings of C_{ij} as we show below. We consider a two parameter approach by setting $C_{ij} = \alpha < 0$ if x_i and x_j have the same class label and $C_{ij} = \beta > 0$ otherwise. In other words we simultaneously minimize the distance between projected pairwise points in the same class and maximize the same distance for points in different classes. For a given dataset we obtain α and β by 1-nearest neighbor cross-validation.

The straightforward eigendecomposition solution requires at least quadratic space in the dimensions of x_i. With graph Laplacians we can employ a singular value decomposition (SVD) approach to avoid this problem (as originally given in [3]) and thus apply it to high dimensional data. Below we describe our approach in detail followed by experimental results.

2   Methods

Suppose we are given the vectors $x_i \in R^d$ for $i = 0...n - 1$ and a real matrix $C \in R^{n \times n}$. Let X be the matrix containing x_i as its columns (ordered x_0 through x_{n-1}). Now consider the optimization problem

$$\arg\max_w \frac{1}{2n} \sum_{i,j} C_{ij}(w^T(x_i - x_j))^2 \tag{3}$$

where $w \in R^d$ and C_{ij} is the entry in C corresponding to the ith row and j^{th} column. This is in fact a more general representation of PCA and MMC.

2.1   Principal Component Analysis

To obtain PCA we set $C_{ij} = \frac{1}{n}$ and Equation 3 becomes (without the $\arg\max$ part)

$$\frac{1}{2n} \sum_{i,j} \frac{1}{n}(w^T(x_i - x_j))^2 =$$

$$\frac{1}{2n} \sum_{i,j} \frac{1}{n} w^T(x_i - x_j)(x_i - x_j)^T w =$$

$$\frac{1}{2n} \sum_{i,j} \frac{1}{n} w^T(x_i x_i^T - x_i x_j^T - x_j x_i^T + x_j x_j^T)w =$$

$$\frac{1}{2n} w^T \frac{1}{n}(\sum_{i,j}(x_i x_i^T - x_i x_j^T - x_j x_i^T + x_j x_j^T))w =$$

$$\frac{1}{2n} w^T \frac{1}{n}(2 \sum_{i,j} x_i x_i^T - 2 \sum_{i,j} x_i x_j^T)w =$$

$$\frac{1}{2n} w^T \frac{1}{n}(2n \sum_i x_i x_i^T - 2n^2 m m^T)w =$$

$$\frac{1}{n} w^T(\sum_i x_i x_i^T - n m m^T)w =$$

$$w^T(\frac{1}{n} \sum_i (x_i - m)(x_i - m)^T)w =$$

$$w^T S_t w$$

where $S_t = \frac{1}{n}\sum_i (x_i - m)(x_i - m)^T$ and is called the total scatter matrix. Inserting the optimization criterion into the last step yields $\arg\max_w w^T S_t w$ which is exactly the PCA optmization criterion [1].

2.2 Maximum Margin Discriminant

To obtain the MMC discriminant (a supervised learning method) first recall that the MMC optimization criterion is defined as $\arg\max_w w^T(S_b - S_w)w$ where S_b is the between-class scatter matrix and S_w is the within-class scatter matrix [2]. Since $S_b - S_w = S_t - 2S_w$ where S_t is the total scatter matrix, this can be written as $\arg\max_w w^T(S_t - 2S_w)w$ [4]. In practice though we would use the weighted maximum margin discriminant which is given by $\arg\max_w w^T(S_b - \alpha S_w)w$ [5]. We now set the weights C_{ij} to obtain this discriminant.

Suppose class labels $y_i \in \{+1, -1\}$ are provided for each x_i and n_k is the size of class k. Define C_{ij} to be $\frac{1}{n}$ if i and j have different class labels and $\frac{1}{n} - 2\frac{1}{n_k}$ if i and j have the same class labels. We can then write Equation 3 as

$$\arg\max_w \frac{1}{2n}\left(\sum_{i,j} G_{ij}(w^T(x_i - x_j))^2 - \sum_{i,j} 2L_{ij}(w^T(x_i - x_j))^2\right) \qquad (4)$$

where $G_{ij} = \frac{1}{n}$ for all i and j and $L_{ij} = \frac{1}{n_k}$ if i and j have class labels k and 0 otherwise. By substituting the values of G_{ij} and L_{ij} into Equation 4 and some symbolic manipulation we obtain the MMC discriminant

$$\frac{1}{2n}\sum_{i,j} w^T(G_{ij}(x_i - x_j)(x_i - x_j) - 2L_{ij}(x_i - x_j)(x_i - x_j)^T)w =$$

$$\frac{1}{2n}(\sum_{i,j}\frac{1}{n}w^T(x_i - x_j)(x_i - x_j)^T w - 2\sum_{k=1}^c \sum_{cl(x_j)=k, cl(x_i)=k}\frac{1}{n_k}w^T(x_i - x_j)(x_i - x_j)^T w) =$$

$$\frac{1}{2n}(2\sum_i^n w^T(x_i - m)(x_i - m)w - 2\sum_{k=1}^c \frac{1}{n_k}\sum_{cl(x_j)=k, cl(x_i)=k} w^T(x_i x_i^T - x_i x_j^T - x_j x_i^T + x_j x_j^T)w) =$$

$$\frac{1}{2n}(2\sum_i^n w^T(x_i - m)(x_i - m)w - 2\sum_{k=1}^c \frac{1}{n_k}\sum_{cl(x_j)=k, cl(x_i)=k} w^T(2x_i x_i^T - 2x_i x_j^T)w) =$$

$$\frac{1}{2n}(2\sum_i^n w^T(x_i - m)(x_i - m)w - 2\sum_{k=1}^c \frac{1}{n_k}\sum_{cl(x_i)=k} w^T(2n_k x_i x_i^T - 2n_k^2 m_k m_k^T)w) =$$

$$\frac{1}{n}(\sum_i^n w^T(x_i - m)(x_i - m)w - 2\sum_{k=1}^c \sum_{cl(x_i)=k} w^T(x_i x_i^T - n_k m_k m_k^T)w) =$$

$$\frac{1}{n}(\sum_i^n w^T(x_i - m)(x_i - m)w - 2\sum_{k=1}^c \sum_{cl(x_i)=k} w^T(x_i - m_k)(x_i - m_k)^T)w) =$$

$$w^T(S_t - 2S_w)w$$

where m_k is the mean of points in k and $cl(x)$ returns the class of point x. The last equation in the above steps is just the MMC discriminant.

Equation 3 can be rewritten as $\arg\max_w \frac{1}{n}w^T XLX^T w$ where $L = D - C$ and $D_{ii} = \sum_i C_{ii}$ [6]. The matrix L is called the Laplacian of the weight matrix C. Using Lagrange multipliers one can show that the largest eigenvector of $\frac{1}{n}XLX^T$ (i.e. eigenvector with largest eigenvalue) is the solution to w [6]. Thus, the largest eigenvector is also the solution to PCA and MMC.

2.3   Laplacian Linear Discriminant Analysis

Following the Laplacian framework we can write the MMC discriminant (Equation 4) as $\arg\max_w \frac{1}{n}w^T X(L_g - 2L_l)X^T w$ where L_g is the Laplacian of G and L_l is the Laplacian of L [3,4]. This form of the the maximum margin discriminant is also called Laplacian linear discriminant analysis and has been studied for unsupervised learning [4]. As in PCA and MMC the largest eigenvector of $\frac{1}{n}X(L_g - 2L_l)X^T$ is the solution to the Laplacian discriminant.

Notice that C_{ij} in Equation 3 can take on arbitrary values. With suitable settings we obtained PCA and MMC. How does one select the best values C_{ij} for a particular problem? Our solution is to collapse values of C into two parameters and select their values that minimize error on the training data.

2.4   Two Parameter Weighted Maximum Variance Discriminant

As shown above the MMC discriminant is obtained by setting $G_{ij} = \frac{1}{n}$ for all i and j and $L_{ij} = \frac{1}{n_k}$ if i and j have class labels k and 0 otherwise in Equation 4. We consider a different setting for L below which gives us the two parameter weighted maximum variance discriminant (2P-WMV). We also show that this yields a class-wise unnormalized within-class scatter matrix and a pairwise inter-class scatter matrix.

Define the matrix $G \in R^{n \times n}$ as $G_{ij} = \frac{1}{n}$ for all i and j and $L \in R^{n \times n}$ as

$$L_{ij} = \begin{cases} \alpha & \text{if } y_i = y_j \\ \beta & \text{if } y_i \neq y_j \\ 0 \text{ if } y_i \text{ or } y_j \text{ is undefined} \end{cases}$$

Substituting these values into Equation 4 we obtain

$$\frac{1}{2n}(\sum_{i,j}\frac{1}{n}w^T(x_i-x_j)(x_i-x_j)w$$
$$-2\sum_{cl(x_i)=cl(x_j)}\alpha w^T(x_i-x_j)(x_i-x_j)^Tw$$
$$-2\sum_{cl(x_i)\neq cl(x_j)}\beta w^T(x_i-x_j)(x_i-x_j)^Tw)=$$

$$\frac{1}{2n}(2\sum_i^n w^T(x_i-m)(x_i-m)w$$
$$-2\sum_{k=1}^c\alpha 2n_k\sum_{cl(x_j)=k}w^T(x_j-m_k)(x_j-m_k)^Tw$$
$$-2\beta\sum_{c=1}^k\sum_{d=c+1}^k\sum_{cl(x_i)=c,cl(x_j)=d}w^T(x_i-x_j)(x_i-x_j)^Tw)=$$

$$\frac{1}{n}\sum_i^n w^T(x_i-m)(x_i-m)w$$
$$-2\alpha\frac{1}{n}\sum_{k=1}^c n_k\sum_{cl(x_j)=k}w^T(x_j-m_k)(x_j-m_k)^Tw$$
$$-2\beta\frac{1}{n}\sum_{c=1}^k\sum_{d=c+1}^k\sum_{cl(x_i)=c,cl(x_j)=d}w^T(x_i-x_j)(x_i-x_j)^Tw=$$

$$w^TS_tw-2(\alpha w^TS'_ww+\beta w^TS'_bw)=$$

$$w^T(S_t-2(\alpha S'_w+\beta S'_b))w$$

where

$$S'_w=\frac{1}{n}\sum_{k=1}^c n_k\sum_{cl(x_j)=k}(x_j-m_k)(x_j-m_k)^T$$
$$S'_b=\frac{1}{2n}\sum_{c=1}^k\sum_{d=c+1}^k\sum_{cl(x_i)=c,cl(x_j)=d}(x_i-x_j)(x_i-x_j)^T$$

Note the similarity of S'_w to the standard within-class matrix used in MMC given by $S_w=\frac{1}{n}\sum_i^k\sum_{cl(x_j)=i}(x_j-m^i)(x_j-m^i)^T$. S_w is the class-wise normalized version of S'_w. Thus, the discriminant yielded by our approach is given by the standard total scatter matrix, a modified within-class matrix, and a pairwise inter-class scatter matrix. We can obtain MMC by setting $\alpha=\frac{1}{n_k}$ if $y_i=k,y_j=k$ and $\beta=0$. This discards the inter-class scatter matrix and makes $S'_w=S_w$.

After defining L and G compute L_g the Laplacian of G, L_l the Laplacian of L, and the matrix $\frac{1}{n}X(L_g-L_l)X^T$ (the 2P-WMV discriminant). The solution to 2P-WMV is w that maximizes $\frac{1}{n}w^TX(L_g-L_l)X^Tw$ which is in turn is given by the largest eigenvector of $\frac{1}{n}X(L_g-L_l)X^T$ [4].

3   Results

To evaluate the classification ability of our extracted features we use the simple and popular 1-nearest neighbor (1NN) algorithm. In 10-fold and 5-fold cross-validation experiments we apply the 1-nearest neighbor classification algorithm to features extracted from our method 2P-WMV, the weighted maximum margin discriminant (WMMC), PCA, and the features as they are (denoted simply as 1NN). We calculate average error rates across 50 randomly selected datasets shown in Table 1 from the UCI Machine Learning Repository [7].

Table 1. Datasets from the UCI Machine Learning repository that we used in our study [7]

Code	Dataset	Classes	Dimension	Instances
1	Liver-disorders	2	6	345
2	Diabetes	2	8	768
3	Breast Cancer	2	10	683
4	Page block	5	10	5473
5	Wine-quality-red	11	11	1599
6	Wine quality	11	11	4898
7	Wine	3	13	178
8	Heart	2	13	270
9	Australian Credit Approval	2	14	690
10	EEG Eye State	2	14	14980
11	Pen-Based Recognition	10	16	10992
12	Climate	2	18	540
13	lymphography	4	18	148
14	Statlog image	7	19	2310
15	Two norm	2	20	7400
16	Ring	2	20	7400
17	Cardiotocography	10	21	2126
18	Thyroid	3	21	7200
19	Waveform	3	21	5000
20	Statlog German credit card	2	24	1000
21	Steel faults	7	27	1941
22	Breast cancer	2	30	569
23	Ionosphere	2	34	351
24	Dermatology	6	34	366
25	Statlog	7	36	6435
26	Texture	11	40	5500
27	Waveform	3	40	5000
28	Qsar	2	41	1055
29	SPECTF heart	2	44	267
30	Mlprove	6	51	6118
31	Spambase	2	57	4597
32	Sonar	2	60	208
33	Digits	2	63	762
34	Ozone	2	72	1847
35	Insurance company coil2000	2	85	5822
36	Movement libras	15	90	360
37	Hill valley	2	100	606
38	BCI	2	117	400
39	Gas sensor array drift	6	128	13910
40	Musk	2	166	476
41	Coil	6	241	1500
42	Scene classification	6	294	2230
43	Madelon	2	500	2600
44	Smartphone	6	561	10299
45	Secom	2	591	1567
46	Mfeat	10	649	2000
47	CNAE-9	9	857	1080
48	ACASVA actions	2	960	11288
49	Micromass	2	1300	931
50	Gisette	2	5000	1000

3.1 Experimental Methodology

We compare four classification algorithms: 2P-WMV+1NN, PCA+1NN, WMMC+1NN, and 1NN where the first three are 1NN applied to features extracted from each of the three dimensionality reduction algorithms. We use 10-fold cross-validation on each real dataset with the same set of splits for each algorithm. However, for datasets with fewer than 300 instances we use 5-fold cross-validation to obtain a large enough validation set. For dimensionality reduction we find the best parameters and number of dimensions by cross-validating further on the training dataset (also 10-fold).

In 2P-WMV we let β range from $\{-2,-1.9,-1.8,-1.7,-1.6,-1.5,-1.4,-1.3,-1.2,-1.1,-1,-.9,-.8,-.7,-.6,-.5,-.4,-.3,-.2,-.1,-.01\}$ and α fixed to 1. For WMMC we let the α parameter range from $\{10^{-7}, 10^{-6}, 10^{-5}, 10^{-4}, 10^{-3}, 10^{-2}, 10^{-1}, 1, 10, 100\}$. Recall that WMMC is given by $\arg\max_w w^T(S_b - \alpha S_w)w$ [5]. For each parameter we reduce dimensionality to 20 and then pick the top $1 <= k <= 20$ features that give the lowest 1NN error on the training. Thus the cross-validation on the training set gives us the best values of α and the reduced number of features (including PCA) which we then apply to the validation set.

We wrote our code in C and R and make it freely available at http://www.cs.njit.edu/usman/wmv/. Our C programs use CLAPACK libraries for performing the eigenvector and singular value decompositions.

3.2 Experimental Results on Fifty Datasets

We compute the balanced error rate [8] for each training-validation split during cross-validation and take the mean to be the average cross-validation error. In Table 2 we show the average cross-validation error on each dataset. Across the the 50 datasets 2P-WMV+1NN achieves the lowest average error of 13.324% and has the lowest error in 21 out of the 50 datasets. The next best is WMMC+1NN that achieves an average error of 15.302% and has the lowest error in 12 out of the 50 datasets. PCA+1NN are 1NN have higher average errors at 18.765% and 18.946% respectively. PCA+1NN and 1NN have the lowest error in 2 and 9 out of the 50 datasets respectively.

We measure the statistical significance with the Wilcoxon rank test [9]. This is a standard test to measure the difference between two methods across a number of datasets. Roughly speaking it shows statistical significance between two methods when one outperforms the other each time on a large number of datasets. In Table 3 the p-values show that 2P-WMV+1NN statistically significantly outperforms the other three method across all 50 datasets.

Table 2. Average cross-validation error of different algorithms on each of the 50 real datasets from the UCI machine learning repository. Shown in bold is the method with the lowest unique error.

Code	Dataset	2P-WMV+1NN	WMMC+1NN	PCA+1NN	1NN
1	Liver-disorders	**0.364**	0.376	0.4	0.404
2	Diabetes	0.31912	0.33382	0.34706	0.31912
3	Breast Cancer	**0.03016**	0.03492	0.37937	0.37937
4	Page block	0.04586	**0.04199**	0.04622	0.04622
5	Wine-quality-red	**0.37718**	0.37785	0.42081	0.42013
6	Wine quality	**0.37582**	0.38381	0.4043	0.40451
7	Wine	0.075	0.075	0.2125	0.2125
8	Heart	**0.21**	0.33	0.425	0.42
9	Australian Credit Approval	**0.20833**	0.21667	0.44167	0.43167
10	EEG Eye State	**0.0198**	0.02094	0.0202	0.0202
11	Pen-Based Recognition	0.00586	0.00614	0.00577	0.00577
12	Climate	**0.066**	0.072	0.14	0.132
13	Lymphography	0.2	0.21786	0.21429	0.2
14	Statlog image	0.03609	**0.03435**	0.03609	0.03565
15	Two norm	**0.0289**	0.02918	0.03342	0.05315
16	Ring	0.14685	**0.14014**	0.15425	0.24274
17	Cardiotocography	0.08398	0.08932	0.08495	**0.0835**
18	Thyroid	**0.03915**	0.06211	0.07014	0.07014
19	Waveform	0.18143	**0.18**	0.18612	0.22857
20	Statlog German credit card	**0.33444**	0.37	0.35667	0.35444
21	Steel faults	0.36126	**0.36073**	0.61885	0.61885
22	Breast cancer	**0.07755**	0.11429	0.09388	0.09388
23	Ionosphere	0.06452	**0.05806**	0.10323	0.10968
24	Dermatology	**0.01538**	0.03462	0.11538	0.11538
25	Statlog	**0.09118**	0.11874	0.09496	0.09512
26	Texture	0.00926	0.01315	0.00944	**0.00796**
27	Waveform	0.18143	0.18755	**0.17898**	0.23837
28	Qsar	0.18211	**0.16211**	0.20316	0.19895
29	SPECTF heart	0.27647	**0.25882**	0.28235	0.26471
30	Mlprove	0.42204	0.44128	0.41941	**0.41382**
31	Spambase	0.08709	**0.08249**	0.17221	0.16565
32	Sonar	0.17222	0.2	0.15556	0.15556
33	Digits	0.01111	0.01806	0.01111	**0.00972**
34	Ozone	0.10904	**0.09718**	0.10678	0.10565
35	Insurance company coil2000	0.1042	0.10262	**0.0965**	0.09685
36	Movement libras	0.10333	0.12333	0.10333	**0.09667**
37	Hill valley	**0.02321**	0.06429	0.41607	0.42143
38	BCI	**0.16333**	0.17667	0.44667	0.41333
39	Gas sensor array drift	0.00878	0.01058	0.00878	0.00885
40	Musk	**0.11957**	0.23696	0.13478	0.1587
41	Coil	0.02286	0.03429	0.02143	**0.01429**
42	Scene classification	0.29454	0.335	0.29636	**0.28909**
43	Madelon	**0.1256**	0.4568	0.1268	0.3444
44	Smartphone	0.04563	0.04194	0.07363	**0.02623**
45	Secom	**0.08027**	0.11429	0.1	0.10204
46	Mfeat	0.05526	**0.05158**	0.05211	0.05263
47	CNAE-9	0.069	**0.065**	0.176	0.132
48	ACASVA actions	**0.11637**	0.18479	0.17809	0.1178
49	Micromass	0.07253	0.06264	0.11209	**0.05934**
50	Gisette	**0.04889**	0.05111	0.09556	0.08222
	Average error	0.13324	0.15302	0.18765	0.18946

Table 3. Wilcox rank test p-values (two-tailed test) between all pairs of methods

	WMMC+1NN	PCA+1NN	1NN
2P-WMV+1NN	.0004	< .0001	.0001
WMMC+1NN		.0232	.0536
PCA+1NN			.0949

4 Discussion

Both 2PWMV+1NN and WMMC+1NN reduce dimensionality by determining optimal parameters specific to the given dataset. This approach is better than the unsupervised PCA and the non-parametric MMC (results not shown here). In fact 1NN applied to the raw data can be better than non-parameteric MMC most of the time.

In this study we fixed α for 2PWMV and varied only β. If we cross-validated α we could potentially obtain lower error but at the cost of increased running time. In the current experiments 2PWMV+1NN and WMMC+1NN are the slowest methods yet still tractable for large datasets.

We chose 1NN as the classification method for this study due to its simplicity and its popularity with dimensionality reduction programs. Other classifiers such as the support vector machine [1] may perform better when replaced with 1NN. However, in that case the regularization parameter would also need to be optimized via cross-validation which increases the total runtime.

5 Conclusion

We introduce a two parameter variant of the weighted maximum variance discriminant and optimize it with cross-validation followed by 1-nearest neighbor for classification. Compared to existing approaches our method obtains the lowest average error with statistical significance across several real datasets from the UCI machine learning repository.

References

1. Alpaydin, E.: Machine Learning. MIT Press (2004)
2. Li, H., Jiang, T., Zhang, K.: Efficient and robust feature extraction by maximum margin criterion. In: Thrun, S., Saul, L., Schölkopf, B. (eds.) Advances in Neural Information Processing Systems 16. MIT Press, Cambridge (2004)
3. Tang, H., Fang, T., Shi, P.F.: Rapid and brief communication: Laplacian linear discriminant analysis. Pattern Recogn. 39(1), 136–139 (2006)
4. Niijima, S., Okuno, Y.: Laplacian linear discriminant analysis approach to unsupervised feature selection. IEEE/ACM Transactions on Computational Biology and Bioinformatics 6(4), 605–614 (2009)
5. Zheng, W., Zou, C., Zhao, L.: Weighted maximum margin discriminant analysis with kernels. Neurocomputing 67, 357–362 (2005)

6. He, X., Niyogi, P.: Locality preserving projections. In: Thrun, S., Saul, L., Schölkopf, B. (eds.) Advances in Neural Information Processing Systems 16. MIT Press, Cambridge (2004)
7. Asuncion, A., Newman, D.: UCI machine learning repository (2007)
8. Guyon, I., Gunn, S., Ben-Hur, A., Dror, G.: Result analysis of the nips 2003 feature selection challenge. In: Advances in Neural Information Processing Systems, pp. 545–552 (2004)
9. Kanji, G.K.: 100 Statistical Tests. Sage Publications Ltd. (1999)

Improved Performance of Computer Networks by Embedded Pattern Detection

Angel Kuri-Morales[1] and Iván Cortés-Arce[2]

[1] Instituto Tecnológico Autónomo de México, ITAM, D.F., México
akuri@itam.mx
[2] Universidad Nacional Autónoma de México, IIMAS, D.F., México
ivan.eduardo.uzzy@gmail.com

Abstract. Computer Networks are usually balanced appealing to personal experience and heuristics, without taking advantage of the behavioral patterns embedded in their operation. In this work we report the application of tools of computational intelligence to find such patterns and take advantage of them to improve the network's performance. The traditional traffic flow for Computer Network is improved by the concatenated use of the following "tools": a) Applying intelligent agents, b) Forecasting the traffic flow of the network via Multi-Layer Perceptrons (MLP) and c) Optimizing the forecasted network's parameters with a genetic algorithm. We discuss the implementation and experimentally show that every consecutive new tool introduced improves the behavior of the network. This incremental improvement can be explained from the characterization of the network's dynamics as a set of emerging patterns in time.

Keywords: Load Balancing, Computer Networks, Intelligent Agents, Neural Networks, Genetic Algorithms.

1 Introduction

Computer networks are frequently balanced appealing to heuristics or, simply, the experience of the administrator of the network [5, ch. 1], [27, ch. 3]. This typical practice suffers from the severe inconvenient of not taking into consideration the behavioral patterns which may be discovered if the appropriate tools are used. To begin with, it is very convenient to consider a dynamic link between the elements of the network. If this is achieved, it is possible to apply machine learning and optimization techniques to improve their performance. This realization is the main motivation to merge, in one scheme, the following tools: statistical protocol adaptation, intelligent agents, MLPs and genetic algorithms (GA). The main purpose is to improve the channel utilization and all related computer network resources. It should also consider the impact of these tools under *steady* and *error regime* conditions (see below). It is true that there are solutions [1], [9] based on well-known algorithms [2], [3], [4]. These,

J.F. Martínez-Trinidad et al. (Eds.): MCPR 2014, LNCS 8495, pp. 21–30, 2014.
© Springer International Publishing Switzerland 2014

however, do not consider congestion problems. The Traffic Engineering Performance Objectives are described in [10]. They are either 1) Traffic oriented or 2) Resource oriented. The key traffic oriented performance objectives include minimization of packet loss, minimization of delay and maximization of throughput. Minimization of packet loss is one of the most important traffic oriented performance objectives. The routing algorithms typically consider link state [3] or distance vector [2] to select routing paths based on static link weights or costs. These, however, do not allow us to use all alternate and available paths leading to the same destination. This fact increases the probability of congestion traffic as mentioned in [1] since the routing algorithm does not change in time as the traffic flow does. In this paper we will prove that the use of the appropriate computational intelligence tools minimizes packet loss and maximizes channel utilization. To achieve this, the behavior of the traffic flow along the full network must be known. Such global knowledge allows us, in principle, to attempt accurate forecasting. If this is achieved then it is possible to establish the best values of the variables involved such that the traffic is maximized. We have selected an implementation of the Bellman-Ford distance vector algorithm [2, 5] as a benchmarking standard with which to compare our algorithm and we have set the minimization of the number of lost packets as the routing metric. In Section 2, the necessary concepts and definitions are introduced; in Section 3 we present a brief explanation of the method applied. In section 4 we present the experimental results. Finally in section 5 we present our conclusions.

2   Preliminaries

Suppose that there is a computer network in which there are N routing devices and L links which correspond to the communication channels. We denote the sources of the traffic by G; d is the bandwidth of the channel; p is the packet size; q_t is the percentage utilization of the channel and t is the number of the sample; λ is the network traffic flow given in packets per second [24]; r_n is the n-th adaptive routing device; $g_k(\lambda)$ is the k-th input traffic source; l_k is the number of links associated with r_n; $l_k^{(i)}$ is the input traffic flow of channel k; $l_k^{(o)}$ is the output traffic flow of channel k; $l_{g(k)}^{(i)}$ is the input traffic flow of the channel which connects r_k to $g_k(\lambda)$; $l_k^{(i)}, l_k^{(o)} \in l_k$ where i is the input and o is the output; $\sum \rho_n(\omega)^{(i)}$, $\sum \rho_n(\omega)^{(o)}$ are, respectively, the sums of all optimized input and output traffic flows on device r_i; w_0, w_1 are the linear regression coefficients of the forecasted channel's utilization in time. $S(p)$ is the single path routing algorithm; $M(p)$ is the adaptive path routing algorithm.

3   Adaptive Process on Computer Network

The adaptive model's performance is incrementally improved through consecutive application of: a) Agents [17, 22], b) MLPs [18] and c) GAs [14]. Along this paper, the results refer to the network illustrated in Fig. 1:

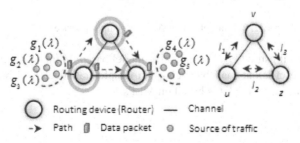

Fig. 1. Schematic architecture of the Computer Network

From Figure 1 we have: $G = \{g_1(\lambda), g_2(\lambda), g_3(\lambda), g_4(\lambda), g_5(\lambda)\}$; $N = \{r_u, r_v, r_z\}$; $L = \{l_1, l_2, l_3\}$; every r_i on the network is fully connected by a link l_k, $r_{u, z}$ are connected to $g_k(\lambda)$ by link $l^{(i)}_{g(k)}$; $r_{u, z}$ are the external nodes connected with $g_k(\lambda)$; r_v is an internal node. For convenience we use $M(p)$ instead of $S(p)$ [2], [5] (since $S(p)$ does not allow the *ad hoc* use of all available paths). $S(p)$, thus, increases the probability of traffic congestion. In our model each r_i is provided with tools such as: a) $A_{(r)}$ [set of intelligent agents (daemons) running in r_i]. $A_{(r)} = \{a_1,...,a_k\}$; $k = |A|$ where a_k is the *k-th* agent in r_i; b) NN is a MLP and c) *ega* which is the GA-based [26] optimization algorithm. The use of the tools and adoption of $M(p)$ allows us to consecutively improve the network's performance. In what follows we will describe the different tools applied in every stage.

3.1   Agents

The initial adaptive model implements *wlb*, a simple initial statistical load balancing method which distributes traffic to all routing nodes. When r_i detects traffic, $A_{(r)}$ is started; before this, the agents have not been active. It is here that they get ready to sample the channel's behavior. This they do until they have enough data, at which point an optimization task is started. Each r_i on the network works as an autonomous entity which takes its own decisions derived from the knowledge other agents give. Channel's sampling is described by Equation (1):

$$A(s)_r = \{u_1(t), u_2(t), ..., u_n(t)\} \tag{1}$$

Where $u_i(t) = \{q_1,..., q_n\}$; $u_i(t)$ is resource sampled in r_i. Once $A_{(r)}$ has sufficiently sampled the channel (as per $s = \{u_1(t), u_2(t),...,u_n(t)\}$) it forecasts the future channel's utilization from linear extrapolation, whose detailed equations are:

$$w_0 \leftarrow w_0 + \alpha \sum_i [u_i - f_w(t_i)]; \quad w_1 \leftarrow w_1 + \alpha \sum_i [u_i - f_w(t_i)] \times t_i$$

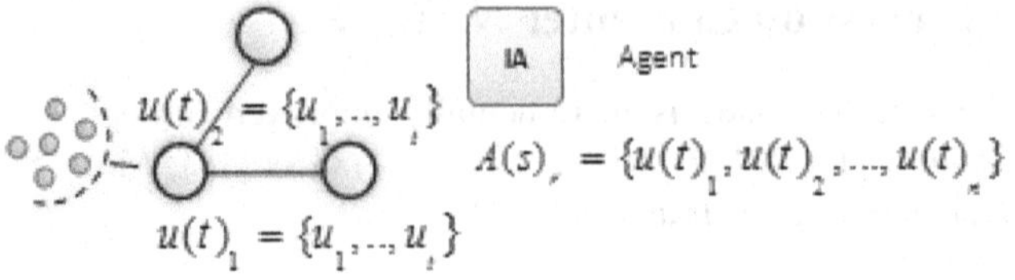

$$u(t)_i = \{u_1, ..., u_i\}$$

$$A(s)_r = \{u(t)_1, u(t)_2, ..., u(t)_n\}$$

$$u(t)_1 = \{u_1, ..., u_i\}$$

Agent

Fig. 2. Example of an Agent's sampling process

In Figure 2 we illustrate how the adaptive model based on linear prediction acts on ri to find a more efficient load balancing via simple statistical load balancing. The next step of the adaptive model is based on MLPs.

3.2   MLP's

Our aim is to improve on the basic linear prediction by discovering the behavioral patterns in the data of the channel. It is well known [25] that MLPs are universal approximators which, as argued in [18], are accurate regardless of the probability distribution function of the variables under observation. If we want to get the future values to prevent potential network traffic problems, MLPs are a proven reliable choice. Therefore, once enough data have accumulated, we are able to take ad-vantage of the embedded behavioral patterns (uncovered by the MLP) and replace linear forecast with the superior MLP forecast. We denote our BMLP (Backpropagation Multi-Layer Perceptron) model with $NN_{(i)}$. In Figure 3 we illustrate a possible MLP architecture. In our model each adaptive routing device has an associated MLP to perform forecasting. Given samples $s = \{u_1(t), u_2(t),...,u_n(t)\}$ provided by each $A_{(r)}$ in a previous time step, we want to find $U(\tau) = \{u_1(t), u_2(t),...,u_n(\tau)\}$ (described in [13]) such that:

$$u_i(\tau) = f_i(u_i(t), ..., u_n(t)) \text{ for } i = 1, .., n \tag{2}$$

$\tau = t + k$ where t represents time and k is time displacement relative to future period to characterize. Forecasted values will be denoted by $u'_i(\tau)$. Such values will have an expected approximation error ε_i such that $u'_i(\tau) = u_i(\tau) \pm \varepsilon_i$

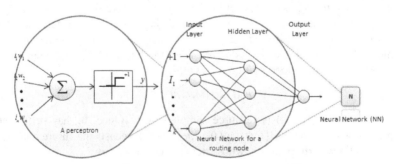

Fig. 3. A Neural Network Model

Taking in consideration all of above we denote the forecasted values with $u'_i(\tau)$ and

$$u'_i(\tau) = NN_{(i)}(u_1(t), ..., u_n(t))$$ (3)

MLP's error is $\varepsilon(NN_{(i)})_t$. Then we can compare it with the previous one $\varepsilon(LR_{(i)})_t$ found by $A_{(r)}$ *without* an MLP. $A_{(r)}$ selects the smaller one for every r_i.

3.3   Genetic Algorithm

EGA [26] gets values from $u'_i(\tau)$ to optimize traffic flow. For convenience, traffic flow is given in mbps (megabits per second). In Fig. 4 is shown a typical genome for this application.

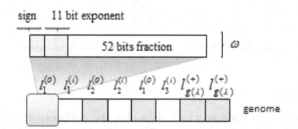

Fig. 4. Representation of the Genome

Henceforth we use the following equation to transform $u'_i(\tau)$ into suitable units.

$$\omega(u'_i(\tau)) = \sum_{i=1}^{\tau}(u'_i(\tau) \times r(l_k))$$ (4)

Where ω is the traffic flow at time i; r is the bandwidth l_k and (4) allows us to compute forecasted values at time τ. To exemplify, assume that our fitness function (which we want to maximize) is determined by $ega(\omega)$ and has the following form:

$$ega(\omega) = max\left(\sum_{n=1}^{N}(\sum \rho_n(\omega)^{(i)} - \sum \rho_n(\omega)^{(o)})\right)$$ (5)

In Equation (5) (Fitness function) i and o represent the incoming and outgoing channels. When $ega(\omega)$ has optimized from the forecasted values it supplies them to A(r) which will communicate parameter's values to all the agents.

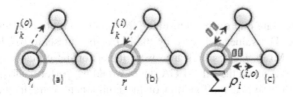

Fig. 5. a) Output Traffic Flow, b) Input Traffic Flow, c) Accumulated Traffic Flow

Figures 5a, 5b, 5c show how the adaptive model optimizes using all available resources from the network. The learning process can be summarized as in Figure 6 which shows the adaptive model with all the stages working in unison.

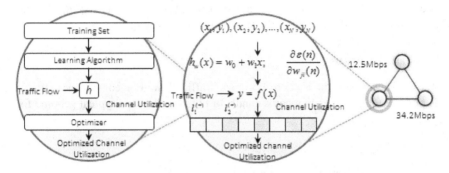

Fig. 6. Adaptive Routing with all stages working in unison

4   Results

We have performed experiments which show that the performance of our model is better than typical ones under similar conditions [2], [3], [5]. We have extensively simulated the behavior of various networks on OMNET++ [23]. The behavior of the system was performed for 25 simulated seconds (corresponding to processing ~57,000 packets; roughly 2,300 packets per second). By *Steady regime* we mean that the network is stable (no errors occur); while the *Error regime* corresponds component errors being considered.

Packet loss may occur from network congestion and overflow at queues in routers and/or switches. It results in wasted bandwidth. Recalling that one of the key traffic oriented performance objectives is the minimization of packet loss, the evident superiority of our method is shown in Table 1.

Table 1. Difference betweeen packets generated and packets arrived

Routing Strategy	Packet Received	Relative Loss	Packet Lost	Relative Efficiency
Distance Vector	39,662	23.56%	17,544	46.75%
Adaptive with Agents	40,257	21.73%	16,949	48.39%
Adaptive with MLP	41,088	19.27	16,118	50.88%
Adaptive with EGA	49,005	0.00%	8,201	100.00%

Notice the outstanding improvement resulting from optimal routing assignment which is achieved from a) The values delivered by the EGA; this attests to b) The successful forecast which the MLPs yield; c) Clearly, were it not for the efficient update of the network's status (via Agents) the MLP-EGA stages would not perform adequately.

If errors (due to assumed malfunction of the components) are included, the behavior of the network varies accordingly. To this effect, exponentially distributed component failures were induced. Error recovery times were also assumed exponentially distributed, although the parameters of the exponential distributions for both error and recovery times were different for every router. A performance comparison of the network in steady and error regimes is shown in Table 2.

Table 2. Comparative of the Routing Protocol Performance

Routing Strategy	Packet Lost (Stable Regime)	Relative Efficiency (Error regime)
Distance Vector	4,355	21,854
Adaptive with Agents	2,911	5,427
Adaptive with MLP	0	3,101
Adaptive with EGA	0	3,101

The experiments based on the adaptive model display a degradation both when MLPs and/or GAs are included if a relatively large number of network failures is simulated. This is due to the fact that the underlying patterns (which are the basis for adequate forecasting) tend to vanish because of the simulated errors. However, our method automatically folds-back to the simple routing algorithm in such a case. We have also included a graph that shows how load balancing methods are ap-proaching the optimal one with our proposed model. Optimality was calculated by exhaustive enumerative analysis.

Figure 7 illustrates a classification of the number of lost packets.

Several comparisons between the network's behavior under the different options are possible. For reasons of space we are unable to annotate them all. We wish to point out, however, that introducing agents (and, thus, making the global information available to all routers) yields immediate benefits. For example, let us consider node u when connected to a 34.2 Mbps channel (l1) and simultaneously connected to a 12.5 Mbps channel (l2). Two alternative methods are considered: a) Statistical (no agents) and b) Agents. With method (a) 2.91 Mbps are transported on l1 and 6.85 Mbps on l2; with method (b) 68.76 Mbps are transported on l1 and 179.91 on l2. This is a remarkable improvement of 23.54:1 for l1 and 26.26:1 for l2 when agents are considered.

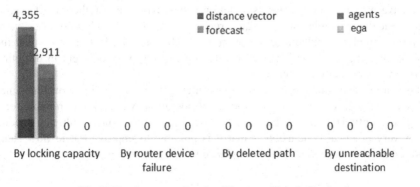

Fig. 7. Routing strategies classifications (Steady Regime)

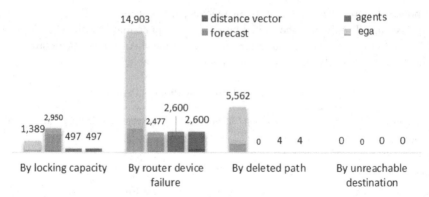

Fig. 8. Routing strategies classification (with errors)

Table 3. Comparative among Load Balancing Methods

Method	34.2Mbps Transported Load (%)	12.5Mbps Transported Load (%)
Theoretical load balancing	0.7323	0.2670
Statistical load balancing	0.7015	0.2984
Intelligent Load balancing	0.7234	0.2765

5   Conclusions

We used a new approach to improve a computer's network resources. We worked with a) Agents, b) Neural Networks, c) Genetic Algorithms. We have shown that our model minimizes the number of packets lost, increasing the network's performance. We have shown that every time that a new component is added to the adaptive model, it further improves the network's performance. On the other hand, when fail-ures are considered, the MLP attempting to forecast from the network's past behavior is unable to uncover (the non-existent) patterns. Regardless of this, the adaptive model still behaves reasonably well because agents are still effective in attempting to globally optimize the system.

We have presented preliminary simulation results based on a rather simple archi-tecture. But the principles are the same regardless of the network's complexity. In fact, more complex architectures are prone to exhibit more intricate patterns and the tools we implemented have been repeatedly shown to be very efficient in detecting patterns in complex environments.

This is a prime example of computational intelligence working in an on-line simu-lation environment. Given all of the above considerations we think that reliable fore-casting and optimization can be improved working, to be sure, with non-chaotic data. A very practical conclusion is that it is possible to improve traffic flow at no software/hardware cost when network balance is based on this approach.

References

1. Mahlous, A.: Multipath Routing Using Max Flow Algorithms For Internet Traffic: Development and Performance Evaluation of Max Flow Multipath Routing Schemes for the Internet using Max Flow Algorithms. Lambert Academic Publishing (2009)
2. Bellman, R.: On A Routing Problem. RAND Corporation, Santa Monica (1958)
3. Dijkstra, E.: A note on Two Problems in Connexion with Graphs. Numerische Mathmaik 1, 269–271 (1959)
4. Aceves, J.: Loop Free Routing Using Diffusing Computations. IEEE/ACM Transactions on Networking 1(1) (1993)
5. Kurose, J., Ross, K.: Computer Networking: A Top Down Approach, pp. 374–387. Addison Wesley (2010)
6. Awdche, D., Malcom, J., O'Dell, M., MacManus, J.: Requirements for Traffic Engineering Over MPLS. RFC 2702. Internet Society (1999)
7. Akami Technologies, Internet Bottlenecks: The Case for Edge Delivery Services (2000), http://www.cse.cuhk.edu.hk/~cslui/CSC5480/akamai-bottlenecks.pdf
8. Sinha, R., Papadopoulus, C., Heidenmann, J.: Internet Packet Size Distributions: Some Observations. University of Southern California (2005)
9. Ahmad, I., Ghafoor, A., Mehrotra, K., Mohan, C., Ranka, S.: Performance modeling of load balancing algorithms using neural networks. L.C. Smith College of Engineering and Computer Science. Syracuse University (1994)
10. Awdche, D., Malcom, J., O'Dell, M., MacManus, J.: Requirements for Traffic Engineering Over MPLS. RFC 2702. Internet Society (1999)
11. Mitchell, M.: An Introduction to Genetic Algorithms. MIT Press (1996)
12. Kuri-Morales, Á.F.: Pattern Recognition via Vasconcelos' Genetic Algorithm. In: Sanfeliu, A., Martínez Trinidad, J.F., Carrasco Ochoa, J.A. (eds.) CIARP 2004. LNCS, vol. 3287, pp. 328–335. Springer, Heidelberg (2004)
13. Kuri-Morales, A.: Application of a Method Based on Computational Intelligence for the Optimization of Resources Determined from Multivariable Phenomena. In: Batyrshin, I., Mendoza, M.G. (eds.) MICAI 2012, Part II. LNCS, vol. 7630, pp. 292–303. Springer, Heidelberg (2013)
14. Kuri-Morales, A.: A Universal Eclectic Genetic Algorithm for Constrained Optimization. In: Proceedings 6th European Congress on Intelligent Techniques & Soft Computing, EUFIT 1998 (1998)
15. Goldberg, D.: Genetic Algorithms in Search, Optimization, and Machine Learning. Addison Wesley (1989)
16. Anand, V., Spears, W.: A Study of Crossover Operators in Genetic Programming. In: Raś, Z.W., Zemankova, M. (eds.) ISMIS 1991. LNCS, vol. 542, pp. 409–418. Springer, Heidelberg (1991)
17. Russell, S., Norving, P., Artificial Intelligence: A Modern Approach. Prentice Hall (2010)
18. Haykin, S.: Neural Networks.: A comprehensive Foundation. Prentice Hall (1999)
19. Stallings, W.: Queuing Analysis Notes (2013), http://www.computersciencestudent.com/
20. Kleinrock, L.: On modeling and Analysis of Computer Networks. Proceedings of the IEEE 81(8) (August 1993)
21. Hertz, J., Krogh, A., Palmer, R.: Introduction to the Theory of Neural Computation. A Lecture Notes Editorial Board (1990)

22. Wooldridge, M., Jennings, N.: Intelligent Agents: theory and practice. The Knowledge Engineering Review 10(2), 115–152 (1995)
23. Vargas, A.: OMNeT++ User Manual Version 4.3.1. OpenSim Ldt. (2011)
24. Sinha, R., Papadopoulos, C., Heidemann, J.: Internet packet size distributions: Some observations. USC/Information Sciences Inst (2007),
    `http://netweb.usc.edu/~rsinha/pkt-sizes`
25. Hornik, K., Stinchcombe, M., White, H.: Multilayer feedforward networks are universal approximators. Neural Networks 2(5), 359–366 (1989)
26. Kuri-Morales, A., Aldana-Bobadilla, E.: The Best Genetic Algorithm Part I. In: Castro, F., Gelbukh, A., González, M. (eds.) MICAI 2013, Part II. LNCS, vol. 8266, pp. 1–15. Springer, Heidelberg (2013)
27. Graziani, R., Johnson, A.: Routing Protocols and Concepts, CCNA exploration companion guide. Cisco Press (2007)

On Two Definitions of Reduct*

Manuel S. Lazo-Cortés, José Fco. Martínez-Trinidad,
and J.A. Carrasco-Ochoa

Instituto Nacional de Astrofísica, Óptica y Electrónica
Mexico
{mlazo,fmartine,ariel}@ccc.inaoep.mx

Abstract. This paper studies the relationship between the two most common definitions of reduct. Although there are other definitions, almost all the literature published in the framework of the Theory of Rough Sets, uses one of the two definitions we study here. However, there is an ambiguity in the use of these definitions and often authors do not previously declare what definition they refer to. Moreover, there are no publications where the relation between these two definitions is widely discussed, just that is what this paper addresses. We enunciate and demonstrate several properties expressing relations between both definitions including some illustrative examples.

1 Introduction

Object classification is normally accompanied and usually preceded by a task of feature selection, which reduces the dimension of the space of representation of objects. Intensive research on feature selection and pattern discovery has given us several new representations and approaches that use different formalisms. In the framework of the Rough Set Theory [7], the basic concept for the mentioned aim is the concept of reduct for a decision table. Informally, the concept of reduct, refers to a subset of attributes that retains the same ability to discern between object pairs in a table as the full set of attributes do.

In the literature, there are several definitions of reduct, see for example [3–8, 11]. Nevertheless, reducts, in any definition, combine two properties, the capacity of preserving certain property of the set of all attributes (normally associated to differentiating power) and being of minimal cardinality among all subsets fulfilling this property. It means that attributes in a reduct are jointly sufficient and individually necessary to differentiate among object descriptions.

We decided to examine the relation between the two definitions more commonly used in the literature.

This document is organized as follows. Section 2 provides the formal background for the study of both definitions of reduct. In this section, we include

---

* This work was partly supported by the National Council of Science and Technology of Mexico (CONACyT) through the project grants CB2008-106443 and CB2008-106366.

J.F. Martínez-Trinidad et al. (Eds.): MCPR 2014, LNCS 8495, pp. 31–40, 2014.

several examples for supporting our discussion. Section 3 contains a list of theoretical relations between both types of reducts, including a case study. Our remarks are summarized in Section 4.

2   Basic Concepts

In many data analysis applications, information and knowledge are stored and represented as an information table because this information table provides a convenient way to describe a finite set of objects within a universe through a finite set of attributes [7]. Reduct is a key concept within the Rough Set Theory, defined for information systems or decision tables.

Definition 1. *(information system) An information system is a pair $S = (U, A_t^*)$ where U is a finite non-empty set of objects, A_t^* is a finite non-empty set of conditional (descriptive) attributes. Each $a \in A_t^*$ corresponds to the function $I_a :$ $U \to V_a$ called evaluation function, where V_a is called the value set of a.*

An *information table* is the simplest form of an information system. It can be represented as a matrix, in which rows are associated to objects, columns to attributes and cells to values of attributes on objects. Without loss of generality, in this paper, we focus our discussion on a type of information table called decision table.

Definition 2. *(decision table) A special type of information table is denoted as $S_d = (U, A_t = A_t^* \cup \{d\})$, where A_t^* is a set of conditional attributes and d is a decision attribute ($\{d\}$=D) indicating the decision class for each object in the universe. Such information table is called a decision table.*

When considering decision tables, it is important to distinguish between the so called *consistent* and the *inconsistent* ones. A decision table is said to be *consistent*, if each combination of values of descriptive attributes uniquely determines the value of the decision attribute, and *inconsistent*, otherwise. Later we will define these concepts formally.

For introducing the concept of reduct, the indiscernibility relation plays a special role.

Definition 3. *(indiscernibility relation) Given a subset of conditional attributes $A \subseteq A_t^*$, the indiscernibility relation $IND(A) \subseteq U \times U$ for an information system is defined as*

$$IND(A) = \{(u, v) \in U \times U : \forall a \in A; I_a(u) = I_a(v)\}$$

For a decision table S_d, we can define the relative indiscernibility relation as

$$IND(A|D) = \{(u, v) \in U \times U : \forall a \in A, [I_a(u) = I_a(v)] \vee [I_d(u) = I_d(v)]\}$$

In practice, it is quite common that decision tables contain descriptions of a finite sample $\mathcal{U}$ of objects from a larger (possibly infinite) universe U, where values of descriptive attributes are always known for all objects from U, but decision is in general a hidden function except for those objects from the sample $\mathcal{U}$. The main problem of learning theory is to generalize the decision function (defined on the sample $\mathcal{U}$) to the whole universe U. In this case, we formally have a decision table $\mathcal{S}_d = (\mathcal{U}, A_t = A_t^* \cup \{d\})$ and an information table $\mathcal{S} = (U, A_t^*)$, being $\mathcal{U} \subseteq U$. The decision attribute allows partitioning the universe into blocks determined by all possible decisions.

Definition 4. *(decision class) For $k \in V_d$, a decision class is defined as $U_k = \{u \in U : I_d(u) = k\}$. Let us denote the cardinality of U_k by m_k ; so $|U_k| = m_k$. Based on this definition, we can write $U/IND(D) = \{U_1, U_2, \ldots, U_{|V_d|}\}$.*

Based on the relative indiscernibility relation, a reduct [8] is defined as follows.

Definition 5. *(reduct for a decision table) Given a decision table $\mathcal{S}_d$, an attribute set $R \subseteq A_t^*$ is called a reduct, if R satisfies the following two conditions:*

(i) $IND(R|D) = IND(A_t^*|D)$ (if R satisfies (i) it is called a super reduct);
(ii) For any $a \in R, IND((R - \{a\})|D) \neq IND(A_t^*|D)$.

Other definition widely used requires that a certain region of the universe be preserved, this region is called *positive region*. Next, we will introduce it.

Definition 6. *(lower and upper approximations) Let $A \subseteq A_t$ be a subset of attributes and let $[u]_A$ be the block (class) of the partition $U \mid IND(A)$ containing $u \in U$. We define the A-lower approximation of a set $X \subseteq U$ as follows:*

$$\underline{A}(X) = \{u \in U : [u]_A \subseteq X\}$$

The A-upper approximation of X is defined as

$$\overline{A}(X) = \{u \in U : [u]_A \cap X \neq \emptyset\}$$

The set $\overline{A}(X) - \underline{A}(X)$ is called the boundary region of X.

The notion of rough set is associated to the boundary region.

Definition 7. *(rough set) X is a rough set if it has a non-empty boundary region (i.e. $\overline{A}(X) - \underline{A}(X) \neq \emptyset$). Otherwise X is a crisp set.*

Definition 8. *(positive region) Given a decision table $\mathcal{S}_d = (U, A_t = A_t^* \cup \{d\})$ and a subset of attributes $A \subseteq A_t^*$. The A-positive region with respect to d is defined as*

$$POS_{\{d\}}(A) = \bigcup_{X \in U/IND(\{d\})} \underline{A}(X)$$

We say that a decision table $\mathcal{S}_d = (U, A_t = A_t^* \cup \{d\})$ is *deterministic or consistent* if $POS_{\{d\}}(A_t^*) = U$. Otherwise, we call it *non-deterministic or inconsistent*. Another commonly used definition of reduct is [9]:

Definition 9. *(relative reduct) Given a decision table* $S_d = (U, A_t = A_t^* \cup \{d\})$, *an attribute subset* $R \subseteq A_t^*$ *is called a relative reduct, if* R *satisfies the two conditions:*

(i) $POS_{\{d\}}(R) = POS_{\{d\}}(A_t^*)$; *(if* R *satisfies (i) is called a relative super reduct)*

(ii) $POS_{\{d\}}(R - \{a\}) \neq POS_{\{d\}}(A_t^*)$ *for any* $a \in R$.

As an initial step in understanding the relationship between the two definitions of reduct, let analyze the following example.

Example 1. Let us consider the decision table in Table 1 where $U = \{u_1, u_2, u_3, u_4, u_5, u_6, u_7\}$, $A_t^* = \{a_1, a_2, a_3, a_4\}$ and $D = \{d\}$. Notice that Table 1 is inconsistent, see for example that $I_{\{a_1,a_2,a_3,a_4\}}(u_2) = I_{\{a_1,a_2,a_3,a_4\}}(u_6) = (0,0,0,0)$ but $0 = I_d(u_2) \neq I_d(u_6) = 1$.

We have that
$IND(A_t^*|D) = \{(u_1, u_1), (u_2, u_2), (u_3, u_3), (u_4, u_4), (u_5, u_5), (u_6, u_6), (u_7, u_7),$
$\langle u_1, u_2 \rangle, \langle u_1, u_3 \rangle, \langle u_1, u_4 \rangle, \langle u_2, u_3 \rangle, \langle u_2, u_4 \rangle, \langle u_3, u_4 \rangle, \langle u_5, u_6 \rangle, \langle u_5, u_7 \rangle, \langle u_6, u_7 \rangle,$
$\langle u_2, u_6 \rangle, \langle u_3, u_6 \rangle, \langle u_4, u_5 \rangle\}$, where $\langle u_i, u_j \rangle$ denotes the two elements (u_i, u_j) and (u_j, u_i).

Let us consider the attribute set $R = \{a_1, a_2, a_3\}$, then
$IND(R) = \{(u_1, u_1), (u_2, u_2), (u_3, u_3), (u_4, u_4), (u_5, u_5), (u_6, u_6), (u_7, u_7),$
$\langle u_2, u_3 \rangle, \langle u_2, u_6 \rangle, \langle u_3, u_6 \rangle, \langle u_4, u_5 \rangle\} = IND(A_t^*)$,
therefore $IND(R|D) = IND(A_t^*|D)$.

Following definition 5, R is a super reduct for this decision table.

Let analyze if R is a reduct, and for this purpose let consider the subsets $R_1 = R - \{a_1\} = \{a_2, a_3\}$, $R_2 = R - \{a_2\} = \{a_1, a_3\}$ and $R_3 = R - \{a_3\} = \{a_1, a_2\}$, for which we have that
$IND(R_1|D) = IND(A_t^*|D) \cup \{\langle u_2, u_5 \rangle, \langle u_3, u_5 \rangle, \langle u_4, u_6 \rangle\}$; $IND(R_2|D) = IND(A_t^*|D) \cup \{\langle u_1, u_7 \rangle\}$ and $IND(R_3|D) = IND(A_t^*|D) \cup \{\langle u_1, u_6 \rangle\}$.

Table 1. An inconsistent decision table

U	a_1	a_2	a_3	a_4	d
u_1	0	0	1	1	0
u_2	0	0	0	0	0
u_3	0	0	0	0	0
u_4	1	0	0	0	0
u_5	1	0	0	0	1
u_6	0	0	0	0	1
u_7	0	1	1	0	1

According to condition *(ii)* in definition 5, we can say that R is a reduct for this decision table.

Now, let us consider the definition 9, we need to calculate $POS_{\{d\}}(R)$; then

$U/IND(\{d\}) = \{\{u_1, u_2, u_3, u_4\}, \{u_5, u_6, u_7\}\};$
$U/IND(A_t^*) = \{\{u_1\}, \{u_2, u_3, u_6\}, \{u_4, u_5\}, \{u_7\}\}$ and
$\underline{A_t^*}(\{u_1, u_2, u_3, u_4\}) = \{u_1\} = \underline{R}(\{u_1, u_2, u_3, u_4\});$
$\underline{A_t^*}(\{u_5, u_6, u_7\}) = \{u_7\} = \underline{R}(\{u_5, u_6, u_7\}),$
and therefore $POS_{\{d\}}(A_t^*) = \{u_1, u_7\} = POS_{\{d\}}(R);$
so R satisfies condition *(i)* of definition 9 and we can say that R is a relative super reduct.

Let analyze condition *(ii)*:
$U/IND(R_1) = \{\{u_1\}, \{u_2, u_3, u_4, u_5, u_6\}, \{u_7\}\};$
$U/IND(R_2) = \{\{u_1, u_7\}, \{u_2, u_3, u_6\}, \{u_4, u_5\}\}$ and
$U/IND(R_3) = \{\{u_1, u_2, u_3, u_6\}, \{u_4, u_5\}, \{u_7\}\};$ then
$\underline{R_1}(\{u_1, u_2, u_3, u_4\}) = \{u_1\},$
$\underline{R_2}(\{u_1, u_2, u_3, u_4\}) = \emptyset$ and
$\underline{R_3}(\{u_1, u_2, u_3, u_4\}) = \emptyset$ and
$\underline{R_1}(\{u_5, u_6, u_7\}) = \{u_7\},$
$\underline{R_2}(\{u_5, u_6, u_7\}) = \emptyset$ and
$\underline{R_3}(\{u_5, u_6, u_7\}) = \{u_7\};$
thence $POS_{\{d\}}(R - \{a_1\}) = POS_{\{d\}}(A_t^*)$. It means that R does not fulfill condition *(ii)* of definition 9. We can conclude that R is a reduct of the decision table in Table 1 according to definition 5, but it is not a reduct if we use definition 9.

It should be emphasized that although in some publications the equivalence between both definitions of reduct here included (5 and 9) is handled lightly; in [9] it is accurately established (Proposition 5.6, page 351) that this equivalence holds if $IND(A) = IND(\{d\})$. Meanwhile, Bazan and Szczuka [2] also remark that in the presence of an inconsistent table the notion of generalized decision, which is defined below, has to be used.

Definition 10. *(generalized decision) Let $\mathcal{S}_d = (U, A_t = A_t^* \cup \{d\})$ be a decision table, the generalized decision function ∂ is defined as $\partial(u) = \{k \in V_d : \exists v \in U \ [(u,v) \in IND(A_t^*) \wedge I_d(v) = k]\}$. Any set consisting of all objects with the same generalized decision value is called a generalized decision class.*

Now, we can say that $\mathcal{S}_d$ is consistent or deterministic if $|\partial(u)| = 1$ for any $u \in U$. An important consequence of the last definition is that it is possible to transform an arbitrary inconsistent decision table $\mathcal{S}_d = (U, A_t = A_t^* \cup \{d\})$ into a consistent decision table $\mathcal{S}_\partial = (U, A_t^* \cup \{\partial\})$.

We will differentiate with names and notations between the reducts defined by definition 5 (we will call them *discerning decision reducts* and we will denote the set of all these reducts of a decision table $\mathcal{S}_d$ by $RED_{ind}(\mathcal{S}_d)$) and those defined by definition 9 (which we will call *positive region decision reducts*, and we will denote the set of all positive region decision reducts of a decision table $\mathcal{S}_d$ by $RED_{pos}(\mathcal{S}_d)$), analogously we will denote as $DS_{ind}(\mathcal{S}_d)$ and $DS_{pos}(\mathcal{S}_d)$ the set of super reducts determined by definitions 5 and 9 respectively. Sometimes, to point out that the generalized decision is being used, we will use the notation $\mathcal{S}_\partial$ instead of $\mathcal{S}_d$.

3   Relations

In this section, we present the theoretical relations between both types of reducts. Since $\mathcal{S}_\partial$ is a consistent table, first we can derive the following fact.

Lemma 1. *Let $\mathcal{S}_d = (U, A_t = A_t^* \cup \{d\})$ a decision table, then $RED_{pos}(\mathcal{S}_d) = RED_{ind}(\mathcal{S}_\partial) = RED_{pos}(\mathcal{S}_\partial)$.*

The following theorem establishes a relation between the set of discerning decision super reducts and the set of positive region decision super reducts of a decision table.

Theorem 1. *Let $\mathcal{S}_d = (U, A_t = A_t^* \cup \{d\})$ a decision table, then $DS_{ind}(\mathcal{S}_d) \subseteq DS_{pos}(\mathcal{S}_\partial)$. If $\mathcal{S}_d$ is consistent the equality holds.*

Proof. The implication $[IND(R)=IND(A_t^*)] \Rightarrow [POS_{\{d\}}(R) = POS_{\{d\}}(A_t^*)]$ naturally follows from definition of relative indiscernibility relation and definitions 8 and 6. From this is immediate that $DS_{ind}(\mathcal{S}_d) \subseteq DS_{pos}(\mathcal{S}_d)$.

Now let $\mathcal{S}_d$ be a consistent table and let $R \in DS_{pos}(\mathcal{S}_d)$; it means that $POS_{\{d\}}(R) = POS_{\{d\}}(A_t^*) = U$.

Let us suppose that $IND(R|D) \neq IND(A_t^*|D)$, obviously in this case $IND(A_t^*|D) \subset IND(R|D)$. Let $(u,v) \in IND(R|D) - IND(A_t^*|D)$; it means that A_t^* discerns between u and v but R does not. Hence we have that $I_R(u) = I_R(v)$ and $I_d(u) \neq I_d(v)$.

Let us denote as $[u]_{\{d\}}$ and $[u]_R$ respectively the class to which u belongs in $U/IND(d)$ and $U/IND(R)$. We have that $[u]_{\{d\}} \neq [v]_{\{d\}}$ but $[u]_R = [v]_R$, then $[u]_R \not\subseteq [u]_{\{d\}}$ and $[v]_R \not\subseteq [v]_{\{d\}}$ and hence $u \notin POS_{\{d\}}(R)$ and $v \notin POS_{\{d\}}(R)$ which is a contradiction.

Thus we have that $IND(R|D) = IND(A_t^*|D)$ and therefore $R \in DS_{ind}(\mathcal{S}_d)$ and hence $DS_{ind}(\mathcal{S}_d) = DS_{pos}(\mathcal{S}_d)$.

It is important to highlight that sometimes the equality holds even if we do not have consistent tables, as it can be seen from Example 2.

Example 2. Consider the decision table $\mathcal{S}_d$ in Table 2 being $U = \{u_1, u_2, u_3, u_4, u_5, u_6\}$, $A_t^* = \{a_1, a_2, a_3\}$ and $D = \{d\}$. Notice that Table 2 is inconsistent since $I_{\{a_1,a_2,a_3\}}(u_2) = I_{\{a_1,a_2,a_3\}}(u_5) = (1,0,H)$ and $0 = I_d(u_2) \neq I_d(u_5) = 1$.

Table 2. Another inconsistent table

U	a_1 a_2 a_3 d
u_1	0 1 H 0
u_2	1 0 H 0
u_3	1 1 V 0
u_4	0 1 N 1
u_5	1 0 H 1
u_6	0 1 V 0

We have that

$IND(D) = \{(u_1, u_1), (u_2, u_2), (u_3, u_3), (u_4, u_4), (u_5, u_5), (u_6, u_6), \langle u_1, u_2 \rangle,$
$\langle u_1, u_3 \rangle, \langle u_1, u_6 \rangle, \langle u_2, u_3 \rangle, \langle u_2, u_6 \rangle, \langle u_3, u_6 \rangle, \langle u_4, u_5 \rangle \}.$

$U/IND(D) = \{\{u_1, u_2, u_3, u_6\}, \{u_4, u_5\}\}$

$IND(A_t^*) = \{(u_1, u_1), (u_2, u_2), (u_3, u_3), (u_4, u_4), (u_5, u_5), (u_6, u_6), \langle u_2, u_5 \rangle)\}.$

$U/IND(A_t^*) = \{\{u_1\}, \{u_2, u_5\}, \{u_3\}, \{u_4\}, \{u_6\}\}$

$IND(A_t^*|D) = \{(u_1, u_1), (u_2, u_2), (u_3, u_3), (u_4, u_4), (u_5, u_5), (u_6, u_6), \langle u_1, u_2 \rangle,$
$\langle u_1, u_3 \rangle, \langle u_1, u_6 \rangle, \langle u_2, u_3 \rangle; \langle u_2, u_6 \rangle, \langle u_3, u_6 \rangle, \langle u_4, u_5 \rangle, \langle u_2, u_5 \rangle\}$

Let us consider the subsets $R_1 = A_t^* - \{a_1\} = \{a_2, a_3\}$, $R_2 = A_t^* - \{a_2\} = \{a_1, a_3\}$ and $R_3 = A_t^* - \{a_3\} = \{a_1, a_2\}$.

We have that

$IND(R_1|D) = IND(R_2|D) = IND(A_t^*|D)$ and

$IND(R_3|D) = IND(A_t^*|D) \cup \{\langle u_1, u_4 \rangle, \langle u_4, u_6 \rangle\}.$

From this we have that $DS_{ind}(\mathcal{S}_d) = \{R_1, R_2, A_t^*\}$ and $RED_{ind}(\mathcal{S}_d) = \{R_1, R_2\}$. Notice that $IND(\{a_3\}|D) = IND(A_t^*|D) \cup \{\langle 1_2, u_5 \rangle\}$ therefore $\{a_3\} \notin DS_{ind}(\mathcal{S}_d)$, being $\{a_1\} \subset R_3$ and $\{a_2\} \subset R_3$ no singleton in U is a super reduct.

Now, let us calculate the corresponding positive regions

$\underline{A_t^*}(\{u_1, u_2, u_3, u_6\}) = \{u_1, u_3, u_6\}$

$\underline{A_t^*}(\{u_4, u_5\}) = \{u_4\}$

and therefore $POS_{\{d\}}(A_t^*) = \{u_1, u_3, u_4, u_6\}$

$U/IND(R_1) = \{\{u_1\}, \{u_2, u_5\}, \{u_4\}, \{u_3, u_6\}\} = U/IND(R_2)$ and

$U/IND(R_3) = \{\{u_1, u_4, u_6\}, \{u_2, u_5\}, \{u_3\}\}$

then $\underline{R_1}(\{u_1, u_2, u_3, u_6\}) = \{u_1, u_3, u_6\} = \underline{R_2}(\{u_1, u_2, u_3, u_6\})$

and $\underline{R_3}(\{u_1, u_2, u_3, u_6\}) = \{u_3\}$

$\underline{R_1}(\{u_4, u_5\}) = \{u_4\} = \underline{R_2}(\{u_4, u_5\})$ and $\underline{R_3}(\{u_4, u_5\}) = \emptyset$;

and thence $POS_{\{d\}}(R_1) = POS_{\{d\}}(R_2) = POS_{\{d\}}(A_t^*) = \{u_1, u_3, u_4, u_6\}$ and $POS_{\{d\}}(R_3) = \{u_3\}$.

Then we have that $DS_{pos}(\mathcal{S}_d) = \{R_1, R_2, A_t^*\}$ and $RED_{pos}(\mathcal{S}_d) = \{R_1, R_2\}$. In this case, despite being an inconsistent table, we have that $DS_{ind}(\mathcal{S}_d) = DS_{pos}(\mathcal{S}_d)$.

Let $\mathcal{S}_d = (U, A_t^* \cup \{d\})$ be a (possibly inconsistent) decision table, and let us introduce the decision attribute Δ defined as

$$\Delta(u) = \begin{cases} [u]_\partial & if \ [u]_\partial \subseteq [u]_{\{d\}} \\ [u]_{A_t^*} & otherwise \end{cases} \tag{1}$$

Theorem 2. *Let $\mathcal{S}_d = (U, A_t^* \cup \{d\})$ be a decision table and let $\mathcal{S}_\Delta = (U, A_t^* \cup \{\Delta\})$ being Δ defined as in (1), then $\mathcal{S}_\Delta$ is consistent.*

Proof. Let suppose that $\mathcal{S}_d$ is consistent, then for every $u \in U$ we have that $[u]_\partial = [u]_{\{d\}}$ and hence $[u]_\Delta = [u]_\partial = [u]_{\{d\}}$. It means that $U/IND(\{\Delta\}) = U/IND(\{\partial\}) = U/IND(\{d\})$ so $\mathcal{S}_\Delta$ consistent.

Let us now consider that $\mathcal{S}_d$ is inconsistent and let $u \in U$ such that $[u]_\partial \subseteq [u]_{\{d\}}$; in this case, from (1) we have that $[u]_\Delta = [u]_\partial \subseteq [u]_{\{d\}}$.

Let suppose now that $[u]_\partial \nsubseteq [u]_{\{d\}}$, then from (1) $[u]_\Delta = [u]_{A_t^*}$ and from definition of generalized decision (definition 10) we can conclude that $[u]_{A_t^*} \subseteq$

$[u]_\partial$; thereby $U/IND(\{\Delta\})$ is a finer partition than $U/IND(\{\partial\})$. Therefore $\mathcal{S}_\Delta$ is consistent.

From theorem 2, since $\mathcal{S}_\Delta$ is consistent, it is immediate the following.

Corollary 1. Let $\mathcal{S}_d = (U, A_t^* \cup \{d\})$ be a decision table and let $\mathcal{S}_\Delta = (U, A_t^* \cup \{\Delta\})$ built as above. Then $RED_{ind}(\mathcal{S}_\Delta) = RED_{pos}(\mathcal{S}_\Delta)$.

From theorem 2 and from the definitions of $\Delta(u)$ and $\partial(u)$ we also have that:

Corollary 2. Let $\mathcal{S}_d = (U, A_t^* \cup \{d\})$ be a decision table and let $\mathcal{S}_\Delta = (U, A_t^* \cup \{\Delta\})$ built as above. Then $RED_{ind}(\mathcal{S}_d)=RED_{pos}(\mathcal{S}_\Delta)$.

The theorems and properties enunciated in this section confirm the non-equivalence between the two definitions of reduct. But even more, our study gives us the possibility of using algorithms to compute one type of reducts in contexts where algorithms to compute other type are used and vice versa. For example Corollary 2 provides a method for computing discerning decision reducts (definition 5) for an inconsistent table by using a software like RSES [2] which was designed for computing positive region decision reducts (definition 9).

3.1   Case Study

Here we illustrate the non-equivalence between the two definitions of reduct using the dataset Spect from the UCI Machine Learning Repository [1].

The Spect dataset consists of two non-disjoint classes, each class containing 40 objects and 22 descriptive attributes, but there are several coincidences in object descriptions. Table 3 shows these coincidences.

Description (I) $a_1 = a_2 = a_3 = a_4 = a_5 = a_6 = a_7 = a_8 = a_9 = a_{10} = a_{11} = a_{12} = a_{13} = a_{14} = a_{15} = a_{16} = a_{17} = a_{18} = a_{19} = a_{20} = a_{21} = a_{22} = 0$ appears 12 times in class 0 and twice in class 1. Obviously none reduct can discern among these objects. Likewise, description (II) $a_1 = a_2 = a_3 = a_4 = a_5 = a_6 = a_7 = a_8 = a_9 = a_{10} = a_{11} = a_{12} = a_{13} = a_{14} = a_{15} = a_{16} = a_{17} = a_{18} = a_{19} = a_{20} = a_{21} = 0$, $a_{22} = 1$ appears 3 times in class 0 and once in class 1. Descriptions (III) $a_1 = a_2 = a_3 = a_4 = a_5 = a_6 = a_7 = a_8 = a_9 = a_{10} = a_{11} = a_{12} = a_{13} = a_{14} = a_{15} = a_{16} = a_{17} = a_{18} = a_{19} = a_{21} = a_{22} = 0$, $a_{20} = 1$ and (IV) $a_1 = 1$, $a_2 = a_3 = a_4 = 0$, $a_5 = 1$, $a_6 = a_7 = a_8 = a_9 = 0$, $a_{10} = 1$, $a_{11} = a_{12} = a_{13} = a_{14} = a_{15} = a_{16} = a_{17} = a_{18} = 0$, $a_{19} = 1$, $a_{20} = a_{21} = a_{22} = 0$ appear once in each class. The last two columns in Table 3 (T(0) and T(1)) show the times each description appears in class 0 and class 1 respectively.

From the Spect dataset we created two modified datasets: Spect3c and Spect6c. Spect3c results from creating a new class containing the intersection between the two original classes and Spect6c results from separating each repeated description as a new class. Notice that Spect3c is the table resulting from applying generalized decision; in Table 4 we denote it by $\mathcal{S}_\partial$, meanwhile Spect6c corresponds to $\mathcal{S}_\Delta$.

Table 4 presents the amount of discerning decision reducts (column (A)) and positive region decision reducts (column(B)) from the original Spect dataset and

Table 3. Repeated objects in the Spect dataset

	a_1	a_2	a_3	a_4	a_5	a_6	a_7	a_8	a_9	a_{10}	a_{11}	a_{12}	a_{13}	a_{14}	a_{15}	a_{16}	a_{17}	a_{18}	a_{19}	a_{20}	a_{21}	a_{22}	T(0)	T(1)
(I)	0	0	0	0	0	0	0	0	0	0	0	0	0	0	0	0	0	0	0	0	0	0	12	2
(II)	0	0	0	0	0	0	0	0	0	0	0	0	0	0	0	0	0	0	0	0	0	1	3	1
(III)	0	0	0	0	0	0	0	0	0	0	0	0	0	0	0	0	0	0	0	1	0	0	1	1
(IV)	1	0	0	0	1	0	0	0	0	1	0	0	0	0	0	0	0	0	1	0	0	0	1	1
																								17	5

Table 4. Discerning decision reducts and positive region decision reducts for the Spect dataset

Dataset	Descriptive attributes	Classes	Objects	(A) $\lvert RED_{ind}(S_*)\rvert$	(B) $\lvert RED_{pos}(S_*)\rvert$
Spect=$(\mathcal{S}_d)$	22	2	80	26	70
Spect3c=$\mathcal{S}_\partial$	22	3	80	70	70
Spect6c=$\mathcal{S}_\Delta$	22	6	80	26	26

$* \in \{d, \partial, \Delta\}$.

for each one of the two modified datasets before described. Although Table 4 contains only quantities and not the sets, we can see the equalities $\lvert RED_{ind}(\mathcal{S}_d)\rvert = \lvert RED_{pos}(\mathcal{S}_\Delta)\rvert$ (Corollary 2) and $\lvert RED_{pos}(\mathcal{S}_d)\rvert = \lvert RED_{pos}(\mathcal{S}_\partial)\rvert$ (Lemma 1). Since $\mathcal{S}_\partial$ and $\mathcal{S}_\Delta$ are consistent tables, values in columns (A) and (B) in second and third rows show that $\lvert RED_{ind}(\mathcal{S}_\partial)\rvert = \lvert RED_{pos}(\mathcal{S}_\partial)\rvert$ and $\lvert RED_{ind}(\mathcal{S}_\Delta)\rvert = \lvert RED_{pos}(\mathcal{S}_\Delta)\rvert$. For this experiment, reducts were computed by using RSES [2].

4   Conclusions

This paper studies the relation between the two most important definitions of reduct demonstrating and illustrating that although in many cases (particularly when classes are disjoint, and tables are consistent) the two concepts coincide, in general they are not the same. As we show in the study case, our study gives us, as an immediate result, the possibility of using algorithms to compute reducts by definition 5, in contexts where algorithms to compute reducts by definition 9 are used and vice versa. Knowledge of the true relationship between these concepts can make proper use of each approach. This study can be a starting point for further considerations regarding other definitions of reduct.

References

1. Bache, K., Lichman, M.: UCI Machine Learning Repository. University of California, School of Information and Computer Science, Irvine, CA (2013),
   http://archive.ics.uci.edu/ml

2. Bazan, J.G., Szczuka, M.S.: The Rough Set Exploration System. In: Peters, J.F., Skowron, A. (eds.) Transactions on Rough Sets III. LNCS, vol. 3400, pp. 37–56. Springer, Heidelberg (2005)
3. Chen, D.G., Wang, C.Z., Hu, Q.H.: A new approach to attribute reduction of consistent and inconsistent covering decision systems with covering rough sets. Information Sciences 177, 3500–3518 (2007)
4. Kryszkiewicz, M.: Comparative studies of alternative type of knowledge reduction in inconsistent systems. International Journal of Intelligent Systems 16, 105–120 (2001)
5. Mi, J.S., Wu, W.Z., Zhang, W.X.: Approaches to knowledge reduction based on variable precision rough set model. Information Sciences 159(3), 255–272 (2004)
6. Miao, D.Q., Zhao, Y., Yao, Y.Y., Li, H.X., Xu, F.F.: Relative reducts in consistent and inconsistent decision tables of the Pawlak rough set model. Information Sciences 179(24), 4140–4150 (2009)
7. Pawlak, Z.: Rough sets. International Journal of Computer Information and Science 11, 341–356 (1982)
8. Pawlak, Z.: Rough Sets: Theoretical Aspects of Reasoning About Data. Kluwer Academic Publishers, Dordrecht (1991)
9. Skowron, A., Rauszer, C.: The discernibility matrices and functions in information systems. In: Słowiński, R. (ed.) Intelligent Decision Support, Handbook of Applications and Advances of the Rough Sets Theory, System Theory, Knowledge Engineering and Problem Solving, vol. 11, pp. 331–362. Kluwer Academic Publishers, Dordrecht (1992)
10. Ślęzak, D.: Approximate entropy reducts. Fundamenta Informaticae 53(3-4), 365–390 (2002)
11. Zhao, Y., Yao, Y., Luo, F.: Data analysis based on discernibility and indiscernibility. Information Sciences 177(22), 4959–4976 (2007)

A Family of Two-Dimensional Benchmark Data Sets and Its Application to Comparing Different Cluster Validation Indices

Jorge M. Santos[1,2] and Mark Embrechts[3]

[1] ISEP, School of Engineering, Polytechnic of Porto - Dept. of Mathematics
[2] INEB, Biomedical Engineering Institute, Porto - Portugal
[3] Rensselaer Polytechnic Institute - Dept. Ind. Systems Eng., Troy, NY - USA

Abstract. There are two main objectives in this paper: the first one is
to introduce a collection of two-dimensional benchmark data sets with a
wide variety of clustering characteristics that are typical for real-world
data sets. These simple 2-D data sets allow the user to easily evaluate
clustering solutions from a variety of different clustering algorithms; the
second one is to evaluate four different commonly used clustering validation indices by using these 2-D benchmark data sets. It is shown that
even for simple 2-D data sets there is a large discrepancy on the ideal
number of clusters suggested by traditional cluster validation indices.
The performed experiments also suggest that the Dunn and the GAP
statistic seems to be more robust cluster validation indices, even though
they still fail to comply with common sense clustering solutions in more
than 50% of the cases.

1 Introduction

The aim of clustering for a given data set is to identify different groups in such
a way that (i) data within each group are similar to each other and (ii) different
groups are dissimilar to each other. Clustering is a very complex and problem
dependent task. There are several different clustering algorithms and it is well
known that the resulting clusters are not unique: vastly different acceptable clustering solutions for the same data set can (and often will) occur. Two popular
clustering algorithms will be applied in this paper to compare cluster validation
indices: (i) the standard agglomerative average link hierarchical clustering with
Euclidean distance and (ii) the K-means clustering. Hierarchical agglomerative
clustering starts by assigning each data point to a single cluster and then enlarg-
ing the clusters by joining clusters based on cluster similarity measures (which
can be based on different distance metrics (e.g., the Euclidean, and the Man-
hattan distance). The K-means algorithm on the other hand starts with a given
number of cluster prototypes, then it iteratively assigns data points to these
prototypes and updates them accordingly.

Because there isn't a known a priori solution for a clustering problem, cluster
validation indices are often utilized (i) to evaluate and compare different proposed clustering solutions and (ii) to assess the cluster solution quality. There

J.F. Martínez-Trinidad et al. (Eds.): MCPR 2014, LNCS 8495, pp. 41–50, 2014.
© Springer International Publishing Switzerland 2014

is a variety of cluster validation indices. In this work four popular cluster validation indices will be applied as explained in Sect. 3. Cluster validation indices are typically used to determine the optimal number of clusters for a particular clustering method.

There are few two-dimensional benchmark data sets for clustering: in most cases such 2-D benchmark data are limited to two or more partially overlapping Gaussian blobs. An example of a set of 2-D data sets with a small set of different clustering situations can be found in [1]. In addition, there are some data sets for image segmentation with clustering solutions proposed by humans [2,3]. We introduce in this paper a benchmark data and make it available for benchmarking new clustering algorithms. 2-D data sets offer the advantage that it can easily be visualized to evaluate the proposed clustering solution.

For high-dimensional data sets one usually relies on cluster validation indices for assessing the clustering quality. It will be shown in this paper that these indices are a weak tool at best to assess cluster quality: even with very simple data sets such cluster validation indices often fail to identify the proper number of clusters using the most common clustering algorithms.

2   The Data Sets

The data sets presented in this work were first proposed by Santos et al. in 2005 [4] and are available via [5]. They consist of a set of 30 two-dimensional artificial data sets as depicted in Fig. 5 and they were specifically designed for assessing human clustering on two-dimensional data. All 30 data sets were manually constructed and it was attempted to create the different situations typically encountered in clustering-related tasks.

The 30 benchmark data sets can be divided in different groups according to specific characteristics such as

- Connectedness - Probably the most basic feature leading someone to join points into clusters whenever connecting paths are perceived. This feature is valued in the data set of Fig. 1a when a human "sees" one cluster instead of two.
- Structuring direction - This feature leads us to "see" the two arms of the cross in Fig. 1b instead of only one cluster. Humans are good at perceiving structuring directions in data set graphs, independently of those directions being straight or curved lines.
- Structuring density - This feature leads us to "see" two clusters in Fig. 1c instead of only one.
- Structuring morphology - This feature leads us to "see" two clusters in Fig. 1d instead of only one, deciding differently of the similar Fig. 1a. The reason is that, contrary to Fig. 1a, we now identify the bulging out wart of Fig. 1d with a known form.

A set of manual clustering experiments were performed with control groups of adults and children in order to grasp the clustering process and divide the results

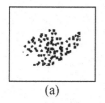
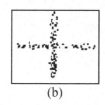
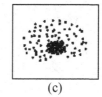
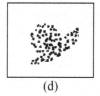

| (a) | (b) | (c) | (d) |

Fig. 1. Clustering features: a) connectedness; b) structuring direction; c) structuring density; d) structuring morphology

according to different kinds of data sets such as data sets (i) with well-separated clusters; (ii) with different density clusters; (iii) with crossing clusters; (iv) with nested-clusters; (v) with spiral-shaped clusters.

Experimental results showed that solutions proposed by adults are more consistent, exhibiting fewer solutions for each data set than the ones proposed by children (6-7 years). A more detailed analysis on children solutions revealed that a large percentage of them usually build clusters with a small number of points. It seems that they pay particular attention to small groups. An example of such behavior is shown in Fig. 2. In this case we may consider as outliers points belonging to extremely small clusters. Adults produce more consistent solutions but also very different. An example of four different solutions proposed for a data set with different point densities is depicted in Fig. 3(a-d).

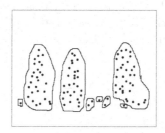

Fig. 2. One clustering solution proposed by children for 'Anthills'

It is well known that there is no unique solution for clustering and the results of the experiments reported in [4] show exactly that.

The 2-D benchmark data sets can also be used for evaluating the performance of clustering algorithms by comparing their solutions with the ones proposed by humans in [4] or with solutions proposed by a specific person. Although the benchmark data sets are relatively small, they can be easily transformed to big data sets by generating additional data points scattered around the original data points. Similarly for the benchmarking of outlier detection algorithms it would be straightforward to produce some outliers for these data sets. In addition we colored in plausible clusters that can be interpreted as different classes for

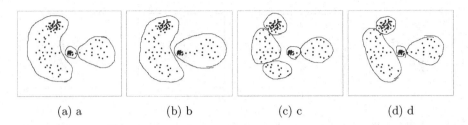

(a) a   (b) b   (c) c   (d) d

Fig. 3. Four different clustering solutions proposed by adults for 'Anchor' (a-d)

benchmarking supervised learning algorithms. For other possible solutions we refer to [4].

3   Cluster Validation Indices

In this work we chose to use some of the most common cluster validation indices like Davies-Bouldin, Dunn and Silhouette indices but also the GAP statistics, not so well known but that proved to be a very interesting index. In the following we will briefly present these indices.

3.1   Davies-Bouldin Index

The Davies-Bouldin (DB) cluster validation index [6] is a measure that helps to estimate the ideal number of clusters (K) in a dataset and it is based on the average ratio between the within cluster scatter (S_l) for all clusters and the distance D between two clusters. The DB Index is computed by:

$$DB = \frac{1}{N} \sum_{l=1}^{N} R_l \qquad (1)$$

with

$$R_l = \max_{l \neq m} R_{lm} \qquad (2)$$

$$R_{lm} = \frac{S_l + S_m}{D_{lm}} \qquad (3)$$

$$D_{lm} = \|\mathbf{v}_l - \mathbf{v}_m\| = \sqrt{\sum_{k=1}^{N} |v_{kl} - v_{km}|^2} \qquad (4)$$

$$S_l = \sqrt{\frac{1}{N_l} \sum_{m=1}^{N_l} |\mathbf{x}_m - \mathbf{v}_l|^2} \qquad (5)$$

where N is the number of clusters for which we are computing the DB index, S_l is the within cluster scatter for cluster l, $\mathbf{v}_l$ is the n dimensional cluster centroid for cluster l, $v_i l$ is the ith component of $\mathbf{v}_l$, $\mathbf{x}_l$ representes an individual data point in cluster l, and N_l and N_m are the number of data in clusters l and m respectively. D_{lm} is the distance between vectors which are chosen as characteristic of clusters l and m. In formulas 4 and 5 we use the Euclidian distance but the original ones use the Minkowski distance.

A lower DB index indicates a better cluster quality.

3.2   Dunn Index

The Dunn index [7] is simpler but similar to the Davies-Bouldin index because it is also based on relations between within-cluster distance and between-clusters distance. The within-cluster distance Δl is computed as the maximum distance between two points in the same cluster l and the between-clusters distance $\delta(l, m)$ between cluster l and cluster m is computed as the smallest distance between two points in different clusters (l and m). The Dunn index is defined as the minimum ratio between the between-clusters distance, $\delta(l, m)$, and the within-cluster distance Δl,

$$Dunn = \frac{\delta(l, m)}{\Delta l} \tag{6}$$

with

$$\Delta l = \max_{x,y \in l}(d(x, y)) \tag{7}$$

$$\delta(l, m) = \min_{x \in l, y \in m}(d(x, y)) \tag{8}$$

A higher Dunn index indicates a better cluster quality.

3.3   Cluster Silhuette Width Index

The cluster silhouette width (SHW) index [8] is a measure that compares cluster tightness and cluster separation and it is based on the silhouette width for each sample, the average silhouette width for each cluster, and the overall average silhouette width for all the data. The optimal number of clusters maximizes the cluster silhouette width index:

$$SHW = \frac{1}{N} \sum_{l=1}^{N} \frac{1}{N_l} \sum_{i=1}^{N_l} s_i \tag{9}$$

with

$$s_i = \frac{b_i - a_i}{max\{a_i, b_i\}}$$

$$a_i = \frac{1}{N_A} \sum_{\substack{x_i, x_j \in A \\ i \neq j}} d(x_i, x_j)$$

$$b_i = \underset{A \neq C}{\text{minimum }} d(x_i, C)$$

where N is the number of clusters, N_l is the number of data in cluster l, a_i is the average within-cluster distance, b_i is the minimal average between-cluster distance between two clusters, $d(x_i, x_j)$ is the dissimilarity between objects x_i and x_j of the same cluster, and $d(i, C)$ is the average dissimilarity of object x_i to all objects of C. The silhouette value varies from $-1 \leq S \leq 1$ and a value close to unity for a sample indicates that the sample is 'well-clustered', a value close to -1 is indicative of a possible misclassification and a value close to 0 means that that sample could also be assigned to another cluster.

A higher SHW index indicates a better cluster quality.

3.4   GAP Statistic

The GAP statistic was introduced in [9] and is used to estimate the number of clusters in a data set by comparing the cluster dispersion obtained for a clustering algorithm against the cluster dispersion obtained with the same algorithm for a uniformly random distribution of the same number of data with the same number of attributes. Cluster dispersion is algorithmic dependent. For hierarchical clustering, cluster dispersion is defined as:

$$Gap(k) = \mathbf{E}\{\log(W_k)\} \tag{10}$$

with

$$W_k = \sum_{r=1}^{k} \frac{1}{2n_r} D_r \tag{11}$$

where $\mathbf{E}\{.\}$ is the expectation operator for the reference uniformly random distribution, k is the number of clusters, W_k is the pooled within-cluster sum of squares around the cluster means, and D_r is the sum of all pairwise distances in cluster r. The GAP statistic is a function of the number of clusters in a given dataset, meaning that one usually computes it for a different number of clusters k and take as the possible number of clusters the one for which there is a sudden jump in the difference of the cluster dispersion between the actual data and the random gauge data.

4   Experiments

We performed an exhaustive number of experiments with the 30 data sets using both K-means [10] and hierarchical clustering algorithms [11]. In both cases Euclidean distance-based similarity measures were used. The purpose of these experiments is to demonstrate that (even for simple 2-D data sets) different cluster validation indices often result in different assessments for the optimal number of clusters. In these experiments the suggested number of clusters for both clustering algorithms was determined for each of the four cluster validation indices. We show in Fig. 4 the clustering indexes results obtained with K-means (left) and the hierarchical clustering (right) on the 'Citroen' data set. As one can see, there is a considerable difference on the results obtained for both clustering

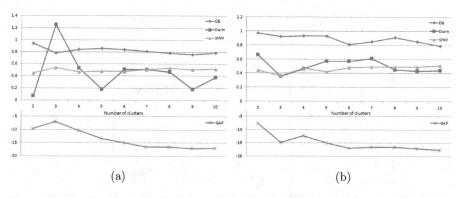

Fig. 4. Davies-Bouldin, Dunn, Silhuette and GAP indices values for data set Citroen for both K-means (a) and hierarchical (b) clustering algorithms

algorithms and also very different values for the different clustering indices. In this case, the suggested number of clusters for K-means clustering was DB=9, Dunn=3, SHW=3, GAP=3 and for hierarchical clustering was DB=10, Dunn=2, SHW=10, GAP=2.

We did not attempt to reconcile the results of obtained number of clusters with the 'real' number of clusters (as suggested by human evaluations). Only in data sets with well-separated and globular shaped clusters one can observe a match between the number of clusters obtained from cluster validation indices and human assessments.

5   Results

Results of the performed experiments with 29 data sets are presented in Table 1. We do not present any results for data set 'One' because there is only 1 cluster

Table 1. Clustering results for the 29 data sets

		Three	Kites	Citroen	Bermuda	Clock	Snake	Anthills	Birds	Anvils	Anchor	Cross	Starfish	Swarm	Helix	Eye	Hockey	Bean	Rings	Boomer.	Stamp	Layers	Sticks	Lips	Duck	Food	Epiglottis	Penguin	Sunset	Spiral	Hits
	Sep.	n	n	n	n	y	y	y	y	y	y	n	n	n	n	y	n	n	n	n	n	y	y	y	y	y	n	n	n	n	n
	Clust.	3	2	2	4	3	2	3	3	2	4	2	5	6	2	2	2	2	2	4	3	3	2	2	2	4	2	2	3	2	
K-means	DB	3	3	9	8	3	2	7	3	2	5	5	12	8	3	6	4	5	2	8	6	10	2	6	11	12	7	9	4	8	7
K-means	Dunn	3	2	3	3	4	2	2	2	2	3	2	5	3	2	2	2	3	2	2	8	3	2	6	2	2	8	9	3	3	14
K-means	SHW	2	4	3	6	3	2	6	3	2	3	5	8	5	3	6	3	5	8	10	6	10	2	6	8	11	7	3	3	7	6
K-means	GAP	3	2	3	9	4	2	6	3	2	5	1	1	6	3	3	4	1	2	2	1	2	5	2	3	2	2	3	3	3	10
Hierarch.	DB	3	3	10	8	3	2	9	3	2	5	5	12	8	3	8	4	4	9	10	7	9	2	9	12	12	7	10	5	7	6
Hierarch.	Dunn	3	2	2	2	3	2	2	2	2	6	2	6	2	5	2	4	4	2	2	6	2	2	7	3	2	8	10	3	3	11
Hierarch.	SHW	2	5	10	8	3	2	11	3	2	3	5	7	5	3	5	3	4	7	6	6	7	2	5	4	11	7	4	3	6	6
Hierarch.	GAP	3	2	2	3	3	2	2	3	2	4	4	7	3	3	3	5	3	2	3	3	3	2	2	4	2	2	4	4	3	14
	Hits	6	4	2	0	6	8	0	6	8	1	2	1	1	1	2	1	0	5	0	1	2	7	2	1	0	2	0	5	0	

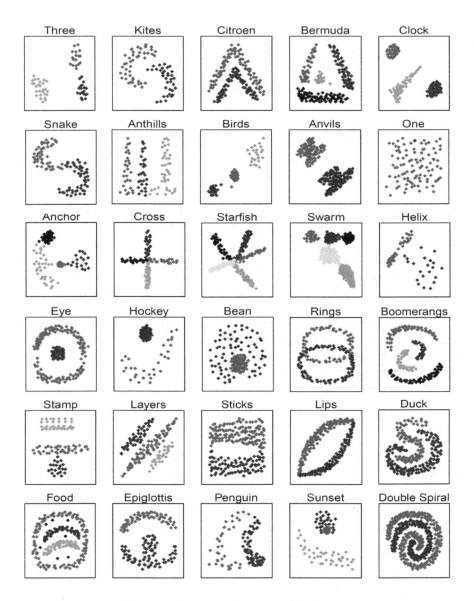

Fig. 5. The 30 Two-dimensional data sets

and several indices exhibit numerical difficulties to yield a single cluster as a valid assessment. The first row (Sep.) shows if the clusters are linearly separable meaning that the clustering problem is an easier one and the second row (Clust.) shows the number of suggested clusters. In the last row we present the number of times there is a coincidence between the number of clusters given by the cluster validation index and the number of suggested clusters. The last column shows the number of times each cluster validation index gives the correct number of clusters.

As one can see, there is a significant difference in the number of clusters proposed by each clustering validation index for each data set and each clustering algorithm. The difference is related with the way these indices use the within cluster or between clusters distances. Different cluster shapes and structure also represent a problem for clustering algorithms. A closer view to the results may suggest that the Davies-Bouldin and the Cluster Silhuette Width Indices are the indices presenting the worst results and the Dunn and the GAP statistics indices being the ones presenting the best results. We can also see that the results are better for 'simple' data sets as those marked as linearly separable compared with those more 'complex' data sets where the results are quite bad. There are almost 50% of the data sets where the number of hits is zero or one meaning that almost every clustering algorithm and cluster validation index fail to give the correct number of clusters. One can see for example the case of the Bermuda data set that presents 4 distinct clusters and the results of the cluster validation indices are quite different none of them with the correct answer.

We must emphasize again that the purpose of these experiments was not to compare clustering solutions with those proposed in [4] but only to evaluate the results for the number of clusters. If we have done such a comparison we can assume that the results would have been much worst because apart from the bad results on the number of clusters one should add the expected bad results on the clustering solutions because the clustering algorithms used in the experiment would have failed on given the correct solution in several data sets.

6 Conclusions

We have presented in this work a novel set of two-dimensional benchmark data sets for evaluating clustering algorithms and clustering validation indices. Because 2-D data can be visualized, it is easy to assess the resulting clustering solutions and compare them with the 'natural' clustering provided by humans. The natural clustering solution were obtained from a previous experiment using human subjects but they can be substituted by the users own preferred labeling. The presented data sets can also be easily transformed in big data sets by adding data points randomly distributed in the neighborhood of each point.

The benchmark data sets were used to assess the performance of cluster validation indices with two different popular clustering algorithms. This study demonstrates that even for data sets that would be perceived as 'easy' to cluster, the optimal number of clusters as suggested by the cluster validation indices can vary widely.

References

1. Ultsch, A.: Clustering with som: U*c. In: Workshop on Self-Organizing Maps, pp. 75–82 (2005), www.uni-marburg.de/fb12/datenbionik/Daten

2. Martin, D., Fowlkes, C., Tal, D., Malik, J.: A database of human segmented natural images and its application to evaluating segmentation algorithms and measuring ecological statistics. In: Proc. 8th Int'l Conf. Computer Vision, vol. 2, pp. 416–423 (July 2001)

3. Alpert, S., Galun, M., Basri, R., Brandt, A.: Image segmentation by probabilistic bottom-up aggregation and cue integration. In: Proceedings of the IEEE Conference on Computer Vision and Pattern Recognition (June 2007)

4. Santos, J.M., Marques de Sá, J.: Human clustering on bi-dimensional data: An assessment. Technical Report 1, INEB - Instituto de Engenharia Biomédica, Porto, Portugal (October 2005)

5. Santos, J.M.: Bi-dimensioanl data sets, http://www.dema.isep.ipp.pt/~jms/datasets

6. Davies, D., Bouldin, D.: A cluster separation measure. IEEE Transactions on Pattern Analysis and Machine Intelligence 1, 224–227 (1971)

7. Dunn, J.C.: Well separated clusters and optimal fuzzy partitions. Journal of Cybernetics 4(1), 95–104 (1974)

8. Rousseeuw, P.J.: Silhouettes: A graphical aid to the interpretation and validation of cluster analysis. Computational and Applied Mathematics 20, 53–65 (1987)

9. Tibshirani, R., Walther, G., Hastie, T.: Estimating the number of clusters in a data set via the gap statistic. Journal of the Royal Statistical Society: Series B (Statistical Methodology) 63(2), 411–423 (2001)

10. Jain, A.K.: Data clustering: 50 years beyond k-means. Pattern Recognition Letters 31(8), 651–666 (2010)

11. Xu, R., Wunsch, D.: Clustering. IEEE Press Series on Computational intelligence. IEEE (2008)

Studying Netconf in Hybrid Rule Ordering Strategies for Associative Classification

Raudel Hernández-León[1], José Hernández-Palancar[1],
J.A. Carrasco-Ochoa[2], and José Fco. Martínez-Trinidad[2]

[1] Centro de Aplicaciones de Tecnologías de Avanzada (CENATAV),
7a ♯ 21406 e/ 214 and 216, Rpto. Siboney, Playa, C.P. 12200, La Habana, Cuba
{rhernandez,jpalancar}@cenatav.co.cu
[2] Instituto Nacional de Astrofísica, Óptica y Electrónica (INAOE)
Luis Enrique Erro No. 1, Sta. María Tonantzintla, Puebla, C.P. 72840, México
{ariel,fmartine}@ccc.inaoep.mx

Abstract. In Associative Classification, building a classifier based on Class Association Rules (CARs) consists in finding an ordered CAR list by applying a rule ordering strategy. Since this CAR list will be used to build a classifier, it is important to develop a good rule ordering strategy. In this paper, we introduce four novel hybrid rule ordering strategies; the first three combine the Netconf measure with Support-Confidence based rule ordering strategies. The fourth strategy, called Hybrid Specific Rules/Netconf (SR/NF), combines the Netconf measure with a rule ordering strategy based on the CAR's size. The experiments show that the proposed strategies obtain better classification accuracy than the best ordering strategies reported in the literature.

Keywords: Classification, class association rules, rule ordering strategy.

1 Introduction

Associative Classification, also known as Classification Association Rule Mining (CARM) is a well-known Data Mining technique for the extraction of Class Association Rules (CARs) from a given class-transaction dataset. The aim of Associative Classification is to build a classifier to predict the class of "unseen" transactions. In general, a CAR describes an implicative co-occurring relationship between a set of items (itemset) and a pre-defined class, expressed as "$\langle item_1, \ldots, item_n \rangle \Rightarrow class$".

Associative classification has been applied to many tasks including text classification [6], automatic image annotation [19], automatic error detection [16], determination of cotton yarn quality [2], among others.

In CARM, it is assumed that a set of items $I = \{i_1, i_2, \ldots, i_n\}$, a set of pre-defined classes $C = \{c_1, c_2, \ldots, c_m\}$ and a class-transaction dataset T are given. Each transaction $T_j \in T$ comprises a set of items $I_j \subseteq I$ and a class $c \in C$. A CAR has the form $X \Rightarrow c$, with $X \subseteq I$ and $c \in C$. The rule $X \Rightarrow c$ holds in the dataset T with certain Support s and Confidence α, where s is the fraction

J.F. Martínez-Trinidad et al. (Eds.): MCPR 2014, LNCS 8495, pp. 51–60, 2014.
© Springer International Publishing Switzerland 2014

of transactions in T that contain $X \cup \{c\}$, and α is the ratio of the number of transactions in T containing $X \cup \{c\}$ from the total number of transactions containing X; "alpha" represents how "strongly" the antecedent X implies the consequent c.

Several classifiers based on CARs have been developed [15, 14, 9, 22, 12, 13]. Regardless of the CARM approach, a CAR based classifier is usually presented as an ordered list of CARs based on a rule ordering strategy. Therefore, we could obtain a more accurate classifier by developing a better rule ordering strategy.

In this paper, we propose four novel hybrid rule ordering strategies, which combine the Netconf measure with four rule ordering strategies based on Support and Confidence, as well as with a rule ordering strategy based on the CAR's size. Our experiments were conducted using several datasets taken from the UCI Machine Learning Repository [3], all of them used in other representative works [20–22]. The results obtained using the proposed hybrid rule ordering strategies show good performance, regarding the accuracy of classification, compared against the best hybrid rule ordering strategies reported in the literature.

This paper is organized as follows: The next section describes the related work. In Section 3, the new hybrid rule ordering strategies are introduced. In Section 4, experimental results comparing our hybrid rule ordering strategies against the best ones reported in the literature are shown. Finally, our conclusions are given in Section 5.

2   Related Work

Broadly, the CAR-based classifiers can be categorized into two groups according to the way the CARs are generated: (1) **Two stage classifiers** where all CARs satisfying the Support and Confidence thresholds are mined in a first stage; and later, in a second stage, a classifier is built by selecting an ordered subset of CARs (CBA [15], CMAR [14]), and (2) **Integrated classifiers** where a reduced set of CARs is built in a single step (TFPC [9]), these algorithms avoid the coverage process by directly generating a subset of CARs.

2.1   Case Satisfaction Mechanisms

In [22], the authors summarize three case satisfaction mechanisms that have been employed for classifying "unseen" transactions in CAR based classifiers.

1. **Best Rule:** This mechanism selects, according to an ordering imposed on the list of CARs [22], the first (the best) rule that satisfies the transaction to be classified, and it assigns to this transaction the class associated to the best rule.
2. **Best K Rules:** For each pre-defined class, this mechanism selects the first (top) K rules satisfying the transaction to be classified and it assigns the class for this transaction applying an averaging process as those used in [20].
3. **All Rules:** This mechanism selects all rules satisfying the given transaction and it assigns the class applying an averaging process [14].

2.2 Rule Ordering Strategies

Once a subset of CARs has been obtained, regardless the way they were generated, the CARs are ordered. In [4, 20–22] the authors established six main CAR ordering strategies divided in two groups:

Group 1: Based on Support-Confidence

a) CSA (Confidence - Support - Antecedent size): The CSA rule ordering strategy sorts the rules in descending order according to their Confidence. Those CARs with the same Confidence value are sorted in descending order according to their Supports, and if the tie persists, CSA sorts the rules in ascending order according to their antecedent sizes [15, 14].

b) ACS (Antecedent size - Confidence - Support): The ACS rule ordering strategy is a variation of CSA, but it takes into account the antecedent size as first ordering criterion followed by Confidence and Support criteria [9].

c) L^3: This rule ordering strategy was proposed in [4] and it is also a variation of CSA, but it sorts the rules in descending order according to their antecedent size, as third ordering criterion.

Group 2: Based on Weighting

e) WRA (Weighted Relative Accuracy): The WRA rule ordering strategy, proposed in [9], assigns to each CAR a weight (based on their Support and Confidence) and then sorts the set of CARs in descending order according to these weights. The weight for a CAR $X \Rightarrow c$ is computed as $Sup(X)(Conf(X \Rightarrow c) - Sup(X))$.

f) LAP (Laplace Expected Error Estimate): The LAP rule ordering strategy was introduced in [8] and it been used to sort the CARs in some classifiers [21]. LAP rule ordering strategy is similar to WRA but LAP defines the weight of the CARs in a different way, also based on their Support and Confidence. Given a rule $X \Rightarrow c$, LAP is defined as $\frac{Sup(X \Rightarrow c)+1}{Sup(X)+|C|}$, where C is the set of predefined classes.

g) χ^2 (Chi-Square): The χ^2 rule ordering strategy is a well-known technique in statistics, which can be used to determine whether two variables are independent or related. After computing an additive χ^2 value for each CAR (also based on their Support and Confidence), these values are used to sort the rules in descending order [14].

Additionally, hybrid rule ordering strategies have been proposed in [20–22] by combining one rule ordering strategy taken from the Support-Confidence based group (group 1) and another one taken from the Weighting based group (group 2). In general, let A, B be rule ordering strategies from groups 1 and 2 respectively. The rule ordering strategy "Hybrid A/B" is defined as follows:

– For each predefined class, this ordering strategy selects, from the original list, the Best K Rules in B manner; the remainder of the original list is sorted in A manner; after, this strategy reorders the selected K Rules in A manner. Finally, these K Rules are put at the front of the remainder of the original rule list which has been already sorted in A manner.

The experiments in [20–22] showed that the obtained classification accuracies using these hybrid rule ordering strategies were better than the ones obtained using their "parents", e.g., the obtained accuracy using the Hybrid CSA/WRA rule ordering strategy was better than the accuracies obtained using CSA and WRA separately.

In [7], the authors proposed a hybrid rule ordering strategy, called MLRP (Multi-level Rule Priority), which sorts the CARs using rule priority to reduce the influence of rule dependence. The rule dependence problem occurs when (during the database coverage analysis) a training transaction O is covered by several CARs concurrently and one of them is used first for classifying O [7]. In this case, because the transaction O has been classified, the confidences of all other CARs covering O are recalculated excluding the transaction O, implying possible changes in the CARs order.

In a first step, MLPR adopts the L^3 rule ordering strategy as initial order. The L^3 strategy gives higher priority to higher confidence and longer rules. In a second step, rule dependencies are computed and stored in a matrix EWM (Effective Weight Matrix), and later, these dependencies are used to obtain the final order of the CARs [7].

In [13], a novel measure called Netconf [1] (see Eq. 1) was used to compute and sort the set of CARs; in this paper we will call Netconf rule ordering strategy (NF) to this approach. Some useful properties of the Netconf measure are the following:

– Netconf holds the statistical independence property, therefore $Netconf(X \Rightarrow c) = 0 \Leftrightarrow Sup(X \Rightarrow c) = Sup(X)Sup(c)$.
– $Netconf(X \Rightarrow c) \neq Netconf(c \Rightarrow X)$ if $Sup(X) \neq Sup(c)$, which means that Netconf is not symmetric, therefore, it can indicate the strength of implication in both directions.
– Netconf takes values in $[-1, 1]$, positive values represent positive dependencies, negative values represent negative dependencies and a zero value represents independence.
– Netconf satisfies some properties which, according to Shapiro [17], should be satisfied by every good quality measure used for separating strong rules from weak rules.

$$Netconf(X \Rightarrow c) = \frac{Sup(X \Rightarrow c) - Sup(X)Sup(c)}{Sup(X)(1 - Sup(X))} \tag{1}$$

In addition, in [13] the authors showed that Netconf solves the drawbacks of the Support and Confidence measures, which have been mentioned in several works [5, 18]. According to the above defined groups, the Netconf measure can be considered as a rule ordering strategy belonging to the Weighting based group. Therefore, in this paper, we investigate the use of the Netconf rule ordering strategy combined with rule ordering strategies from the Support-Confidence group in order to determine whether it is possible to obtain better hybrid rule ordering strategies than those proposed in the literature.

3   Novel Hybrid Rule Ordering Strategies

In this section, we present four novel hybrid rule ordering strategies. Following the results reported in [13], we propose to combine the Netconf rule ordering strategy (NF) with the well known Support-Confidence based rule ordering strategies (CSA, ACS and L^3), which gives as results the next three hybrid rule ordering strategies: (1) Hybrid CSA/NF, (2) Hybrid ACS/NF and (3) Hybrid L^3/NF.

Our hypothesis is that Netconf combined with CSA, ACS and L^3 can outperform the best hybrid strategies reported in the literature [20–22, 7].

A fourth hybrid rule ordering strategy based on Netconf (NF strategy) and the CAR's size (Specific Rules strategy) is also introduced in this paper. As it was shown in [12, 13], the Specific Rule strategy (SR) considers the CAR's size in descending order, favoring specific (large) rules since specific rules would involve more items from the unseen transactions than general (short) rules [13]. Notice that all rule ordering strategies of group 1 are also based on the CAR's size but this criterion is considered in ascending order (CSA and ACS), favoring general rules. In the case of L^3, the CAR's size is considered in descending order but it is applied after the Confidence and Support criteria (both applied in descending order), therefore, the general rules are favored because of the Support download closure [7]. Unlike the L^3 strategy, the SR strategy considers the CAR's size as first (and unique) criterion order, favoring specific rules. Thus, this new hybrid rule ordering strategy is called Hybrid Specific Rules/Netconf (Hybrid SR/NF).

In this case, as in the former proposed hybrid rule ordering strategies, our hypothesis is that Netconf combined with the CAR's size can outperform the best hybrid strategies reported in the literature [20–22, 7]. The overall procedure of the above fifth hybrid rule ordering strategies is shown in Algorithm 1.

In lines $2 - 5$, for all CARs belonging to list L, their Netconf are calculated and stored in the list L^{NF}. In line 6, the list L^{NF} is sorted in descending order according to the Netconf value. In line 7, the top K CARs of L^{NF} are selected and stored in L^{topK}. Later, the remainder of the L^{NF} list is stored in the L^X list (line 8). In lines $9 - 10$ both lists L^{topK} and L^X, are sorted in X manner. Finally, in line 11, the list L^{topK} is placed at front of the list L^X.

4   Experimental Results

In this section, we aim to evaluate the novel hybrid rule ordering strategies introduced in this paper; comparing their accuracy of classification against the best hybrid rule ordering strategies reported in the literature [20–22, 7]. The evaluation of all strategies was obtained using the TFPC classifier [10] coupled with the "Best K Rules" case satisfaction mechanism (with K equal to 5 as proposed in

---

Algorithm 1. Hybrid X/NF

Input: A list of CARs L

Output: A re-ordered list of CARs L^{Hybrid} ordered in a hybrid manner

1 $L^{NF} = L^{topK} = L^X = L^{Hybrid} \leftarrow \emptyset$

2 **forall** $r \in L$ **do**

3 $\quad$ **calculate** the *Netconf* Γ of r

4 $\quad$ **add** r jointly with its Γ value to L^{NF}

5 **end**

6 **sort** L^{NF} in a descending order according to Γ

7 $L^{topK} \leftarrow$ **select** the top K CARs $\in L^{NF}$

8 $L^X \leftarrow L^{NF} - L^{topK}$

9 **sort** L^{topK} in X manner

10 **sort** L^X in X manner

11 $L^{Hybrid} \leftarrow$ **put** L^{topK} at front of L^X

12 **return** L^{Hybrid}

---

[20]), although any classifier coupled with the "Best K Rules" case satisfaction mechanism could be used. In our experiments, for CSA/NF, ACS/NF, L^3/NF and SR/NF strategies, we also compute the Netconf value of the CARs in order to apply the proposed ordering strategies. Our tests were run on a 1.86 GHz Intel(R) Core(TM)2 CPU with 1.00 GB DDR2 of RAM, running Windows XP SP2.

The experiments were conducted using the datasets reported in [20–22], all of them taken from the UCI Machine Learning Repository [3]. It should be noticed that our experiments were done using ten-fold cross-validation, reporting the average over the ten folds. The same folds were used to evaluate all the rule ordering strategies. Additionally, in order to perform a fair comparison as it was reported in other works [14, 10, 22, 13], we set the Confidence threshold to 0.5, the Support threshold to 0.01 and the Netconf threshold to 0.5. Finally, for Algorithm 1 (see Section 3), we set K equal to 5 (the same value used in other works [20–22]).

In the first four columns of Table 1, we show the average accuracy that we get at applying the best no-hybrids rule ordering strategies, based on Support-Confidence [22]; additionally, in the last two columns we show the average accuracy that we get at applying NF and SR rule ordering strategies, respectively. From this set of results, it can be seen that the NF rule ordering strategy worked better than all other evaluated ordering strategies since as we can see from Table 1, NF gets the maximum accuracy in 13 out of the 19 datasets.

As we announced at section 3 of this paper, our hypothesis is that Netconf combined with CSA, ACS, L^3 and SR can overcome the best hybrid strategies reported in the literature. Thus, in order to test our hypothesis, we performed an experiment comparing the results of our novel hybrid rule ordering strategies against the best rule ordering strategies reported in the literature [20–22, 7].

Table 1. Classification accuracy using the main non-hybrid rule ordering strategies from group 1 as well as using the Netconf (NF) and Specific Rule (SR) ordering strategies

Dataset	CSA	ACS	L³	NF	SR
adult	80.80	74.70	80.80	**81.68**	81.43
anneal	88.29	75.58	88.51	**92.21**	**92.21**
breast	**89.99**	**89.99**	**89.99**	84.12	83.76
connect4	**65.83**	65.18	**65.83**	62.05	62.05
flare	84.30	84.30	84.52	85.87	**86.21**
glass	64.97	50.74	64.97	**67.49**	67.12
heart	51.42	39.76	51.42	**54.45**	**54.45**
hepatitis	81.83	48.50	82.03	**84.16**	**84.16**
horseColic	79.07	41.11	79.39	**82.56**	81.73
ionosphere	**86.34**	64.67	**86.34**	83.92	84.09
iris	95.33	95.33	95.33	**95.76**	95.21
led7	68.72	64.22	68.72	**73.32**	**73.32**
mushroom	99.04	64.92	99.04	**99.40**	98.36
pageBlocks	89.99	89.99	89.99	**91.83**	**91.83**
pima	74.37	73.85	75.06	**76.79**	76.01
nursery	77.75	55.08	77.75	**78.12**	77.96
soybean-large	88.01	86.10	88.01	**89.35**	88.73
ticTacToe	67.10	39.03	**67.45**	66.69	66.12
wine	71.51	50.28	71.51	71.23	**71.72**
Average	79.19	65.96	79.30	**80.05**	79.81

In the last four columns of Table 2, we show the accuracies obtained by our proposed Hybrid strategies CSA/NF, ACS/NF, L³/NF and SR/NF (see columns 5–8). In columns 2–4 of the same table we show the results of the best rule ordering strategies reported in the literature (CSA/χ^2, ACS/LA and MLRP). The first interesting thing that we can observe from our experiments is that, as it was established in [20–22], an Hybrid A/B strategy obtains better classification accuracy results than its "parents" A or B separately. For example, we can see in Table 2 that the classification accuracy obtained using Hybrid SR/NF (81.55) is greater than the accuracies obtained by its "parents" (see Table 1) SR (79.81) and NF (80.05). Analogously, the classification accuracies obtained by using Hybrid CSA/NF, Hybrid ACS/NF and Hybrid L³/NF are greater than the accuracies obtained by their "parents". From our results reported in Table 2, we can see that all the rule ordering strategies proposed in this paper outperform the best rule ordering strategies reported in the literature. It means that our hypothesis is true for all the proposed strategies except for ACS/NF. This occurs because the ACS strategy, different from CSA, L³ and SR strategies, favors short rules.

As we mentioned above, we evaluate all hybrid rule ordering strategies applying the "Best K Rules" case satisfaction mechanism (with K equal to 5 as in [20]). However, in order to show that these strategies are independent of the case satisfaction mechanism used, we performed the same experiments of

Table 2. Classification accuracy using hybrid rule ordering strategies

Dataset	CSA/χ^2	ACS/LA	MLRP	CSA/NF	ACS/NF	L^3/NF	SR/NF
adult	80.08	83.86	82.56	82.78	**84.25**	82.78	83.37
anneal	89.92	80.73	**93.77**	93.48	88.51	93.64	93.72
breast	**91.00**	89.59	83.66	84.12	89.60	84.12	85.26
connect4	65.88	65.28	62.06	62.13	65.41	62.15	62.37
flare	84.51	84.49	86.29	86.26	85.85	86.35	**86.52**
glass	65.59	60.82	67.80	67.71	65.40	67.73	**68.02**
heart	51.14	50.66	54.09	54.52	53.31	54.54	**56.51**
hepatitis	80.50	76.83	84.47	84.38	83.94	84.65	**86.43**
horseColic	81.24	81.01	82.90	82.56	81.85	82.88	**83.25**
ionosphere	84.05	84.90	83.75	84.10	**85.23**	84.10	84.31
iris	95.33	95.33	95.82	95.87	95.33	95.91	**96.93**
led7	68.92	64.85	73.41	73.50	73.06	73.47	**74.69**
mushroom	98.52	98.82	98.96	99.40	98.52	99.40	**99.52**
pageBlocks	90.72	90.16	92.22	91.91	91.47	91.88	**92.61**
pima	74.63	74.50	77.18	76.84	75.87	77.23	**77.65**
nursery	78.52	66.83	79.50	79.25	78.41	79.19	**80.12**
soybean-large	88.23	77.66	89.93	89.98	89.03	89.94	90.56
ticTacToe	67.94	63.16	66.74	66.69	66.31	66.86	**72.43**
wine	74.52	72.31	71.21	71.44	71.95	71.44	**75.14**
Average	79.54	76.94	80.33	80.36	80.17	80.43	**81.55**

Table 2 applying the other two case satisfaction mechanisms ("Best Rule" and "All Rules"); all these results appear in Table 3. Something interesting that can be seen from these results is that if we rank the strategies based on the accuracy they reach for the three case satisfaction mechanisms, we get the same ranking (see the last row in Table 3). However, the best average accuracies are obtained when the "Best K Rules" mechanism is used.

Table 3. Average classification accuracy throughout the 19 datasets using other Case Satisfaction Mechanisms (CSM)

CSM	CSA/χ^2	ACS/LA	MLRP	CSA/NF	ACS/NF	L^3/NF	SR/NF
Best Rule	79.46	76.86	80.26	80.29	80.12	80.37	81.48
All Rules	78.08	74.63	78.82	78.90	78.66	79.11	80.16
Best K Rules	**79.54**	**76.94**	**80.33**	**80.36**	**80.17**	**80.43**	**81.55**
Ranking	6	7	4	3	5	2	1

From our experiments we can conclude that in general our hybrid rule ordering strategies outperform the best hybrid strategies reported in the literature. We can see in Table 2 that the Hybrid SR/NF strategy gets an average accuracy, throughout the 19 datasets, of 81.55; it represents an improvement of 1.12 percentage points in accuracy with respect to the second place (Hybrid L^3/NF).

Finally, in order to determine if the results shown in Table 2 are statistically significant, we performed a pairwise comparison between all tested hybrid rule ordering strategies. Each cell (i, j), in Table 4, contains the number of datasets where the strategy of row i significantly Win/Lose to the strategy of column j. We detected ties using a one-tailed T-Test [11] with significance level of 0.05. The results in the pairwise comparison reveal that the proposed Hybrid SR/NF rule ordering strategy beats in accuracy all other evaluated rule ordering strategies, over most of the tested datasets.

Table 4. Pairwise comparison between all evaluated hybrid rule ordering strategies. Each cell (i, j) contains the number of datasets where the strategy of row i significantly Win/Lose to the strategy of column j, over the 19 selected datasets.

	CSA/χ^2	ACS/LA	MLRP	CSA/NF	ACS/NF	L^3/NF	SR/NF
CSA/χ^2		8/1	4/11	4/10	6/4	3/9	2/14
ACS/LA	1/8		5/12	4/12	0/3	4/12	1/14
MLRP	11/4	12/5		0/0	4/4	0/0	0/7
CSA/NF	10/4	12/4	0/0		7/4	0/0	0/9
ACS/NF	4/6	3/0	4/4	4/7		3/3	3/13
L^3/NF	9/3	12/4	0/0	0/0	3/3		0/5
SR/NF	14/2	14/1	7/0	9/0	13/3	5/0	

5 Conclusions

In this paper, we have proposed four novel hybrid rule ordering strategies based on the Netconf measure. Our experimental results show the proposed hybrid strategies always reached better classification accuracies than those obtained by their parents rule ordering strategies, as occurs with other hybrid strategies. From the experiments, we can conclude that our novel hybrid rule ordering strategies (with exception of ACS/NF) have better performance than the best hybrid rule ordering approaches reported in the literature. In particular, our Hybrid SR/NF strategy reached the best classification accuracy.

Acknowledgements. This work was partly supported by the National Council of Science and Technology of Mexico (CONACyT) through the project grants CB2008-106443 and CB2008-106366.

References

1. Ahn, K.I., Kim, J.Y.: Efficient Mining of Frequent Itemsets and a Measure of Interest for Association Rule Mining. Information and Knowledge Management 3(3), 245–257 (2004)
2. Amin, A.E.: A novel Classification Model for Cotton Yarn Quality based on Trained Neural Network using Genetic Algorithm. Knowledge-Based Systems 360, 124–132 (2013)

3. Asuncion, A., Newman, D.J.: UCI Machine Learning Repository (2007),
   http://www.ics.uci.edu/~mlearn/MLRepository.html
4. Baralis, E., Garza, P.: A Lazy Approach to Pruning Classification Rules. In: Proc.
   of the ICDM, pp. 35–42 (2002)
5. Berzal, F., Blanco, I., Sánchez, D., Vila, M.A.: Measuring the Accuracy and Interest
   of Association Rules: A new framework. Intelligent Data Analysis 6(3), 221–235
   (2002)
6. Buddeewong, S., Kreesuradej, W.: A new Association Rule-Based Text Classifier
   Algorithm. In: Proc. of the 17th IEEE International Conference on Tools with
   Artificial Intelligence, pp. 684–685 (2005)
7. Chun-Hao, C., Rui-Dong, C., Cho-Ming, L., Chih-Yang, C.: Improving the Performance of Association Classifiers by Rule Prioritization. Knowledge-Based Systems 36, 59–67 (2012)
8. Clark, P., Boswell, R.: Rule Induction with CN2: Some Recent Improvments. In:
   Kodratoff, Y. (ed.) EWSL 1991. LNCS, vol. 482, pp. 151–163. Springer, Heidelberg
   (1991)
9. Coenen, F., Leng, P.: An Evaluation of Approaches to Classification Rule Selection.
   In: Proc. of the ICDM, pp. 359–362 (2004)
10. Coenen, F., Leng, P., Zhang, L.: Threshold Tuning for Improved Classification
    Association Rule Mining. In: Ho, T.-B., Cheung, D., Liu, H. (eds.) PAKDD 2005.
    LNCS (LNAI), vol. 3518, pp. 216–225. Springer, Heidelberg (2005)
11. Demšar, J.: Statistical Comparisons of Classifiers over Multiple Data Sets. J. Mach.
    Learn. Res. 7, 1–30 (2006)
12. Hernández, R., Carrasco, J.A., Martínez, F.J., Hernández, J.: Classifying using
    Specific Rules with High Confidence. In: Proc. of the MICAI, pp. 75–80 (2010)
13. Hernández, R., Carrasco, J.A., Martínez, F.J., Hernández, J.: CAR-NF: A Clas-
    sifier based on Specific Rules with High Netconf. Intelligent Data Analysis 16(1),
    49–68 (2012)
14. Li, W., Han, J., Pei, J.: CMAR: Accurate and Efficient Classification based on
    Multiple Class-Association Rules. In: Proc. of the ICDM, pp. 369–376 (2001)
15. Liu, B., Hsu, W. and Ma, Y.: Integrating Classification and Association Rule Min-
    ing. In: Proc. of the KDD, pp. 80–86, 1998.
16. Malik, W.A., Unwin, A.: Automated Error Detection using Association Rules.
    Intelligent Data Analysis 15(5), 749–761 (2011)
17. Shapiro, G.: Discovery, Analysis, and Presentation of Strong Rules. In: Knowledge
    Discovery in Databases. LNCS, pp. 229–238 (1991)
18. Steinbach, M., Kumar, V.: Generalizing the notion of Confidence. Knowl. Inf.
    Syst. 12(3), 279–299 (2007)
19. Teredesai, A.M., Ahmad, M.A., Kanodia, J., Gaborski, R.S.: CoMMA: a Frame-
    work for Integrated Multimedia Mining using Multi-Relational Associations.
    Knowl. Inf. Syst. 10(2), 135–162 (2006)
20. Wang, Y.J., Xin, Q., Coenen, F.: A Novel Rule Weighting Approach in Classi-
    fication Association Rule Mining. In: International Conference on Data Mining
    Workshops, pp. 271–276 (2007)
21. Wang, Y.J., Xin, Q., Coenen, F.: A Novel Rule Ordering Approach in Classifica-
    tion Association Rule Mining. In: Perner, P. (ed.) MLDM 2007. LNCS (LNAI),
    vol. 4571, pp. 339–348. Springer, Heidelberg (2007)
22. Wang, Y.J., Xin, Q., Coenen, F.: Hybrid Rule Ordering in Classification Associa-
    tion Rule Mining. Trans. MLDM 1(1), 1–15 (2008)

Multilayer Neural Network with Multi-Valued Neurons in Time Series Forecasting of Oil Production

Igor Aizenberg[1], Leonid Sheremetov[2], and Luis Villa-Vargas[3]

[1] Texas A&M University-Texarkana, USA
igor.aizenberg@tamut.edu
[2] Mexican Petroleum Institute, Mexico
sher@imp.mx
[3] Computer Science Research Center of the IPN, Mexico
lvilla@cic.ipn.mx

Abstract. In this paper, we discuss the long-term time series forecasting using a Multilayer Neural Network with Multi-Valued Neurons (MLMVN). This is complex-valued neural network with a derivative-free backpropagation learning algorithm. We evaluate the proposed approach using a real-world data set describing the dynamic behavior of an oilfield asset located in the coastal swamps of the Gulf of Mexico. We show that MLMVN can be efficiently applied to univariate and multivariate multi-step ahead prediction of reservoir dynamics. This paper is not only intended for proposing a novel model of forecasting but to study carefully several aspects of the application of ANN models to time series forecasting that could be of the interest for pattern recognition community.

Keywords: time series forecasting, MLMVN neural networks, oil production.

1 Introduction

An oilfield is described by a set of time series (TS) of fluids from petroleum wells (oil, gas and water), which are characterized by different starting points and mutual influence. Production performance is both controlled by the reservoir properties and is affected by operational constraints and surrounding wells performance. Since the rock and fluid properties of the reservoirs are highly nonlinear and heterogeneous in nature, production TS comprise high-frequency multipolynomial components, represent a long memory process and are often discontinuous (or piecewise continuous).

Several important tasks of petroleum reservoir engineering are concerned with the forecasting of oil production from the reservoir. Usually, production prediction problem is considered within several different settings [1]: i) prediction of existing wells based on that well's previous production data, ii) spatial prediction of a new infill drilling well based on the reservoir's model, and iii) backward prediction, known as "backcasting", for some brown fields with no record of the measured wells' production. In this paper, we limit the discussion to the former case.

Traditional methods of production prediction in petroleum engineering include decline curve analysis (DCA), black oil model history matching, exploration analogies

J.F. Martínez-Trinidad et al. (Eds.): MCPR 2014, LNCS 8495, pp. 61–70, 2014.

and exploration trend extrapolations. The main disadvantage of such tools is that they are based on subjective data interpretation: to pick the proper slope, to tune the parameters of the numerical simulation model in such a way that they keep the reasonable values, to interpret reservoir geology [2].

The underlying idea of TS forecasting is that patterns associated with past values in a data series can be used to project future values [3]. In real-life dynamic systems the task for a TS forecasting can be stated as follows: given measurements of one component of the state vector, reconstruct the (possibly) chaotic dynamics of the phase space and thereby predict the evolution of the measured variable [4]. The paper studies an oilfield behavior reflected in the oil well's monthly production TS analyzing both the architecture and the parameters (time lag, memory size, etc.) which better describe and are able to predict its dynamics on long time intervals.

Recently, we reported the application of pattern recognition techniques (the associative model) to oil production prediction [5]. The Gamma model showed very competitive behavior on short prediction horizons (up to one year) but, in the current state of the development of forecasting algorithm, had some difficulties on longer intervals. Several artificial neural networks (ANN) topologies have been studied in the literature in their application to the prediction of oil and gas production both in univariate and multivariate settings. Multi-layer perceptron (MLP) and recursive neural networks (RNN), such as NARX, Elman and Jordan RNN, can be applied for multi-step-ahead TS forecasting. In [1, 6] a forecasting model based on the use of MLP was suggested to predict existing and infill oil well performance using only production data. Garcia and Mohaghegh [8] used recurrent neural networks for forecasting natural gas production in the United States. In [9] the NARX networks have been studied for univariate forecasting of oil monthly production, Chakra et al. described higher order neural networks (HONN) applied to forecast water, oil and gas production [10]. On relatively short-term (6 - 18 months) forecasting intervals and rather small data sets (up to 10 TS) most of these models outperformed DCA results with mean absolute percentage error (MAPE) about 14 – 16% [6], but long-term forecasting is still a challenge.

In this paper, we analyze the problem of long-term forecasting using a Multilayer Neural Network with Multi-Valued Neurons (MLMVN) introduced in [11] and further developed in [12, 13]. We illustrate the representation of TS patterns with MLMVN, several aspects of the prediction problem as the prediction horizon increases (for up to 5-15 years) and compare the univariate and multivariate forecasting with real data from an oilfield located in the coastal swamps of the Gulf of Mexico.

2   The MLMVN Neural Network in Time Series Forecasting

MLMVN [13] consists of multi-valued neurons (MVN) with complex-valued weights, and this is its main distinction from a classical feedforward neural network. Using complex-valued inputs/outputs, weights and activation functions, it is possible to increase the functionality of a single neuron and a neural network, to improve their performance, and to reduce the training time [13, 14].

The discrete MVN was introduced in [15]. It implements a mapping between n inputs and a single output. Let $\varepsilon_k = e^{i2\pi/k}$, where i is an imaginary unit, be the primitive k-th root of unity. Let $E_k = \{\varepsilon_k^0, \varepsilon_k, \varepsilon_k^2, ..., \varepsilon_k^{k-1}\}$. An MVN input/output mapping is described by a function of n variables $f(x_1, ..., x_n)$, which can be either of $f: E_k^n \to E_k$ or $f: O^n \to E_k$ (discrete MVN) or $f: O^n \to O$ (continuous MVN), where O is a set of points located on the unit circle. Such a function can be represented using $n+1$ complex-valued weights as follows [13]:

$$f(x_1, ..., x_n) = P(w_0 + w_1 x_1 + ... + w_n x_n), \tag{1}$$

where $x_1, ..., x_n$ ($x_j \in E_k$, $j=1, ..., n$) are neuron inputs and $w_0, w_1, ..., w_n$ are the weights. P is the activation function of the neuron, which is for a discrete MVN:

$$P(z) = e^{i2\pi j/k}, \text{ if } 2\pi j / k \leq \arg z < 2\pi(j+1)/k, \tag{2}$$

where $j=0, 1, ..., k-1$ are values of the k-valued logic, $z = w_0 + w_1 x_1 + ... + w_n x_n$ is the weighted sum, $\arg z$ is the argument of the complex number z. Function (2) divides a complex plane onto k equal sectors and maps the whole complex plane into a subset of points belonging to the unit circle.

The MVN learning is based on the error-correction learning rule [16]:

$$W_{r+1} = W_r + \frac{C_r}{(n+1)|z_r|}(D-Y)\bar{X}, \tag{3}$$

where $\bar{X}$ is the vector of neuron inputs complex-conjugated, n is the number of neuron inputs, D is the desired output of the neuron, $Y = P(z)$ is the actual output of the neuron, r is the number of the learning step, W_r is the current weighting vector, W_{r+1} is the following weighting vector, C_r is a learning rate (it is complex-valued in general, but in all simulations, which we have done in this work, we used $C_r = 1$), and $|z_r|$ is the absolute value of the weighted sum obtained on the rth learning step.

The use of MVN as a basic neuron in a MLMVN was suggested in [11, 16]. It's most important advantage is the derivative-free backpropagation learning algorithm [11-13], which is constructed in the following way. Let w_i^{js} be the weight corresponding to the ith input of the js^{th} neuron (j^{th} neuron of the sth layer), Y_{js} be the actual output of the jth neuron from the sth layer ($j=1, ..., m$), and N_s be the number of the neurons in the sth layer. It means that the neurons from the $s+1^{st}$ layer have exactly N_j inputs. Let $x_1, ..., x_n$ be the network inputs. To obtain the local errors for all neurons, the global error ($\delta_{jm}^* = D_{jm} - Y_{jm}$) must be shared with these neurons. Hence, the errors of the mth (output) layer neurons are:

$$\delta_{jm} = \delta^*_{jm} / t_m ,$$
(4)

where jm specifies the jth neuron of the mth layer; $t_m = N_{m-1} + 1$. The errors of the hidden layers neurons are calculated as follows:

$$\delta_{js} = \frac{1}{t_s} \sum_{j=1}^{N_{s+1}} \delta_{js+1} (w_i^{js+1})^{-1} ,$$
(5)

where js specifies the jth neuron of the sth layer ($j=1,...,m$-1); $t_s = N_{s-1} + 1$, $s = 2,...,m$ is the number of all neurons in the layer s-1, and $t_1 = n+1$ (n is the number of network inputs). The weights for all neurons are corrected using the error-correction learning rule (3) adapted to MLMVN.

3   Time Series Prediction Using MLMVN

Time series prediction using MLMVN was first considered in [13], where univariate forecasting of finacial time series was studied. It was shown that MLMVN learning capability does not depend on the size of the network, a big network can be successfully used for a long term time series prediction. We use here two natural models, which are very suitable for MLMVN.

3.1   Univariate Forecasting Model

The model of a "classical time series" [17], is based on the assumption that the following series member depend only on a certain amount of its direct predecessors. Suppose we have historical data for some TS $x_0, x_1, ..., x_{n-1}, x_n, x_{n+1}, ..., x_r$ and there exist some functional dependence among the series members, according to which the $n+1^{st}$ member's value is a function of the preceding n members' values (6). Our task is to predict the following members of the series, that is $x_{r+1}, x_{r+2}, ...$, which are not known. According to our assumption, (6) holds for our TS, but f is unknown. However, we can approach this function using some machine learning tool. This means that we have to form a learning set from the known TS members. Since the first r members of the TS are known, and according to (6) each following member is a function of the preceding n members, our learning set should contain the learning samples and desired outputs. As soon as the learning process is completed, f can be implemented as its approximation $\hat{f}$, which is resulted from the learning process, and future members of the TS can be predicted according to (7). The heat sign in (7) means that the corresponding value is not a true value, but the predicted one.

3.2   Multivariate Forecasting Model

This model is a generalization of the first model for such a case when a TS member to be predicted depends not only on the preceding members of the same series, but on the members of another TS. Let $y_0 = y(t_0), y_1 = y(t_1),..., y_n = y(t_n),...$ be another TS changing and measured synchronously with the first one. Let us suppose that there exist some functional dependence among the series members, according to which the $n+1^{st}$ member's value is a function of the preceding n members' values of both series.

$$x_n = f\left(x_0,...,x_{n-1}\right)$$
$$x_{n+1} = f\left(x_1,...,x_n\right),$$
$$x_{n+2} = f\left(x_2,...,x_{n+1}\right), \qquad (6)$$
$$...$$
$$x_{n+j} = f\left(x_j,...,x_{n+j-1}\right).$$

$$\hat{x}_{r+1} = \hat{f}\left(x_{r-n+1},...,x_r\right)$$
$$\hat{x}_{r+2} = \hat{f}\left(x_{r-n+2},...,x_r,\hat{x}_{r+1}\right),$$
$$\hat{x}_{r+3} = \hat{f}\left(x_{r-n+3},...,x_r,\hat{x}_{r+1},\hat{x}_{r+2}\right), \qquad (7)$$
$$...$$

Suppose we have historical data for some TS $x_0, x_1,..., x_{n-1}, x_n, x_{n+1},..., x_r$ and $y_0, y_1,..., y_{n-1}, y_n, y_{n+1},..., y_r$. Suppose that there exist the functional dependence (8) among their members. Our task is to predict the following members of the series, that is $x_{r+1}, x_{r+2},...$, which are not known. According to our assumption, (8) holds for our TS, but f is unknown. In the same way as for the first model, f can be implemented as its approximation $\hat{f}$, which is resulted from the learning process, and future members of the time series can be predicted as in (9).

$$x_n = f\left(x_0, y_0...,x_{n-1},y_{n-1}\right)$$
$$x_{n+1} = f\left(x_1,y_1,...,x_n,y_n\right),$$
$$x_{n+2} = f\left(x_2,y_2,...,x_{n+1},y_{n+1}\right), \qquad (8)$$
$$...$$
$$x_{n+j} = f\left(x_j,y_y,...,x_{n+j-1},y_{n+j-1}\right).$$

$$\hat{x}_{r+1} = \hat{f}\left(x_{r-n+1},y_{r-n+1}...,x_r,y_r\right)$$
$$\hat{x}_{r+2} = \hat{f}\left(x_{r-n+2},y_{r-n+2}...,x_r,y_r,\hat{x}_{r+1},y_{r+1}\right), \qquad (9)$$
$$\hat{x}_{r+3} = \hat{f}\left(x_{r-n+3},y_{r-n+3},...,x_r,y_r,\hat{x}_{r+1},y_{r+1},\hat{x}_{r+2},y_{r+2}\right)$$
$$...$$

4   Experimental Settings and Results

In order to test the proposed forecasting model, it was applied to the data set comprising monthly production from 15 wells of an oilfield asset located in the coastal swamps of the Gulf of Mexico. Both models (7) and (9) have been tested using MLMVN software simulators. For the multivariate model only two dynamic inputs: oil and gas-oil ratio (GOR) were used. From a number of experiments it follows that $n=60$ is an optimal value in (7) and (9). Since the series members were measured once in a month, then this means that a current member depends on the ones for the preceding 60 months (exactly 5 years). The optimal length of the learning set corresponds to 120 months (exactly 10 years). This makes it possible to perform a long-term prediction (5 years or even more) using both models. Thus, the wells from the data set meet the following criterion: to have a production history for at least 15 years.

4.1   Experimental Settings

The first model (univariate) was tested using MLMVN 60→2→32768→1 (60 inputs, 2 neurons in the 1st hidden layer, 32768 neurons in the 2nd hidden layer, and 1 output neuron). The second model (multivariate) was tested using MLMVN 120→8→1 (120 inputs - they still correspond to 60 months -, 8 hidden neurons in a single hidden layer, and 1 output neuron).

To transform TS values into numbers located on the unit circle (to be able to use them as MLMVN inputs and outputs), the following transformation was used:

$$u_j \in [a,b] \Rightarrow \varphi_j = \frac{u_j - a}{b-a}(2\pi - \delta) \in [0, 2\pi - \delta[\ ; x_j = e^{i\varphi_j} \ ; j = 0,...,n, \tag{10}$$

where $u_0, u_1, ..., u_n$ is the original time series. If $u_{min} = \min\limits_{j=0,1,...,n} u_j$ and $u_{max} = \max\limits_{j=0,1,...,n} u_j$,

then a and b were chosen in the following way $a = \begin{cases} y_{min} - 0.125(y_{max} - y_{min}), y_{min} > 0 \\ 0, y_{min} = 0 \end{cases}$

and $b = y_{max} + 0.125(y_{max} - y_{min})$. This extension of the range is important to avoid closeness to each other of the numbers on the unit circle corresponding to minimal and maximal values of a time series. For the same purpose, a shift δ was used. In our experiments, we used $\delta = \pi/4$. Evidently, to return back to the original data scale, the inverse transformation is necessary:

$$x \in O, \arg x = \varphi; \ u = \frac{\varphi(b-a)}{2\pi - \delta} + a \tag{11} \qquad x \in e^{is2\pi/k}; \ u = \frac{s(b-a)}{k-1} + a \tag{12}$$

According to previous experimental results [13], the MLMVN software simulator shows better accuracy when the standard deviation of the TS data is "squeezed" to a value of order $[0.1, 10.0]$. To achieve this effect, the initial data were normalized by division of all the series members by 10,000 or 100,000 depending on their initial range. The resulting series members were multiplied by the same number accordingly.

Since the MLMVN software simulator supporting the multivariate model can produce only discrete output (the output neuron of the network is discrete, that is (2) is its activation function), to approach the continuous output, the large number of sectors (k=4096) was used. This makes a sector's angular size negligently small and the neuron's performance is practically equivalent to the continuous case. To transform the actual data into the format suitable for MVN/MLMVN and vice versa, the equations (10) - (11) should be accordingly transformed into equation (12).

To control the learning process, the root mean square error (RMSE) was used. The results are compared on two different error measures: the Mean Square Error (MSE) and the adjusted Mean Absolute Percent Error, also known as symmetric (though actually it is not symmetric since over- and under-forecasts are biased) MAPE (SMAPE) normalized between 0% and 100%. These error metrics are computed as shown in equations (13) and (14) respectively, where y_i is the actual and $\hat{y}_i$- is the predicted value.

$$E_{MSE} = \frac{1}{n}\sum_{i=1}^{n}(y_i - \hat{y}_i)^2, \qquad (13) \qquad\qquad E_{SMAPE} = \frac{1}{n}\sum_{i=1}^{n}\frac{|y_i - \hat{y}_i|}{(|y_i| + |\hat{y}_i|)} \qquad (14)$$

4.2   Experimental Results

Experimental results are resumed in Table 1, which contains both the results for reference models (exponential smoothing – ES, ARIMA (1,1,2) and NARX neural network [10]) and the errors for learning and prediction periods measured in a number of time points. All the TS were used in all models but for different forecasting periods. It is important to note, that reference models were used for much shorter prediction periods than MLMVN (12 months for the NARX model and 24 months for smoothing and ARIMA) since there accuracy drastically degrades with time when stationarity hypothesis fails. It can be seen for W3, W7 and W13 cases (shadowed) on the observed 2-years intervals. The NARX model gives competitive results on a one-year period, but it requires more study to be applied for longer periods. In turn, the univariate MLMVN model was studied on a 5-years period and the multivariate one – for up to 15 years period. Fig. 1 illustrates the forecasting for two typical TS with low (W1) and high (W11) errors.

Table 1. Experimental results

	Mean	W1	W2	W3	W4	W5	W6	W7	W8	W9	W10	W11	W12	W13	W14	W15
Period		24	24	24	24	24	24	24	24	24	24	24	24	24	24	24
SMAPE (ES), %	26.02	4.49	5.14	59.04	28.98	10.69	7.58	100	1.42	8.91	14.75	2.39	4.01	100	7.08	35.78
SMAPE (ARIMA), %	17.28	7.68	5.30	60.81	8.38	4.96	6.98	18.10	1.85	8.84	5.31	1.09	1.61	91.82	7.45	28.96
Period		12	12	12	12	12	12	12	12	12	12	12	12	12	12	12
SMAPE (NARX), %	12.20	6.08	11.22	18.57	12.93	10.88	9.58	38.42	7.52	10.63	10.70	4.61	3.93	N/A	9.29	16.47
Period		120	122	142	113	121	145	156	141	163	165	156	130	52	44	63
MSE (LM)		4.30E+08	3.32E+07	1.25E+08	4.25E+08	4.64E+08	6.40E+07	2.39E+07	9.87E+08	2.19E+08	9.33E+07	3.98E+08	6.87E+08	4.76E+06	1.32E+07	1.37E+08
SMAPE (LM), %		2.3	1.97	1.68	2.41	1.47	1.53	1.11	6.32	3.87	15.1	3.12	3.47	8.28	1.53	7.43
Period		60	61	61	61	61	61	61	61	61	61	61	61	41	31	61
MSE (M1)		1.96E+08	1.76E+09	2.75E+09	9.57E+08	3.95E+09	2.24E+10	1.54E+09	1.55E+09	7.97E+08	8.58E+08	2.67E+09	2.67E+07	1.42E+07	1.57E+08	2.88E+07
SMAPE (M1), %	25.99	3.05	25.05	9.57	25.65	17.54	33.16	26.32	44.84	23.96	26.62	81.1	4.48	36.12	8.72	23.74
Period		144	61	61	71	120	144	154	80	102	104	95	129	21	13	62
MSE (M2)		9.51E+08	1.68E+08	6.89E+08	1.39E+09	1.34E+10	1.50E+09	3.68E+08	6.34E+08	1.26E+08	2.03E+08	4.57E+07	7.91E+07	1.27E+07	1.17E+09	4.66E+07
SMAPE (M2), %	17.81	7.87	9.36	28.54	27.05	29.84	12.31	10.51	13.13	14.92	17.34	6.14	11.51	25.78	N/A	35.03

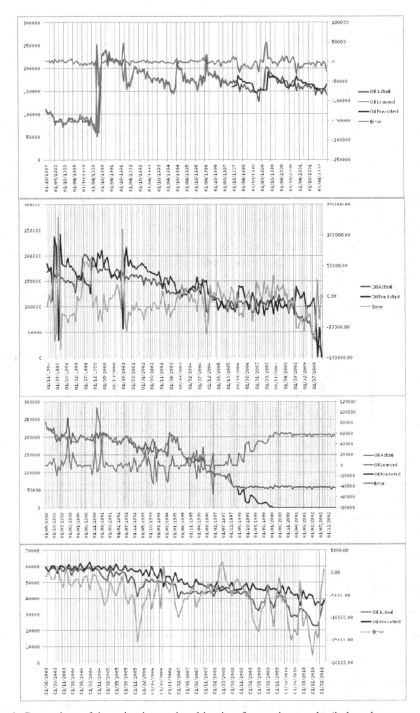

Fig. 1. Comparison of the univariate and multivariate forecasting results (in barrels per month): TS W1 model 1, TS W1 model 2, TS W11 model 1 and TS W11 model 2

Since only in one case (W3) the MSE and SMAPE showed the opposite results for both models, we'll use SMAPE for the rest of the discussion. As we can see the average SMAPE for the learning period is about 4%, being higher than 10% only for one TS (W10). In general, multivariate forecasting showed better performance (average SMAPE of 17% vs. 25%), though for several TS (W1, W3-W5, W12, W15) the univariate model showed better results (shadowed cells in Table 1). As we can see, the average error of model 2 is comparable to the errors reported in the literature (see the Introduction) for short-term forecasting models. Moreover, it permitted to considerably reduce the error for a number of TS which used to be very difficult for univariate forecasting (W2, W6-W11).

Let us consider the example of the W11 TS, showing extremely high error of 81% for the univariate model. For the forecasting period (comprising 12 years) the GOR pattern was relatively similar to the training period. As we can see from Fig. 1, for longer periods, the univariate model doesn't reflect properly the changes in the well's behavior: during the 10-years long training period till April 1998 the univariate network learns the declined behavior of the well and predicts it's shut-off for February 2000. Such prediction, by the way, is consistent with the DCA results for the same period (if the last slop is selected). Nevertheless, the bivariate model behaves differently and shows the SMAPE of 6.14% on a 12 years horizon. This example clearly shows the difference between DCA and ANN forecasting for long-term intervals.

Both models showed considerable difficulties while learning from (W10) and predicting (W3-W5, W13-W15) TS with zero values of production, which unfortunately is a typical situation when the wells are closed for some time for workovers or due to an accident. An interesting observation is that for the wells with high errors (average SMEPE 29%), the error of cumulative oil production for the tested period was as low as 6%. Another advantage of the multivariate model is the ability of forecasting of infill wells (mentioned as a second forecasting task in the Introduction), but this discussion is out of the scope of this paper.

Given that the network has up to 32768 neurons, it took about one hour to learn the model on the Xeon X5550 CPU @ 2.67 GHz (CPU mark 5414) and 64 bits OS.

5   Conclusions

In this paper, the application of MLMVN to long-term TS prediction has been studied on a real-life example of oil monthly production. Both univariate and multivariate models were developed. Compared to DCA method the advantage of ANN forecasting models is that prediction allows local variation instead of smooth curve projection as in the DCA.

As the experimental results showed, both models can be efficiently used and achieve results which are significantly better than prior published work in terms of the predicted interval and enables long-term prediction for up to 15 years (see W7, model 2). When there are no "gaps" in the data or these gaps are minimal, the qualitative long-term predictions are possible.

Acknowledgements. The authors would like to thank the CONACYT-SENER project 146515 for partial support of this work.

References

1. He, Z., Yang, L., Yen, J., Wu, C.: Neural-Network Approach to Predict Well Performance Using Available Field Data. In: SPE Western Regional Meeting, Bakersfield, California, pp. 26–30. SPE 68801 (March 2001)
2. Weiss, W.W., Balch, R.S., Stubbs, B.A.: How artificial intelligence methods can forecast oil production. In: SPE/DOE Improved Oil Recovery Symposium, Tulsa, Oklahoma, April 13-17, pp. 1–16 (2002)
3. Batyrshin, I., Sheremetov, L.: Perception based approach to time series data mining. J. of Applied Soft Computing. Elsevier Science 8(3), 1211–1221 (2008)
4. Davey, N., Hunt, S.P., Frank, R.J.: Time series prediction and neural networks. J. of Intelligent and Robotic Systems 31(1-3), 91–103 (1999)
5. López-Yáñez, I., Sheremetov, L., Yáñez-Márquez, C.A.: Novel Associative Model for Time Series Data Mining. Pattern Recognition Letters 41, 23–33 (2014)
6. Olivares-Velazquez, G., Escalona-Quintero, C., Gimenez, E.: Production monitoring using artificial intelligence. SPE paper 149594 (2012)
7. Silva, L.C.F., Portella, R.C.M., Emerick, A.A., Ebecken, N.F.F.: Predictive Data-Mining Technologies for Oil-Production Prediction in Petroleum Reservoir. SPE 107371 (2007)
8. Garcia, A., Mohaghegh, S.D.: Forecasting of natural gas production into year 2020: a comparative study. SPE 91413 (2004)
9. Sheremetov, L.B., González-Sánchez, A., López-Yáñez, I.: Time Series Forecasting: Applications to the Upstream Oil and Gas Supply Chain. In: IFAC Conference on Manufacturing Modelling, Management, and Control, vol. 7(1), pp. 957–962 (2013)
10. Chakra, C., Song, K.-Y., Saraf, D.N., Gupta, M.M.: Production forecasting of petroleum reservoir applying higher-order neural networks (HONN) with limited reservoir data. Int. J. of Computer Applications 72(2), 23–35 (2013)
11. Aizenberg, I., Moraga, C.: Multilayer Feedforward Neural Network based on Multi-Valued Neurons and a Backpropagation Learning Algorithm. Soft Computing 11(2), 169–183 (2007)
12. Aizenberg, I., Paliy, D., Zurada, J., Astola, J.: Blur Identification by Multilayer Neural Network based on Multi-Valued Neurons. IEEE Transactions on Neural Networks 19(5), 883–898 (2008)
13. Aizenberg, I.: Complex-Valued Neural Networks with Multi-Valued Neurons. SCI, vol. 353. Springer, Heidelberg (2011)
14. Hirose, A.: Complex-Valued Neural Networks, 2nd edn. SCI, vol. 400. Springer, Heidelberg (2012)
15. Aizenberg, N., Aizenberg, I.: CNN Based on Multi-Valued Neuron as a Model of Associative Memory for Gray-Scale Images. In: Proc. of the 2nd IEEE Int. Workshop on Cellular Neural Networks and their Applications, Munich, Germany, pp. 36–41 (1992)
16. Aizenberg, I., Moraga, C., Paliy, D.: A Feedforward Neural Network based on Multi-Valued Neurons. In: Reusch, B. (ed.) Comp. Intelligence, Theory and Applications. Advances in Soft Computing, vol. XIV, pp. 599–612. Springer, Heidelberg (2005)
17. Box, G., Jenkins, G., Reinsel, G.: Time series analysis: forecasting and control, 4th edn. Wiley (2008)

Developing Architectures of Spiking Neural Networks by Using Grammatical Evolution Based on Evolutionary Strategy

Andrés Espinal[1], Martín Carpio[1], Manuel Ornelas[1], Héctor Puga[1],
Patricia Melín[2], and Marco Sotelo-Figueroa[1]

[1] Instituto Tecnológico de León, Av. Tecnológico S/N. León, Gto, México
andres.espinal@itleon.edu.mx
[2] Instituto Tecnológico de Tijuana, Calz. del Tecnológico S/N. Tijuana, B.C., México

Abstract. The Artificial Neural Networks (ANNs) have been used for solving problems in many theoretical and practical areas. Advances on the field of ANNs have derived in Spiking Neural Networks (SNNs); which are considered as the third generation of ANNs. SNNs receive/send the information by timing of events (spikes) instead by the spike rate; as their predecessors do. Although SNNs are capable to solve some functions with fewer neurons than networks of previous generations, there aren't rules to set the architecture of any kind of ANN for solving a specific task; usually the architecture is set empirically based on the designer's experience and the neural network's performance over the problem. Recently, metaheuristic algorithms are being implemented to optimize some aspect on ANNs such as weight, connections and even the architecture. This work proposes a generic framework for automatic construction of Fully-Connected Feed-Forward Spiking Neural Networks through an indirect representation by means of Grammatical Evolution (GE) based on Evolutionary Strategy (ES) algorithm. Two well-known benchmarks datasets of pattern recognition were used for testing the proposal of this paper.

1 Introduction

Artificial Neural Networks (ANNs) are mathematical models inspired in biology, which have been successfully applied to solve problems in fields such as pattern recognition, segmentation, regression, etc. Advances on ANNs field have derived in Spiking Neural Networks (SNNs), which are considered as the third generation of ANNs [17]. The SNNs are formed by spiking neurons, which deal with information encoded in timing of events (spikes), are computationally stronger than sigmoid neural networks [16]; in fact, there is evidence that fewer spiking neurons are required for solving some functions than neurons of previous generations [17].

Several topologies have been proposed for ANNs, which are defined around three aspects: computing nodes (neuron models), communications links (synapse connections) and message types (coding schemes) [13]. Although the aspects for

J.F. Martínez-Trinidad et al. (Eds.): MCPR 2014, LNCS 8495, pp. 71–80, 2014.

defining an ANN with a particular topology can be chosen, there isn't a rule to set how many computing nodes are required to solve an specific task, this last is an important criteria due to the fact that they have a strong impact on ANNs' performance [5].

Recently, methauristic algorithms have been used for dealing with the problem designing ANNs for solving some given problem [5] [22]. Metaheuristics can design ANNs by either direct or indirect representation; with a direct representation the algorithm tries to modified some aspects of pre-set ANNs [7] in order to improve the performance of it and with an indirect representation, aspects of an ANN are codified, and the algorithm tries to design with that an ANN for a given problem [3].

In this work a generic framework is presented for designing SNNs to solve pattern recognition problems. The paper is organized as follows: section 2 gives all the fundamentals required for this work, section 3 explains the proposal of this work, in section 4 some experiments and their results are explained and showed, and finally, section 5 gives the conclusions of this work and proposes future work.

2 Backgrounds

2.1 Spiking Neural Networks

The Spiking Neural Networks (SNNs) are formed by the interconnection of spiking neurons, which handle the information by timing of events (spikes). When a SNN is applied to solve pattern recognition problems, original patterns can not be fed into the SNN; they need to be transformed as spikes in an interval of time by using an encoding scheme. Several encoding schemes have been proposed, such as the Gaussian Receptive Fiels (GRFs); this encoding scheme has been extensively used in [2], [1], [21]. Basically, this encoding scheme requires for encoding a variable, m neurons (with Gaussian functions) used for covering the whole range of the variable, γ as a coefficient for setting the width of Gaussian functions and the encoding simulation time τ . For detailed information about GRFs and other encoding schemes authors suggest to check [12].

After transforming original vectors into spikes in an interval of time, they can be fed into the SNN. The architecture of the SNN can vary depending on the kind of the problem to solve. This work focuses on SNNs with architecture known as Fully-Connected Feed-Forward as used in [2], [1] and [11]. There are several spiking neuron models that can be implemented in a SNN, this work use the Spike Response Model which is detailed in next section.

Spike Response Model

The Spike Response Model (SRM) [8] [9] is an approximation of the dynamics of the integrate-and-fire neuron. For this work, the spiking neurons use the time-to-first-spike as coding scheme for sending/receiving messages. Due to the coding scheme being used, a reduced version of the SRM is implemented, which has been used in [2], [1] and [21].

The reduced SRM is defined according [1] as follows. Let us consider that a neuron j has a set Γ_j of immediate predecessors called presynaptic neurons and recives a set of spikes with firing times t_i, $i \in \Gamma_j$. Neurons fire when their state variable $x(t)$, called membrane potential, reaches a certain threshold θ. The internal state of a neurons is determined by eq. (1), where w_{ji} is the synaptic weight to modulate $y_i(t)$, which is the unweighted postsynaptic potential of a single spike coming from neuron i and impinging on neuron j.

$$x_j(t) = \sum_{i \in \Gamma_j} w_{ji} y_i(t) \tag{1}$$

The unweighted contribution $y_i(t)$ is given by eq. (2), this uses a function $\varepsilon(t)$; which describes the form of the postsynaptic potential and its input parameter are formed by the next three values: t is the current time, t_i is the firing time of the presynaptic neuron i and d_{ji} is the associated synaptic delay.

$$y_i(t) = \varepsilon(t - t_i - d_{ji}) \tag{2}$$

The form of the postsynaptic potential $\varepsilon(t)$ is given by eq. (3), the function has a τ parameter, that is the membrane potential time constant defining the decay time of the postsynaptic potential.

$$\varepsilon(t) = \begin{cases} \frac{t}{\tau} e^{1 - \frac{t}{\tau}} & \text{if } t > 0 \\ 0 & \text{else} \end{cases} \tag{3}$$

Each neuron fires once at most, the firing time t_j of neuron j is determined as the first time the state variable crosses the threshold from below.

2.2 Evolutionary Strategy

The Evolutionary Strategies (ES) [19], deal natively with problems in real domain. In [1] was designed a Self-Adaptive ES originally for training SNNs, but it could be used to solve other optimization problems. In this ES each population member consists of n-dimensional vectors. The population at any given generation g is denoted as $P(g)$. Each individual is taken as a pair of real-valued vectors, (x_i, η_i), where x_i's are objective variables which depend of the optimization problem, and η_i's are standard deviations for mutations. Each individual generates a single offspring (x_i', η_i'), where each variable $x_i'(j)$ of the offspring can be randomly defined by either eq. (4) (local search) or eq. (5) (global search) and the standard deviation for mutation of the offspring is defined by eq. (6).

$$x_i'(j) = x_i(j) + \eta_i(j) N_j(0, 1) \tag{4}$$

$$x_i'(j) = x_i(j) + \eta_i(j) \delta_j \tag{5}$$

$$\eta_i'(j) = \eta_i(j) exp(\tau' N(0, 1) + \tau N_j(0, 1)) \tag{6}$$

Algorithm 1. Self-adaptive ES

1: Generate the initial population of μ individuals.
2: Evaluate the fitness score for each individual$(x_i, \eta_i), i = 1, \ldots, \mu$ of the population based on the fitness function.
3: **while** the maximum iteration is not reached **do**
4:    Each parent (x_i, η_i) generates a single offspring (x'_i, η'_i)
5:    Calculate the fitness of each offspring $(x'_i, \eta'_i), i = 1, \ldots, \mu$.
6:    Generate a new population $P(g)$ using tournament selection and elitism to keep track of the best individual at each generation
7: **end while**

---

where:

- $N(0, 1)$ denotes a normally distributed one dimensional random number with $\mu = 0$ and $\sigma = 1$.
- $N_j(0, 1)$ indicates that the random number is generated anew for each value of j.
- δ_j is a Cauchy random variable, and it is generated anew for each value of j (Scale = 1).
- Factor $\tau = \frac{1}{\sqrt{2\sqrt{n}}}$
- Factor $\tau' = \frac{1}{\sqrt{2n}}$

The Self-adaptive ES is presented in the algorithm 1.

2.3   Grammatical Evolution

Grammatical Evolution (GE) [20] is a grammar-base form of Genetic Programming (GP) [15]. GE joins the principles from molecular biology, which are used by the GP, and the power of formal grammars. Unlike GP, the GE adopts a population of lineal genotypic integer strings, or binary strings, which are transformed into functional phenotypic through a genotype-to-phenotype mapping process, this process is also know as Indirect Representation [6]. This transformation is governed through a Backus Naur Form grammar (BNF). Genotype strings are evolved with no knowledge of their phenotypic equivalent, only use the fitness measure.

Eventhough the GE uses the Genetic Algorithm (GA) [4, 10, 20] as search strategy it is possible to use another search strategy like the Particle Swarm Optimization, called Grammatical Swarm (GS) [18]. In the GE each individual is mapped into a program using the BNF.

Mapping Process

When approaching a problem using GE, initially a BNF grammar must be defined. This grammar specifies the syntax of desired phenotypic programs to be produced by GE. The development of a BNF grammar also affords the researcher the ability to incorporate domain biases or domain-specific functions.

A BNF grammar is made up of the tuple N, T, P, S; where N is the set of all non-terminal symbols, T is the set of terminals, P is the set of production rules that map $N \rightarrow T$, and S is the initial start symbol where $S \in N$. Where there are a number of production rules that can be applied to a non-terminal, a "|" (or) symbol separates the options.

Using the grammar as the GE input, eq. (7) is used to choose the next production based-on the non-terminal symbol.

$$Rule = c\%r \tag{7}$$

where c is the codon value and r is the number of production rules available for the current non-terminal.

An example of the mapping process employed by GE is shown in Figure 1.

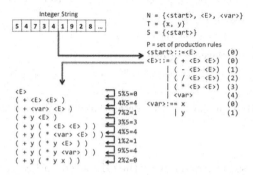

Fig. 1. An example a transformation from genotype to phenotype using a BNF Grammar. It begins with the start symbol, if the production rule from this symbol is only one rule, then the production rule gets instead of the start symbol, and the process begins to choose the productions rules base on the current genotype. It is taking each genotype and the non-terminal symbol from the left to realize the next production using eq. (7) until all the genotypes are mapped or there aren't more non-terminals in the phenotype.

3   Proposal

This paper proposes a generic framework for designing architectures of SNNs to solve pattern recognition problems. The proposed framework (see fig. 2) requires as inputs: training and testing sets from the pattern recognition problem to solve, a BNF grammar as indirect representation of the architectures of SNN and the output firing times for each class in the dataset. The indirect representation is defined by Grammar 1.1, which can specify a Fully-Connected Feed-Forward SNN. The specified SNN architecture will be defined by the number of GRFs for encoding patterns, one or several hidden layers with their respective number of neurons and a single output neuron in the output layer.

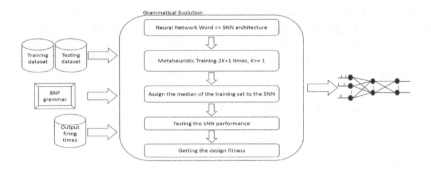

Fig. 2. Generic Framework Diagram for designing SNNs architectures

$$\langle \text{network} \rangle \models \langle \text{receptiveFields} \rangle - \langle \text{layers} \rangle$$
$$\langle \text{receptiveFields} \rangle \models \langle \text{digit} \rangle$$
$$\langle \text{layers} \rangle \models \langle \text{layer} \rangle \mid \langle \text{layer} \rangle, \langle \text{layers} \rangle$$
$$\langle \text{layer} \rangle \models \langle \text{digit} \rangle$$
$$\langle \text{digit} \rangle \models 1 \mid 2 \mid 3 \mid 4 \mid 5 \mid 6 \mid 7 \mid 8 \mid 9$$

Grammar 1.1. BNF grammar for SNN design based on the first approach proposed in [3]

The design process is carried out by the GE based on ES (the used ES is that proposed in [1]), which basically by means of the BNF grammar and the mapping process creates architectures of SNNs candidates. The GE evaluates the quality of its candidates by using a fitness function and evolves them trying to improve the candidates by minimizing their fitness values. The eq. (8) is proposed as a fitness function for looking over the search space of SNNs architectures.

This fitness function of design requires of three stages to be calculated. The first stage consists in training $2K + 1$ (with $K \geq 1$) times the candidate architecture using the input training set, the desired firing output times and the supervised-learning based on ES for training SNNs used in [1]. The second stage consist in assigning to the candidate architecture, the median training process from the training set generated in the first stage. Finally, the third stage consist in obtaining the performance of the candidate architecture of SNN (trained) over unseen patterns using the input testing set.

$$f = \frac{\#feat * \#GRFs}{9 * \#feat} + \sum_{i=1}^{\#nhl_i} i * \frac{\#nhl_i}{9} + ((1 - perfTest) * 100) \quad (8)$$

where:

- $\#feat$ is the number of original features.
- $\#GRFs$ is the number of GRFs selected by the GE.

- $\#nhl_i$ is the number of neurons in the $i - th$ hidden layer set by the GE.
- $perfTest$ is the performance of the trained SNN with the candidate architecture over the input testing set.

The fitness function of design showed in eq. (8) was designed for trying to find compact SNNs architectures with a high classification performance over unseen patterns in the search space of architectures.

4 Experiments and Results

The proposed framework for developing architectures of SNNs was tested over two well-known benchmark datasets form the *UCI Machine Learning Repository*:

Iris plant: The iris plant dataset contains 3 classes (*Iris Setosa, Iris Versicolour* and *Iris Virginica*). One class is linearly separable from the other 2; the latter are not linearly separable. There are 50 instance patterns for each class. Each pattern is described by 4 attributes.

Wine: The wine dataset contains 3 classes. There are 59, 41 and 48 instance patterns for classes 1, 2 and 3 respectively. Each patter is described by 13 attributes.

Usually in the pattern recognition area, a classifier is tested by using some accuracy estimation method such as K-folds cross validation [14]. In this work is used the leave-one-out version of this method, not to test a classifer but to obtain a test instances set for each benchmark dataset; each benchmark dataset was splitted with $K = 10$, giving a set of 10 test instance. For each test instance was designed a SNN using the proposed framework.

As both benchmark datasets have three classes, the same configuration was used through all their test instances; some parameters were chosen empirically, others were taken from the checked works for this paper and others parameters were defined by the framework. The configuration of the experiments is presented next.

GE based on ES. The parameters *size of population* = 30, *function calls* = 600 and *boundaries* $\in [0, 255]$.

Supervised-learning based on ES. The parameters *size of population* = 30, *function calls* = 15000, *weights* $\in [-1000, 1000]$ and *delays* $\in [0.1, 16]$.

GRFs. m could be from 1 to 9, which is defined by the framework. The parameters $\tau = 4$ ms and $\gamma = 1.5$.

SRM. The parameters $\theta = 1.0$ mV, $\tau = 9.0$ ms, *simulation start time* = 5 ms and *simulation end time* = 19 ms.

Output firing times for the classes 1,2 and 3 where 6.0 ms, 10.0 ms, 14 ms respectively.

The tables 1 and 2 show for each test instance the designed architectures and the performance of the trained SNN over the training and testing patterns. The last row shows an accuracy value of the obtained performance over training and testing patterns through all tests.

Table 1. Classification performance of the designed SNNs over training and testing patterns through 10 tests for Iris Plant Dataset

# test	Architecture	Performance training	Performance testing
1	$4(5) - 3 - 1$	0.8740	1.0
2	$4(4) - 7 - 1$	0.9481	1.0
3	$4(5) - 2 - 1$	0.8592	1.0
4	$4(3) - 7 - 1$	0.9111	1.0
5	$4(9) - 6 - 1$	0.9185	1.0
6	$4(6) - 6 - 1$	0.8666	1.0
7	$4(7) - 6 - 1$	0.9407	1.0
8	$4(5) - 3 - 1$	0.9777	1.0
9	$4(5) - 5 - 1$	0.9333	1.0
10	$4(7) - 4 - 1$	0.9333	1.0
	Accuracy	0.91625	1.0

Table 2. Classification performance of the designed SNNs over training and testing patterns through 10 tests for Wine Dataset

# test	Architecture	Performance training	Performance testing
1	$13(7) - 3 - 1$	0.6037	0.6842
2	$13(4) - 8 - 1$	0.8187	0.9444
3	$13(8) - 6 - 1$	0.8000	0.8333
4	$13(7) - 7 - 1$	0.7687	0.9444
5	$13(7) - 9 - 1$	0.7750	0.8333
6	$13(5) - 7 - 1$	0.7937	0.9444
7	$13(8) - 3 - 1$	0.8062	0.8888
8	$13(4) - 8 - 1$	0.7625	0.8333
9	$13(7) - 8 - 1$	0.8757	0.8823
10	$13(4) - 6 - 1$	0.9012	1.0
	Accuracy	0.79054	0.87884

The proposal was compared against an ANNs trained by means of Backpropagation algorithm only for the Iris Plant dataset. The ANN has an architecture of 4 neurons in the input layer, 7 neurons in the hidden layer and 3 neurons in the output layer; this ANN was trained for each test instance. The accuracy achieved for the SNN over the tests for known patterns was 0.91625 and 1.0 for unknown patterns, againts the accuracy achieved for the ANN for known patterns was 0.99407 and for unkown patterns was 0.96. This comparison shows that the proposal can design SNN with better generalization than an ANN with empirical design.

5   Conclusions

This work presents a generic framework for designing Fully-Connected Feed-Forward SNNs to solve pattern recognition problems no matter how many features represent the patterns in the dataset. The framework requires few parameters (population size for the GE based on ES and BNF grammar) to do the design process due that uses an ES, which is self-adaptive; the other parameters are dependant of the characteristics for the SNNs to be designed and they aren't cosider to be part of the framework.

Analyzing the BNF grammar, it was possible to define a fitness function for the GE based on ES. The fitness function looks for SNNs with compact architectures over the search space, which have acceptable performance for both known and unknown patterns. The resulting SNNs have a good generalization performance due that the fitness function besides that it tries to looks for compact architectures, it chooses architectures which have maximum performance for unknown patterns.

A remarkable advantage of the proposed framework is that it can handle different grammars as indirect representation for designing architectures of SNNs.

As future work, authors propose to define a grammar, which integrates additional inherent aspects of SNNs for their design. Besides to implement other metaheuristics for the optimization process and compare them.

Acknowledgments. The authors thank to Consejo Nacional de Ciencia y Tecnología (CONACyT) and *Instituto Tecnológico de León* (ITL) for the support to this research.

References

1. Belatreche, A.: Biologically Inspired Neural Networks: Models, Learning, and Applications. VDM Verlag, Saarbrücken (2010)
2. Bohte, S.M., Kok, J.N., LaPoutre, H.: Error-backpropagation in temporally encoded networks of spiking neurons. Neurocomputing 48, 17–37 (2002)
3. De Mingo Lopez, L.F., Gomez Blas, N., Arteta, A.: The optimal combination: Grammatical swarm, particle swarm optimization and neural networks. Journal of Computational Science 3(1-2), 46–55 (2012)
4. Dempsey, I., O'Neill, M., Brabazon, A.: Foundations in Grammatical Evolution for Dynamic Environments. SCI, vol. 194. Springer, Heidelberg (2009)
5. Ding, S., Li, H., Su, C., Yu, J., Jin, F.: Evolutionary artificial neural networks: A review. Artif. Intell. Rev. 39(3), 251–260 (2013)
6. Fang, H.-L., Ross, P., Corne, D.: A promising genetic algorithm approach to job-shop scheduling, rescheduling, and open-shop scheduling problems. In: Proceedings of the Fifth International Conference on Genetic Algorithms, pp. 375–382. Morgan Kaufmann (1993)
7. Garro, B.A., Sossa, H., Vazquez, R.A.: Design of artificial neural networks using a modified particle swarm optimization algorithm. In: Proceedings of the 2009 International Joint Conference on Neural Networks, IJCNN 2009, pp. 2363–2370. IEEE Press, Piscataway (2009)

8. Gerstner, W.: Time structure of the activity in neural network models. Physical Review E 51(1), 738–758 (1995)
9. Gerstner, W., Kistler, W.: Spiking Neuron Models: Single Neurons, Populations, Plasticity. Cambridge University Press (2002)
10. Holland, J.: Adaptation in natural and artificial systems. University of Michigan Press (1975)
11. Hong, S., Ning, L., Xiaoping, L., Qian, W.: A cooperative method for supervised learning in spiking neural networks. In: CSCWD, pp. 22–26. IEEE (2010)
12. Johnson, C., Roychowdhury, S., Venayagamoorthy, G.K.: A reversibility analysis of encoding methods for spiking neural networks. In: IJCNN, pp. 1802–1809 (2011)
13. Judd, J.S.: Neural Network Design and the Complexity of Learning. Neural Network Modeling and Connectionism Series. Massachusetts Institute Technol. (1990)
14. Kohavi, R.: A study of cross-validation and bootstrap for accuracy estimation and model selection. In: IJCAI, pp. 1137–1145 (1995)
15. Koza, J.R., Poli, R.: Genetic programming. In: Burke, E.K., Kendall, G. (eds.) Search Methodologies: Introductory Tutorials in Optimization and Decision Support Techniques, pp. 127–164. Kluwer, Boston (2005)
16. Maass, W.: Noisy spiking neurons with temporal coding have more computational power than sigmoidal neurons, pp. 211–217. MIT Press (1996)
17. Maass, W.: Networks of spiking neurons: The third generation of neural network models. Neural Networks 10(9), 1659–1671 (1997)
18. O'Neill, M., Brabazon, A.: Grammatical differential evolution. In: International Conference on Artificial Intelligence (ICAI 2006), Las Vegas, Nevada. CSEA Press (2006)
19. Rechenberg, I.: Evolutions Strategie: optimierung technischer systeme nach prinzipien der biologischen evolution. Frommann-Holzboog (1973)
20. Ryan, C., Collins, J.J., Neill, M.O.: Grammatical evolution: Evolving programs for an arbitrary language. In: Banzhaf, W., Poli, R., Schoenauer, M., Fogarty, T.C. (eds.) EuroGP 1998. LNCS, vol. 1391, pp. 83–95. Springer, Heidelberg (1998)
21. Shen, H., Liu, N., Li, X., Wang, Q.: A cooperative method for supervised learning in spiking neural networks. In: CSCWD, pp. 22–26. IEEE (2010)
22. Yao, X.: Evolving artificial neural networks. Proceedings of the IEEE 87(9), 1423–1447 (1999)

Problem Solving Environment Based on Knowledge Based System Principles

A.M. Martinez-Enriquez[1], G. Escalada-Imaz[2], and Aslam Muhammad[3]

[1] Department of Computer Science, Centre of Research and Advanced Studies
(CINVESTAV-IPN), Mexico D.F., Mexico
[2] Artificial Intelligence Research Institute (IIIA-CSIC), Spanish Council
for Scientific Research (CSIC), Barcelona, Spain
[3] Department of CS & University of Engineering and Technology, Lahore, Pakistan
ammartin@cinvestav.mx, gonzalo@iiia.csic.es, maslam@uet.edu.pk

Abstract. This paper describes how to solve numerical problems by a
non computer user based on Knowledge Based Systems (KBSs) principles. The aims of our approach is to handle numerical information of the
problem, by using Backward Logical inferences, deducing whether or not
the required mathematical composition functions exist. We implemented
a backward inference algorithm which is bounded by $O(n)$, n being the
size of KBS. Moreover the inference engine proceeds in a top-down way,
so scans a small reduced search space compared to those of the forward
chaining algorithms. Our experimental example deals with some statistical analysis and its application to clustering and concept formation.

Keywords: backward inference engine, concept formation.

1 Introduction

This paper focuses on the deduction and the composition of mathematical functions including in the inference rules along with an efficient inferences engine
(IE) that access them to satisfy a user-query (Q). IE combines several deduc-
tive rules to resolve explicitly asked function including in the query (Q). In this
way, we designed a knowledge based system including the binary logical relation
of specific solution. The deduction of these relationships relies on an efficient
Backward Inference Engine detailed in Section 3.

We have chosen as an experimental framework, the analysis and resolution of
statistical problems that can be applied into different domains like clustering,
pattern recognition. Our logical framework detailed in Section 2, is composed
by: a base of facts (BF), a knowledge base of implication rules (BR), a user
query noted (Q), and an Inference Engine (IE) responsible to determine/deduce
whether or not a particular statistical function exists (Section 3).

The paper is organized as follows: Section 2 describes our main framework for
discovering statistical functions using logical inference. Also, some examples of
application are presented. Section 3 explains the inference mechanism. Section
4 analyzes the experimental results. Section 5 concludes and draws future work.

J.F. Martínez-Trinidad et al. (Eds.): MCPR 2014, LNCS 8495, pp. 81–91, 2014.

2 System Framework

This is the standard case where it is necessary to know if a client query (Q) can be deduced from BF and BR : $BF \wedge BR \vdash Q$. The elements of Q, BF, and BR form a set of propositional Horn clauses. This classical deduction problem, in our studied case, can be formulated as follows:

Given

- *BF*: a set of propositions $\{mf_1, \ldots, mf_j, \ldots, mf_m\}$, where mf_j represents the confirmed existence of a particular mathematical function that has been implemented and tested, such that each proposition mf_j is evaluated to either True or False;
- *BR*: a set of implication rules $\{rf_1, \ldots, rf_i, \ldots, rf_n\}$, where a set of rf_i rules models a composition solution. Each rf_i, $mf_1 \wedge \ldots \wedge mf_n \to mf_i$, indicates that if the n mf in the antecedent exist then the existence of this statistical function mf_i in the consequent of this rule (rf_i) exist too. In fact, each registered rf_i into BR is true because the functionality it represents has been implemented, tested, and verified before; and
- *Q*: a user query representing whether a mf_s composition exists.
  This query is expressed by a disjunction of conjunctions of propositions: $Q = (q_{11} \wedge \ldots \wedge q_{1n1}) \vee \ldots \vee (q_{k1} \wedge \ldots \wedge q_{knk})$

Goal: To determine whether or not Q can be deduced from BF and BR performing sound inferences: BF $\wedge$ BR $\vdash$ Q.

In order to achieve this goal, we proposed and implemented a Backward Inference Engine being linear and logically correct, described later (Section 3).

2.1 Mathematical Functions

Each required useful functionality is provided by IE, which can be grouped as :

- **Input/Output.** In order to solve heterogeneous data mismatch, we implemented some data-format transforming functions for reading and exporting files containing numbers in different formats: ASCII, integer, float or double. ASCII files can have numbers laid out either with a number per line, a line with various numbers separated with a space, or several lines each with several numbers. From the inference point of view, this data transformation is represented by the following pattern. Next we write some particular rules.

$$experimentDta \wedge treatDta \to stdDta$$

Where: *experimentDta* stands for the existence of the input data in any layout format provided by the client user.
treatDta is the existing mf_j which processes the input data : *experimentDta*
stdDta refers to the existence of the transformed data. On the other hand, the proposition *stdDta* represents the existence of the output of the function (*treatDta*) which transforms *experimentDta* to the required format to be processed (if needed).

The following rules represent examples of the input data transformation (experimentDta) with numerical binary data into numerical ASCII string, which is the format used by our mathematical functions.

$$integer D \wedge binary Double Big Endian \rightarrow ASCII string$$
$$integer 4 byts \wedge binary Integer Big Endian \rightarrow ASCII string$$
$$short D \wedge binary Short Big Endian \rightarrow ASCII string$$
$$float D \wedge binary short Litle Endian \rightarrow ASCII string$$
$$double D \wedge binary Double Big Endian \rightarrow ASCII string$$
$$long 8 byt D \wedge binary Long Big Endian \rightarrow ASCII string$$
$$long 8 byt Little ED \wedge binary Long Little Endian \rightarrow ASCII string$$

As explained before $integer D$, $integer 4 byts$, ... idem $ASCII string$ are propositions that test the existence of these input/output data type.

Similarly $binary Double Big Endian$, $binary Integer Big Endian$, ... are propositions testing the existence of functions mf_s registered in our infrastructure.

- **Plotting** draws data. For instance, giving two sets of input data, a regression line can be calculated and graphical representation can be displayed, as described by the following rule.

$$stdDta - of X \wedge stdDta - of Y \wedge regressline \rightarrow plot RE$$
$$stdDta - of X \wedge y - axis Intercpt \wedge regr Coeff \rightarrow regressline$$
$$stdDeviation of X \wedge stdDeviation of Y \wedge correlt Coeff fof XY \rightarrow regr Coeff$$
$$mean of X \wedge mean of Y \wedge regr Coeff \rightarrow y - axis Intercept$$

Where $stdDta - of X$, $stdDta - of Y$ represent the existence of two sets of input data, $regressline$ stands for the regression line equation, $y - axis Intercpt$ is the ordinate, $regr Coeff$ represents the correlation coefficient (see Table 1), and $plot RE$ the resulting plot.

- **Mathematical functions** compute numerical measures and analysis. The symbolic name associated to mf_s is a proposition stored in BF which validates the existence of an implemented and tested mf_s, such that $mean Opr$, $mode Opr$, $median Opr$.

Our test bed environment solves problems using inference rules, e.g., giving the experimental data as required by $stdDta$, it is possible to calculate several numerical functions associated to the following classical implication rules, such that if a user asks for the standard Deviation (R_5), IE deduces that it is required to apply firstly $\{[R_4], [R_1]\}$:

$[R_1] stdDta \wedge mean Opr \rightarrow mean$ $[R_2] stdDta \wedge mode Opr \rightarrow mode$
$[R_3] stdDta \wedge media Opr \rightarrow media$ $[R_4] stdDta \wedge mean \wedge variance Opr \rightarrow variance$
$[R_5] square Root \wedge variance \rightarrow stdDeviation$

Moreover, users are able to store an inference rule into BR with the set of deduced propositions, the rule can be named as user wants e.g., $Experimental App1$. This rule can be executed as many times it is required for the same kind of experimentation analysis :

$$mean \wedge mode \wedge stdDeviation \rightarrow Experimental\,App1$$

Giving two sets of data several rules take place, the semantic is as follows:

$[R6] variance - ofX \wedge variance - ofY \wedge covarianceOpr \rightarrow covariance - ofXY$

Semantic : Once *variance − ofX*, *variance − ofY* have been calculated (they are True), and the function *covarianceOpr* has been implemented and tested (it is True), so the computation of *covariance − ofXY* is launched.

2.2   Combining Logical and Numerical Information

A proposition P in KBS is evaluated to true iff its associated cells memory $[P]$ contains a numerical value x. If the cell memory $[P]$ is undefined, P is evaluated

Table 1. Some statistics functions and related inference rules. Input data are: d, X, and Y. Lowered indexes x and y refer to values in sets X and Y respectively, N is the number of data, and $N - a$ grades of freedom.

Statistics Equation	Related Rules
Mean $$M = \frac{1}{N}\sum_{i=1}^{N} d_i$$	$stdDta \wedge meanOpr \rightarrow mean$ $stdDta \wedge modeOpr \rightarrow mode$ $stdDta \wedge medianOpr \rightarrow median$
Standard deviation $$SD = \sqrt{\frac{1}{N-1}\sum_{i=1}^{N}(d_i - M)^2}$$	$stdDta \wedge mean \wedge varianceOpr \rightarrow variance$ $sqrt \wedge variance \rightarrow stdDeviaton$
Mean of X	$stndDta - ofX \wedge meanOpr \rightarrow meanofX$
Standard deviation of X	$stdDta - ofX \wedge meanofX \rightarrow stdDeviation - ofX$
Standard deviation of Y	$stdDta - ofY \wedge meanofY \rightarrow stdDeviation - ofY$
Correlation coefficient $$r = \frac{\sum_{i=1}^{N}(X_iY_i)-NM_xM_y}{(N-1)SD_xSD_y}$$	$stdDeviatn - ofX \wedge stdDeviatn - ofY \wedge$ $grdsFreedom \wedge rOpr \rightarrow correltCoeff - ofXY$
Student's test t $$t = r\sqrt{\frac{N-2}{1-r^2}}$$	$stdDta - ofX \wedge stdDta - ofY \wedge$ $correltCoeff - ofXY \wedge tOpr \rightarrow stdentTtest$
Regression line $Y = a + bX$	$stdDta - ofX \wedge stdDta - ofY \wedge YOpr$ $y - axsIntercpt \wedge regrCoeff \rightarrow regressline$
Regr. coefficient(slope) $$b = r\frac{SD_y}{SD_x}$$	$stdDeviatn - ofX \wedge stdDeviatn - ofY \wedge$ $correltCoeff - ofXY \wedge coeRegOpr \rightarrow regrCoeff$
y-axisIntercpt(ordinate) $a = (M_y - bM_x)$	$mean - ofX \wedge mean - ofY \wedge regrCoeff \wedge$ $aOpr \rightarrow y - axsIntercpt$
Residual Std. deviation $$D_{res} = \sqrt{\frac{SD_y^2(1-r^2)(n-1)}{n-2}}$$	$stdDta - ofY \wedge stdnDeviaton - ofY \wedge DresOpr \wedge$ $correltCoeff - ofXY \rightarrow resStdDeviation$
Slope's std. error $$SE_b = \frac{D_{res}}{\sqrt{\sum_{i=1}^{N}(X_i-M_x)^2}}$$	$stndDta - ofX \wedge meanofX \wedge resStdDeviation \wedge$ $SEbOpr \rightarrow slopeStdErr$

to false. The consequent of an implication rule P is evaluated to true iff all its antecedent variables P' are true, i.e. [P'] contains a numerical value x, and iff the function f representing the logical implication is computationally calculable. The value assigned to its cell memory $[P]$ is derived from the computing function f applied upon the numerical values x, i.e. $f(x_1, x_2, \ldots, x_n) = y$ associated to its antecedent propositions. Once the computation of the function f has been performed, the truth of P is confirmed and its cell memory $[P]$ is set to y.

A rule within BR models a fragment of a solution. That means that generally the whole solution is represented by a set of rules and facts within KBS.

3   Inference Mechanism

We can distinguish two type of strategies in KBSs to deduce new facts:

- **Forward** chaining precedes from the knowledge base of facts (BF) and uses the knowledge base of rules (BR) to infer a client query (Q). During the inference process the consequent P of the rule is added to BF, since all propositions of the antecedent of the rule: $P1, \ldots, Pn$ are already in BF. It is means, a rule is triggered whenever its antecedent has been previously deduced, i.e. when all propositions in the antecedent have been added to BF. Case in which the consequent is added to BF.
- **Backward** chaining begins by Q. Instead of knowing if the consequent P is deduced from BF and BR, the problem is to know if the antecedent of the rule $P1, \ldots Pn$ whose consequent is P, can be deduced from BF and BR. In other words, in an inference step it is asked whether a proposition P can be deduced which leads to ask whether the propositions $P_1, P_2, \ldots, P_k$ in the antecedent of a rule whose consequent is P can be deduced.

Some linear algorithms to solve the problem of deducing a goal from BR and BF have been proposed in [1] [3] [4]. All of them rely on a bottom-up control strategy; hence they develop a larger search space than that required by a top-down search focused on the explicitly given goal. Indeed, Forward Chaining Algorithms deduce all the implicit knowledge that is logical consequence of the BF and BR. Contrary to this, Backward Chaining processes only inferences that are goal directed, i.e. they only scan rules and facts related to the current query.

The Backward Inference Engine algorithm (BackwardIE) employed here has a strict linear complexity and proceeds in top-down way [2]. Due to the top-down strategy, a goal is proved or disproved with a reduced search space.

The BackwardIE algorithms in KBSs remain however quite crude: usually a priori bounded depth-first or backtrack search strategies relying on the assumption of a loop-free search space. Because of the indirect-recursive problem (as in the two rules $Q \land R \to P$, $P \land S \to Q$) such an assumption is rarely met.

The only existing linear backward algorithm scanning a search space considering recursion in the BR is that presented in [2]. The formal description and proofs of the logical and complexity properties is beyond the space of the present article. Thus we will give a rough description of the strategy to scan the search space modeling the deduction backward problem by means of a given example.

The proof of a goal can be represented as a search problem in an And/Or graph G. As a running example, let us consider the following set of rules:

$$P_2 \wedge P_8 \rightarrow P_1, \qquad P_9 \wedge P_{10} \rightarrow P_1 \qquad P_{11} \wedge P_{12} \rightarrow P_{10} \qquad P_5 \wedge P_3 \wedge P_6 \rightarrow P_2$$
$$P_2 \wedge P_4 \rightarrow P_3, \qquad P_2 \rightarrow P_4 \qquad P_7 \wedge P_1 \rightarrow P_4$$
$$P_3 \wedge P_{14} \rightarrow P_{13} \qquad P_4 \wedge P_{10} \rightarrow P_{13} \qquad P_{15} \wedge P_{16} \rightarrow P_{17}$$

Each proposition P in BR is associated with a node labeled P in the And/Or graph G and each rule is associated with a connector linking its consequent P with its set of antecedents $(P_1, P_2, \ldots, P_k)$. The propositions P in BF are marked as true nodes. Q is also a connector in G (see Figure 1). The proof of $Q = ((P_1 \wedge P_{13}) \vee P_{17})$ with $BF = \{P_5, P_7, P_9, P_{11}, P_{12}, P_{15}\}$ is a search in the graph shown in Figure 1. The below data structures are used to search in the And/Or graph. To deduce Q we need to search a tree T rooted at Q with the property that all its nodes P are either in BF or have a sub-tree routed in P in T. Its proof is in [2].

$$c(P) \text{ is the set of connectors issued from P.}$$
$$r(C) \text{ is the node from which C is issued.}$$
$$s(C) \text{ the set of successors nodes of } r(C) \text{ along connector C.}$$

IE is based on a recursive depth-first search. For each node P visited, the set $c(P)$ of connectors outgoing from P is sequentially examined (Or-Expand) until one leads a solution. Visiting a connector C involves the expansion of all non leaf successor nodes in $s(C)$(And-Expand) until one fails to lead a solution. Initially nodes in BF are marked SOLVED, and all other nodes are marked OPEN. A node P being expanded is marked EXPANDING until either: **a)** P has a solved connector: one along which every successor node is SOLVED: In that case P is marked SOLVED; or **b)** is shown to have no such connector: P is marked FAILED.

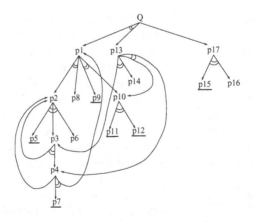

Fig. 1. And/Or graph G

There is a loop if during the expansion of a node P_i one of its successors P_j is found *EXPANDING*. The sequence of nodes in the loop $[P_j, \ldots, P_k, P_{k+1}, \ldots, P_j]$ is a last-in first-out stack; P_j will be called its *source* node. A node P_k is said to be *confined* on the loop if its connector on this loop is solved except for the successor node P_{k+1} in the loop (marked EXPANDING) and if P_k has no other solved connector. If all nodes in the loop are confined, then all will be marked FAILED. If P_i is confined and later on P_j is found SOLVED, then P_i will also be marked SOLVED. This marking of confined nodes as SOLVED is propagated backward up to to the source node. In general, a node P can have more than one EXPANDING successor: it may be on several overlapping loops. If it is confined for one or several loops, then the algorithm backtracks, leaving P EXPANDING. The final marking of P will depend on that of its EXPANDING successors. Two data structures will be needed for that:

- **Followers**(P): nodes on which the marking of confined node P depends, arranged as a formula in disjunctive form, e.g. **Followers**$(P_4) = P_2 \vee P_1$; P_4 is solved iff either P_2 or P_1 is solved (Figure 1).
- **Leaders**(P'): list of predecessor nodes of P' that are confined on the loops, e.g. **Leaders**$(P_2) = (P_3, P_4)$

If P' appears in **Followers**(P) then P belongs to **Leaders**(P').

Let us illustrate the use of these structures on the running example (Figure 1). Node Q and then successively P_1, P_2, P_3 are expanded. At this step P_2 is found EXPANDING. Since P_3 is not yet proved to be confined on the loop, we proceed to the next recursion. Two successors of P_4 are EXPANDING, P_7 is SOLVED, and thus P_4 is confined. We set **Followers**$(P_4)=P_2 \vee P_1$, **Leaders**$(P_1)=$**Leaders**$(P_2)=(P_4)$, and backtrack. Node P_3 is now found to be confined: **Followers**$(P_3)=P_2 \wedge P_4$. **Leaders**$(P_2)=(P_3, P_4)$, **Leaders**$(P_4)=(P_3)$. Back to P_2: we find P_6 FAILED; thus P_2 is also marked FAILED. **Leaders** of P_2 are not examined, and nothing will happen to pending nodes.

We backtrack to P_1, skip P_8 and visit successively P_9, P_{10}, P_{11} and P_{12}. P_{10} and then P_1 are marked SOLVED. Before backtracking to Q, node P_4 in **Leaders**(P_1) is examined:

Followers$(P_4)=(P_2 \vee P_4)$ leads us to mark P_4 SOLVED. Thus P_3 in **Leaders**(P_4) is also examined: **Followers**$(P_3)=P2 \wedge P_4$, so P_3 cannot be SOLVED; it remains EXPANDING. This ends the expansion of P_2. Since it is the last source node, all pending nodes that remain EXPANDING (only P_3) are marked FAILED.

Finally node P_{13} is expanded, its successor P_3 is FAILED, P_{14} is skipped and P_4 and P_10 are SOLVED; P_{13} is marked SOLVED. A solution is found, and the rest of the graph is not examined.

To summarize, the algorithm proceeds as follows: if the source node P_j of a loop is marked SOLVED, then nodes in **Leaders**(P_j) are sequentially visited. For every node P_i in this list, the formula **Followers**(P_i) is evaluated. If it leads to P_i SOLVED, then the list **Leaders**(P_i) is in turn examined. Nodes that remain EXPANDING after the end of the expansion of the last source node must be marked FAILED. For that, all nodes confined in a loop are put in a list called

Pending. The different evaluations of the formulas **Followers**(P_i) can be done in an efficient way with suitable data structure (see [2]).

The result obtained from IE is as follows:

Input

$Q = ((P_1 \wedge P_{13}) \vee P_{17})$, $BF = \{P_5, P_7, P_9, P_{11}, P_{12}, P_{15}\}$, P_i marked as SOLVED
$BR = \{R_0, \ldots, R_{11}\}$, where P_0 represents Q, i.e., $\{R_0, R_1\}$

$[R_0]$ $P_1 \wedge P_{13} \to P_0$ $\quad$ $[R_1]$ $P_{17} \to P_0$ $\quad$ $[R_2]$ $P_2 \wedge P_8 \to P_1$ $\quad$ $[R_3]$ $P_9 \wedge P_{10} \to P_1$
$[R_4]$ $P_5 \wedge P_3 \wedge P_6 \to P_2$ $[R_5]$ $P_2 \wedge P_4 \to P_3$ $[R_6]$ $P_2 \to P_4$ $\quad\quad$ $[R_7]$ $P_7 \wedge P_1 \to P_4$
$[R_8]$ $P_4 \wedge P_{10} \to P_{13}$ $\quad$ $[R_9]$ $P_3 \wedge P_{14} \to P_{13}$ $[R_{10}]$ $P_{15} \wedge P_{16} \to P_{17}$ $[R_{11}]$ $P_{11} \wedge P_{12} \to P_{10}$

Output

Return from : $AND_{EXTENSION}(R_6: P_2 \to P_4)$
$\{$ $Result_{AND} = Cycle; r_{UNDEFINED} = \{P_2\}$ $\}$
Return from : $AND_{EXTENSION}(R_7: P_7 \wedge P_1 \to P_4)$
$\{Result_{AND} = Cycle; r_{UNDEFINED} = \{P_1\}$ $\}$
call to: $OR_{EXTENSION}(P_4)$
$\{$ $Val = EXT; Order = 4; PConnector(P_4) = \{R_6, R_7\}; C_{SUCCESSOR}(P_4) = \{$ $\}$ $\}$
Return from : $AND_{EXTENSION}(R_5: P2 \wedge P_4 \to P3)$
$\{Result_{AND} = Cycle; r_{UNDEFINED} = \{P_4, P_2\}\}$
callto : $OR_{EXTENSION}(P_3)$;
$\{Val = EXT; Order = 3; PConnector(P_3) = \{R_5\}; C_{SUCCESSOR}(P_3) = \{\}\}$
call to: $OR_{EXTENSION}(P_6)$;
$\{Val = F; Order = 5; PConnector(P_6) = \{\}; C_{SUCCESSOR}(P_6) = \{$ $\}$ $\}$
Return from : $AND_{EXTENSION}(R_4: P5 \wedge P_3 \wedge P_6 \to P_2)$ $\{Result_{AND} = F\}$
call to : $OR_{EXTENSION}(P_2)$;
$\{$ $Val = F; Order = 2; PConnector(P_2) = \{R_4\}; C_{SUCCESSOR}(P_2) = \{R_6, R_5\}$ $\}$
Return from : $AND_{EXTENSION}(R_2 : P_2 \wedge P_8 \to P1)$ $\{Result_{AND} = F\}$
Return from : $AND_{EXTENSION}(R_{11} : P_{11} \wedge P_{12} \to P_{10})$ $\{Result_{AND} = V\}$
call to : $OR_{EXTENSION}(P_{10})$
$\{$ $Val = V; Order = 6; PConnector(P_{10}) = \{R_{11}\}; C_{SUCCESSOR}(P_{10}) = \{\}$ $\}$
Return from : $AND_{EXTENSION}(R_3 : P_9 \wedge P_{10} \to P_1)$ $\{Result_{AND} = V$ $\}$
call to : $OR_{EXTENSION}(P_1)$
$\{$ $Val = V; Order = 1; PConnector(P_1) = \{R_2, R_3\}; C_{SUCCESSOR}(P_1) = \{R_7\}$ $\}$
Return from : $AND_{EXTENSION}(R_8 : P_4 \wedge P_{10} \to P_{13})$ $\{$ $Result_{AND} = V\}$
call to : $OR_{EXTENSION}(P_{13})$;
$\{$ $Val = V; Order = 7; PConnector(P_{13}) = \{R_8, R_9 : (P_3 \wedge P_{14} \to P_{13})\};$
$C_{SUCCESSOR}(P_{13}) = \{\}\}$
Return from : $AND_{EXTENSION}(R_0 : (P_1 \wedge P_{13} \to P_0) \vee (P_{17} \to P_0))$
$\{$ $Result_{AND} = V$ $\}$
call to : $OR_{EXTENSION}(P_0)$
$\{$ $Val = V; Order = 0; PConnector(P_0) = \{R_0, R_1\}; C_{SUCCESSOR}(P_0) = \{\}$ $\}$

Thus, P_0, i.e., Q is deduced from BR and BF: $BR \wedge BF \vdash Q$

The BackwardIE algorithm was implemented in ANSI C, it runs either on Windows or Unix. The numerical calculation can be executed either in sequential or in concurrent, or in parallel or from different sites, according with the architecture of the problem solving environment.

4   Numerical Solution

The aim of our approach is to solve numerical problems for users who not necessary know how to treat them. Once IE deduces the sequence of mathematical functions (mf_s) that deduce the proposed (Q), this sequence forms a composition of services, ready to be computed. Suppose we have a cluster of observations that are characterized by several symbolic and numerical attributes-values, and a new observation arrives, but this new item has some missing values, because it has been impossible to measure them, so it could be interesting to calculate approximated values. Thus the system takes into account the maximum number of known attributes-values that makes similar the new observation with a cluster. Then the most similar cluster is processed statistically, for instance, the correlation is measured and the linear equation is used to predict missing attributes-values of the new observation.

Let be a cluster C1:{Cs,RB,Na,Li} and the new observation {Fr}. Table 2 shows the set of numerical attributes describing the members of C1 and the new observation [5].

Table 2. Description of the Numerical attributes-values of Cluster C1:{Li,Na, K,Rb,Cs}

Name	1 BL	2 ML	3 D	4 AW	7 CR	8 AR	9 AV	10 IE	11 SH	12 EL	13 HV	14 HF	15 EC	16 TC
Li_3	1330	180.5	0.53	6.939	1.23	1.55	13.1	124	0.79	1.0	32.48	0.72	0.108	0.17
Na_{11}	892	97.8	0.97	22.9898	1.54	1.90	23.7	119	0.295	0.9	24.12	0.62	0.218	0.32
K_{19}	760	63.7	0.86	39.102	2.03	2.35	45.3	100	0.177	0.8	18.9	0.55	0.143	0.23
Rb_{37}	688	38.9	1.53	85.47	2.16	2.48	55.9	96	0.080	0.8	18.1	0.55	0.080	NIL
Cs_{55}	690	28.7	1.90	132.905	2.35	2.67	70	90	0.052	0.7	16.3	0.50	0.053	NIL
Fr_{87}	677	27	NIL	223	NIL	NIL	NIL	NIL	NIL	0.7	NIL	NIL	NIL	NIL
AprxVal			2.74		2.5	3.3	72	67	0.02		6.7	0.5		

Firstly, IE deduces the sequence of mathematical functions as a composition of services. Secondly, the numerical calculation is launched. To simplify the obtained result, we only present here the necessary inference rules. The concept formation concerns only the relationship between Atomic Number (data X) vs Density (data Y), identified by A3 (i.e., proposition P3).

Input

$Q = (regressline, slopeStdErr)$
$BF = \{stsDta, stdDtaofX, stdDtaofY, meanOpr, modeOpr, varianceOpr, sqrt,$
$grdsFreedom, rOpr, tOpr, YOpr, bOpr, aOpr, DresOpr\}$ marked as SOLVED
$BR = \{R_0, \ldots, R_{16}\}$, where P_0 represents Q, i.e., $\{R_0\}$
$[R_0] : regressline \wedge slopeStErr \rightarrow P_0$

$[R_6] stDtaofY \wedge meanOpr \rightarrow meanofY$ $[R_7] stDtaofX \wedge meanOpr \rightarrow meanofX$
$[R_8] sdtDtaofX \wedge varianceofX \rightarrow stdDeviationofX$
$[R_9] stDtaofY \wedge varianceofY \rightarrow stdDeviationofY$
$[R_{10}] stdDeviationofX \wedge stdDeviationofY \wedge$
$$grdsFreedom \wedge rOpr \rightarrow correltCoeffofXY$$
$[R_{11}] stdDtaofX \wedge stdDtaofY \wedge correltCoeffofXY \wedge tOpr \rightarrow stdentTtest$
$[R_{12}] stdDeviationofX \wedge stdDeviationofY \wedge$
$$correltCoeffofXY \wedge bOpr \rightarrow regrCoeff$$
$[R_{13}] meanofY \wedge meanofX \wedge regrCoeff \wedge aOpr \rightarrow y - axsIntercept$
$[R_{14}] stdDtaofY \wedge stdDtaofX \wedge YOpr \wedge yaxsIntercpt \wedge regrCoeff \rightarrow regressline$
$[R_{15}] stdDtaofX \wedge stdDtaofY \wedge stdDeviatonofY \wedge$
$$correltCoeffofXY \wedge DresOpr \rightarrow resStdDeviation$$
$[R_{16}] stdDtaofX \wedge stdDtaofY \wedge meanofX \wedge$
$$resStdDeviation \wedge SEbOpr \rightarrow slopeStdErr$$
$[R_{17}] stDtaofX \wedge meanofX \wedge varianceOpr \rightarrow varianceofX$
$[R_{18}] stDtaofY \wedge meanofY \wedge varianceOpr \rightarrow varianceofY$

Numerical Output

Return from : $Apply(R7, meanofX : stdDtaofX, meanOpr)\{Val(meanofX) => 25\}$;
Return from : $Apply(R17, varianceofX : stDtaofX, meanofX, varianceOpr)$
    $\{Val(varianceofX) => 440\}$;
Return from : $Apply(R8, stdDeviationofX : sdtDtaofX, varianceofX)$
    $\{Val(stdDeviationofX) => 20.9762\}$;
Return from : $Apply(R6, meanofY : stDtaofY, meanOpr)\{Val(meanofY) = 1.587\}$;
Return from: $Apply(R18, varianceofY : stDtaofY, meanofY, varianceOpr)$
    $\{Val(varianceofY) => 0.30187\}$;
Return from : $Apply(R9, stdDeviationofY : stDtaofY, varianceofY)$
    $\{Val(stdDeviationofY) => 0.549426974\}$;
Return from: $Apply(R10, correltCoeffofXY : stdDeviationofX, stdDeviationofY,$
    $grdsFreedom, rOpr)\{Val(correlCoeffofXY) => 0.97528152\}$;
Return from: $Apply(R12, regrCoeff : stdDeviationofX, stdDeviationofY,$
    $correlCoeffofXY, bOpr)\{Val(regrCoeff) => 0.0255455\}$;
Return from: $Apply(R13, y - axsIntercept : meanofY, meanofX, regrCoeff, aOpr)$
    $\{Val(y - axsIntercept) => 0.51936363\}$;
Return from: $Apply(R14, regressLine : stDtaofY, stDtaofX, YOpr,$
    $y - axsIntercept, regrCoeff)$
$\{Val(P17, regressLine) => Y = 0.519368 + 0.0255455X\}$;
Return from: $Apply(R15, resStdDeviation : stDtaofX, stDtaofY, stdDeviationofY,$
    $correltCoeffofXY, DresOpr)\{Val(resStdDeviation) => 0.140186\}$;
Return from: $Apply(R16, slopStdErr : stDtaofX, stDtaofY,$
    $meanofXresStdDeviation, SEbOpr)\{Val(lopeStdErr) => 0.00334155\}$;
Return from: $Apply(R0)\{Val(P0, slopeStdErr) => 0.00334155\}$;

Thanks to R_{14}, it was possible to approximate the density-value (A3) of the new observation (Fr), i.e 2.7. By creating the specific inference rule, it is possible to apply the same process automatically to all numerical attributes and to obtain the missing values when a correlation exists among the members of C1 and the new observation Fr (see last row of Table 2).

5   Conclusion

The principal contribution of our approach is performing inferences to solve problems in a numeric domain like clustering, as an example we used statistical rules. The implemented Backward Inference Engine algorithm is correct and linear. Besides, thanks to its top-down strategy, it only computes a small search space. This strategy assures real cases applications.

Our approach takes advantages of the well-know positives properties of KBSs. The rules can be created, modified, adapted, and re-organized, independent of the inference engine which remains the same. Each time a new rule is approved by users, it is added to BR. Currently we are increasing the statistical functionalities of our framework to be applied for different scientific domains. In addition we study other cases for re-using mathematical formulae.

References

1. Dowling, W.F., Gallier, J.H.: Linear-Time Algorithms for Testing the Satisfiability of Propositional Horn Formulae. J. Logic Programming 3, 267–284 (1984)
2. Ghallab, M., Escalada-Imaz, G.: A linear control algorithm for a class of rule-based systems. The Journal of Logic Programming (11), 117–132 (1991)
3. Gallo, G., Urbani, G.: Algorithms for Testing the Satisfiability of Propositional Formulae. J. Logic Programming 7(1), 45–61 (1989)
4. Itai, A., Makowsky, J.A.: Unification as a Complexity Measure for Logic Programming. J. Logic Programming 4, 105–177 (1987)
5. Scerri, E.R.: The periodic table: its story and its significance. Editor Oxford University Press (2007)

Positive and Negative Local Trend Association Patterns in Analysis of Associations between Time Series

Ildar Batyrshin[1] and Valery Solovyev[2]

[1] Mexican Petroleum Institute, Mexico, D.F.
batyr1@gmail.com
[2] Kazan Federal University, Kazan, Russia

Abstract. The paper introduces new time series shape association measures based on Euclidean distance. The method of analysis of associations between time series based on separate analysis of positively and negatively associated local trends is discussed. The examples of application of the proposed measures and methods to analysis of associations between historical prices of securities obtained from Google Finance are considered. An example of time series with inverse associations between them is discussed.

Keywords: Time series shape association measure, moving approximation transform, local trend associations, hierarchical clustering, Google Finance.

1   Introduction

Many time series similarity measures have been introduced in time series data mining during last two decades [1,2,8-11, 14,15]. These measures usually used in time series clustering and similarity search in time series databases. The following examples of the similarity queries over sequence databases have been mentioned in [1]:

- Identify companies with similar pattern of growth;
- Determine products with similar selling patterns;
- Discover stocks with similar movement in stock prices.

In [3-4], it was pointed out a need in the measures of associations between time series that additionally to similarity between time series could measure inverse relationships between them. Additionally to considered above examples such measures could be used for finding sequences of competitive companies or products with inverse patterns when the rising patterns of one sequence correspond to falling patterns of another one. In [3], the measures of local trend associations (LTA) based on Moving Approximation Transform (MAT) have been introduced and examples of their application to analysis of possible relationships between elements of economic and financial systems have been considered. In [5], the method of construction of positive and negative local trend association patterns for any pair of time series based on MAT with window size $k=2$ has been proposed. An application of this method to analysis of associations between well production data in petroleum reservoirs has been

J.F. Martínez-Trinidad et al. (Eds.): MCPR 2014, LNCS 8495, pp. 92–101, 2014.
© Springer International Publishing Switzerland 2014

considered. In [6,7], the general methods for constructing association measures based on distance and similarity measures have been introduced. These methods generate sample Pearson's correlation coefficient as a particular case. Based on these results in this paper the new measures of association between time series are introduced and the method of analysis of positive and negative association patterns in time series proposed in [5] is generalized on sliding window with size $k \geq 2$. The methods are demonstrated on example of time series of end-of-day prices of securities downloaded from Google Finance [13].

The paper is organized as follows. The definition and examples of time series shape association measures are considered in Section 2. Section 3 introduces new time series shape association measures. In Sections 4 and 5 these measures and local trend association patterns based on MAT are used in clustering and analysis of associations of time series from Google Finance. The last section contains conclusions.

2   Time Series Shape Association Measures

A time series of length n, $(n \geq 1)$, is a sequence of real values $x = (x_1,\ldots,x_n)$. Denote X a set of such time series. Suppose p, q $(p \neq 0)$ are real values. Denote $q(n)$ a constant time series of the length n with all elements equal to q. We will write $x = const$ if $x = q(n)$ for some q, and $x \neq const$ if $x_i \neq x_j$ for some $i \neq j$ from $\{1,\ldots,n\}$. Denote $px+q = (px_1+q, \ldots,px_n+q)$, $x+y = (x_1+y_1, \ldots,x_n+y_n)$.

Difinition [4]. A time series shape association measure is a function $A{:}X{\times}X{\to}$ $[-1,1]$ satisfying for all $x,y \in X$ the properties:

A1. $A(x,y) = A(y,x)$,   (symmetry)

A2. $A(x,x) = 1$,   (reflexivity)

A3. $A(x,-x) = -1$,   (inverse reflexivity)

A4. $A(x,-y) = -A(x,y)$, $x,y \neq const$,   (inverse relationship)

A5. $A(x,y+q) = A(x,y)$,   for any $q \geq 0$.   (translation invariance)

A shape association measure is referred to as scale invariant if it satisfies:

A6. $A(x,py) = A(x,y)$, if $p > 0$.   (scale invariance)

A sample Pearson correlation coefficient:

$$corr(x, y) = \frac{\sum_{i=1}^{n}(x_i-\bar{x})(y_i-\bar{y})}{\sqrt{\sum_{i=1}^{n}(x_i-\bar{x})^2 \sum_{i=1}^{n}(y_i-\bar{y})^2}} \tag{1}$$

is an example of a translation and scale invariant time series shape association measure. The correlation coefficient is often considered as a measure of linear relationship between variables. A slightly modified example of time series from [5] given in

Table 1 and Fig. 1 shows that the correlation coefficient is not so good for measuring time series shape associations. It is reasonable to suppose that there are positive association between time series x and y and negative association between x and $-y$ but we have for them $corr(x,y) = corr(x,-y) = 0$.

Table 1. Example of three synthetic time series with $corr(x,y) = corr(x,-y) = 0$

i	1	2	3	4	5	6	7	8	9	10
x	100	80	50	60	90	150	200	250	180	140
y	200	120	10	20	40	50	60	70	40	20
$-y$	-200	-120	-10	-20	-40	-50	-60	-70	-40	-20

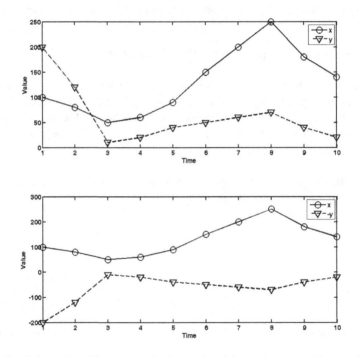

Fig. 1. Example of three synthetic time series with $corr(x,y) = corr(x,-y) = 0$

In [3], it was considered a measure of local trend associations (LTA) based on Moving Approximation Transform (MAT). MAT transforms time series $x = (x_1,...,x_n)$ into a sequence $MAT_k(x) = (a_1, ..., a_{n-k+1})$ of slope values (local trends) of simple linear regressions $f_i = a_i t + b_i$, of time series values $(x_i,...,x_{i+k-1})$, $i \in \{1,..., n-k+1\}$ in sliding window of size k. Suppose $x = (x_1,...,x_n)$ and $y = (y_1,...,y_n)$ are two time series and $MAT_k(x) = (a_{x1},...,a_{xm})$, $MAT_k(y) = (a_{y1}, ..., a_{ym})$, $k \in \{2,...,n-1\}$, $m = n-k+1$, are their MATs. The function (2) is called a measure of local trend associations:

$$lta_k(x,y) = \frac{\sum\limits_{i=1}^{m} a_{xi} \cdot a_{yi}}{\sqrt{\sum\limits_{i=1}^{m} a_{xi}^2 \cdot \sum\limits_{j=1}^{m} a_{yj}^2}} \quad , \quad k \in \{2,\dots,n\text{-}1\}. \tag{2}$$

It is easy to see that this measure for all $k \in \{2,\dots,n\text{-}1\}$ satisfies A1-A6. This measure evaluates associations between local trends and depends on the size of sliding window (see Table 2). For window size $k = 10$, the (global) trends have different signs: $MAT_{10}(x) = 0.7697$, $MAT_{10}(y) = -0.5582$, $MAT_{10}(-y) = 0.5582$ with association values $lta_{10}(x,y) = -1$, $lta_{10}(x,-y) = 1$. In spite of the global trends of x and y have different signs, i.e. x is "increasing" and y in "decreasing" with negative global trend association $lta_{10}(x,y) = -1$, the local trend associations between time series x,y (Table 2) have positive association values for small windows showing similarity in shapes of these time series and similar dynamics of them.

Table 2. Local trend associations for time series from Table 1 for all window sizes k

K	2	3	4	5	6	7	8	9	10
$lta_k(x,y)$	0.534	0.517	0.452	0.340	0.162	-0.094	-0.505	-0.895	-1
$lta_k(x,-y)$	-0.534	-0.517	-0.452	-0.340	-0.162	0.094	0.505	0.895	1

In [5], it was proposed the following shape association measure:

$$A_{UDk}(x,y) = \frac{\sum\limits_{i=1}^{m} A_{xi} \cdot A_{yi}}{\sqrt{\sum\limits_{i=1}^{m} A_{xi}^2 \cdot \sum\limits_{j=1}^{m} A_{yj}^2}} \quad , \quad k \in \{2,\dots,n\text{-}1\}. \tag{3}$$

such that in (2) all slope values are replaced by their sign values $A_i = \text{sign}(a_i) \in \{-1, 0,1\}$. For example from Table 1 this measure takes value $A_{UDk}(x,y) = 1$ for window size $k=2$ that corresponds to our perceptions that time series x and y are positively associated because both of them synchronously move up and down. For time series x and $-y$ we have $A_{UD2}(x,-y) = -1$ that reflects inverse dynamics of these time series. This measure also depends on window size like original lta_k measure.

3   New Time Series Shape Association Measures

The general procedure of construction of time series shape association measures introduced in [6,7] contains several components: 1) a time series standardization $F(x)$, 2) a dissimilarity (distance) measure $D(F(x),F(y))$, 3) a transformation of D into a similarity measure S, 4) a transformation of S into an association measure A. Each component should satisfy some conditions to define shape association measure A satisfying properties A1-A5 and, perhaps, A6. For example, the sample Pearson's correlation coefficient (1) can be constructed using the standardization (4), the Euclidean distance (5), the similarity measure (6) and the formula (7) for an association measure:

$$F(x)_i = \frac{x_i - \bar{x}}{\sqrt{\sum_{j=1}^{n}(x_j - \bar{x})^2}}, \qquad \bar{x} = \frac{1}{n}\sum_{j=1}^{n} x_j. \tag{4}$$

$$D(x,y) = \sqrt[2]{\sum_{i=1}^{n}|F(x)_i - F(y)_i|^2}, \tag{5}$$

$$S(x,y) = 1 - \frac{1}{4}D^2(x,y) = 1 - \frac{1}{4}\sum_{i=1}^{n}|F(x)_i - F(y)_i|^2, \tag{6}$$

$$A_{S,L}(x,y) = S(x,y) - S(x,-y). \tag{7}$$

The papers [6,7] have considered odd standardizations $F(x)$ satisfying the property: $F(-x) = -F(x)$. We introduce here shape association measures based on standardization

$$F(x)_i = \frac{x_i - MIN(x)}{MAX(x) - MIN(x)}, \text{ where } MIN(x) = min\{x_1,\ldots,x_n\}, MAX(x) = max\{x_1,\ldots,x_n\}, \tag{8}$$

that satisfies the property: $F(x) + F(-x) = 1$. Note that standardization (8) is widely used in time series data mining. We use the similarity measure $S(x,y)$ based on Euclidean distance (9) and two association measures (10), (11), where $x,y \neq const$, (see [6,7]):

$$S(x,y) = 1 - \frac{1}{n}D^2(x,y) = 1 - \frac{1}{n}\sum_{i=1}^{n}|F(x)_i - F(y)_i|^2. \tag{9}$$

$$A_{S,M}(x,y) = \begin{cases} S(x,y), & \text{if } S(x,y) > S(x,-y) \\ -S(x,y), & \text{if } S(x,y) < S(x,-y) \\ 0, & \text{otherwise} \end{cases} \tag{10}$$

$$A_{S,P}(x,y) = (S(x,y) - S(x,-y))/(1 - min(S(x,y),S(x,-y))). \tag{11}$$

The resulting association measures can be presented as follows:

$$A_{S,M}(x,y) = sign(\sum_{i=1}^{n}(2F(x)_i - 1)(2F(y)_i - 1)) \cdot$$

$$\left[1 - \frac{1}{n}min\{\sum_{i=1}^{n}|F(x)_i - F(y)_i|^2, \sum_{i=1}^{n}|F(x)_i + F(y)_i - 1|^2\}\right], \tag{12}$$

$$A_{S,P}(x,y) = \frac{\sum_{i=1}^{n}(2F(x)_i - 1)(2F(y)_i - 1)}{max(\sum_{i=1}^{n}|F(x)_i - F(y)_i|^2, \sum_{i=1}^{n}|F(x)_i + F(y)_i - 1|^2)}. \tag{13}$$

From the construction it follows that these measures are translation and scale invariant association measures. Note that these measures and the correlation coefficient are not defined for constant time series due to division by 0 in (4) and (8).

For benchmark example given in Table 1 and Fig. 1 we have $A_{S,M}(x,y) = 0.806$, $A_{S,M}(x,-y) = -0.806$, $A_{S,P}(x,y) = 0.313$, $A_{S,P}(x,-y) = -0.313$. Note that we have for this example $corr(x,y) = 0$, $corr(x,-y) = 0$. Hence, from this point of view the new time series shape association measures give better choice than correlation coefficient.

4   Time Series Clustering Based on Association Measures

Consider an example of time series of end-of-the-day prices of securities downloaded from Google Finance [13] and denoted here as follows: 1-XRX, 2-HPQ, 3-ERIC, 4-NOK, 5-BBRY, 6-AAPL, 7-IBM, 8-LNVGY. Each time series contains 251 data measured during period 19.02.2013 – 14.02.2014 and smoothed by moving average with window size 5 (see Fig. 2). Using different association measures $A(x,y)$ we calculated associations between these time series and converted them to similarity measures: $S(x,y) = abs(A(x,y))$. Applying single linkage clustering [15] to these similarity measures we obtained the hierarchical clusterings of time series.

For association measure $A_{S,M}$ it was constructed the clustering: {{{{C1, C2} C3}, C4}, C5} with the following two clusters joined on high level of similarity:

- C1:{{1-XRX (Xerox), 6-AAPL (Apple)}, 4-NOK (Nokia)}, securities with "rising" price, and
- C2:{5-BBRY (BlackBerry), 7-IBM (IBM)}, securities with "falling" price.

The clusters C1 and C2 are joined together because they have high negative associations defining high similarity between them.

- C3:{8-LNVGY (Lenovo)} is joined with these two clusters because it has high positive associations with cluster C1.
- C4:{2-HPQ (Hewlett Packard)} and C5:{3-ERIC (Ericsson)} are joined with other clusters on lower levels of similarity. C4 has positive association with 1-XRX and C5 has negative association with 2-HPQ.

For association measure $A_{S,P}$ we obtained the similar clustering. It is surprising that for correlation coefficient we obtained almost the same clustering with small difference in cluster C1:{{6-AAPL (Apple), 4-NOK (Nokia)}, 1-XRX (Xerox)}.

Based on the analysis of association values we can propose a hypothesis that the companies of the cluster C2 are competitive with the companies from the cluster C1 because the time series from these two clusters have negative association values. This analysis is based on association measures defined by metrics. Applying single linkage clustering to similarity measure $S(x,y) = abs(lta_{100}(x,y))$ we have obtained the following clustering of companies: {{D1, D2}, D3}, where

D1:{{6-AAPL, 4-NOK}, 8-LNVGY},

D2:{{5-BBRY, 7-IBM}, 1-XRX}, where 1-XRX has high negative associations with other two time series from this cluster. D2 is joined with D1 because 1-XRX has high positive association with 6-AAPL.

D3:{2-HPQ, 3-ERIC}. These time series have sufficiently high negative association. D3 joined with D1 and D2 on lower level of similarity due to similarity between 2-HPQ and 1-XRX.

Local trend association measures give possibility to find associations between "increasing" and "decreasing" trend patterns important in many applications of time

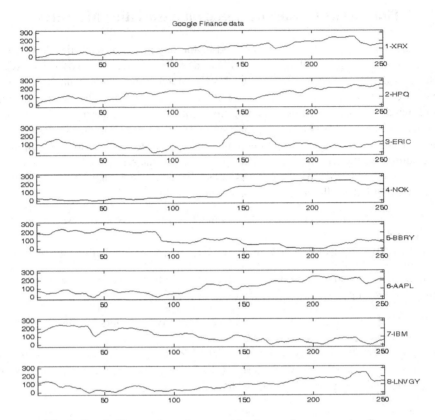

Fig. 2. Google Finance data after smoothing by moving average (w=5)

series analysis while distance based measures $A_{S,P}$, $A_{S,M}$ and correlation coefficient *corr* evaluate associations between "high" and "small" values of time series with respect to their "mean" values. In the following section we propose the method of analysis of positively and negatively associated trend patterns of time series.

5   Analysis of Positively and Negatively Associated Trend Patterns in Time Series

In [5], it was proposed the method of construction of positively and negatively associated patterns of time series based on linear regressions constructed by MAT for window size k=2. Two linear regressions computed in the same window for time series x and y are considered as positively associated if they have the slope values with the same sign, i.e. both are positive or both are negative. These linear regressions are considered as negatively associated if they have opposite signs. In last case when one time series is increasing another one is decreasing in the same window and vice versa. The maximal sequences of positively (negatively) associated linear regressions in

consecutive windows of size 2 have been considered as positively (negatively) associated patterns for considered two time series. This method was used in [5] in analysis
of associations between monthly well production data in oilfields.

An application of this technique for highly oscillating data, for example for time
series of daily prices of securities in stock market, requires to smooth time series data
and/or to consider local trends for windows larger than $k=2$ that also smooth data
fluctuations. Here we propose the method of visualization of positively and negatively
associated patterns in time series when MAT applied for windows with size greater
than 2. By changing window size in MAT it is possible to do more detailed analysis
of local trend associations. Separate analysis of positively and negatively associated
local trend patterns for window size $k=30$ is presented in Fig. 3 in comparative analysis of 5-BBRY and 6-AAPL time series. The local trend association for these time
series is negative and equals to -0.7433. Positively associated and negatively associated local trends (linear regressions) of these time series are presented separately on
the top and on the down of Fig. 3 correspondingly. It is interesting, that the Up-Down
association measure (3) for these local trends of time series takes value zero:
$A_{UDk}(x,y)= 0$, because exactly one half of local trends of time series are positively
associated and another half is negatively associated. The positively associated local
trends are located mostly on the left side of the domain (see two upper charts in
Fig. 3). The negatively associated local trends are located mostly on the right side of
the domain, see two lower charts in Fig. 3. The right part of these charts in presented
also in Fig. 4. From Fig. 4 we see that only 10 local trends (11%) in this part of chart
are positively associated and 79 local trends (89%) are negatively associated. An
analysis of Figures 3 and 4 gives possibility to generate a hypothesis that
BLACKBERRY and APPLE companies are competitive companies due to the large
number of negatively associated local trends of considered time series.

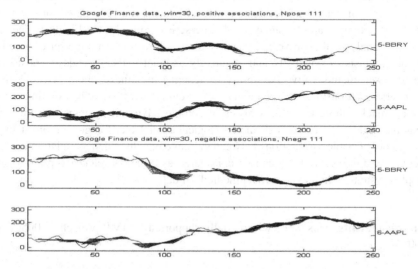

Fig. 3. Positively and negatively associated moving approximations of Google Finance data in
sliding window of size $k = 30$

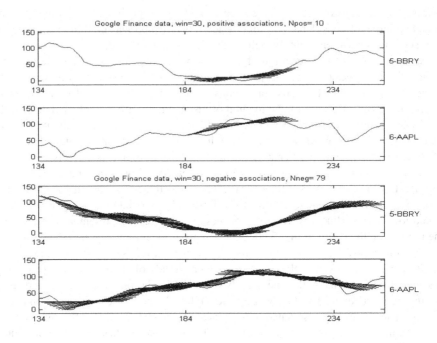

Fig. 4. The right part of Fig. 3 with high number of negatively associated local trends

6   Conclusion

The new time series shape association measures based on Euclidean distance and on popular type of data standardization are introduced and compared on synthetic benchmark example and on analysis of time series from Google Finance. The new method of analysis of positive and negative associations between time series based on separate analysis of positively and negatively associated local trends is considered. The proposed methods give possibility to generate hypothesis about possible direct and inverse relationships between complex system elements described by time series. This approach can be used for analysis of complex dynamic systems like financial, economic, industrial, ecological, meteorological, social etc. for generation of hypothesis about possible associations between system elements. Such association analysis of complex dynamic systems can be considered as a part of data-driven analysis of complex system including additional methods of data analysis.

Aknowledgments. This work was partially supported by IMP projects D.00507 and H.0016.

References

1. Agrawal, R., Faloutsos, C., Swami, A.: Efficient Similarity Search in Sequence Databases. In: Lomet, D.B. (ed.) FODO 1993. LNCS, vol. 730, pp. 69–84. Springer, Heidelberg (1993)
2. Agrawal, R., Lin, K.-I., Sawhney, H.S., Shim, K.: Fast Similarity Search in the Presence of Noise, Scaling, and Translation in Time-Series Databases. In: 21st International Conference on Very Large Databases, pp. 490–501. Morgan Kaufmann, San Francisco (1995)
3. Batyrshin, I., Herrera-Avelar, R., Sheremetov, L., Panova, A.: Moving Approximation Transform and Local Trend Associations in Time Series Data Bases. In: Batyrshin, I., Kacprzyk, J., Sheremetov, L., Zadeh, L.A. (eds.) Perception-based Data Mining and Decision Making in Economics and Finance. SCI, vol. 36, pp. 55–83. Springer, Heidelberg (2007)
4. Batyrshin, I., Sheremetov, L., Velasco-Hernandez, J.X.: On Axiomatic Definition of Time Series Shape Association Measures. In: Workshop on Operations Research and Data Mining, ORADM 2012, Cancun, pp. 117–127 (2012)
5. Batyrshin, I.: Up and Down Trend Associations in Analysis of Time Series Shape Association Patterns. In: Carrasco-Ochoa, J.A., Martínez-Trinidad, J.F., Olvera López, J.A., Boyer, K.L. (eds.) MCPR 2012. LNCS, vol. 7329, pp. 246–254. Springer, Heidelberg (2012)
6. Batyrshin, I.: Constructing Time Series Shape Association Measures: Minkowski Distance and Data Standardization. In: BRICS CCI 2013, Brasil, Porto de Galhinas (2013)
7. Batyrshin, I.: Association Measures and Aggregation Functions. In: Castro, F., Gelbukh, A., González, M. (eds.) MICAI 2013, Part II. LNCS, vol. 8266, pp. 194–203. Springer, Heidelberg (2013)
8. Das, G., Gunopulos, D.: Time Series Similarity and Indexing. In: Handbook on Data Mining, pp. 279–304. Lawrence Erlbaum Associates (2003)
9. Fu, T.-C.: A Review on Time Series Data Mining. Engineering Applications of Artificial Intelligence 24, 164–181 (2011)
10. Goldin, D.Q., Kanellakis, P.C.: On Similarity Queries for Time-Series Data: Constraint Specification and Implementation. In: Montanari, U., Rossi, F. (eds.) CP 1995. LNCS, vol. 976, pp. 137–153. Springer, Heidelberg (1995)
11. Liao, T.W.: Clustering of Time Series Data – A Survey. Pattern Recognition 38, 1857–1874 (2005)
12. Rafiei, D., Mendelzon, A.O.: Querying Time Series Data Based on Similarity. IEEE Transactions on Knowledge and Data Engineering 12, 675–693 (2000)
13. Google Finance, Historical Prices, http://www.google.com/finance (February 19, 2013-February 14, 2014)
14. Buza, K., Nanopoulos, A., Schmidt-Thieme, L.: Fusion of Similarity Measures for Time Series Classification. In: Corchado, E., Kurzyński, M., Woźniak, M. (eds.) HAIS 2011, Part II. LNCS, vol. 6679, pp. 253–261. Springer, Heidelberg (2011)
15. Everitt, B.S., Landau, S., Leese, M., Stahl, D.: Cluster Analysis, 5th edn. John Wiley & Sons, Ltd., Chichester (2011)

An Effective Permutant Selection Heuristic for Proximity Searching in Metric Spaces[*]

Karina Figueroa[1] and Rodrigo Paredes[2]

[1] Facultad de Ciencias Físico-Matemáticas, Universidad Michoacana, México
[2] Departamento de Ciencias de la Computación, Universidad de Talca, Chile
karina@fismat.umich.mx, raparede@utalca.cl

Abstract. The permutation based index has shown to be very effective in medium and high dimensional metric spaces, even in difficult problems such as solving reverse k-nearest neighbor queries. Nevertheless, currently there is no study about which are the desirable features one can ask to a permutant set, or how to select good permutants. Similar to the case of pivots, our experimental results show that, compared with a randomly chosen set, a good permutant set yields to fast query response or to reduce the amount of space used by the index. In this paper, we start by characterizing permutants and studying their predictive power; then we propose an effective heuristic to select a good set of permutant candidates. We also show empirical evidence that supports our technique.

1 Introduction

Proximity or *similarity* searching is the problem of, given a data set and a similarity criterion, finding elements within the set that are close or similar to a given query. This is a natural extension of the classical problem of exact searching. It is motivated by data types that cannot be queried by exact matching, such as multimedia databases containing images, audio, video, documents, and so on. In this framework, the exact comparison is just a type of query, while close or similar objects can be queried as well.

There exist several computer applications where the concept of similarity retrieval is of interest (see [4] for a comprehensive survey on those applications). Some examples are *machine learning and classification*, where a new element must be classified according to its closest existing element; *image quantization and compression*, where only some samples can be represented and those that cannot must be coded as their closest representable one; *text retrieval*, where we look for words in a text database allowing a small number of errors, or we look for documents similar to a given query or document; *computational biology*, where we want to find a DNA or protein sequence in a database allowing some errors due to typical variations; and *function prediction*, where past behavior is extrapolated to predict future behavior, based on function similarity.

---

[*] This work is partially funded by National Council of Science and Technology (CONACyT) of México, Universidad Michoacana de San Nicolás de Hidalgo, México, and Fondecyt grant 1131044, Chile.

J.F. Martínez-Trinidad et al. (Eds.): MCPR 2014, LNCS 8495, pp. 102–111, 2014.

Proximity/similarity queries can be formalized using the metric space model [4,7,10,12]. The model assumes that there is a universe $\mathbb{X}$ of objects and a non-negative distance function $d : \mathbb{X} \times \mathbb{X} \to R^+ \cup \{0\}$ defined among them. Objects in $\mathbb{X}$ do not necessarily have coordinates (think, for instance, in strings, images, audio, or video). On the other hand, the distance function gives us a dissimilarity criterion to compare objects from the universe. Therefore, the smaller the distance between two objects, the more "similar" they are.

The distance satisfies the following properties that make the tuple $(\mathbb{X}, d)$ a metric space: $d(x, y) \geq 0$ (*positiveness*), $d(x, y) = d(y, x)$ (*symmetry*), $d(x, x) = 0$ (*reflexivity*), and $d(x, z) \leq d(x, y) + d(y, z)$ (*triangle inequality*). These properties hold for many reasonable similarity functions.

In the typical scenario of the metric space search problem, there is a finite database or dataset of interest $\mathbb{U} \subset \mathbb{X}$. Later, when a new query object $q \in \mathbb{X} \setminus \mathbb{U}$ arrives, its proximity query consists in retrieving objects from $\mathbb{U}$ that are relevant (that is, similar) to q. There are two basic kinds of queries. The first is the *range query* $d(q, r)$, which retrieves all the elements in $\mathbb{U}$ which are within distance r to q. Formally, $(q, r) = \{u \in \mathbb{U}, d(q, u) \leq r\}$. The second is the *$k$-nearest neighbor query* $NN_k(q)$, which retrieves the k closest-to-q elements in $\mathbb{U}$. This is, $|NN_k(q)| = k$, and $\forall\, u \in NN_k(q)$ and $v \in \mathbb{U} \setminus NN_k(q)$, $d(u, q) \leq d(v, q)$.

Given the database, these similarity queries can be trivially answered by performing $n = |\mathbb{U}|$ distance evaluations. Yet, as the distance function is assumed to be expensive to compute (think, for instance, when comparing two fingerprints), it is customary to define the complexity of the search as the number of distance evaluations performed, disregarding other components such as CPU time for side computations and even I/O time. Thus, the ultimate goal is to build offline an index in order to speed up online queries.

The Permutation Index [3] is one of the most effective similarity search indices. It is particularly well suited for medium and high dimensional spaces. Despite that its practical version is focused in the case of retrieving an approximate answer for a given query, its effectiveness allows us to consider it as an (almost) exact answer. As a matter of fact, experimental results shown in [3] reveal that the Permutation Index is extremely promissory. Nevertheless, there is no study about which are the desirable features one can ask to a permutant set, or how to select good permutants. This is the main focus of this paper.

Similar to the case of traditional pivots [1,2], our experimental results show that a good permutant set yields to fast query response or to reduce the amount of space used by the index compared to a randomly chosen set. In fact, in the metric space of Flickr images, we only need to review a 1.15% of the dataset to obtain the nearest neighbor of a given query.

The rest of this paper is organized as follows. In Section 2, we cover related work on metric space indices. Then, in Section 3, we start by characterizing permutants and studying their prediction power, and then we propose an effective heuristic to select a good permutant candidate set. Next, Section 4 shows the empirical evidence that supports our technique. We finally draw our conclusions and future work directions in Section 5.

2   Related Work

2.1   Previous Work on Choosing Pivots

The pivot based indices are one of the most popular in the field of metric space searching. These algorithms select a set of pivots $\{p_1 \ldots p_k\} \subseteq \mathbb{U}$ and store a table of kn distances $d(p_i, u)$, $i \in \{1 \ldots k\}, \forall\, u \in \mathbb{U}$. To solve a range query (q, r), pivot-based algorithms measure $d(q, p_i)$ for all the pivots, and use the fact that, because of the triangle inequality, $d(q, u) \geq |d(q, p_i) - d(u, p_i)|$, so they can discard every $u \in \mathbb{U}$ such that $|d(q, p_i) - d(u, p_i)| > r$, since this implies $d(q, u) > r$ (which any of the pivots). The elements u that still cannot be discarded at this point are directly compared against q.

In general, these indices choose the pivots randomly among the database objects. However, there are some preliminary attempts to choose pivots [11,8] which are based in two ideas: good pivots are far away from the rest of the database, and also, far away of each other pivots. These techniques have good performance in some metric spaces but they fail in others.

There are two works [1,2] on how to systematically select a good pivot set.

In [1], the authors propose an efficiency measure to compare two pivot sets, maximizing the mean of the distance distribution among pivots. Based on that criterion, they also provide three optimization techniques to select good sets of pivots: (i) produce several pivot sets at random and choose the set with the highest average distance; (ii) choose pivots incrementally, the first pivot p_1 is the object that have the maximum average distance to other objects, the second one p_2 is selected so that the subset $\{p_1, p_2\}$ has the maximum average distance, and so on until selecting all the pivots; and (iii) starting with a random set of pivot, in each iteration the pivot having the smallest contribution to the average distance is removed and replaced by a better pivot.

In [2], the authors propose a dynamic pivot selection technique, which combines the third alternative in [1] with the Sparse Spatial Selection (SSS) technique [9]. The idea is to use the same SSS's pivot insertion criterion but checking if any of the already selected pivots becomes redundant (in the sense that its contribution to some efficiency criterion is low) or the new pivot candidate is redundant with respect to the current pivot set.

2.2   The Permutation Based Index

Let $\mathbb{P} \subset \mathbb{U}$ be a subset of permutants (in the literature, they are also called anchors). Each element $u \in \mathbb{U}$ induces a preorder $\leq_u$ given by the distance from u towards each permutant, defined as $y \leq_u z \Leftrightarrow d(u, y) \leq d(u, z)$, for any pair $y, z \in \mathbb{P}$. The relation $\leq_u$ is a preorder and not an order because some permutants can be at the same distance of u. So, it could be possible to find $y, z \in \mathbb{P}$, such that $y \leq_u z \wedge z \leq_u y$.

Let $\Pi_u = i_1, i_2, \ldots, i_{|\mathbb{P}|}$ be the permutation of u, where permutant $p_{i_j} \leq_u p_{i_{j+1}}$. Permutants at the same distance take an arbitrary but consistent order. Every object in $\mathbb{U}$ computes its preorder of $\mathbb{P}$ and associates it to a permutation, which is stored in the index (this index does not store distances). Thus, a simple implementation needs $n|\mathbb{P}|$ space.

The crux of this index is that two equal objects must have the same permutation, while similar objects will hopefully have similar ones. So if Π_u is similar to Π_q we expect that u is close to q. Thus, we have changed the problem from searching the dataset $\mathbb{U}$ to searching the permutation set.

At query time, we compute Π_q and compare it with all the permutations stored in the index. So, we traverse $\mathbb{U}$ in the order $\leq_{\Pi_q}$ induced by Π_q (by increasing permutation dissimilarity). If we limit the number of distance computations, we obtain a probabilistic search algorithm (in the sense that with some probability, we are able to find the right answer to the query). Fortunately, the order $\leq_{\Pi_q}$ induced is extremely promissory, as reported in [3] for range queries.

Similarity between the permutations of q and u can be measured by Kendall Tau K_τ, Spearman Footrule S_F, or Spearman Rho S_ρ metric [5], among others. K_τ can be seen as the number of swaps that a bubble-sort-like algorithm has to do in order to make two permutations equal. On the other hand, using $\Pi_u^{-1}(i_j)$ to denote the position of permutant p_{i_j} in the permutation Π_u, S_F and S_ρ are defined as follows:

$$S_F(\Pi_u, \Pi_q) = \sum_{j=[1,|\mathbb{P}|]} |\Pi_u^{-1}(i_j) - \Pi_q^{-1}(i_j)| \tag{1}$$

$$S_\rho(\Pi_u, \Pi_q) = \sqrt{\sum_{j=[1,|\mathbb{P}|]} |\Pi_u^{-1}(i_j) - \Pi_q^{-1}(i_j)|^2} \tag{2}$$

As S_ρ is monotonous, we can simple use S_ρ^2. For example, let $\Pi_u = (42153)$ and $\Pi_q(32154)$ be the object $u \in \mathbb{U}$ and query $q \in \mathbb{X} \setminus \mathbb{U}$ permutations, respectively. So, $K_\tau(\Pi_u, \Pi_q) = 7$, $S_F(\Pi_u, \Pi_q) = 8$ and $S_\rho^2 = (\Pi_u, \Pi_q) = 32$.

3   Finding Good Permutants

In the following, we will describe our approach to select good permutants. It is based on experimental observations that lead us to the final methodology to obtain a good permutant set. We start by characterizing the permutants, and then we propose a heuristic to select a permutant set.

3.1   Characterizing the Permutants

Let us consider a single permutant p from the set $\mathbb{P}$. For this permutant, the maximum difference of positions between the query permutation Π_q and the permutation of any object in the database Π_u is $|\mathbb{P}| - 1$. This is obvious, however it suggests a simple way to determine how much a permutant can contribute in the searching process. Permutants at the beginning or the end of a permutation can produce an important increase in the permutation distance, while the ones in the middle of the permutation produce a mild increase. Note that, such increase is the one that changes the order $\leq_{\Pi_q}$ (induced by the permutation of the query).

Based in this observation, we start our study by considering how much contributes a portion of the permutation to the order $\leq_{\Pi_q}$. To illustrate our point we perform the following experiment. We divide the permutation Π_q in three equal portions, and show the results when searching in a metric space using the permutants that fall in two thirds of the permutation Π_q (that is, we exclude a portion). To do this, we compute the permutation distance using Equation 3.

$$S_F(\Pi_u, \Pi_q) = \sum_{j=[1,|\mathbb{P}|\wedge \Pi_q^{-1}(i_j)\notin\texttt{portion}]} |\Pi_q^{-1}(i_j) - \Pi_u^{-1}(i_j)| \qquad (3)$$

For this experiment, we use $(\mathbb{R}^D, L_2)$ considering a uniform dataset composed by 80,000 vectors with dimension $D \in [8, 128]$, and show the average over 100 randomly chosen queries. According to the results of [3] we use permutant sets of size $D \pm 2$, that is, a direct relation with the dimension of data.

Fig. 1 shows the results when we discard either the left, middle, or right portions of the permutation. The figure shows that the best results are obtained when we discard the middle portion; this is in agreement with the intuition that the permutants that fall in this section do not heavily increase the permutation distance. On the other hand, the figure also says that the permutants in the left portion are the most important ones in terms of inducing the order $\leq_{\Pi_q}$, since in high dimension ($D = 128$), removing the left partition produces the biggest degradation in the search efficiency.

This observation leads us to the core of our method to find good permutants. The main idea is trying to pick permutants that do not fall in the middle portion. To do this, we can look for permutants that concentrate their occurrences in some portions of the object permutations (hopefully in the left one).

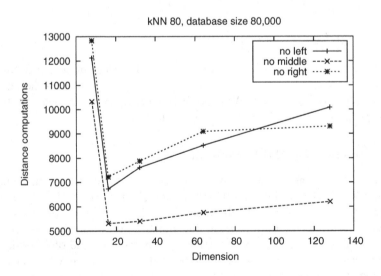

Fig. 1. Retrieval performance when excluding one portion of the permutation

3.2 A Simple Heuristic to Find Good Permutants

Given a permutant, one can compute the histogram of its positions in the permutations of all the elements in $\mathbb{U}$. If that histogram is not concentrated, its variance is large when compared with a random permutant.

Therefore, we now perform another preliminary experiment in order to verify this assumption. In this experiment we compare the retrieval performance of three sets. The first is a randomly chosen permutant set of size D, the second is composed by D permutants having low variance in their histogram of positions, and the third are the D permutants with high variance. This experiment was done using the same setup of the previous section.

To choose permutant sets with low and high variance, we take a random sample of size $c = \left\lfloor \frac{1+\sqrt{1+8n}}{2} \right\rfloor$ (where $n = |\mathbb{U}|$). We select this value since the full comparison among all the elements in the sample requires $\frac{c(c-1)}{2} < n$ distance computations. So, we maintain controlled the number distance computations. If $D > c$, we repeat the process until we have enough permutants to make the selection. But, in practical cases $D = O(\sqrt{n})$, so with one iteration is enough.

Fig. 2 shows that the best similarity query performance is verified with the set whose permutants present the largest variance. The difference is clearly noticeable, in particular in high dimensional spaces. In fact, in dimension $D = 128$, the high variance set needs 79% of the distance computations required by the random set; and for $D = 64$, the high variance set requires just 76%. The second performance is achieved by the random chosen set. This behavior is counter intuitive as we would expect that having a criterion is better that choosing permutants at random.

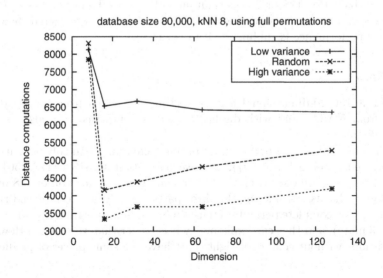

Fig. 2. Search performance of a random permutant set versus low and high variance permutant sets

4   Experimental Evaluation

We show the performance of our heuristic in two real-world spaces of images.

4.1   Flickr

The set of image objects were taken from Flickr, using the URL provided by the SAPIR collection [6]. The content-based descriptors extracted from the images were: Color Histogram $3 \times 3 \times 3$ using RGB color space (27 dimension vector), Gabor Wavelet (48 dimension vector), Efficient Color Descriptor (ECD) 8×1 using RGB color space (32 dimension vector), ECD 8×1 using HSV color space (32 dimension vector), and Edge Local 4×4 (80 dimension vector). For each image, all the components are concatenated in a single vector of 219 components. We compare the vectors using Euclidean distance. The dataset contains 1 million of images.

Fig. 3 shows the performance of our technique when solving k-nearest neighbor queries. We test three values of k, namely 1, 10, and 20, and the three criteria used in Section 3.2, that is, excluding the each one of the three portions (left, middle and right). We repeat the experiment using permutant set of size 128 and 256. Notice that we also compare our criteria with the complete permutation of 128 or 256 permutants, respectively. These experiments show that we make almost the same computational effort using two thirds of the permutations than using the complete one. In practice, the center or the right portion does not really give much information.

Usually, users retrieve a few numbers of images per query. So for illustrate our results, we remark that with $k = 1$, we need to compare only 1.15% to 0.89% of the database (for 128 or 256 permutants). If we use higher values of k, our index needs to review a larger fraction of the database, as expected; however, the query performance is sublinear with respect to k.

4.2   Nasa

A set of 40,150 20-dimensional feature vectors, generated from images downloaded from NASA[1] and with duplicate vectors eliminated. We also use Euclidean distance.

At Fig. 4, we show the performance of our technique when solving k-nearest neighbor queries ($k \in \{1, 10, 20\}$), and two permutant set sizes $\{128, 256\}$. Notice that we compare our criteria with the complete permutation of 128 or 256 permutants (that is, considering the three parts, namely, left, center and right). Once again, the complete permutation uses more permutants than the others (exactly $\mathbb{P}/3$ more), and that can explain why it is better than the others. However, permutations without center (or right) part have the same power of prediction.

---

[1] At http://www.dimacs.rutgers.edu/Challenges/Sixth/software.html

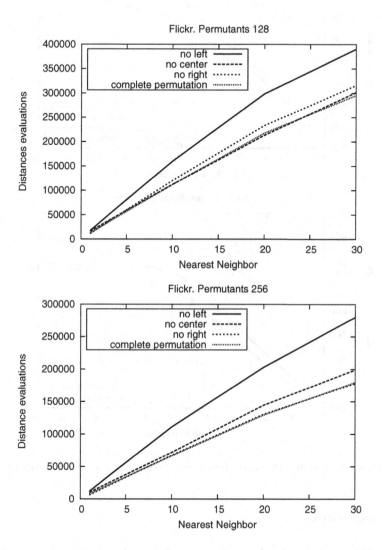

Fig. 3. Performance of our technique using real database (FLICKR images)

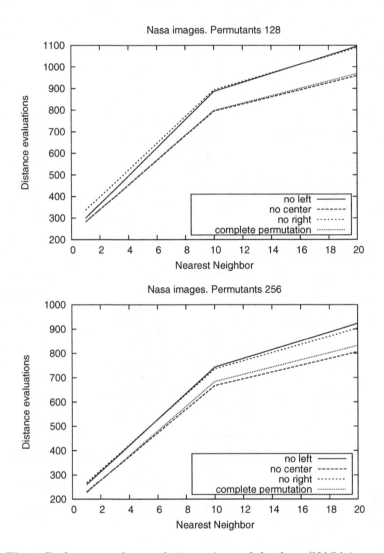

Fig. 4. Performance of our technique using real database (NASA images)

5   Conclusions

In this paper we started by characterizing permutants and studying their prediction power. Next, we proposed an effective heuristic to select a good permutant candidate set. We also showed empirical evidence that supports our technique. The experimental results shows that our approach is very promising when retrieving objects from high dimensional spaces and also from real-world datasets.

In fact, in the Flickr real-world metric space, which contains 1 million of images represented with a vector of 219 dimensions, using 128 permutants, we only need to review 1.15% of the dataset to obtain the nearest neighbor of a given query. We obtain a similar performance in the space of Nasa images (represented by 20-dimensional feature vectors), where, using a permutant set of size 128 and our criteria, we need to review 2.24% of the dataset in order to retrieve the 10 nearest neighbors of a given query.

In the future work, we are interesting on compressing the permutants through removing the middle of the permutations, as we state here. We are also very interested in how to characterize better the set of permutants. Finally, the high variance permutant set of Fig. 2 is composed by permutants that concentrate their occurrences in some specific positions of the permutation. In future work we also study how to we refine this permutant set.

References

1. Bustos, B., Navarro, G., Chávez, E.: Pivot selection techniques for proximity searching in metric spaces. Pattern Recognition Letters 24(14), 2357–2366 (2003)
2. Bustos, B., Pedreira, O., Brisaboa, N.R.: A dynamic pivot selection technique for similarity search. In: Proc. 1st Workshop on Similarity Search and Applications (SISAP 2008), pp. 105–112 (2008)
3. Chávez, E., Figueroa, K., Navarro, G.: Effective proximity retrieval by ordering permutations. IEEE Trans. on Pattern Analysis and Machine Intelligence (TPAMI) 30(9), 1647–1658 (2009)
4. Chávez, E., Navarro, G., Baeza-Yates, R., Marroquin, J.: Searching in metric spaces. ACM Computing Surveys 33(3), 273–321 (2001)
5. Fagin, R., Kumar, R., Sivakumar, D.: Comparing top k lists. SIAM J. Discrete Math. 17(1), 134–160 (2003)
6. Falchi, F., Kacimi, M., Mass, Y., Rabitti, F., Zezula, P.: SAPIR: Scalable and distributed image searching. In: SAMT (Posters and Demos). CEUR Workshop Proceedings, vol. 300, pp. 11–12 (2007)
7. Hjaltason, G., Samet, H.: Index-driven similarity search in metric spaces. ACM Transactions Database Systems 28(4), 517–580 (2003)
8. Micó, L., Oncina, J., Vidal, E.: A new version of the nearest-neighbor approximating and eliminating search (AESA) with linear preprocessing-time and memory requirements. Pattern Recognition Letters 15, 9–17 (1994)
9. Pedreira, O., Brisaboa, N.R.: Spatial selection of sparse pivots for similarity search in metric spaces. In: van Leeuwen, J., Italiano, G.F., van der Hoek, W., Meinel, C., Sack, H., Plášil, F. (eds.) SOFSEM 2007. LNCS, vol. 4362, pp. 434–445. Springer, Heidelberg (2007)
10. Samet, H.: Foundations of Multidimensional and Metric Data Structures. Morgan Kaufmann (2006)
11. Yianilos, P.: Data structures and algorithms for nearest neighbor search in general metric spaces. In: Proc. 4th ACM-SIAM Symposium on Discrete Algorithms (SODA 1993), pp. 311–321 (1993)
12. Zezula, P., Amato, G., Dohnal, V., Batko, M.: Similarity Search – The Metric Space Approach. Advances in Database System, vol. 32. Springer (2006)

Study of Overlapping Clustering Algorithms
Based on Kmeans through FBcubed Metric

Argenis A. Aroche-Villarruel[1], J.A. Carrasco-Ochoa[1], José Fco. Martínez-Trinidad[1],
J. Arturo Olvera-López[2], and Airel Pérez-Suárez[3]

[1] Computer Science Department, Instituto Nacional de Astrofísica, Óptica y Electrónica,
Luis Enrique Erro No. 1, Sta. María Tonantzintla, Puebla, CP: 72840, México
{argenis,ariel,fmartine}@inaoep.mx
[2] Faculty of Computer Sciences, Benemérita Universidad Autónoma de Puebla,
Av. San Claudio y 14 sur. Ciudad Universitaria. Puebla, Pue., México
aolvera@cs.buap.mx
[3] Advanced Technologies Application Center, 7ma A #21406 e/ 214 y 216, Rpto. Siboney,
Playa. C.P. 12200. La Habana, Cuba
asuarez@cenatav.co.cu

Abstract. In this paper we present a study of the overlapping clustering algorithms OKM, WOKM and OKMED, which are extensions to the overlapping case
of the well known Kmeans algorithm proposed for building partitions. Different
to other previously reported comparisons, in our study we compare these algorithms using the external evaluation metric FBcubed which takes into account the
overlapping among clusters and we contrast our results against those obtained by
F-measure, a metric that does not take into account the overlapping among clusters and that has been previously used in another reported comparison.

Keywords: Clustering, Overlapping Clustering, Clustering Validation.

1 Introduction

Among the clustering algorithms, those building overlapping clusters are useful in
different applications, where it is common that objects belong to more than one cluster. Some examples of this kind of applications are information retrieval [1], social
network analysis [2], text segmentation [3], among others. In the literature, several
algorithms have been proposed for overlapping clustering [4, 5, 6, 7, 8, 9, 10, 11],
which are different according to their mathematical basis and clustering strategies, as
well as the type of datasets they can process.

Due to their simplicity, the Kmeans algorithm [12] together with its variants are
clustering algorithms that have been widely used in several applications. However,
since these algorithms do not produce overlapping clusterings therefore, they could be
non suitable for applications needing this kind of clustering. The algorithms OKM
[8], WOKM [9] and OKMED [9], have been proposed as extensions to the overlapping clustering case of the Kmeans algorithm [12], weighting Kmeans [13], and k-
medoids (Partitioning Around Medoids) algorithms [14], respectively.

J.F. Martínez-Trinidad et al. (Eds.): MCPR 2014, LNCS 8495, pp. 112–121, 2014.
© Springer International Publishing Switzerland 2014

In [9] an experimental evaluation of these algorithms is reported; however, in this work the efficacy of the algorithms was assessed using F-measure that is not defined for evaluating overlapping clustering. Taking into account that some metrics have been recently proposed for evaluating overlapping clusterings, we perform an experimental evaluation of the above commented algorithms employing these metrics. In this way, we will be able to know how good really are these algorithms for overlapping clustering problems.

This paper is organized as follows: Section 2 briefly describes the algorithms OKM, WOKM and OKMED. Section 3 reports the experimental study in which we compare these algorithms using some standard overlapping datasets. Finally, in section 4 some conclusions are presented.

2   OKM, WOKM and OKMED Algorithms

The problem of clustering a set of objects $X = \{x_1, x_2, \dots x_n\}$ in k clusters (a priori parameter), using the Kmeans algorithm [12] is formulated as an optimization problem, where the objective function (1) is minimized.

$$Q(\pi) = \sum_{j=1}^{k} \sum_{x_i \in \pi_j} d^2(x_i, z_j) \tag{1}$$

being $\pi = \{\pi_1, \dots \pi_k\}$ is a set of k clusters, $\pi_i \cap \pi_j = \emptyset$, for $i \neq j$; $Z = \{z_1, \dots z_k\}$ is a set such that z_i is the centroid of π_i, for $i = 1, \dots, k$; and $d(x_i, z_j)$ is the Euclidean distance between objects x_i and z_j.

2.1   OKM

The OKM algorithm [8], extends the objective function used in Kmeans [12], to consider the possibility of overlapping clusters. In this algorithm, the objective function is defined as in (2).

$$Q'(\pi) = \sum_{i=1}^{n} d^2(x_i, \phi(x_i)) \tag{2}$$

where π, Z and d are as in (1), removing the condition of $\pi_i \cap \pi_j = \emptyset$, for $i \neq j$; $\phi(x_i)$ is the "image" of x_i, which is defined as a combination of the centroids (z_j) of the clusters π_j where x_i belongs to, computed as in (3).

$$\phi(x_i) = (\phi_1(x_i), \dots, \phi_p(x_i)) \text{ with } \phi_v(x_i) = \frac{\sum_{z_j \in A_i} z_{j,v}}{|A_i|} \tag{3}$$

where $A_i = \{z_j | x_i \in \pi_j\}$

There are two important differences between Kmeans and OKM. The first one is in the way the objects are assigned to one or more clusters and, the second, is in the way the centroid of each cluster is computed. The assignment step for an object x_i, consists in scrolling through the list of centroids, from the nearest to the farthest, and assigning x_i to the respective cluster while $d(x_i, \phi(x_i))$ decreases. The new assignment list is stored only if it is better than the previous one.

The centroid z_j for the cluster π_j is updated as follows:

$$z_{j,v} = \frac{1}{\sum_{x_i \in \pi_j} \frac{1}{\delta_i^2}} \sum_{x_i \in \pi_j} \frac{1}{\delta_i^2} \cdot \tau_{i_v}^j \qquad (4)$$

where: $z_{j,v}$ denotes the $v - th$ feature of the centroid z_j, δ_i is the number of clusters to which x_i belongs to ($\delta_i = |A_i|$) and $\tau_{i_v}^j$ is computed as follows:

$$\tau_{i_v}^j = \delta_i \times x_{i,v} - \sum_{z_j \in A_i/\{z_i\}} z_{j,v} \qquad (5)$$

where A_i is as in (3).

2.2   WOKM

In WOKM [9] the objective function of weighting-Kmeans [13] is extended to take into account feature weights into each cluster; therefore, it is necessary to redefine the concept of "image". In this algorithm the image for x_i is defined through a weighted average of the cluster centroids for x_i as follows:

$$\phi(x_i) = (\phi_1(x_i), \dots, \phi_p(x_i)) \text{ with } \phi_v(x_i) = \frac{\sum_{z_j \in A_i} \lambda_{j,v}^\beta z_{j,v}}{\sum_{z_j \in A_i} \lambda_{j,v}^\beta} \qquad (6)$$

where $z_{j,v}$ is defined as in (4); $\lambda_{j,v} \in [0,1]$ denotes the weight associated to the feature v in the cluster j (initially this value is $1/p$); β is a parameter ($\beta > 1$) that regulates the influence of the weights in the algorithm.

The vector of weights γ_i for the images $\phi(x_i)$ is defined as follows:

$$\gamma_{i,v} = \frac{\sum_{z_j \in A_i} \lambda_{j,v}}{|A_i|} \qquad (7)$$

From this definition the objective function for the algorithm WOKM is given by:

$$Q''(\pi) = \sum_{x_i \in X} \sum_{v=1}^p \gamma_{i,v}^\beta |x_{i,v} - \phi_v(x_i)|^2 \qquad (8)$$

where π and Z are as in (1).

The assignment step is similar to the corresponding step in the OKM algorithm, i.e., an object is assigned to its nearest clusters while $\sum_{v=1}^p \gamma_{i,v}^\beta |x_{i,v} - \phi_v(x_i)|^2$ decreases.

The new centroid z_j^* for the cluster π_j is obtained from the set $\{(\tau_i^j, w_i)|x_i \in \pi_j\}$; τ_i^j like in OKM, allows those objects that belong to more clusters to have less impact on the position of the new centroid; w_i denotes the weight vector and it is defined as follows:

$$w_{i,v} = \frac{\gamma_{i,v}^\beta}{(\sum_{z_l \in A_i} \lambda_{l,v}^\beta)^2} \qquad (9)$$

For computing the weights WOKM introduces a heuristic based in the one proposed in [15]; the heuristic for each class consists in:

- Computing a new weight $\lambda_{j,v}$ for the cluster π_j by estimating on each feature the variance of the objects that belong only to π_j:

$$\lambda_{j,v} = \frac{(\Sigma_{\{x_i \in \pi_j \,|\, |A_i|=1\}}(x_{i,v}-z_{j,v})^2)^{1/(1-\beta)}}{\Sigma_{u=1}^{p}(\Sigma_{\{x_i \in \pi_j \,|\, |A_i|=1\}}(x_{i,v}-z_{j,v})^2)^{1/(1-\beta)}} \qquad (10)$$

- Store the weight only if it improves the objective function (8).

2.3   OKMED

OKMED [9] is based on the k-medoids algorithm, which uses medoids instead of centroids. With this purpose, the objective function is extended from the OKM algorithm, so that we can use any dissimilarity function between objects. Assuming that $d(,)$ is a dissimilarity function from $X \times X \to \mathbb{R}^+$, the objective function for OKMED is given by (2).

The notion of image was redefined using cluster medoids instead of centroids. The image $\phi(x_i)$ of x_i in the cluster π_j is then defined as the object from X that minimizes the sum of the dissimilarities with all the medoids of the clusters where x_i belongs to:

$$\phi(x_i) = arg \, min_{x_j \in X} \Sigma_{z_l \in A_i} d^2(x_j, z_l) \qquad (11)$$

Notice that, in this new definition, the computation of an image requires to test all the objects in the collection.

The assignment of an object to one or more clusters is done in the same way as in OKM, but using a medoid for each cluster instead of a centroid.

For updating the medoid OKMED tests each object x_i in the cluster π_j, until finding the first object that improves the objective function with respect to the current medoid, that object will be the new medoid for π_j.

3   Experimental Analysis

For our study we propose to use the FBcubed validation metric [16], since this, unlike most external metrics reported in the literature, allows to evaluate overlapping clustering algorithms. Additionally, we compare our results against those results reported in [9]. The clustering algorithms were programmed in ANSI C.

F-measure combines Precision and Recall taking into account a labeled dataset and the result of clustering the same dataset. Let N_c be the set of pairs of objects belonging to the same class (same label) and N_π the set of pairs of objects belonging to the same cluster, the Precision, Recall and F-measure metrics are defined as:

$$Precision = \frac{|N_\pi \cap N_C|}{|N_\pi|} \tag{12}$$

$$Recall = \frac{|N_\pi \cap N_C|}{|N_C|} \tag{13}$$

$$F - measure = \frac{2 \times Precision \times Recall}{Precision + Recall} \tag{14}$$

FBcubed is calculated using the Bcubed Precision and Bcubed Recall metrics as proposed in [16]. The Bcubed Precision and Bcubed Recall are based on the Multiplicity Precision and Multiplicity Recall metrics respectively; which are defined as:

$$Multiplicity\ Precision(x_i, x_j) = \frac{Min(|\pi(x_i) \cap \pi(x_j)|, |C(x_i) \cap c(x_j)|)}{|\pi(x_i) \cap \pi(x_j)|} \tag{15}$$

$$Multiplicity\ Recall(x_i, x_j) = \frac{Min(|\pi(x_i) \cap \pi(x_j)|, |C(x_i) \cap c(x_j)|)}{|C(x_i) \cap c(x_j)|} \tag{16}$$

where x_i and x_j are two objects, $C(x_i)$ are the classes associated to x_i, $\pi(x_i)$ are the clusters associated to x_i. These formulas are only defined when x_i and x_j share at least one cluster (15) and when they share at least one class (16).

Let $D(x_i)$ be the set of objects that share at least one cluster with x_i including x_i. The Bcubed Precision metric of x_i is defined as:

$$Bcubed_{Precision}(x_i) = \frac{\sum_{x_j \in D(x_i)} Multiplicity\ Precision(x_i, x_j)}{|D(x_i)|} \tag{17}$$

Let $H(x_i)$ be the set of objects that share at least one class with x_i including x_i. The Bcubed Recall metric of x_i is defined as:

$$Bcubed_{Recall}(x_i) = \frac{\sum_{x_j \in H(x_i)} Multiplicity\ Recall(x_i, x_j)}{|H(x_i)|} \tag{18}$$

Finally, the FBcubed metric is defined as follows:

$$FBcubed = \frac{2\left(\frac{1}{n}\sum_i^n Bcubed_{Precision}(x_i)\right)\left(\frac{1}{n}\sum_i^n Bcubed_{Recall}(x_i)\right)}{\left(\frac{1}{n}\sum_i^n Bcubed_{Precision}(x_i)\right) + \left(\frac{1}{n}\sum_i^n Bcubed_{Recall}(x_i)\right)} \tag{19}$$

Where n is the number of objects in the dataset.

In [16] the authors present an analysis of different external metrics for clustering evaluation, and based on this analysis they propose some constraints, that these metrics should satisfy. They conclude that FBcubed satisfies all constraints, but F-measure does not, therefore, F-measure is unable to distinguish certain undesirable situations at evaluating overlapping clusters:

In order to show an example of these situations, suppose a dataset $X = \{x_1, x_2, x_3, x_4, x_5, x_6, x_7, x_8, x_9, x_{10}\}$, which is divided in three overlapping classes

$C_1 = \{x_1, x_2, x_3, x_4, x_5, x_6\}$, $C_2 = \{x_5, x_7, x_8\}$, and $C_3 = \{x_6, x_9, x_{10}\}$. Now suppose that two clustering algorithms obtained the following clusters:

$$\pi_{1,1} = \{x_1, x_2, x_3, x_4, x_5, x_6\}, \quad \pi_{1,2} = \{x_6, x_7, x_8\}, \quad \pi_{1,3} = \{x_5, x_9, x_{10}\}$$
$$\pi_{2,1} = \{x_1, x_2, x_3, x_4, x_5, x_6\}, \quad \pi_{2,2} = \{x_5, x_7, x_{10}\}, \quad \pi_{2,3} = \{x_6, x_9, x_8\}$$

Both results have two objects in a wrong cluster but in $\pi_{1,2}$ and $\pi_{1,3}$ the error is in the objects x_5, x_6, which belong to the overlapping with $\pi_{1,1}$. While in $\pi_{2,2}$ and $\pi_{2,3}$ the error is in the objects x_8, x_{10}, which belong to only one cluster, clearly both errors are different. However, when the assessment is done through F-measure in both cases we get the same result (0.8095), while if we do the assessment through FBcubed it allows to distinguish these different errors, obtaining 0.8166 and 0.7750; indicating that the first clustering algorithm obtains a better result than the second one. Based on the situations above commented it is noteworthy that F-measure may not be adequate for evaluating overlapping clusters; as it will be analyzed in the following experiments.

For our experiments, we used three datasets taken from the MULAN repository[1] (see table 1). These data sets were chosen because they are the same used in [9] where the clustering algorithms OKM, WOKM, and OKMED were compared through F-measure.

Table 1. Description of datasets used in the experiments

Name	Domain	#Objects	#Features	#Labels	Overlapping
Emotions[17]	Music	593	72	6	1.869
Scene[18]	Image	2307	294	6	1.074
Yeast[19]	Biology	2417	103	14	4.237

Since the WOKM algorithm uses the β parameter to regulate the influence of feature weights. In order to study the behaviour of β, as first experiment, several values, 1.1, 1.5, 1.9, 2, 2.1, 2.5 and 3, for β were tested, these values were used in [13]. Table 2 shows the results of F-measure (FM), Fbcubed (FBC), and the relative overlapping[2] (RO) of these experiments, the best result for each column is boldfaced.

From Table 2, it can be seen that a higher value of the parameter β does not necessarily mean a better result. According to F-measure, the values of β that produced the best results were 3 for Emotions and Scene, and 2.5 for Yeast. But, according to Fbcubed the best values are 3, 1.5 and 2.5, respectively.

---

[1] http://mulan.sourceforge.net/datasets.html

[2] Relative overlapping is computed dividing the overlapping of the clustering result by the overlapping of the original dataset. Values close to 1 mean that the overlapping build by the clustering algorithm is close to the original overlapping, values greater than 1 mean that the original dataset has more overlapping than the overlapping built by the clustering algorithm and values lesser than 1 represent the opposite.

Table 2. F-measure (FM) and FBcubed (FBC) results of the algorithm WOKM for different values of the parameter β, the relative overlapping (RO) is also reported

β	Emotions			Scene			Yeast		
	FM	FBC	RO	FM	FBC	RO	FM	FBC	RO
1.1	0.5575	0.4957	1.127	0.3528	0.2701	2.385	0.8150	0.6698	1.077
1.5	0.4549	0.4227	0.651	0.3342	**0.2935**	1.826	0.8149	0.6698	1.078
1.9	0.5423	0.5146	0.688	0.3545	0.2727	2.383	0.8146	0.6694	1.077
2	0.5624	0.5265	0.833	0.3545	0.2727	2.383	0.8150	0.6698	1.077
2.1	0.5897	0.5607	0.658	0.3548	0.2743	2.373	0.8157	0.6706	1.079
2.5	0.5803	0.5557	0.610	0.3558	0.2754	2.376	**0.8167**	**0.6718**	1.082
3	**0.5929**	**0.5653**	0.610	**0.3574**	0.2786	2.370	0.8150	0.6700	1.078

Analyzing with more detail the results in Table 2, for the Scene dataset, we can observe that $\beta = 1.5$ produces the worst clustering result according to F-measure, while for the same value of β, according to FBcubed, it obtains the best result. In order to better understand what is happening, notice that the clustering result evaluated through F-measure for $\beta = 1.1$ is 0.3528, while for $\beta = 1.5$ is 0.3342, and the relative overlapping obtained for $\beta = 1.1$ is 2.385 and for $\beta = 1.5$ is 1.826, i.e. F-measure gives a better evaluation in the case where more overlapping is obtained. This is a clear example of what happens when the clustering built by an algorithm has a higher rate of overlapping with respect to the overlapping in the original classes. If there is a high overlapping in the clusters, it means objects belong to more than one cluster; increasing the intersection of object pairs in the same cluster and class, and consequently, it makes the Recall increases. Precision is affected only by the number of pairs of objects belonging to the same cluster[3]. Conversely, if the overlapping is not high, Recall will have a lower value and Precision will only be slightly higher compared to the high overlapping scenario. It explains why F-measure gets a higher values (better results) for $\beta = 1.1$ in comparison to $\beta = 1.5$. Contrarily, FBcubed obtains better results for $\beta = 1.5$ in comparison to $\beta = 1.1$, since it is formulated for considering the amount of classes and clusters to which each object belongs instead of only taking into account if they are in the same cluster or class.

We present another experiment, reported in table 3, for comparing WOKM, OKM and OKMED algorithms using F-measure (FM) and Fbcubed (FBC). For WOKM we report the best result obtained in the previous experiment after testing different values of β, for OKMED we use as dissimilarity function the Euclidean distance. For the three algorithms the parameter k was set as the number of classes in the dataset. In order to have a fair comparison, the same seeds were used in the initialization of each algorithm. In Table 3, also the relative overlapping (RO) obtained by each algorithm is reported.

---

[3] The same happens when the classes have a higher rate of overlapping with respect to the clusters built by an algorithm, Precision will be higher and Recall will be lower.

Table 3. Values obtained for the OKM, WOKM, and OKMED algorithms on all datasets with the F-measure (FM) and FBcubed (FBC) metrics. The relative overlapping (RO) is reported also.

Dataset	*OKM*			*WOKM*			*OKMED*		
	FM	FBC	RO	FM	FBC	RO	FM	FBC	RO
Emotions	0.5575	0.4957	1.1268	**0.5929**	**0.5653**	0.6096	0.5013	0.4588	0.9770
Scene	0.3552	0.2744	2.3766	0.3574	0.2935	1.8264	**0.3749**	**0.3689**	1.6855
Yeast	0.8146	0.6693	1.0764	**0.8167**	**0.6718**	1.0817	0.2029	0.1102	0.2679
Average	0.5758	0.4798	1.5266	**0.5890**	**0.5102**	1.1726	0.3597	0.3126	0.9768

In Table 3, we can see that the only dataset where OKMED obtained the best result compared to OKM and WOKM was Scene dataset, contrarily to the results reported in [9] where the author reports that both OKMED and OKM obtained a similar result for this dataset, since he used F-measure and in terms of this metric the F-measure results didn't show a great difference. However in our experiments evaluating using FBcubed a different result is obtained, and clearly OKMED outperforms OKM and WOKM. Notice that Scene is a dataset with little overlapping (1.074) and OKMED obtains less overlapping than the other clustering algorithms. From our experiments we can see that OKMED builds clusterings with low overlapping therefore it is a good algorithm at those datasets were we expect a clustering with low overlapping. From this experiment we also can see that WOKM algorithm obtained the best results in average. From this, we can deduce that the use of weights helps to get better results in most cases, the problem with WOKM algorithm lies in finding an adequate value for β that allows getting a good result, and if it is not possible to determine what value of β is the best, possibly WOKM is not the best choice. Finally the OKM algorithm is a good choice since it only requires, as input, the number of clusters, moreover, in terms of quality OKM results are very close to the results obtained by WOKM and both algorithms are good at datasets were we expect a clustering with high overlapping.

4   Conclusions

This paper presents a study of the overlapping clustering algorithms OKM, WOKM and OKMED, which are based on the Kmeans algorithm. Different to other previously reported comparisons, in our study we compare these algorithms using the external evaluation metric FBcubed which takes into account the overlapping among clusters. From our experiments we can conclude that in general WOKM algorithm obtains the best results in comparison to OKM and OKMED however it is not easy to finding out an adequate value for β parameter, while OKM results are very close to the results obtained by WOKM and it only requires, as input, the number of clusters, moreover in terms of overlapping both algorithms produce similar clusterings with high overlapping. On the other hand, OKMED builds clusterings with low overlapping but unlike OKM and WOKM it has the characteristic that can use any dissimilarity function.

Finally, and the most important, we can conclude that for evaluating overlapping clustering algorithms a metric that takes into account the overlapping must be used, since the use of other metrics as F-measure cannot correctly evaluate the results obtained by this kind of algorithms.

Acknowledgment. This work was partly supported by the National Council of Science and Technology of Mexico (CONACyT) through the project grants CB2008-106443 and CB2008-106366; and the scholarship grant 362371.

References

1. Aslam, J., Pelekhov, E., Rus, D.: The star clustering algorithm for static and dynamic information organization. Journal of Graph Algorithms and Applications 8(1), 95–129 (2004)
2. Davis, G., Carley, K.: Clearing the FOG: Fuzzy, overlapping groups for social networks. Social Networks 30(3), 201–212 (2008)
3. Abella-Pérez, R., Medina-Pagola, J.E.: An incremental text segmentation by clustering cohesion. In: Proceedings of HaCDAIS 2010, pp. 65–72 (2010)
4. Pons-Porrata, A., Ruiz-Shulcloper, J., Berlanga-Llavorí, R., Santiesteban-Alganza, Y.: Un algoritmo incremental para la obtención de cubrimientos con datos mezclados. In: Proceedings of CIARP 2002, pp. 405–416 (2002)
5. Zamir, O., Etziony, O.: Web document clustering: A feasibility demonstration. In: Proceedings of the 21st Annual International ACM SIGIR Conference, pp. 46–54 (1998)
6. Aslam, J., Pelekhov, E., Rus, D.: Static and dynamic information organization with star clusters. In: Proceedings of the Seventh International Conference on Information and Knowledge Management, pp. 208–217 (1998)
7. Gil-García, R.J., Badía-Contelles, J.M., Pons-Porrata, A.: Extended star clustering algorithm. In: Sanfeliu, A., Ruiz-Shulcloper, J. (eds.) CIARP 2003. LNCS, vol. 2905, pp. 480–487. Springer, Heidelberg (2003)
8. Cleuziou, G.: An Extended Version of the k-Means Method for Overlapping Clustering. In: 19th ICPR Conference, Tampa, Florida, USA, pp. 1–4 (2008)
9. Cleuziou, G.: Two Variants of the OKM for Overlapping Clustering. In: Guillet, F., Ritschard, G., Zighed, D.A., Briand, H. (eds.) Advances in Knowledge Discovery and Management. SCI, vol. 292, pp. 149–166. Springer, Heidelberg (2010)
10. Gil-García, R.J., Badía-Contelles, J.M., Pons-Porrata, A.: Parallel algorithm for extended star clustering. In: Sanfeliu, A., Martínez Trinidad, J.F., Carrasco Ochoa, J.A. (eds.) CIARP 2004. LNCS, vol. 3287, pp. 402–409. Springer, Heidelberg (2004)
11. Suárez, A.P., Pagola, J.E.M.: A clustering algorithm based on generalized stars. In: Perner, P. (ed.) MLDM 2007. LNCS (LNAI), vol. 4571, pp. 248–262. Springer, Heidelberg (2007)
12. MacQueen, J.B.: Some Methods for classification and Analysis of Multivariate Observations. In: Proceedings of 5th Berkeley Symposium on Mathematical Statistics and Probability, pp. 281–297. University of California Press (1967)
13. Chan, E.Y., Ching, W.K., Ng, M.K., Huang, J.Z.: An optimization algorithm for clustering using weighted dissimilarity measures. Pattern Recognition 37(5), 943–952 (2004)

14. Kaufman, L., Rousseeuw, P.J.: Clustering by means of medoids. In: Dodge, Y. (ed.) Statistical Data Analysis based on the L1 Norm, pp. 405–416 (1987)
15. Bezdek, J.C.: Pattern Recognition with Fuzzy Objective Function Algorithms. Plenum Press, New York (1981)
16. Amigó, E., Gonzalo, J., Artiles, J., Verdejo, F.: A comparison of extrinsic clustering evaluation metrics based on formal constraints. Information Retrieval, 461–486 (2009)
17. Trohidis, K., Tsoumakas, G., Kalliris, G., Vlahavas, I.: Multilabel Classification of Music into Emotions. In: Proc. 2008 International Conference on Music Information Retrieval (ISMIR 2008), pp. 325–330 (2008)
18. Boutell, M.R., Luo, J., Shen, X., Brown, C.M.: Learning multi-label scene classiffication. Pattern Recognition 37(9), 1757–1771 (2004)
19. Elisseeff, A., Weston, J.: A kernel method for multi-labelled classification. In: Advances in Neural Information Processing Systems, vol. 14 (2002)

Contextualized Hand Gesture Recognition with Smartphones

Enrique Garcia-Ceja, Ramon Brena, and Carlos E. Galván-Tejada

Tecnológico de Monterrey, Campus Monterrey, Av. Eugenio Garza Sada 2501 Sur,
Monterrey, N.L., México
{A00927248,ramon.brena}@itesm.mx, ericgalvan@uaz.edu.mx

Abstract. Most of the previous works in hand gesture recognition focus in increasing the accuracy and robustness of the systems, however little has been done to understand the context in which the gestures are performed, i.e, the same gesture could mean different things depending on the context and situation. Understanding the context may help to build more user-friendly and interactive systems. In this work, we used location information in order to contextualize the gestures. The system constantly identifies the location of the user so when he/she performs a gesture the system can perform an action based on this information.

Keywords: hand gesture recognition, context-aware, accelerometer, Wifi, smartphone, DTW.

1 Introduction

In recent years, people have been devising new ways to communicate and interact with machines, e.g., voice commands, touch screens, gestures, etc. Coupled with this, the use of devices with sensors like accelerometers, gyroscopes, magnetometers, among others, has increased rapidly. Examples of this devices are smartphones, smart watches [1], tablet pc's, fitness monitoring bracelets [2], etc. In this work we focus on wearable sensors for gesture detection. Advantages of using wearable sensors over video cameras for gesture recognition are that they do not require a fixed infrastructure, their range is not limited to a particular area and they raise less privacy concerns. For the rest of this work, a *hand gesture* refers to the movement of the hand and the arm to form certain patterns. The difference with pure hand signals is that in this form of communication, the position of the fingers is relevant to identify the overall hand shape.

Most of the previous works in hand gesture recognition focus in increasing the accuracy and robustness of the systems, however little has been done to understand the context in which the gestures are performed, i.e, the same gesture could mean different things depending on the context and situation. Understanding the context may help to build more user-friendly and interactive systems. For example, a set of gestures $\{g_1...g_n\}$ may be used to turn on the lights in different locations inside a house. In this case the user would have to memorize a gesture for each light he would like to turn on. It may be more practical to have

J.F. Martínez-Trinidad et al. (Eds.): MCPR 2014, LNCS 8495, pp. 122–131, 2014.

a single gesture to perform that action and let the system choose which light to turn on depending on the context of the person.

In this work, we used location information in order to contextualize the gestures. The system constantly identifies the location of the user so when he/she performs a gesture the system could perform an action based on this information. The user's location is identified using the on-range Access Points and their signal strength, the gestures are recognized using Dynamic Time Warping [3]. A smartphone was used to implement a prototype, and unlike other systems that send the information to a server to perform the computations, here, all the processing is made inside the smartphone.

The rest of this document is organized as follows: Section 2 presents the related work. In Sect. 3 we describe the sensing platform we used to collect the data and the data collection process for gestures and locations. Section 4 explains the architecture and design of the system. Section 5 describes the gesture recognition process. Section 6 presents the method we used to identify the user's location. Section 7 describes our experiments and results and finally in Sect. 8 we draw conclusions and propose the future work.

2   Related Work

In recent years, there have been several works in accelerometer based gesture recognition. Specifically, in [4] they used Bayesian classification and Dynamic Time Warping (DTW) to classify 4 gestures (circle, figure eight, square, star) achieving accuracies of 97% and 95% respectively. In [5] they proposed a Frame-based Descriptor and multi-class Support Vector Machine approach with a recognition rate of 95.21% for 12 gestures in the user-dependent case and 89.29% in the user-independent case. They used a Wiimote[1] and the processing was made in a laptop. Akl and Valaee [6] used dynamic time warping, affinity propagation and compressive sensing achieving an accuracy of 99.79% for user-dependent recognition using 18 gestures. For the user-independent recognition, they achieved an accuracy of 96.89% for 8 gestures, however they asked the participants to keep the remote straight. We believe that with these recognition rates it is already possible to implement non critical real world systems for home automation, entertainment, appliance control, etc. There is also a recent work called WiSee [7] in which they used wireless signals such as Wifi to perform the recognition so the user does not need to carry any type of device. Kühnel et al. [8] did a very complete work about gesture recognition for controlling home appliances. They conduct a survey and found that the majority of the respondents liked the idea of controlling appliances with gestures. Also, the majority answered that they would prefer a predefined set of gestures that they could adjust instead of designing their own. Their implementation was made on a smartphone that includes a user interface to select the devices. They also conducted experiments to find a good gesture vocabulary and studied their memorability.

---

[1] Wii http://www.nintendo.com/wii

This work differs from the above mentioned in the sense that we are also taking context into account in order to perform an appropiate action based on the detected gesture.

3   Sensing Platform

An LG Optimus Me smartphone was used to collect the accelerometer and Wifi data. This smartphone has a STMicroelectronics triaxial accelerometer. It returns the acceleration value for each of the axes (x,y,z). Its maximum range is $\pm 19.60 m/s^2$. The x-axis runs parallel to the width of the smartphone, the y-axis parallel to the height of the phone and the z-axis perpendicular to its face (see Fig. 1).

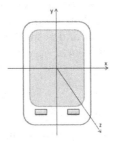

Fig. 1. Acceleration axes

3.1   Data Collection

Gestures. First, we collected the data for 10 different gestures (triangle, square, circle, a, b, c, 1, 2, 3, 4) from 10 persons. We did not instruct the participants to hold the cellphone in any particular manner. These gestures were selected because they encompass three groups of interest: shapes, letters and digits and this is a first attempt to the recognition of the entire set of letters from the english alphabet, the set of decimal digits and a larger set of shapes in a continuous manner(i.e, being able to recognize a sequence of letters and digits to form words and numbers which will be left for future work). Each person performed 5 repetitions of each of the gestures. The sampling rate was set at 50 Hz. To record a gesture the user presses the phone screen with the thumb, performs the gesture and stops pressing the screen. At the end of the process each gesture is represented by the accelerations in each of the three axes (Figure 2).

Locations. The data collection process consisted of generating several instances for every room we want to recognize. To generate one instance we scan the room and record the BSSID (Basic Service Set Identifier) and signal strengths of the detected Access Points, then we perform two more scans with a delay of 500 ms between the scans. The reason behind doing several scans is because in [9] they observed that sometimes one or more Access Points may not be detected

Fig. 2. Performing a triangle gesture

because limited sensitivity of the hardware and/or long beacon interval of some Access Points. Each instance has a List L in which each element is a pair $\langle bssid,$ signal strength$\rangle$ where *signal strength* is the mean signal strength of the 3 scans for that specific BSSID. For each location, we collected 3-4 minutes of data.

4   System Design

The overall system architecture is illustrated in Fig. 3 and consists of four main components: the cellphone application, a Ninja Block[2], Ninja Blocks REST API and the actuators. The cellphone application has three modules: *Gestures, Location* and *Inference*. The functioning of the first two modules is explained in Sections 5 and 6, respectively. The *Inference* module is made up of simple conditional rules. For future work we intend to replace it with some type of probabilistic inference method. Once the user performs a hand gesture, the *Inference* module uses this information along with the current location to select an action, e.g, turn on the lights, activate an alarm, etc. The action is sent in the form of a command to the Ninja Blocks REST API which in turn sends it to the Ninja Block and finally it activates the corresponding actuators. A Ninja Block is a hardware box that makes it easy to build applications that talk to hardware. A video of the prototype is available at `http://youtu.be/47-35YmimN4`.

5   The Gesture Recognition Process

Every time a gesture is performed the phone may be rotated in a slightly different way. To account for variations of this type we compute the magnitude of the three accelerations in order to work in just one dimension.

$$Magnitude(t) = \sqrt{a_x(t)^2 + a_y(t)^2 + a_z(t)^2}, \tag{1}$$

where $a_x(t)$, $a_y(t)$ and $a_z(t)$ are the accelerations at time t.

---

[2] Ninja Blocks website `http://ninjablocks.com/`

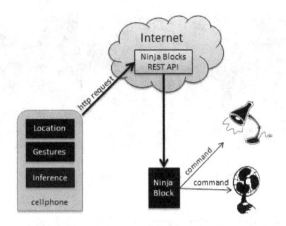

Fig. 3. Overall system architecture

We will call the *query instance* Q the gesture we want to recognize and a *reference instance* R a gesture from the training set of which we know its true class. We used Dynamic Time Warping (DTW)[3] to compute the dissimilarity between the query instance Q and every reference instance R from the training set and return the statistical mode of the k least dissimilar reference instances' class as the predicted gesture. DTW is a method that finds an optimal match between two given time-dependent sequences. It also computes the dissimilarity between those sequences, i.e, if the sequences are the same the dissimilarity will be 0. Let $X = (x_1, x_2, ..., x_{T_x})$ and $Y = (y_1, y_2, ..., y_{T_y})$ be two sequences where x_i and y_i are vectors; $d(i_x, i_y)$ the dissimilarity between vectors x_i and y_i; ϕ_x and ϕ_y are the warping functions that relate i_x and i_y to a common axis k:

$$i_x = \phi_x(k), k = 1, 2, ..., T \tag{2}$$

$$i_y = \phi_y(k), k = 1, 2, ..., T \tag{3}$$

Thus the global dissimilarity is:

$$d_\phi(X, Y) = \sum_{k=1}^{T} d(\phi_x(k), \phi_y(k)) \tag{4}$$

and the problem consists of finding the warping functions that minimize Eq.(4), that is:

$$\min_\phi d_\phi(X, Y) \tag{5}$$

which can be solved efficiently using dynamic programming.

Figure 4 shows the alignment produced by DTW for two triangle gestures with a resulting absolute dissimilarity of 87.30. For the prototype, we used Stan's

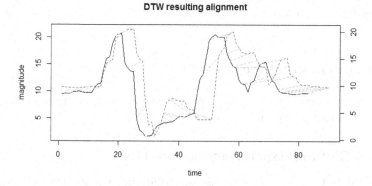

Fig. 4. Resulting DTW alignment. The query instance is represented by the solid line and the reference instance by the dotted line.

approximate DTW algorithm implementation [10] which has linear time and space complexity unlike the exact method which has quadratic complexity.

6   The Location Identification Process

The number of Wifi Access Points around the world has increased significantly in the last years. They are installed in many places such as restaurants, hotels, schools, parks, airports, etc. Since every Access Point has a unique identifier namely, the BSSID (Basic Service Set Identifier), it is possible to use this information along with the signal strength for localization and tracking purposes [11, 12, 13]. In this work we are not focused in computing the absolute or relative location (coordinates on a plane) of the user. Instead, we want to know in which of the n rooms that compose the house or apartment the user is in so this can be seen as a classification problem. Since we do not need the exact coordinates, we can take advantage of the existing Wifi Access Points without any further configuration, i.e., we do not need to know the location of each Access Point.

Once a query instance is generated (as described in Section 3.1), the classification is done using K-Nearest Neighbors with $k = 3$ and distance function $d(q, r) = j(q, r) + s(q, r)$ where q is the query and r is a reference instance from the training set.

$$j(q, r) = 1 - \frac{|L(q) \cap L(r)|}{|L(q) \cup L(r)|} \qquad (6)$$

where the function L returns the list of access points of the specified instance. Eq.(6) is known as the Jaccard distance [14].

$$s(q, r) = 1 - (1/1 + \alpha) \qquad (7)$$

where $\alpha = abs(SD(q,r) - SD(r,q))$ and $SD(p1, p2)$ is a function that returns the standard deviation of the signal strength of all access points of *p1* that are also in *p2*.

7   Experiments and Results

In this section, we describe the hand gesture recognition experiments and results and then, the location experiments and results.

7.1   Hand Gestures Experiments and Results

Two types of tests which are common for validating the accuracy of gesture recognition systems were performed: user-dependent case and user-independent case. The former consists of evaluating the recognition accuracy by training and testing the system with data from the same user. The latter consists of testing the system with data from the user to be evaluated and training the system with data from all other users. The recognition accuracy for each of the persons was evaluated using leave-one-out cross validation [15] for the user-dependent case (Table 1). For testing the user-independent case, leave-one-person-out cross validation [5] was used. The average accuracy for the user-dependent case was 93.8% and for the user-independent case it was 78.4%. Figure 5 shows the confusion matrix for both, the user-dependent and user-independent case. In matrix (a) we can see that shape 'a' was confused 4 times with a circle, 2 times with shape 'b', 1 with 'triangle', 1 with '3' and 1 with '2'.

Table 1. Hand gesture recognition results

Person	user-dependent	user-independent
1	88%	80%
2	90%	82%
3	94%	84%
4	96%	90%
5	94%	72%
6	98%	72%
7	96%	50%
8	92%	86%
9	92%	90%
10	98%	78%
average	93.8%	78.4%

7.2   Location Experiments and Results

The location recognition was tested in 4 different scenarios; two apartments and two houses. In each scenario different locations were chosen to be recognized. For

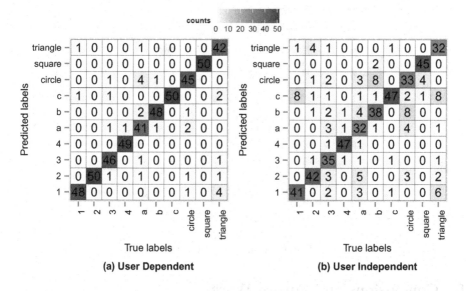

Fig. 5. Confusion matrices. a) user dependent case. b) user independent case.

example, Fig. 6 shows the layout of the third floor of an apartments building. It shows 3 of the 4 tested locations (The lobby is not shown. It is at the same level of bedroom A but in the first floor.) The locations were chosen to be very close to each other.

The experiments consisted of collecting the in range Access Points BSSID and signal strength. For each location the samples were collected for 3-4 minutes. The tests were performed using 10-fold cross validation on each of the scenarios. Table 2 shows the achieved accuracy and the number of locations for each scenario.

The expected combined accuracy (gesture + location) is the product of the two independent accuracies. Thus, for the user-dependent case it is 88.7% and for the user-independent case it is 74.2% however, more robust tests and experiments must be designed in order to conveniently evaluate the contribution of the context and the interactivity of the system in more scenarios which will be left as future work.

Table 2. Location recognition accuracy

Scenario	No. locations	Accuracy
Apartment 1	3	99.0%
Apartment 2	4	92.3%
House 1	5	93.7%
House 2	4	93.6%
	average	94.65%

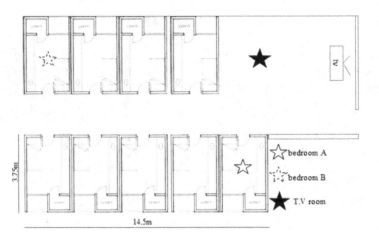

Fig. 6. Apartment 2 layout

8   Conclusions and Future Work

In this work it was shown how contextual information can be used along with the gesture recognition process to build a more user friendly and interactive system. The contextual information consisted of the user's location. A working prototype was implemented using a smartphone. Unlike other systems, all the computation is performed by the smartphone instead of delegating it to an external server. The main contribution of this work was that the gestures were recognized within a location context. This enables the system to be context-aware and thus more interactive and user friendly.

For future work we plan to include more information about the context, e.g, time of the day, temperature, historical data of the user's activities, etc. We also plan to use a probabilistic graphical model as inference engine instead of simple conditional rules.

Acknowledgements. Enrique would like to thank Juan Pablo García for his suggestions and feedback, and to Consejo Nacional de Ciencia y Tecnología (CONACYT) and the AAAmI research group at Tecnológico de Monterrey for the financial support in his PhD. studies.

References

1. Pebble, http://getpebble.com/ (accessed March 22, 2014)
2. Jawbone up, http://jawbone.com/up/ (accessed March 22, 2014)
3. Rabiner, L., Juang, B.-H.: Fundamentals of speech recognition. Prentice hall (1993)
4. Mace, D., Gao, W., Coskun, A.: Accelerometer-based hand gesture recognition using feature weighted naïve bayesian classifiers and dynamic time warping. In: Proceedings of the Companion Publication of the 2013 International Conference on Intelligent User Interfaces Companion, pp. 83–84. ACM (2013)

5. Wu, J., Pan, G., Zhang, D., Qi, G., Li, S.: Gesture recognition with a 3-D accelerometer. In: Zhang, D., Portmann, M., Tan, A.-H., Indulska, J. (eds.) UIC 2009. LNCS, vol. 5585, pp. 25–38. Springer, Heidelberg (2009)
6. Akl, A., Valaee, S.: Accelerometer-based gesture recognition via dynamic-time warping, affinity propagation, & compressive sensing. In: 2010 IEEE International Conference on Acoustics Speech and Signal Processing (ICASSP), pp. 2270–2273. IEEE (2010)
7. Pu, Q., Gupta, S., Gollakota, S., Patel, S.: Whole-home gesture recognition using wireless signals. In: Proceedings of the 19th Annual International Conference on Mobile Computing & Networking, pp. 27–38. ACM (2013)
8. Kühnel, C., Westermann, T., Hemmert, F., Kratz, S., Müller, A., Müller, S.: I'm home: Defining and evaluating a gesture set for smart-home control. International Journal of Human-Computer Studies 69(11), 693–704 (2011)
9. Carlotto, A., Parodi, M., Bonamico, C., Lavagetto, F., Valla, M.: Proximity classification for mobile devices using wi-fi environment similarity. In: Proceedings of the first ACM International Workshop on Mobile Entity Localization and Tracking in GPS-Less Environments, MELT 2008, pp. 43–48. ACM, New York (2008)
10. Salvador, S., Chan, P.: Toward accurate dynamic time warping in linear time and space. Intelligent Data Analysis 11(5), 561–580 (2007)
11. Krumm, J., Horvitz, E.: Locadio: Inferring motion and location from wi-fi signal strengths. In: First Annual International Conference on Mobile and Ubiquitous Systems: Networking and Services (Mobiquitous) (2004)
12. Correa, J., Katz, E., Collins, P., Griss, M.: Room-level wifi locationntracking. Carnegie Mellon Silicon Valley, CyLab Mobility Research Center technical report MRC-TR-2008-02 (2008)
13. Zdruba, G.V., Huber, M., Karnangar, F.A., Chlarntac, I.: Monte carlo sampling based in-home location tracking with minimal rf infrastructure requirements. In: Global Telecommunications Conference, GLOBECOM 2004, November 3-December, vol. 6, pp. 3624–3629. IEEE (2004)
14. Jaccard, P.: Nouvelles recherches sur la distribution florale. Bull. Soc. Vaud. Sci. Nat. (1908)
15. Witten, I.H., Frank, E., Hall, M.A.: Data Mining: Practical Machine Learning Tools and Techniques, 3rd edn. The Morgan Kaufmann Series in Data Management Systems. Elsevier Science (2011)

Introducing an Experimental Framework in C# for Fingerprint Recognition

Miguel Angel Medina-Pérez[1], Octavio Loyola-González[1,2],
Andres Eduardo Gutierrez-Rodríguez[1,2], Milton García-Borroto[3],
and Leopoldo Altamirano-Robles[1]

[1] Instituto Nacional de Astrofísica, Óptica y Electrónica. Luis Enrique Erro No. 1, Sta. María
Tonanzintla, Puebla, México, C.P. 72840
{migue,octavio,andres,robles}@inaoep.mx

[2] Centro de Bioplantas, Universidad de Ciego de Ávila. Carretera a Morón km 9,
Ciego de Ávila, Cuba, C.P. 69450
{octavioloyola,andres}@bioplantas.cu

[3] Instituto Superior Politécnico José A. Echeverría. Calle 114, No. 11901, e/ Ciclovía y
Rotonda, Apartado 6028. Marianao, Habana, Cuba, C.P. 11901
mgarciab@ceis.cujae.edu.cu

Abstract. In this paper, a framework for fingerprint recognition is introduced. The framework contains several algorithms for fingerprint matching and feature extraction, as well as the evaluation protocol for several fingerprint verification competitions. All the algorithms are implemented in C# providing the source code which researchers can review, reuse or modify. In order to show the framework relevance, an experimental comparison among different matching algorithms is presented.

Keywords: biometrics, fingerprint matching, experimental framework.

1 Introduction

When starting a new research project, an important challenge is to find a framework, SDK or library that could be reused to save coding time. While machine learning researchers count with established tools like Weka [13], KEEL [1] and PRTools [9], researchers in the area of fingerprint recognition [18] are more limited. Table 1 shows the limitations of available fingerprint recognition tools according to the following criteria:

a) The users must pay for using the libraries or they must use the tools with time limitations and/or limited amount of fingerprints. For example, "Free Fingerprint Verification SDK" [23] is limited to ten records in the database while "VeriFinger SDK" [23] is limited to a trial period of 30 days, after which users must pay for the SDK.

b) The tools do not contain multiple fingerprint matching and feature extraction algorithms. For instance, the users cannot test different combination schemes with "NIST Biometric Image Software" [29] because it only includes one fingerprint matching algorithm.

J.F. Martínez-Trinidad et al. (Eds.): MCPR 2014, LNCS 8495, pp. 132–141, 2014.

c) The users do not have free access to the source code so they cannot reuse any component of the algorithms. For example, users cannot reuse the segmentation algorithm included at "Fingerprint SDK" [12] without paying to access the source code.

d) The users do not have control over the fingerprint databases and they cannot create an experiment with a custom protocol for performance evaluation. For instance, latent fingerprint identification is a very active research topic at present but users cannot use their own databases with the "FVC-onGoing web-based automated evaluation system" [8] because the system does not allow the users to upload custom databases.

e) The tools do not contain any protocol for performance evaluation. For example, to test "SourceAFIS SDK" [31] in FVC2004 [17] databases, the users have to implement the performance evaluation protocol.

Table 1. This is a representative set of fingerprint recognition tools and their limitations

Fingerprint recognition tools	Limitations				
	a	b	c	d	e
NIST Biometric Image Software [29]		X			X
FVC-onGoing web-based automated evaluation system [8]	X		X	X	
SourceAFIS SDK [31]		X			X
MCC SDK [4, 5, 10]			X	X	X
VeriFinger SDK [23]	X	X	X		X
Fingerprint SDK [12]	X	X	X		X
BiometricSDK [27]		X			X
IDKit PC SDK [14]	X	X	X		X

To deal with all these limitations, this paper introduces a fingerprint recognition framework containing matching algorithms, feature extraction algorithms, and experimental protocols. This framework is implemented in .Net Framework using the C# language for the following reasons:

– .Net Framework and C# have proved to be effective for developing fingerprint recognition tools such as MCC SDK [4, 5, 10] and SourceAFIS SDK [31].
– The C# language is very easy to learn because of its similarities to C and C++ languages.
– .Net Framework includes a large pack of technologies, tools and class libraries that saves coding time. Algorithms in this framework or algorithms developed by researchers based on this framework can be easily included in systems developed for real clients. Take into account that faster implementations may be required for those applications that involve processing high amounts of fingerprints.

While designing the framework, the "high cohesion and low coupling" principle [2] was applied, so users can creatively reuse most components in their own applications without integrating the entire framework or modifying the existing architecture. The framework contains tools for fingerprint matching evaluation where new algorithms can be included using minimum effort without recompiling the framework.

This framework allows carrying out fingerprint matching experiments for several databases according to the evaluation protocols of the Fingerprint Verification Competitions (FVC) [6]. Additionally, users can include experiments with a custom evaluation protocol or different databases.

There is no charge for the use of this framework or its source code and there are no restrictions regarding the amount of time or number of fingerprint used. Source code and documentation are available at http://www.codeproject.com/Articles/97590/A-Framework-in-C-for-Fingerprint-Verification.

In order to show the framework relevance, an experimental evaluation of matching algorithms in the framework over eleven databases is presented. The results are summarized using *critical difference diagrams* (CD diagrams) [7]. This kind of experimental comparison is rarely found in previous research papers because of the limitations of previous experimental frameworks.

This framework was used to create a new version of M3gl [20] which is among the top ten algorithms according to the accuracy indicators in database FMISO-HARD of FVC-onGoing [8].

2 Structure of Our Framework

The framework includes the algorithms that we have implemented in our research projects. Some of these algorithms have hundreds of references according to Google Scholar and, as far as we know, their source code is not available on the web. This framework contains nine minutiae-based fingerprint matching algorithms distributed in the following assemblies:

- [FR.Jiang2000] includes the algorithms JY [15] and MJY [21].
- [FR.Tico2003] includes the algorithms TK [30] and MTK [22].
- [FR.Parziale2004] includes the algorithm PN [24].
- [FR.Qi2005] includes the algorithms QYW [25] and MQYW [21].
- [FR.Medina2011] includes the algorithm MPN [19].
- [FR.Medina2012] includes the algorithm M3gl [20].

The framework contains four algorithms to extract the basic features (orientation image, skeleton image and minutiae) distributed in the following assemblies:

- [FR.Ratha1995] includes the algorithms proposed in [26] to extract orientation image, skeleton image and minutiae.
- [FR.Sherlock1994] includes the algorithm proposed in [28] to extract the orientation image.

The rest of the tools contained in the framework are distributed in the following assemblies:

- [FR.Core] contains the architecture of the framework.
- [FR.FMExperimenter] contains an application that allows conducting fingerprint matching experiments.

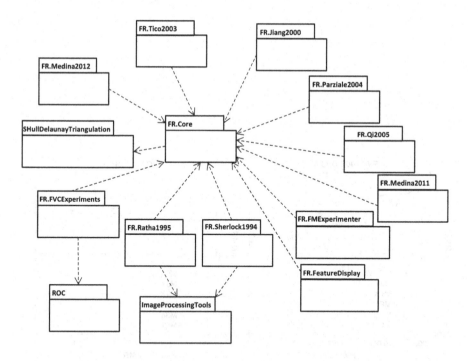

Fig. 1. The package diagram of the fingerprint recognition framework

- [FR.FeatureDisplay] contains an application that allows visualizing fingerprint features.
- [FR.FVCExperiments] contains the performance evaluation protocols of competitions FVC2000, FVC2002 and FVC2004 [6].
- [ROC] contains tools to build ROC curves.
- [ImageProcessingTools] contains tools to process images.
- [SHullDelaunayTriangulation] contains the algorithm available at http://www.s-hull.org/ to compute Delaunay triangulation.

Figure 1 shows the dependency relationships among the assemblies that comprise the framework. It is worth mentioning, that assembly ImageProcessingTool is only used by assemblies FR.Ratha1995 and FR.Scherlock1994 because these are the only two assemblies that perform image processing.

3 Experimental Results

The algorithms are evaluated on databases DB1A, DB2A, DB3A, and DB4A of FVC2002 [16]; databases DB1_A, DB2_A, DB3_A, and DB4_A of FVC2004 [17]; and databases DB2_A, DB3_A, and DB4_A of FVC2006 [3]. The algorithms evaluated are: MCC [4, 5, 10] (SDK v1.4 available in http://biolab.csr.unibo.it/mccsdk.html), M3gl [20], JY [15], TK [30], PN [24], QYW [25], MJY [21], MTK [22], MPN [19], and MQYW [21].

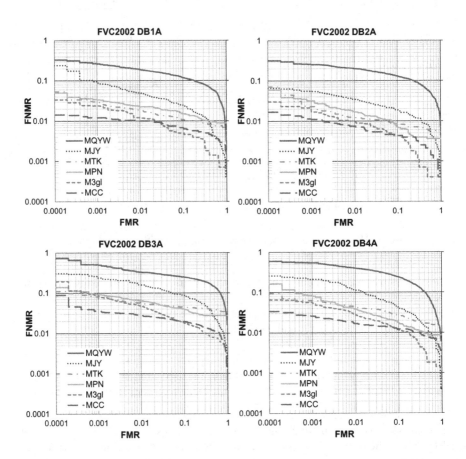

Fig. 2. ROC curves with the performance of the compared algorithms in FVC2002

The algorithms MJY, MTK, MPN, and MQYW are improved versions of JY, TK, PN, and QYW respectively; visualizing the results of JY, TK, PN, and QYW is avoided for the sake of clarity.

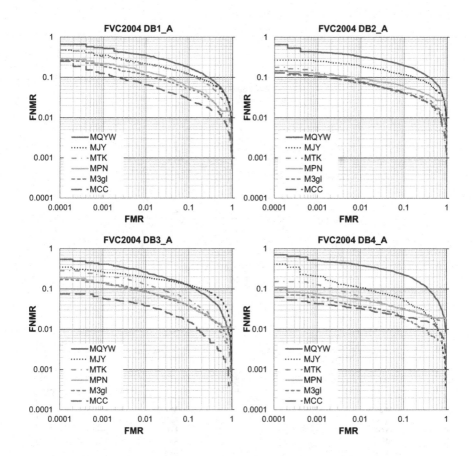

Fig. 3. ROC curves with the performance of the compared algorithms in FVC2004

All the algorithms are evaluated with their default parameters except for algorithm M3gl, whose parameter c (i.e. neighbor count) is changed to 7 (see reference [20]). The evaluation protocols proposed in [6] are used and the ROC curves with the performance of the compared algorithms are shown in Figure 2, Figure 3, and Figure 4.

Figure 2, Figure 3, and Figure 4 show that MCC tends to achieve the lowest FNMR for most of the values of FMR and it is only outperformed by M3gl for some values of FMR.

To further study the differences among the algorithms, the performance indicators proposed in [6] (*EER*, *FMR100*, *FMR1000*, *ZeroFMR*, and *matching time*) are used. 110 experiments (11 databases x 10 algorithms) are performed; so, there are 110 measures

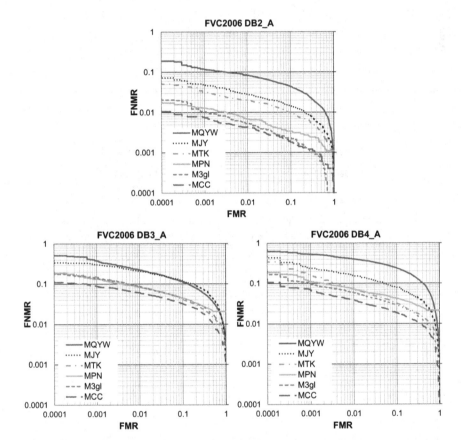

Fig. 4. ROC curves with the performance of the compared algorithms in FVC2006

of every performance indicator. Visualizing these results in a table of 5 columns (performance indicators) and 110 rows (11 databases x 10 algorithms) interferes with their interpretation. That is why the Friedman test [7] and Bergmann-Hommel dynamic post-hoc [11] are used to compare the results. *Critical difference diagrams* (CD diagrams) [7] are used to show the post-hoc results because CD diagrams compactly present the rank of the algorithm according to one performance indicator. CD diagrams also show the magnitude of differences between algorithms and the significance of the observed differences [7]. In a CD diagram, the rightmost algorithm is the best algorithm, while the algorithms sharing a thick line have statistically similar behaviors. Once again, visualizing the results of JY, TK, PN, and QYW is avoided for the sake of clarity.

Figure 5 shows that MCC achieves the best results according to EER, FMR100, FMR1000, and ZeroFMR; but there is no significant statistical difference with M3gl. This is a good result, taking into account that MCC is a patented algorithm for which the source code is not available. Because of the proposed framework, the research community has access to the source code of an algorithm (M3gl) which is not statistically different from MCC, which is one of the most accurate algorithms in state of the art papers.

Figure 5 shows that MCC is the slowest algorithm because its SDK was provided by its authors only for research purposes. A faster version of MCC is available but it is not free.

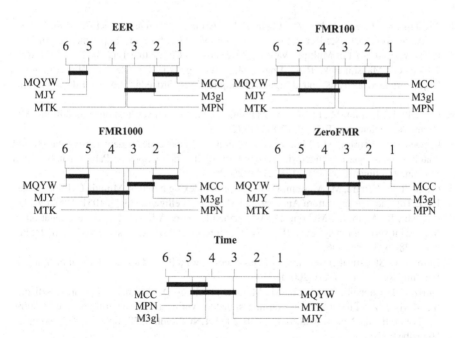

Fig. 5. CD diagrams with the statistical comparison of the algorithms according to EER, FMR100, FMR1000, ZeroFMR and matching time

4 Conclusions

The fingerprint recognition tools available on the web have several limitations. In this paper, a framework is proposed to overcome these limitations. Several matching algorithms are provided not only for experimental purposes, but also to create new applications. The source code for all of the algorithms is provided so users can reuse any part of the code as well as any package of the framework. 110 experiments are performed and the algorithms are compared according to the Friedman test and Bergmann-Hommel dynamic post-hoc. The experiments show that one of the algorithms included in the framework is not statistically different from a well-known patented algorithm. We hope this work motivates more people to collaborate in order to implement other algorithms and improve the fingerprint recognition framework for the benefit of programming and research communities.

Acknowledgment. The authors would like to thank Rebekah Hosse Clark and MSc. Dania Yudith Suárez Abreu for their valuable contributions improving the grammar and style of this paper.

References

1. Alcalá-Fdez, J., Fernández, A., Luengo, J., Derrac, J., García, S.: KEEL Data-Mining Software Tool: Data Set Repository, Integration of Algorithms and Experimental Analysis Framework. Journal of Multiple-Valued Logic and Soft Computing 17(2-3), 255–287 (2011)
2. Booch, G., Maksimchuk, R.A., Engle, M.E., Young, B.J., Conallen, J., Houston, K.A.: Object-oriented analysis and design with applications, 3rd edn. Pearson Education, Inc. (2007)
3. Cappelli, R., Ferrara, M., Franco, A., Maltoni, D.: Fingerprint verification competition 2006. Biometric Technology Today 15(7-8), 7–9 (2007)
4. Cappelli, R., Ferrara, M., Maltoni, D.: Minutia cylinder-code: a new representation and matching technique for fingerprint recognition. IEEE Transactions on Pattern Analysis and Machine Intelligence 32(12), 2128–2141 (2010)
5. Cappelli, R., Ferrara, M., Maltoni, D.: Fingerprint indexing based on Minutia Cylinder-Code. IEEE Transactions on Pattern Analysis and Machine Intelligence 33(5), 1051–1057 (2011)
6. Cappelli, R., Maio, D., Maltoni, D., Wayman, J.L., Jain, A.K.: Performance evaluation of fingerprint verification systems. IEEE Transactions on Pattern Analysis and Machine Intelligence 28(1), 3–18 (2006)
7. Demšar, J.: Statistical comparisons of classifiers over multiple data sets. Journal of Machine Learning Research 7, 1–30 (2006)
8. Dorizzi, B., Cappelli, R., Ferrara, M., Maio, D., Maltoni, D., Houmani, N., Garcia-Salicetti, S., Mayoue, A.: Fingerprint and on-line signature verification competitions at ICB 2009. In: Tistarelli, M., Nixon, M.S. (eds.) ICB 2009. LNCS, vol. 5558, pp. 725–732. Springer, Heidelberg (2009)
9. Duin, R.P.W.: Prtools version 3.0: A matlab toolbox for pattern recognition. In: Proc. of SPIE, p. 1331 (2000)
10. Ferrara, M., Maltoni, D., Cappelli, R.: Noninvertible Minutia Cylinder-Code representation. IEEE Transactions on Information Forensics and Security 7(6), 1727–1737 (2012)

11. García, S., Herrera, F.: An extension on Statistical comparisons of classifiers over multiple data sets for all pairwise comparisons. Journal of Machine Learning Research 9, 2677–2694 (2008)
12. Griaule Biometrics: Fingerprint sdk (2014), http://www.griaulebiometrics.com/en-us/fingerprint_sdk (accessed January 8, 2014)
13. Hall, M., Frank, E., Holmes, G., Pfahringer, B., Reutemann, P., Witten, I.H.: The weka data mining software: an update. SIGKDD Explor. Newsl. 11(1), 10–18 (2009)
14. Innovatrics: Idkit pc sdk (2014), http://innovatrics.com/products/fingerprint-identification-sdk (accessed January 8, 2014)
15. Jiang, X., Yau, W.Y.: Fingerprint minutiae matching based on the local and global structures. In: 15th International Conference on Pattern Recognition, vol. 2, pp. 1038–1041 (2000)
16. Maio, D., Maltoni, D., Cappelli, R., Wayman, J.L., Jain, A.K.: Fvc2002: Second fingerprint verification competition. In: 16th International Conference on Pattern Recognition, vol. 3, pp. 811–814 (2002)
17. Maio, D., Maltoni, D., Cappelli, R., Wayman, J.L., Jain, A.K.: Fvc2004: Third fingerprint verification competition. In: Zhang, D., Jain, A.K. (eds.) ICBA 2004. LNCS, vol. 3072, pp. 1–7. Springer, Heidelberg (2004)
18. Maltoni, D., Maio, D., Jain, A.K., Prabhakar, S.: Handbook of fingerprint recognition, 2nd edn. Springer, Heidelberg (2009)
19. Medina-Pérez, M.A., García-Borroto, M., Gutierrez-Rodríguez, A., Altamirano-Robles, L.: Robust fingerprint verification using m-triplets. In: International Conference on Hand-Based Biometrics (ICHB 2011), Hong Kong, pp. 1–5 (2011)
20. Medina-Pérez, M.A., García-Borroto, M., Gutierrez-Rodríguez, A., Altamirano-Robles, L.: Improving fingerprint verification using minutiae triplets. Sensors 12, 3418–3437 (2012)
21. Medina-Pérez, M.A., García-Borroto, M., Gutierrez-Rodríguez, A., Altamirano-Robles, L.: Improving the multiple alignments strategy for fingerprint verification. In: Carrasco-Ochoa, J.A., Martínez-Trinidad, J.F., Olvera López, J.A., Boyer, K.L. (eds.) MCPR 2012. LNCS, vol. 7329, pp. 147–154. Springer, Heidelberg (2012)
22. Medina-Pérez, M.A., Gutiérrez-Rodríguez, A., García-Borroto, M.: Improving fingerprint matching using an orientation-based minutia descriptor. In: Bayro-Corrochano, E., Eklundh, J.-O. (eds.) CIARP 2009. LNCS, vol. 5856, pp. 121–128. Springer, Heidelberg (2009)
23. NEUROtechnology Inc.: Verifinger (2014), http://www.neurotechnology.com/ (accessed January 8, 2014)
24. Parziale, G., Niel, A.: A fingerprint matching using minutiae triangulation. In: Zhang, D., Jain, A.K. (eds.) ICBA 2004. LNCS, vol. 3072, pp. 241–248. Springer, Heidelberg (2004)
25. Qi, J., Yang, S., Wang, Y.: Fingerprint matching combining the global orientation field with minutia. Pattern Recognition Letters 26(15), 2424–2430 (2005)
26. Ratha, N., Chen, S., Jain, A.K.: Adaptive flow orientation-based feature extraction in fingerprint images. Pattern Recognition 28(11), 1657–1672 (1995)
27. Scott, R.J.: Biometricsdk (2013), http://biometricsdk.sourceforge.net/ (accessed March 8, 2013)
28. Sherlock, B.G., Monro, D.M., Millard, K.: Fingerprint enhancement by directional fourier filtering. IEE Proceedings Vision Image and Signal Processing 141(2), 87–94 (1994)
29. The National Institute of Standards and Technology: NIST Biometric Image Software (2014), http://www.nist.gov/itl/iad/ig/nbis.cfm (accessed January 8, 2014)
30. Tico, M., Kuosmanen, P.: Fingerprint matching using an orientation-based minutia descriptor. IEEE Transactions on Pattern Analysis and Machine Intelligence 25(8), 1009–1014 (2003)
31. Vazan, R.: SourceAFIS SDK (2014), http://www.sourceafis.org/ (accessed January 18, 2014)

A Feasibility Study on the Use of Binary Keypoint Descriptors for 3D Face Recognition

Janez Križaj, Vitomir Štruc, and France Mihelič

Faculty of Electrical Engineering, University of Ljubljana,
Tržaška 25, SI-1000 Ljubljana, Slovenia
{janez.krizaj,vitomir.struc,france.mihelic}@fe.uni-lj.si

Abstract. Despite the progress made in the area of local image descriptors in recent years, virtually no literature is available on the use of more recent descriptors for the problem of 3D face recognition, such as BRIEF, ORB, BRISK or FREAK, which are binary in nature and, therefore, tend to be faster to compute and match, while requiring significantly less memory for storage than, for example, SIFT or SURF. In this paper, we try to close this gap and present a feasibility study on the use of these descriptors for 3D face recognition. Descriptors are evaluated on the three challenging 3D face image datasets, namely, the FRGC, UMB and CASIA. Our experiments show the binary descriptors ensure slightly lower verification rates than SIFT, comparable to those of the SURF descriptor, while being an order of magnitude faster than SIFT. The results suggest that the use of binary descriptors represents a viable alternative to the established descriptors.

Keywords: keypoints, descriptors, face recognition, 3D images.

1 Introduction

Keypoint descriptors pervade in many computer vision tasks, such as object detection, object recognition, image stitching and retrieval and are becoming increasingly popular in the area of 3D face recognition as well. In 3D face recognition systems, the use of keypoint descriptors is motivated by the fact, that different sources of variability plaguing 3D face recognition, such as illumination, changes in facial expression or occlusions, are considered to be either local in nature or their effect is more easily eliminated at the local level. Thus, local keypoint descriptors present an appealing tool for 3D facial surface analysis.

Among descriptor-based techniques proposed for the problem of 3D face recognition, techniques relying on SIFT [12] and SURF [1] features dominate the literature [8,7,2], while only little attention is given to other alternatives, despite the fact that a lot of progress has been made in the area of image descriptors over recent years. Particularly interesting in this regard are the recently proposed binary descriptors such as BRIEF [4], ORB [18], BRISK [10] and FREAK [15], which were shown to represent a viable alternative to established descriptors such as SIFT or SURF for various computer vision task, but to the best of our knowledge have not yet been considered for the task of 3D face recognition.

J.F. Martínez-Trinidad et al. (Eds.): MCPR 2014, LNCS 8495, pp. 142–151, 2014.

In this paper we try to bridge this gap and present a feasibility study on the use of binary descriptors (i.e. BRIEF, ORB, BRISK and FREAK) for 3D face recognition. We assess the descriptors within a 3D face recognition framework similar to the one presented in [9]. We evaluate the performance of the descriptors on three publicly available datasets of 3D face images, namely, the FRGC, UMB and CAISA and show that the binary descriptors represent a viable alternative to SIFT and SURF, as they ensure comparable recognition performance but at the fraction of the computational burden. The findings of our analysis suggest that more research efforts should be devoted to techniques exploiting binary descriptors for 3D face recognition as they seem suitable for building high-performance low-computational cost recognition systems.

The rest of the paper is structured as follows. Section 2 summarizes related work on the topics of image descriptors that can be found in the literature. Section 3 discusses the methodology for the evaluating the descriptors. Section 4 presents the experimental evaluation and Section 5 concludes the paper with some final remarks.

2   Related Work

Computing a local keypoint descriptor typically requires two steps: *i)* detecting a point of interest in an image - the keypoint, and *ii)* computing a descriptor (i.e., a feature vector) in the detected keypoint. Below we briefly survey some of the techniques used for both steps, which together form a descriptor extraction procedure.

2.1   Keypoint Detectors

Keypoint detectors generally find the interest points in an image by searching for points that have corner-like properties. One such approach is the Harris corner detector, proposed in [6], which is often used in conjunction with SIFT and SURF descriptors.

The SIFT descriptor typically relies on a keypoint detector that searches for maxima in the DoG (Difference of Gaussian) scale-space to detect corner-like and edge-like points. Here, the reason for using the DoG scale-space is to achieve scale invariance when searching for keypoints, while unstable edge-like points are removed by the Harris corner detector. The SURF [1] keypoint detector relies on a similar approach, but uses the determinant of the Hessian matrix to detect keypoints.

The more recent FAST [17] keypoint detector is very popular in real-time applications. To classify a pixel as a keypoint, FAST requires at lest p consecutive pixels in the s surrounding circle either being darker or brighter than the center pixel (generally $p = 9$ and $s = 16$). FAST does not produce multi-scale keypoints unless combined with a scale pyramid of an image. A graphical representation of the FAST-keypoint detector approach is shown in Fig. 1. An extension of the FAST was proposed in [13] in the form of the AGAST keypoint detector.

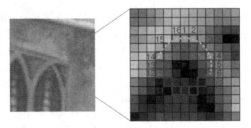

Fig. 1. FAST keypoint detector [17]

The FAST keypoint detector is typically used in conjunction with the BRIEF and ORB descriptors, while the multi-scale AGAST detector is commonly employed with the BRISK and FREAK descriptors.

2.2   Keypoint Descriptors

One of the most popular representatives from the group of keypoint descriptors is SIFT. The SIFT descriptor is obtained from a grid of histograms of oriented gradients. SIFT proved to be highly descriptive and robust to affine image transformations, however, relatively slow to compute and match due to its high dimensionality (128 floating point values). The SURF descriptor is faster to compute and match than SIFT, while with similar matching performance. Similar to SIFT, SURF also relies on local orientation histograms, but uses sums of Haar-like features for histogram computation.

Binary descriptors are designed for high-speed descriptor computation and matching in real-time systems. Binary descriptors are generally obtained by concatenating the results of simple brightness comparison tests. Each test compares the smoothed intensity of two specific pixels on the patch centered at a keypoint, resulting in either 1 or 0, depending on which intensity value in the pair is greater. Different binary descriptors differ in the kernels used to smooth the patches before intensity differencing as well as in the spatial arrangement of the pixel pairs inside the keypoint patch.

The BRIEF descriptor, for example, pre-smooths the whole patch with the Gaussian kernel, while the pixel pairs are sampled from a Gaussian with the center at the keypoint and variance as shown in Fig. 2a. BRIEF is sensitive to scale variation as well as to in-plane rotations.

The ORB descriptor (oriented FAST and rotated BRIEF) is similar to BRIEF, with the difference that ORB also assures invariance to in-plane rotations.

The BRISK descriptor uses deterministic sampling from the points arranged in the sampling pattern shown in Fig. 2b where small circles denote sampling locations and larger dashed circles denote Gaussian kernels used to smooth the intensity values at the sampling points. BRISK is robust both to scale and to rotations.

The FREAK descriptor adopts a biologically inspired sampling pattern (see Fig. 2c). FREAK, similarly as ORB, selects the best pixel pairs from some training data in a way that maximizes the variance of the descriptor elements and minimizes their correlation.

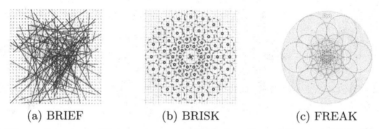

(a) BRIEF   (b) BRISK   (c) FREAK

Fig. 2. Binary descriptors: (a) random sampling of pixel pairs in BRIEF [4], (b) BRISK sampling pattern [10] and (c) FREAK sampling pattern [15]

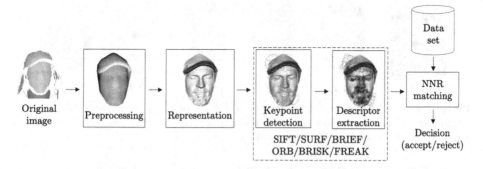

Fig. 3. Conceptual diagram of the evaluation system

3   Methodology

In this section the employed framework for 3D face recognition is described. First, each 3D image is preprocessed, the facial region is localized and segmented from the 3D scan. Localized face images are then represented by various local surface shape metrics. Next, keypoints are detected and descriptors are extracted from each face image. Classification is based on the nearest neighbor ratio method as typically used with the SIFT descriptor [7,11]. Each step of the framework is described in more detail in the following sections, while the schematic diagram of the framework is presented in Fig. 3.

3.1   Image Preprocessing and Localization

Images are initially low-pass filtered to remove high frequency noise, while depth components (z values) are interpolated to a grid of 1.0 mm resolution on the (x, y) plane.

The face localization is similar to the one presented in [19] and is based on K-means clustering. Setting the number of clusters to $K = 3$, this method divides the 3D face image into three regions that most likely correspond to background, body and face/head region. The face region is then selected as the cluster with the lowest average depth value.

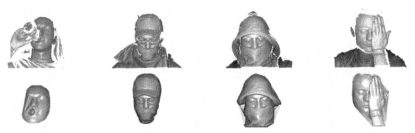

Fig. 4. Examples of original (top row) and localized (bottom row) 3D face images

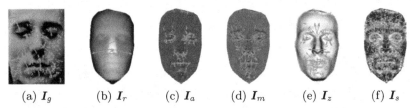

(a) $\boldsymbol{I}_g$ (b) $\boldsymbol{I}_r$ (c) $\boldsymbol{I}_a$ (d) $\boldsymbol{I}_m$ (e) $\boldsymbol{I}_z$ (f) $\boldsymbol{I}_s$

Fig. 5. Variation in the number of detected SIFT keypoints on a different data representations: (a) grayscale, (b) range, (c) maximum curvature, (d) mean curvature, (e) z components of the surface normals, (f) shape index

This face localization procedure assures only rough localization of the facial region (see Fig. 4). However, it is computationally very simple and is able to localize a face even in the presence of severe occlusions and rotations.

3.2   3D Data Representation

Since the assessed keypoint detection and descriptor calculation methods are optimized for the use on 2D images, it is of major importance how 3D data is passed to the keypoint detection and the descriptor calculation module. With an inappropriate representation, the keypoint detector is unable to find a sufficient number of keypoints for the recognition procedure to work. Thus, the facial image needs to be represented in a reasonable form for our assessment to make sense.

In this regard, we consider different metrics of the surface shape, such as range images $\boldsymbol{I}_r$, shape index values $\boldsymbol{I}_s$, mean curvature values $\boldsymbol{I}_m$, maximum curvature values $\boldsymbol{I}_a$ and surface normal coordinates $\boldsymbol{I}_x$, $\boldsymbol{I}_y$ and $\boldsymbol{I}_z$ (see Fig. 5) to be used for the keypoint detection and descriptor calculation steps. In Section 4 we demonstrate how both the keypoint detection and the descriptor calculation steps, are affected by the employed 3D shape representation type. An illustration of the effect of different representations on the keypoint detection step is shown in Fig. 5.

3.3   Keypoints and Descriptors

For the keypoint-detection and descriptor-extraction steps of our framework, we consider all techniques presented in Section 2 - from the established SIFT and SURF descriptors, to the relatively novel binary descriptors like BRIEF, ORB, BRISK and FREAK. While SIFT and SURF methods have its own implementation of keypoint detectors, we use the FAST detector for BRIEF and ORB descriptors and the AGAST keypoint detector for the BRISK and FREAK descriptor.

3.4 Matching

In the last step of our evaluation framework a similarity matrix between the query and the target images needs to be generated, based on which classification of the query images is performed.

The similarity between the two face images, each represented with a number of descriptors, is generally measured based on the number of matching descriptors. Each descriptor from a given query image is matched independently against all descriptors extracted from one target image. Several methods exist that define when the two descriptors match. In this work, we use the most common method called nearest-neighbor ratio (NNR), which was originally introduced in [14]. With this technique, a descriptor from a query image is matched to its nearest neighbor in a target image if the distance ratio between the first and the second nearest neighbor is below some predefined threshold. In this way, ambiguous matches are typically eliminated. Eventually, the number of matching descriptors between the two face images serves as similarity measure.

Matching of binary descriptors is typically performed using the Hamming distance (bitwise XOR followed by bit count), which can be computed very efficiently on today architectures [10]. Note that it is of paramount importance that the correct (i.e. Hamming) distance is used with the binary descriptors. Our preliminary experiments in fact showed that the recognition results using the Euclidean distance are significantly worse than those achieved by applying the Hamming distance.

4 Experiments

For the experimental assessment of the descriptors, we utilize three datasets, i.e. the FRGCv2 [16], UMB-DB [5] and CASIA dataset. The FRGCv2 dataset serves for evaluating the recognition performance ensured by the descriptors in the case of a large number of subjects with near frontal orientations and major expression variations; the UMB-DB dataset is used to examine the robustness of the descriptors (within our framework) to occlusions; while the robustness to pose variations is assessed on the CASIA dataset.

We mainly focus on the overall performance of the face recognition system and thus do not use the otherwise more commonly used metrics for evaluation of detectors and descriptors, i.e. recall and precision, defined in [14]. Therefore, the experimental results show the verification performance and are presented in the form of the verification rate (true accept rate, TAR) at a 0.1% false accept rate (FAR).

Table 1. Influence of different 3D data representation techniques on the keypoint detection step and the recognition rate (TAR @ 0.1% FAR, FRGC v2, *neut. vs neut.*; all descriptors are extracted on the shape index representation)

Method	I_r	I_z	I_a	I_s	I_m
	\multicolumn{5}{c}{Data representation for the keypoint detection}				
SIFT	21.5 (6)*	90.0 (72)	82.2 (62)	**94.3** (396)	81.6 (81)
SURF	52.1 (12)	90.9 (107)	88.9 (111)	**91.1** (243)	86.4 (107)
BRIEF	1.9 (3)	86.9 (200)	72.8 (134)	**89.9** (337)	66.8 (132)
ORB	9.6 (3)	89.9 (200)	82.0 (144)	**91.0** (345)	83.7 (140)
BRISK	0.0 (0)	87.9 (179)	89.0 (182)	**91.0** (301)	87.4 (191)
FREAK	2.4 (3)	**92.5** (162)	78.1 (134)	92.4 (349)	76.8 (138)

* Numbers in brackets denote the average number of detected keypoints per one face image.

4.1 Data Representation Assessment

In the first series of experiments we aim at selecting the most appropriate 3D surface-shape representation that eventually serves as input for the keypoint detection and descriptor extraction steps. Recall, that this test is necessary to establish which facial representation is best suited for keypoint detection. From the results in Table 1, where the results of this series of experiments is presented, we can see, that keypoint detection from the shape index representation I_s gives the best recognition results. We argue that this is due to increased variability in shape index representation, resulting in much more detected keypoints and thus better description of the face. Likewise, the highest recognition rate is achieved if descriptors are extracted from the shape index representation, as can be seen in Table 2. This can be explained by increased robustness of descriptors, resulting from the invariance of shape index to scale, translation and rotation [2].

4.2 Robustness Evaluation

In this series of experiments we evaluate the robustness of the keypoint descriptors to expressions, occlusions and pose variations. Next to the comparison of different keypoint descriptor methods, we also compare the standard NNR matching to an alternative matching approach where descriptors are first modeled by the Gaussian mixture models (GMM) via maximum a posteriori adaptation of universal background model, while matching is performed based on the GMM parameters using support vector machines (SVMs) (see [9] for details). Note that the second matching approach is a variation of the Bag-of-Words model, which is commonly used for the task of object recognition, with the difference that the $k-$means clustering step is replaced with the GMM modeling. This second matching procedure is introduced here as one could voice misgivings that the NNR technique is better suited for the SIFT and SURF descriptors than it is for the binary descriptors.

Table 2. Influence of different 3D data representation techniques on the descriptor computation step and the recognition rate (TAR @ 0.1% FAR, FRGC v2, *neut. vs neut.*; all keypoints are detected on the shape index representation)

| Method | Data representation for the descriptor extraction | | |
	I_r	I_z	I_s
SIFT	12.6	79.3	**94.3**
SURF	78.3	88.4	**91.1**
BRIEF	50.3	82.4	**89.9**
ORB	61.2	81.2	**91.0**
BRISK	53.3	67.3	**91.0**
FREAK	72.8	85.6	**92.4**

The results of this series of experiments are presented in Table 3. The upper half of the table summarizes the performance of the NNR framework, while the lower part of the table resumes the GMM-SVM performance. In the presence of expression variation, we can see that GMM-SVM classification outperforms the NNR matcher. On more challenging images from the UMB-DB and CASIA dataset the NNR matcher is mostly superior despite the reputation of the GMM-SVM classifier for its generalization strength that reflects in the robustness to occlusions, missing data and expression variations.

The SIFT-based method for the most part outperforms the other methods, but at the expense of higher computational cost as is observed in Section 4.3. When using the NNR matching approach, FREAK generally performs better than other binary descriptors and also better than SURF. As is expected, the BRIEF descriptor, being scale and rotation sensitive, achieves the lowest performance when using the NNR matcher. However, when coupled with the GMM-SVM classifier, BRIEF surprisingly gives the best results among the assessed methods. We argue that this is due to the fixed pattern of BRIEF descriptor (no orientation and scale normalization). Oriented keypoints present a more uniform appearance to descriptor computation, therefore, the descriptor variance is reduced resulting in diminished discriminativeness of the descriptors and poor estimation of GMM models.

All in all, the results suggest that while the SIFT descriptor still ensures the highest recognition rates, the binary descriptors (especially the FREAK descriptor) are not far behind. As will be shown in the next section, the binary descriptors have a significant edge when it comes to the matter of computational complexity.

4.3   Time Complexity

In the last series of experiments we measure time needed by our framework to verify a test image given different descriptors. All experiments are performed on

Table 3. TAR (%) at a 0.1% FAR of the assessed methods in the presence of expression, occlusion and orientation variations

	Dataset			Method					
Cls.	Name	Target	Query	SIFT	SURF	BRIEF	ORB	BRISK	FREAK
NNR	FRGC	*neutral*	*non-neut.*	81.2	71.1	66.5	73.5	72.5	77.8
	UMB	*non-occl.*	*occluded*	78.2	64.3	48.2	56.7	70.9	75.0
	CASIA	*frontal*	*non-fron.*	53.1	32.4	21.5	36.9	32.6	34.2
SVM	FRGC	*neutral*	*non-neut.*	84.4	73.4	85.3	75.8	78.8	68.8
	UMB	*non-occl.*	*occluded*	64.4	49.3	50.1	47.4	49.6	42.6
	CASIA	*frontal*	*non-fron.*	36.6	30.9	34.5	24.7	20.6	18.5

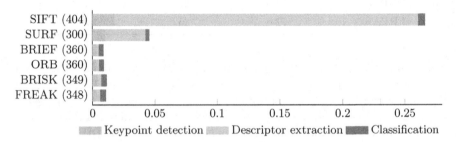

Fig. 6. Average running times (in seconds) of the assessed methods for the verification of one face image (numbers in brackets denote the number of detected keypoints)

an Intel Xeon CPU @ 2.67 GHz personal desktop computer with 12 GB of RAM. The implementation of keypoint detection and descriptor computation procedures are taken from OpenCV [3] and assessed through the recently introduced Matlab wrapper [20]. As can be seen from Fig. 6, the keypoint detection and descriptor extraction times of the binary methods are much lower than those of SIFT and SURF methods. However, the matching times seem to be similar for all methods, which is most likely a consequence of us using the Matlab wrapper. With a purely compiled implementation (without the wrapper) of the matching procedure, the binary descriptors are expected to have an edge in this regard as well.

5   Conclusion

We have assessed the relative usefulness of binary descriptors for the task of 3D face recognition. Among the assessed descriptors, SIFT still exhibits the best performance on all datasets. However, when a significant time efficiency is required (e.g. on mobile devices), binary descriptors are viable option, especially FREAK descriptor giving the best trade-off between performance and speed.

Acknowledgments. The work presented in this paper was supported in parts by the national research programe P2-0250(C) Metrology and Biometric Systems, the European Union's Seventh Framework Programme (FP7-SEC-2011.20.6) under grant agreement number 285582 (RESPECT) and the post-doctoral project 3D-For-REAL (3D Face Recognition in Real World Setting) funded partially by MIZŠ and the European Social Fund, M-1331E (H019001). The authors additionally appreciate the support of COST Actions IC1106 and IC1206.

References

1. Bay, H., Tuytelaars, T., Van Gool, L.: SURF: Speeded Up Robust Features. In: Leonardis, A., Bischof, H., Pinz, A. (eds.) ECCV 2006, Part I. LNCS, vol. 3951, pp. 404–417. Springer, Heidelberg (2006)
2. Bayramoğlu, N., Alatan, A.: Shape Index SIFT: Range Image Recognition Using Local Features. In: Proc. ICPR, pp. 352–355 (2010)
3. Bradski, G.: The OpenCV Library. Dr. Dobb's Journal of Software Tools (2000)
4. Calonder, M., Lepetit, V., Strecha, C., Fua, P.: BRIEF: Binary Robust Independent Elementary Features. In: Daniilidis, K., Maragos, P., Paragios, N. (eds.) ECCV 2010, Part IV. LNCS, vol. 6314, pp. 778–792. Springer, Heidelberg (2010)
5. Colombo, A., Cusano, C., Schettini, R.: UMB-DB: A database of partially occluded 3D faces. In: ICCV Workshops, pp. 2113–2119 (2011)
6. Harris, C., Stephens, M.: A Combined Corner and Edge Detector. In: Proc. of Fourth Alvey Vision Conference, pp. 147–151 (1988)
7. Huang, D., et al.: 3-D Face Recognition Using eLBP-Based Facial Description and Local Feature Hybrid Matching. IEEE TIFS 7(5), 1551–1565 (2012)
8. Inan, T., Halici, U.: 3-D Face Recognition With Local Shape Descriptors. IEEE TIFS 7(2), 577–587 (2012)
9. Križaj, J., Štruc, V., Dobrišek, S.: Combining 3D Face Representations using Region Covariance Descriptors and Statistical Models. In: IEEE FG, pp. 1–7 (2013)
10. Leutenegger, S., Chli, M., Siegwart, R.: BRISK: Binary Robust invariant scalable keypoints. In: Proc. ICCV, pp. 2548–2555 (2011)
11. Lo, T.W.R., Siebert, J.P.: Local Feature Extraction and Matching on Range Images: 2. 5D SIFT. Comput. Vis. Image Underst. 113(12), 1235–1250 (2009)
12. Lowe, D.G.: Distinctive Image Features from Scale-Invariant Keypoints. Int. J. Comput. Vision 60(2), 91–110 (2004)
13. Mair, E., Hager, G.D., Burschka, D., Suppa, M., Hirzinger, G.: Adaptive and Generic Corner Detection Based on the Accelerated Segment Test. In: Daniilidis, K., Maragos, P., Paragios, N. (eds.) ECCV 2010, Part II. LNCS, vol. 6312, pp. 183–196. Springer, Heidelberg (2010)
14. Mikolajczyk, K., Schmid, C.: A Performance Evaluation of Local Descriptors. IEEE TPAMI 27(10), 1615–1630 (2005)
15. Ortiz, R.: FREAK: Fast Retina Keypoint. In: Proc. CVPR, Washington, DC, USA, pp. 510–517 (2012)
16. Phillips, P.J., et al.: Overview of the Face Recognition Grand Challenge. In: Proc. CVPR, pp. 947–954 (2005)
17. Rosten, E., Drummond, T.W.: Machine Learning for High-Speed Corner Detection. In: Leonardis, A., Bischof, H., Pinz, A. (eds.) ECCV 2006, Part I. LNCS, vol. 3951, pp. 430–443. Springer, Heidelberg (2006)
18. Rublee, E., Rabaud, V., Konolige, K., Bradski, G.: ORB: An Efficient Alternative to SIFT or SURF. In: Proc. ICCV, pp. 2564–2571 (2011)
19. Segundo, M., Queirolo, C., Bellon, O.R.P., Silva, L.: Automatic 3D Facial Segmentation and Landmark Detection. In: Proc. ICIAP, pp. 431–436 (2007)
20. Yamaguchi, K.: http://www.cs.stonybrook.edu/~kyamagu/mexopencv/

Robust Head Gestures Recognition for Assistive Technology

Juan R. Terven[1], Joaquin Salas[1], and Bogdan Raducanu[2]

[1] Instituto Politécnico Nacional
Cerro Blanco 141, Colinas del Cimatario, Queretaro, Mexico
jrterven@hotmail.com,
jsalasr@ipn.mx
[2] Centre de Visió per Computador Edifici "O", Campus UAB
08193, Bellaterra, Cerdanyola (Barcelona) Spain
bogdan@cvc.uab.es

Abstract. This paper presents a system capable of recognizing six head gestures: nodding, shaking, turning right, turning left, looking up, and looking down. The main difference of our system compared to other methods is that the Hidden Markov Models presented in this paper, are fully connected and consider all possible states in any given order, providing the following advantages to the system: (1) allows unconstrained movement of the head and (2) it can be easily integrated into a wearable device (*e.g.* glasses, neck-hung devices), in which case it can robustly recognize gestures in the presence of ego-motion. Experimental results show that this approach outperforms common methods that use restricted HMMs for each gesture.

Keywords: assistive technology, social interactions, head gestures recognition, hidden markov models.

1 Introduction

During the last decades, several researchers and companies have developed assistive technology systems to support visually impaired people in tasks such as navigation, orientation, object recognition, and reading printed material [1]. However, few efforts have been devoted in systems to enhance their social interaction [2]. The issue is that during social interactions, a large part of the communication is non-verbal [3] and is given mostly in the form of visual cues such as head and body gestures. Moreover, most sighted people are not aware of the non-verbal signals that they commonly use and make no adjustment when interacting with visually impaired people [2]. In turn, this leaves visually impaired people in disadvantage, promoting in some cases social isolation [4].

Some of the requirements of social interaction devices, in the opinion of Krishna *et al.* [2], include the identification of the following: (1)number of participants, (2)gaze direction, (3)people's identity, (4)people's appearance (face, clothes), (5)facial expressions, and (6)hand and body gestures. Besides these,

J.F. Martínez-Trinidad et al. (Eds.): MCPR 2014, LNCS 8495, pp. 152–161, 2014.
© Springer International Publishing Switzerland 2014

in our research, we have identified the need of inferring the degree of attention that the interlocutor is paying to the speaker during social interactions. This need arises, for instance, when a visually impaired person is engaged in a dyadic interaction (one-to-one) and the interlocutor decides to walk away inadvertently.

In this paper, we develop a highly effective method to recognize head gestures, such as shakes and nods, as they represent an important part of the non-verbal communicative process and, together with the non-verbal backchannels, could signal agreement, disagreement, or the intention for turn-taking [5]. The rest of the paper is structured as follows. In Section 2, we survey previous work on the visual detection of head gestures. Then, in Section 3, we describe our methodology, based largely on the use of Hidden Markov Models (HMM). In section 4, we report experimental results on two datasets. Finally, we conclude and suggest future lines of work.

2 Related Work

In this section we survey previous work on head gesture recognition, highlighting the strengths and weakness for assistive technology applications. According to our review, most head gesture recognition methods divide the process in two steps: motion estimation and temporal sequence analysis.

For motion estimation, several authors have performed head gesture recognition based on eye tracking [6–9]. For instance, Choi & Rhee [6] and Kang et al. [7] segmented the eyes by thresholding, and making use of the head's geometrical characteristics; Kapoor et al. [8] used an infrared sensitive camera and infrared LEDs to track pupils; and Tan & Rong [9] used the cascade classifier from [10] to detect and track the eyes. Nevertheless, a disadvantage of using the eyes as features for motion estimation, is the inability to detect and track faces with sunglasses (commonly worn by visually impaired people). Gunes & Pantic [11] and Fujie et al. [12] estimated head motion using optical flow. More precisely, the head region was extracted by skin color segmentation. This approach works well in controlled environments. Yet, methods based on color are sensitive to changes in illumination and therefore, are not suitable for outdoors. In [11], the head region is detected using the cascade classifier from [10]. However, using [10] for tracking is computationally expensive for an embedded device and the face angles are confined to a limited range. Wei et al. [13] used the Kinect sensor to detect and track the head pose (yaw, pitch, roll). Although this sensor is low cost and provides great capabilities, its use is limited to indoors or dark environments and is not suitable for a wearable device. To overcome these limitations, we use a robust method for motion estimation based on SIFT features [14], capable of detecting and tracking the face even with sunglasses with various illuminations.

The second step of head gesture recognition is temporal sequence analysis. A common approach for this is to use HMMs to recognize each gesture. In fact, all the systems described before make use of two or three HMMs with different states [6–9, 11–13], e.g., up/down for nodding and left/right for shaking. This approach works well if the system is in a fixed position (i.e., third-party perspective), and is commonly use in applications such as robotics and Human Computer Interaction (HCI), where the system should be able to infer the proper gestures and react accordingly. However, if the system is moving, for instance implemented in a wearable assistive device, it should be able to robustly identify the head gestures, despite the ego-motion noise. To account for this, we propose a more flexible approach using identical ergodic HMMs that include all the movements.

3   Methodology

In this section, we describe the process to compute the head pose, and infer nod and shake movements.

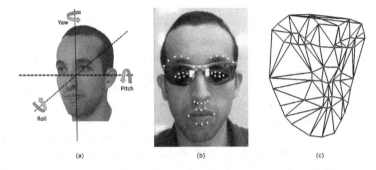

Fig. 1. Head Pose Estimation. (a) If we consider the head as a disembodied rigid object, its pose can be described by yaw, pitch, and roll (b) 2D Face features extracted using the Supervised Descent Method (SDM). (c) 3D anthropometric head model. This 3D model and the 2D features are fed into the POSIT algorithm[15] for head pose estimation.

3.1   Head Pose Estimation

Head pose estimation refers to compute the orientation of a person's head with respect to a camera [16]. If we consider the human head as a rigid object, the pose estimation is limited to three degrees of freedom characterized by *yaw*, *pitch*, and *roll* as shown in Fig. 1(a).

To estimate the head pose, we detect facial landmarks using the *Supervised Descent Method* (SDM) proposed in [17] and freely available online[1]. SDM is used for solving the Non-linear Least Squares (NLS) problem of face alignment. Given a set of n training images $\mathbf{d}^i \in \Re^{m \times 1}, 1 \leq i \leq n$, of m pixels with p landmarks. The system uses SIFT [14] features $\mathbf{h}(\mathbf{d}(x)) \in \Re^{128 \times 1}$ extracted from patches around the landmarks (shown in Fig. 1(b)) to learn a series of descent directions

---

[1] Human Sensing Laboratory: http://www.humansensing.cs.cmu.edu/intraface (Accessed March 25, 2014)

and re-scaling factors such that it produces a sequence of updates in order to converge from the initial estimate (x_0) to the ground truth landmarks (x_*). With this approach, face alignment consists of minimizing the function over Δx

$$f(x_0 + \Delta x) = \|\mathbf{h}(\mathbf{d}(x_0 + \Delta x)) - \mathbf{h}(\mathbf{d}(x_*))\|_2^2 . \qquad (1)$$

Once the face is aligned, *i.e.*, the landmarks converge to the final position, the head pose estimation is obtained following the approach described in [18], where 2D image points and 3D model points are matched, using the POSIT (*Pose from Orthography and Scaling with Iterations*) method [15]. The 3D anthopometric model (Fig. 1(c)) that we used is presented in [18] and it is available online[2].

3.2   Head Nodding and Shaking Detection Using Two HMMs

Once estimated the head pose, the next step is to recognize head gestures such as nodding and shaking. For this purpose, we started developing two HMMs shown in Fig. 2. One is used to recognize nodding, and the other to recognize shaking.

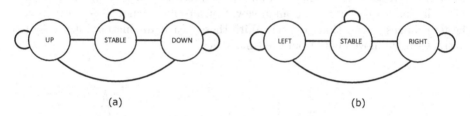

(a)   (b)

Fig. 2. Hidden Markov Models (HMM) designed for head gestures recognition. (a) HMM for nodding recognition, (b) HMM for shaking recognition.

Hidden Markov Models (HMMs). A Hidden Markov Model is a double embedded stochastic process: An underlying stochastic process that is not observable, and a set of stochastic processes that produce the sequence of observations [19]. Each HMM is defined by states, states transition probabilities, observation probabilities, and initial probabilities as follows:

1. The N states in the model $S = \{S_1, S_2, \ldots, S_N\}$. In our case both HMMs have three states: *stable*, *up*, and *down* for the nodding HMM; and *stable*, *left*, and *right* for the shaking HMM.
2. The M observation movements per state $V = \{v_1, v_2, \ldots, v_M\}$. In our system the movements are *stable*, *upward*, *downward*, *leftward*, and *rightward*.
3. The state transition matrix $A = \{a_{ij}\}$, where a_{ij} is the probability that the state S_j is given at time $t + 1$, when the state at time t is S_i.

---

[2] Advance Interaction using Facial Information: http://aifi.isr.uc.pt/index.html (Accessed March 25, 2014).

For example, let's consider $N = 3$, and S_1 is *stable*, S_2 is *up*, and S_3 is *down*. Therefore, a_{11} is the probability of transitioning from *stable* to *stable*. Similarly, a_{12} is the probability of transitioning from *stable* to *up*, and so on.

4. The observation probability matrix $B = \{b_j(k)\}$, where $b_j(k)$ is the probability that the symbol v_k is emitted in the state S_j.

5. The initial state distribution $\pi = \{\pi_i\}$, where π_i is the probability that the model starts at state S_i. In our system we choose $S_1(stable)$ as the initial state.

In practice, the state transition matrix A and the observation probability matrix B are learned during training.

Training. For training and test we collected a database of 10 videos from different people, taken from a static webcam and 10 videos taken with the Pivothead[3] wearable glasses. All the videos contain annotated groundtruth and can be downloaded from the web[4]. Each gesture in the video is translated into a sequence or time series of 20 digits long containing the changes in yaw and pitch in consecutive frames. Fig. 3 shows typical nodding and shaking sequences from the database. From these graphs, we can see that a nodding gesture exhibits larger changes in pitch than in yaw. Conversely, a shaking gesture exhibits larger changes in yaw than in pitch. With these clearly distinctions, it is easy to extract simple movements from the time series.

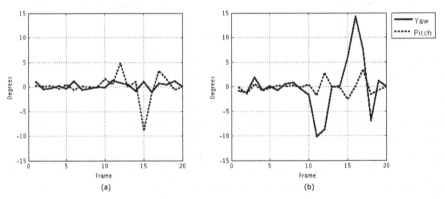

Fig. 3. Yaw and Pitch changes for typical nodding and shaking sequences. (a) shows the yaw and pitch changes (in degrees) for a nodding gesture. (b) shows the yaw and pitch changes (in degrees) for a shaking gesture.

As mentioned before, we defined five observation movements: *stable, upward, downward, leftward,* and *rightward*. Each move is represented by a number (from 1 to 5), and for each training time series, we extracted a sequence of these

---

[3] Pivothead Wearable Imaging: `http://pivothead.com` (Accessed March 25, 2014).

[4] Head Gestures Dataset: `www.jrterven.com/headDataset.html` (Accessed March 25, 2014).

movements from the yaw and pitch changes using the following procedure: Let Δx represent the change in yaw in two consecutive frames. Likewise, Δy represents the change in pitch in two consecutive frames. If $|\Delta y| \gg |\Delta x|$ then the symbol is *up* or *down* (*i.e.*, 2 or 3), now we look at the sign, if Δy is positive, the extracted symbol is 2 (*up*), but, if it is negative, the symbol is 3 (*down*). On the contrary, If $|\Delta x| \gg |\Delta y|$ then the symbol is *left* or *right* (*i.e.*, 4 or 5) and a similar procedure is followed for extracting the final symbol. If none of these conditions are true, the symbol is 1 (*stable*). After this procedure, we are left with a sequence of 20 digits. For example, the sequence (1 1 1 1 2 2 1 1 1 1 1 1 1 3 3 1 1 1 1 1) stands for an *stable* phase followed by *upward* then *stable* followed by *downward*, and the ground truth indicates that this sequence is a nod gesture. The set of all these sequences with their corresponding ground truth constitutes the training data for the HMMs. To select the optimal value for discriminating between vertical and horizontal movements (the $\gg$ threshold), we tested the algorithm with different discriminator thresholds and picked the one with the highest F-score.

The goal of the training phase is to estimate the state transition matrix (A) and the observation probability matrix (B). Using these sequences, we trained two HMMs using the Baum-Welch algorithm: one for nodding and one for shaking. However, the multiple repetitions of the state $S_1(stable)$ produce a very high probability of transition from *stable* to *stable* (≈ 0.74 for nodding and 0.76 for shaking). These high probabilities affect the recognition, because movements containing multiple *stable* states (even a static head) can be regarded as nods or shakes with high probabilities. To address this problem, we removed the repetitions of the *stable* observations from the training and testing sequences. Now, instead of having sequences such as (1 1 1 1 2 2 1 1 1 1 1 1 1 3 3 1 1 1 1 1) for nodding, we are left with sequences like (1 2 2 1 3 3 1). This change improved the recognition stage because now each sequence is shorter and the recognition values are not affected by long chains of *stable* symbols. The repetitions of the other observations are necessary for recognition, because a single observation indicates a fast movement and repetitions of the same observation indicate a slow movement.

Recognition. Given an observation sequence extracted from video, the goal of recognition is to determine which one of the two HMMs is more likely to have generated the sequence. In our case, we used the Baum-Welch algorithm to obtain the probabilities of the observation sequence given each model. To determine the gesture, we selected the model with the highest probability. However, due to the stochastic nature of the algorithm, other movements also return probabilities (although very small). To account for this, we use a threshold value, to discard other gestures. This threshold value is obtained as the minimum probability of all the training sequences given both models (*i.e.*, the lowest recognition result for all training samples).

However, one problem arises with this configuration. Due to the state separation, *left* and *right* states are not defined in the nod HMM. Therefore, if a nodding gesture contains an unexpected leftward or rightward movement, the recognition fails because there is no probability that the observation sequence belongs to the nodding model. A similar case happens with the recognition of the shaking gesture (*up* and *down* states are not defined in the shake HMM), the system fails to recognize a shake if the observation sequence contains an upward or downward movement.

3.3 Head Nodding and Head Shaking Recognition Using Two Complete HMMs

In a second configuration, we created two HMMs including all the possible states for nodding and shaking, like the one shown in Fig. 4. Using these HMMs, it exists a probability (although very low) that during a nodding, a *left* or *right* movement might occur. In other words, a nodding sequence can contain *leftward* or *rightward* observations. Similarly, a shake sequence can contain *upward* or *downward* observations. With this new configuration, the recognition rate increased considerably.

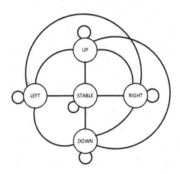

Fig. 4. Second model representation. The model is fully connected and contains all the states and observation movements.

Even though the recognition rate improved, we noticed false positives during live video testing. The false positives appeared when the person being tracked performed a simple movement such as turning right, turning left, looking up or looking down. The observation sequences from these simple movements have high probabilities given the models, *e.g.,* turning right is highly recognized as a shake; sometimes even higher than a shaking gesture. Thus, making the threshold value useless for these situations.

3.4 Head Gestures Recognition Using Six Complete HMMs

In a third configuration, we created six complete HMMs like the ones from the previous approach (Fig. 4). To train these HMMs, we collected another set of 20 videos with left and right movements. The HMMs are trained to recognize each of the following gestures: nodding, shaking, turning left, turning right, looking up, and looking down.

With this configuration, the nodding and shaking recognition-rate improved considerably in live video, because now simple movements are recognized by their own model, minimizing the false positives. Another benefit of this added functionality is that now, we can infer additional information. For instance, we can analyze how much time the interlocutors are looking elsewhere.

4 Experimental Results

We collected a dataset of videos taken from two sources: a static camera and a wearable camera. The static camera dataset consists of 30 videos (from 10 different users) with annotated ground truth, in which half of the videos the participants are wearing sunglasses. In total, this set contains around 100 samples of each gesture: nodding, shaking, turning left, turning right, looking up, and looking down. These videos were created with two software applications: the first application displays 20 *Yes/No* questions. The user answers each question clicking a *Yes* button or a *No* button, and then the user must perform the movement (a nodding for *Yes* or a shaking for *No*). The application records the video and tracks the face for 20 frames (approx. one second) saving in a file the changes in yaw and pitch. The answers given by the user (by clicking the button) serve as ground truth for training and test. The second application requests the user to perform simple movements (turning left, turning right, looking up, and looking down), this application also records the video and tracks the head saving the yaw and pitch changes along with the ground truth (the requested movement). The wearable camera dataset consists of 10 recordings of approximately 3 minutes each, with annotated ground truth (6 gestures). These videos contain moderate ego-motion which affect the tracking.

A random 70% of the data were selected for training and the rest for test. Fig. 5 shows the head nod and shake recognition results for all the 10 videos.

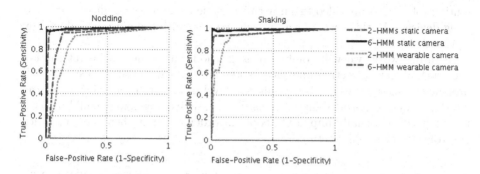

Fig. 5. Recognition curves for the static camera and the wearable camera testing data. (a) shows the head nod recognition curves when varying the discriminator threshold. (b) shows the head shake recognition curves when varying the discriminator threshold.

The ROC curves display the recognition performance of the last two HMMs configurations when varying the discriminator threshold.

Table 1 shows the area under each curve representing the recognition rate for each configuration. We can see from this table that the 6-HMMs configuration performs slightly better on the static camera videos, but performs much better on the wearable camera videos. A video of the system is available from http://www.youtube.com/watch?v=ThvG2VOyJtE&feature=youtu.be.

Table 1. Recognition rates for the two HMMs configurations on the static-camera test data and the wearable-camera test data

	Static camera		Wearable camera	
Gesture	2 HMMs	6 HMMs	2 HMMs	6 HMMs
Nodding	96.6%	98.5%	84.8%	90.6%
Shaking	98.7%	98.7%	92%	95.7%
Left	–	98.5%	–	95.6%
Right	–	98.3%	–	95.6%
Up	–	97.5%	–	90.3%
Down	–	97.4%	–	90.2%

5   Conclusion and Future Work

This paper presents a method for robustly recognize six head gestures (nodding, shaking, turning right, turning left, looking up, and looking down) using what we call *complete Hidden Markov Models*.

The main difference with other methods is that our HMMs consider all possible states in any given order. The selection of this approach provides great flexibility because a head nod that normally contains up and down movements, now, can also contain left and right movements as well. This is an advance over previous methods as it permits unconstrained movements of the head, while presenting robustness on video taken with wearable cameras (*e.g.*, glasses or neck-hung devices). In this case, our approach can deal with the noise introduced by ego-motion.

In future work, we will combine this method with other social interaction cues such as gaze direction and face expressions in a wearable device that will provide the user with cues indicating the level of attention or behavior of the interlocutors during social interactions. Such assistive technology could be used for instance by visually-impaired people in order to strengthen their presence and role during social meetings.

Acknowledgments. This research was partially funded by Fomix CONACYT-GDF under grant 189005 and SIP-IPN under grant 20140325.

References

1. Manduchi, R., Coughlan, J. (Computer) Vision without Sight. Commun. ACM 55(1), 96–104 (2012)
2. Krishna, S., Colbry, D., Black, J., Balasubramanian, V., Panchanathan, S., et al.: A Systematic Requirements Analysis and Development of an Assistive Device to Enhance the Social Interaction of People who are Blind or Visually Impaired. In: Workshop on Computer Vision Applications for the Visually Impaired (2008)
3. Knapp, M.L.: Nonverbal communication in human interaction. Cengage Learning (2012)
4. Wiener, W., Lawson, G.: Audition for the traveler who is visually impaired. Foundations of Orientation and Mobility 2, 104–169 (1997)
5. Dittmann, A.T., Llewellyn, L.G.: Relationship between vocalizations and head nods as listener responses. J. Pers. Soc. Psychol. 9(1), 79–84 (1968)
6. Choi, H., Rhee, P.: Head Gesture Recognition using HMMs. Expert Syst. Appl. 17(3), 213–221 (1999)
7. Kang, S.K., Chung, K.Y., Lee, J.H.: Development of head detection and tracking systems for visual surveillance. Pers. Ubiquit. Comput. 18(3), 515–522 (2014)
8. Kapoor, A., Picard, R.: A Real-Time Head Nod and Shake Detector. In: Workshop on Perceptive user interfaces, pp. 1–5. ACM (2001)
9. Tan, W., Rong, G.: A Real-Time Head Nod and Shake Detector using HMMs. Expert. Syst. Appl. 25(3), 461–466 (2003)
10. Viola, P., Jones, M.: Robust real-time object detection. Int. J. Comput. Vision 4 (2001)
11. Gunes, H., Pantic, M.: Dimensional emotion prediction from spontaneous head gestures for interaction with sensitive artificial listeners. In: Allbeck, J.M., Badler, N.I., Bickmore, T.W., Pelachaud, C., Safonova, A. (eds.) IVA 2010. LNCS, vol. 6356, pp. 371–377. Springer, Heidelberg (2010)
12. Fujie, S., Ejiri, Y., Matsusaka, Y., Kikuchi, H., Kobayashi, T.: Recognition of paralinguistic information and its application to spoken dialogue system. In: Workshop on Automatic Speech Recognition and Understanding, pp. 231–236. IEEE (2003)
13. Wei, H., Scanlon, P., Li, Y., Monaghan, D.S., O'Connor, N.E.: Real-time head nod and shake detection for continuous human affect recognition. In: 14th International Workshop on Image Analysis for Multimedia Interactive Services, pp. 1–4. IEEE (2013)
14. Lowe, D.G.: Distinctive image features from scale-invariant keypoints. Int. J. Comput. Vision 60(2), 91–110 (2004)
15. Dementhon, D.F., Davis, L.S.: Model-based object pose in 25 lines of code. Int. J. Comput. Vision 15(1-2), 123–141 (1995)
16. Murphy-Chutorian, E., Trivedi, M.M.: Head pose estimation in computer vision: A survey. IEEE Trans. Pattern Anal. Machine Intell. 31(4), 607–626 (2009)
17. Xiong, X., De la Torre, F.: Supervised descent method and its applications to face alignment. In: IEEE Conference on Computer Vision and Pattern Recognition (CVPR), pp. 532–539 (2013)
18. Martins, P., Batista, J.: Monocular head pose estimation. In: Campilho, A., Kamel, M.S. (eds.) ICIAR 2008. LNCS, vol. 5112, pp. 357–368. Springer, Heidelberg (2008)
19. Rabiner, L.R.: A tutorial on hidden markov models and selected applications in speech recognition. Proceedings of the IEEE 77(2), 257–286 (1989)

Object Recognition with Näive Bayes-NN via Prototype Generation

Hugo Jair Escalante[1], Mauricio Sotomayor[2],
Manuel Montes[1], and A. Pastor Lopez-Monroy[1]

[1] Computer Science Department, INAOE,
Luis Enrique Erro No. 1, Puebla, 72840, Mexico
{hugojair,mmontesg,pastor}@inaoep.mx
[2] Instituto Tecnologico de Orizaba,
Av. Oriente 9 No. 832, Orizaba, Ver., 66451, Mexico

Abstract. Naïve Bayes nearest neighbors (NBNN) is a variant of the classic KNN classifier that has proved to be very effective for object recognition and image classification tasks. Under NBNN an unseen image is classified by looking at the distance between the sets of visual descriptors of test and training images. Although NBNN is a very competitive pattern classification approach, it presents a major drawback: it requires of large storage and computational resources. NBNN's requirements are even larger than those of the standard KNN because sets of raw descriptors must be stored and compared, therefore, efficiency improvements for NBNN are necessary. Prototype generation (PG) methods have proved to be helpful for reducing the storage and computational requirements of standard KNN. PG methods learn a reduced subset of prototypical instances to be used by KNN for classification. In this contribution we study the suitability of PG methods for enhancing the capabilities of NBNN. Throughout an extensive comparative study we show that PG methods can reduce dramatically the number of descriptors required by NBNN without significantly affecting its discriminative performance. In fact, we show that PG methods can improve the classification performance of NBNN by using much less visual descriptors. We compare the performance of NBNN to other state-of-the-art object recognition approaches and show the combination of PG and NBNN outperforms alternative techniques.

Keywords: NBNN, Prototype generation, KNN, Object recognition.

1 Introduction

Naïve Bayes nearest neighbors (NBNN) is a variant of the KNN classifier that has proved to be very effective in diverse pattern recognition and computer vision tasks. The underlying idea behind NBNN is that the category of an object can be determined by comparing all of the visual descriptors associated to training and test objects. NBNN has outperformed other state-of-the-art methodologies

J.F. Martínez-Trinidad et al. (Eds.): MCPR 2014, LNCS 8495, pp. 162–171, 2014.

(e.g., the bag-of-visual-words) in diverse domains and has motivated research that tries to extend and take advantage of similar ideas [1,26].

In spite of the competitive performance of NBNN, it has a major disadvantage that limits its use for certain applications/domains: it requires of large storage and computational resources. Notwithstanding this limitation of NBNN, its effectiveness and theoretical justification plentifully justify studying ways of improving the efficiency of this methodology. This paper aims at determining whether well known techniques from pattern recognition could amend the efficiency drawback of NBNN without compromising its competitive performance.

We focus on the application of prototype generation (PG) approaches with the goal of reducing the set of visual descriptors that NBNN requires for classifying test instances. PG methods are a type of instance reduction methodology in which a small set prototypical instances are learned, with the constraint that prototypes should be able to effectively represent a whole data set and using the smallest number of prototypes [22]. PG methods have proved to be very effective for KNN classifiers [22,19]. Thus, we hypothesize that PG methods could also be helpful for boosting the performance of NBNN. To the best of our knowledge, the use of PG methods for improving the efficiency of NBNN is a research topic that has not been explored yet.

Along this paper we report a comparative study that considers the most effective PG methods proposed so far and evaluate its usefulness for object recognition using NBNN as classifier. We report experimental results in a database that has been used in previous studies [2] and show that some PG methods indeed are able of reducing the storage and computational requirements of NBNN without compromising its discriminative capabilities. In fact, we show that some methods can even improve the classification performance of NBNN by using much less instances. We compare the performance of NBNN to alternative state-of-the-art approaches and confirm its competitiveness.

2   Considered Object Recognition Methods

This section describes the NBNN [1] method, the pattern classification technique that is focus of our study, and the bag-of-visual-words approach [28], a state-of-the-art object recognition methodology against we compare NBNN.

2.1   Naïve Bayes Nearest Neighbors Method

Recently, it has been shown that pattern recognition techniques based on image-to-image comparisons can obtain state-of-the-art performance in computer vision tasks. This type of techniques rely on direct comparison between descriptors of training and testing objects. One of the most representative methods in this category is NBNN, which is closely related to KNN classification [1].

Under NBNN a set of visual descriptors (e.g., SIFT [16]) are extracted from each training image and they are stored. Each visual descriptor is a numerical vector, thus each image is associated to a set of vectors; in the data set we consider each image has ≈ 450 visual descriptors on average. When a new image has to be classified, we extract its visual descriptors. For each test-image descriptor we estimate its nearest-neighbors in the set of training visual descriptors of each class. That is, for each descriptor we extract nearest-neighbors for each of the classes. For each class, we add the distances of test descriptors to their nearest-neighbors of the class. The class for a test image is assigned by looking at the minimum cumulative distance across classes. NBNN's classification criterion is as follows:

$$\hat{C} = \arg\min_{C} \sum_{i=1}^{n} ||d_i - NN_C(d_i)|| \qquad (1)$$

where $d_{1,...,n}$ is the set of visual descriptors from the test image and $NN_c(d_i)$ is the nearest training neighbor of d_i with class C, note we assume a single nearest neighbor. Boiman et al., argued that the direct comparison of descriptors is more discriminative than vector quantizing the descriptors (e.g., under the bag-of-visual words framework). In fact, they show that under the näive-Bayes assumption, the theoretically optimal image classifier is effectively approximated by NBNN.

One should note that NBNN is a highly inefficient method as one has to estimate distances between all of the training and testing descriptors. Hence, instance reduction methodologies can be applied to improve its efficiency. In this work, we apply PG methods to the set of training visual descriptors, that is, we consider each visual descriptor from each training image an instance of a pattern classification problem (the class of a descriptor is the class corresponding to the image from which the descriptor was extracted). Under these assumptions, PG methods can be applied directly. The goal is to keep only a reduced subset of descriptors and speedup the classification process of NBNN.

2.2 The Bag-of-Visual-Words Representation

The bag-of-visual-words (BoVW) is one of the most used representations for images and videos in many computer vision tasks [28]. The underlying hypothesis is that the content of objects (e.g., images or videos) can be effectively described by histograms that account for the presence of representative features, called visual words. This is in analogy to the bag-of-words representation widely used in information retrieval and text mining. The standard approach for generating visual words is by means of clustering methods, k−means in most of the cases. Low-level descriptors extracted from images are grouped into k−clusters, the k−centers of the learned clusters are considered as visual words. Under the BoVW approach each image is represented by a single vector and standard classifiers can be used, e.g., SVM or KNN. In this paper we compare the performance of NBNN to the BoVWs formulation.

One should note that although unsupervised methods have been used for generating visual vocabularies in BoVWs, object recognition is a supervised classification task and then class information is available for each training visual descriptor. Therefore, it makes sense to ask ourselves whether PG methods could also be used to learn the visual vocabularies: using a PG method to generate discriminative prototypes, playing the role of visual words, instead of applying $k-$means, and use the resultant centers. With the goal of answering this question we also evaluate the suitability of PG methods for generating codebooks for BoVWs representations. Hence, using PG methods for codebook generation is another contribution of this work.

3   Prototype Generation

Prototype-based classification can be seen as a KNN classifier using a subset of the total of training instances [10]. Usually the classification rule is 1NN, and the core of this type of methods lies in the way to obtain a small set of prototypical instances that effectively summarize the whole training set. Many PG[1] methods have been proposed so far. Triguero et al. recently performed a complete experimental study that considered most of the successful PG methods proposed up to 2012.

Among the most effective type of methods are those based on position adjustment and evolutionary algorithms. In evolutionary algorithms the general idea is to consider prototypes as points in the $d-$dimensional input space. The positions of points (prototypes) are updated trying to maximize a criterion related to the classification performance using 1NN in a training or validation set [6,17,7,24,25,4]. Vector quantization methods follow a similar principle, although these methods are based on a gradient-descend like optimization algorithm [27,13,10,8]. Other competitive methods include those based on edition [14] or condensation [3] principles. Alternative strategies include those based on subsampling [9].

For this study we consider all of the PG methods available in the comprehensive KEEL toolbox [11]. This toolbox contains implementations of most PG methods proposed so far. Initially all of the PG methods in the KEEL toolbox were considered, however, we report results on PG for NBNN only for those methods that completed the processing of the considered data set within a 2-weeks period[2]. Table 3 provides a brief description of each of the methods that were used in this study. These methods comprise a wide diversity of methodologies, besides, these are the methods that could be applied efficiently for mid-size data sets. PG methods are applied using the set of visual descriptors extracted from all of the training images, the selected prototypes are then used with NBNN and the BoVWs formulation for object recognition.

---

[1] Prototype selection is also an option [18], in this study we focused on PG techniques as these methods are more general than selective ones (e.g., they can generate prototypes outside the training set). However, for future work we will also study the suitability of prototype selectors.

[2] Experiments were performed in a workstation with Core i7-3820 processor at 3.60Ghz and 64GB in RAM.

Table 1. Considered PG methods `http://sci2s.ugr.es/pr/` for details

Method	Description	Ref.
BST3	Bootstrap technique for nearest neighbor	[9]
Condensation	Condensation PG method	[3]
AVQ	Adaptive vector quantization	[27]
DEGL	Differential Evolution using a Neighborhood-Based Mutation Operator	[24]
DSM	Decision surface mapping	[8]
GENN	Removes instances conservatively trying to maximize classification perf.	[14]
ENPC	Evolutionary algorithm that tries to maximize classification perf.	[6]
VQ/LVQ-X	Variants of the Learning Vector Quantization algorithm	[13]
IPADE	Iterative prototype adjustment based on differential evolution	[25]
MSE	PG using gradient descend and simulated annealing	[4]
POC-NN	Pairwise Opposite Class Nearest Neighbor	[20]
PSCSA	Prototype reduction using an artificial immune system	[7]
PSO	Particle Swarm Optimization	[17]
RSP	Reduction by space partitioning	[21]
SADE	Self-Adaptive Differential Evolution	[24]
SGP	Self-generating Prototypes	[5]

4   Experiments and Results

Experiments were performed using a subset of images from the Caltech-101 data set. We consider 4 categories: *camera, motorcycle, dollar bill* and *wristwatch*, see Figure 1. For each category 20 images were randomly selected for training and another 100 images for testing. This data set was collected by Chang et al. and we use in this paper exactly the same training/test partitions [2].

Fig. 1. Sample images from the training set for each of the considered categories

From each image (either for training or testing) we extracted its SIFT descriptors as described in [16], thus for each image we have a set of $128-$dimensional feature vectors. Raw SIFT-descriptors were used directly for image classification with NBNN. For the BoVW approach, training descriptors were processed with $k-$means to obtain a visual codebook, which was used to represent images; in this aspect, we performed extensive experimentation for determining the optimal value of k. A linear SVM was used as classifier for all of our experiments with BoVW. Table 2 shows some statistics for each category of the data set.

We were able to run all of the PG methods available in the KEEL toolbox. However, only 22 of these methods returned a solution within 400 hours. As future work we will explore the use of stratification [23] for making feasible the application of the rest of PG methods. Default parameters were used for all PG methods (except for $k-$means, see below).

Table 2. Characteristics of the considered data set [2]

Category	Training		Test	
	Imgs.	Descriptors	Imgs.	Descriptors
Camera	20	8,477	100	43,777
Dollar bill	20	9,986	100	66,787
Motorcycle	20	9,236	100	25,836
Wristwatch	20	9,614	100	43,158
Total	80	37,313	400	179,558

Table 3 shows the main results of this paper (see also Figure 2). We show the test-set performance obtained by the two recognition methods (NBNN and BoVW) when using each of the 22 PG techniques. Also, we show for each PG method the number of prototypes/visual words obtained ($|P|$) and, its processing time (comprising the generation of prototypes only). For completion, we report in rows 2 and 3 the performance obtained by the different methods when using (i) all of the descriptors, and (ii) k−means for generating prototypes/visual words, respectively. We emphasize that for k−means we report results obtained with the best value of k we found in preliminary experimentation, this is in order to have a strong baseline.

Several interesting findings can be drawn from Table 3. First, the results when using all of the descriptors confirm those reported in [1]: NBNN performs similarly to the BoVWs formulation (compare columns (i)−NBNN and (ii)−BOW). One should note that even when NBNN did not outperform the performance of BoVWs with k−means, for the latter method we are reporting the best configuration we found after extensive experimentation.

Regarding the suitability of PG methods for NBNN, in terms of accuracy, it can be seen that not all PG methods were useful to obtain prototypes that can compare favorably with NBNN using all of the descriptors. In fact, the performance of NBNN decreases at different rates when using most PG methods. However, the number of instances is reduced dramatically in some cases. For instance, the IPADE [25] method learned only 4 prototypes (one per class) and still it was able to obtain a performance of $\approx 65\%$. On the other hand, methods like VQ, LVQ2 [13], and DSM [8] obtained performances ($\approx 82\%$) that are close to that obtained by NBNN with all descriptors (87%), however, for these PG methods only 10% of the number of original descriptors were used.

Interestingly, prototypes generated with GENN [14] and ENPC [6] methods improved the recognition performance of NBNN, with reduction rates of 39% and 69%, respectively. In fact, results obtained with prototypes generated with the ENPC method outperform any other combination of vocabulary-generation / object-recognition methods. The combination outperforms by more than 5% to the result obtained by NBNN when using all of the descriptors. Hence, by using discriminative prototypes we are able to outperform the popular NBNN approach and using 69% less of descriptors. Therefore, this PG method not only improves the recognition performance of NBNN but also makes more efficient the classification task.

Table 3. Recognition performance for the considered PG methods. For reference we also show the performance obtained when using all of the descriptors.

ID	Description	$|P|$	Time	NBNN	BOW
(i)	All descriptors	37313	–	87.04	75
(ii)	K-means - *optimal k*	22780	01:06:41	81.50	90.50
1	AVQ	8	02:55:41	55.75	56.50
2	BST3	3731	01:03:36	74.75	87.00
3	Condensation	3731	04:04:02	72.50	82.50
4	DEGL	746	96:37:32	74.75	81.50
5	DSM	3731	01:10:36	82.00	89.75
6	ENPC	11244	201:04:57	**92.50**	89.75
7	GENN	22781	372:39:00	89.25	86.50
8	IPADE	4	01:06:14	65.25	65.00
9	LVQ 1	3731	04:32:45	81.50	**90.00**
10	LVQ 2	3731	02:02:17	82.25	**90.00**
11	LVQ 2.1	3731	02:03:45	81.50	89.50
12	LVQ 3 method	746	00:03:51	70.50	86.50
13	LVQ with pruning	3729	02:34:50	80.25	88.50
14	LVQ training counter	4	00:03:07	25.50	31.50
15	MSE	14	00:00:49	25.00	67.75
16	POC-NN	1904	245:55:10	62.25	88.00
17	PSCSA	14	25:27:40	25.00	67.75
18	PSO	746	09:35:57	53.50	78.00
19	RSP	18726	368:50:02	83.00	85.50
20	SADE	746	131:34:07	66.50	83.50
21	SGP	220	00:08:38	32.00	68.00
22	VQ	3731	02:14:36	81.50	89.75
	MAX	22781	372:39:00	92.50	90.00
	AVG.	3988.6	19:04:58	66.23	79.22
	MIN	4	00:00:49	25.00	31.50

NBNN with ENPC prototypes outperforms by 2% to the best result obtained with the BoVWs formulation. This improvement is larger than results reported in previous works that have used discriminative prototypes for codebook generation [12,15]. Actually, ENPC-NBNN outperforms the method in [2] that uses the same database we consider. This approach is based on clustering of descriptors and a Bayesian network. The method in [2] achieves average (throughout classes) recall, precision and accuracy of 90.7%, 93.3% and 94.5%, respectively. Whereas ENPC-NBNN method obtains 92.5%, 92.8% and 96.5%, in the same measures. To the best of our knowledge the results reported in this paper are the best ones so far for the data set we consider.

Regarding the performance of PG methods under the BoVWs formulation, we found that the use of some PG methods for generating the vocabulary can be beneficial: PG methods did not improve the performance of BoWVs but reduced considerably the vocabulary size. For instance, with codebooks generated with LVQ1 and LVQ2 methods one can obtain virtually the same performance as when using k−means with optimized k, but using much less visual words (a reduction of $\approx 83\%$). This result gives evidence that PG methods could be a promising solution for enhancing the BoVWs formulation. Nevertheless, we emphasize that k was optimized for k−means, whereas default parameters were used for all of the other techniques.

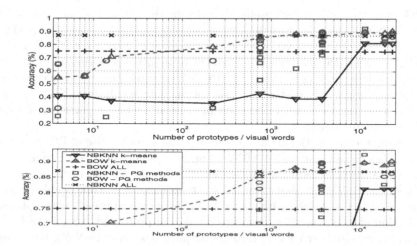

Fig. 2. Performance of NBNN and BoVWs when using the outputs of PG methods. The bottom plot is a zoom of the one in the top.

Figure 2 depicts the performances of NBNN and the BoVWs when using the outputs of PG methods (results are sorted by the number of generated prototypes used). It can be seen that for the data set we considered, the larger the number of prototypes, the better the performances of NBNN and BoVWs. We can clearly see that, for the BoVWs formulation, size seems to be more important than discriminative information: *the larger the size of the vocabulary the higher the performance*, although after $10,000$ BoVWs performance does not change significantly. Under NBNN, several PG methods that obtain more than $\approx 3,000$ prototypes perform similarly to k−means. For instance, methods 5, 9,10, 11 and 22 obtain differences in performance of less than 1% by using 83% less visual words.

Finally, regarding processing time, the most effective PG methods for BoVWs / NBNN classification we identified are also the more computationally expensive (e.g., ENPC and GENN). Although, PG is an off-line process that is performed a single time, it is important to mention that for larger data sets it would be very difficult to apply straight PG-methods. Therefore, efficient PG methods are highly needed, meanwhile stratification approaches can be adopted [23].

5   Conclusions

We described an experimental study that aims at evaluating the suitability of PG for NBNN. We reported experimental results in an object recognition task where we evaluated the performances of NBNN and BoVWs when using prototypes generated with PG methods. The conclusions of this work are as follows:

- PG methods resulted very useful for reducing the training set of descriptors for NBNN. Dramatic reductions were observed and still acceptable performance was obtained, even, when using default parameters for PG methods.
- GENN and ENPC methods improved the recognition performance of NBNN by using less training instances. ENPC achieved the best result overall and reduced significantly ($\approx 69\%$) the size of the data set. In fact, NBNN using prototypes generated with ENPC outperformed the best reported results for the considered data set.
- In general, computational efficiency is a problem on the use of PG methods for object recognition under NBNN. The best performer, ENPC, took more than 200 hours to return a solution for the data set we consider.
- Under the BoVWs formulation, PG methods can obtain comparable performance to that obtained with a traditional k−means approach with optimal selection of k, but using a much less number of prototypes/visual words.
- Vocabulary size is crucial for recognition purposes under BoVWs, but using discriminative visual words does not seem to help considerably.

Future work directions include the development of PG methods that directly optimize the NBNN criterion, and the study of stratification approaches to make scalable the application of PG methods for object recognition problems.

Acknowledgements. This work was partially supported by the LACCIR programm under project id R1212LAC006. We are grateful with I. Triguero for his valuable support on the use of KEEL.

References

1. Boiman, O., Shechtman, E., Irani, M.: In defense of nearest-neighbor based image classification. In: CVPR, pp. 1–8 (2008)
2. Chang, L., Duarte, M.M., Sucar, L.E., Morales, E.F.: A bayesian approach for object classification based on clusters of sift local features. Expert Syst. Appl. 39, 1679–1686 (2012)
3. Chen, C.H., Jozwik, A.: A sample set condensation algorithm for the class sensitive artificial neural network. Pattern Recog. Lett. 17(8), 819–823 (1996)
4. Decaestecker, C.: Finding prototypes for nearest neghbour classification by means of gradient descent and det. annealing. Pattern Recog. 30(2), 281–288 (1997)
5. Fayed, H.A., Hashem, S.R., Atiya, A.F.: Self-generating prototypes for pattern classification. Pattern Recog. 40(5), 1498–1509 (2007)
6. Fernandez, F., Isasi, P.: Evolutionary design of nearest prototype classifiers. Journal of Heuristics 10, 431–454 (2004)

7. Garain, U.: Prototype reduction using an artificial immune system. Pattern Analysis and Applications 11(3-4), 353–363 (2008)
8. Geva, S., Sitte, J.: Adaptive nearest neighbor pattern classification. IEEE Transaction on Neural Networks 2(2), 318–322 (1991)
9. Hamamoto, Y., Uchimura, S., Tomita, S.: A bootstrap technique for nearest neighbor classifier design. IEEE Trans. Pattern Anal. Mach. Intell. 19(1), 73–79 (1997)
10. Hastie, T., Tibshirani, R., Friedman, J.: The Elements of Statistical Learning. Springer (2001)
11. Alcalá-Fdez, J., et al.: Keel: A software tool to assess evolutionary algorithms to data mining problems. Soft Computing 13(3), 307–318 (2009)
12. Jiu, M., Wolf, C., Garcia, C., Baskurt, A.: Supervised learning and codebook optimization for bag-of-words models. Cogn. Comput. 4(4), 409–419 (2012)
13. Kohonen, T.: The self organizing map. Proc. of IEEE 78(9), 1464–1480 (1990)
14. Koplowitz, J., Brown, T.: On the relation of performance to editing in nearest neighbor rules. Pattern Recog. 13(3), 251–255 (1981)
15. Lazebnik, S., Raginsky, M.: Supervised learning of quantizer codebooks by information loss minimization. IEEE Trans. PAMI 31(7), 1294–1309 (2009)
16. Lowe, D.: Distinctive image features from scale-invariant keypoints. International Journal of Computer Vision 60(2), 91–110 (2004)
17. Nanni, L., Lumini, A.: Particle swarm optimization for prototype reduction. Neurocomputing 72(4-6), 1092–1097 (2008)
18. Olvera, A., Carrasco-Ochoa, J.A., Martinez-Trinidad, J.F., Kittler, J.: A review of instance selection methods. Artificial Intell. Rev. 34, 133–143 (2010)
19. Paredes, R., Vidal, E.: Learning prototypes and distances: a prototype reduction technique based on nearest neighbor error minimization. Pattern Recog. 39(2), 180–188 (2006)
20. Raicharoen, T., Lursinsap, C.: A divide-and-conquer approach to the pairwise opposite class-nearest neighbor (poc-nn) algorithm. Pattern Recog. Lett. 26, 1554–1567 (2005)
21. Sánchez, J.S.: High training set size reduction by space partitioning and prototype abstraction. pattern recognition. Pattern Recog. 37(7), 1561–1564 (2004)
22. Triguero, I., Derrac, J., García, S., Herrera, F.: A taxonomy and experimental study on prototype generation for nearest neighbor classification. IEEE Trans. on Systems, Man, and Cybernetics–Part C 42(1), 86–100 (2012)
23. Triguero, I., Derrac, J., Herrera, F., Garcia, S.: A study of the scaling up capabilities of stratified prototype generation. In: NaBIC, pp. 297–302. IEEE (2011)
24. Triguero, I., García, S., Herrera, F.: Differential evolution for optimizing the positioning of prototypes in nearest neighbor classification. Pattern Recog. 44(4), 901–916 (2011)
25. Triguero, I., Garcia, S., Herrera, F.: Ipade: Iterative prototype adjustment for nearest neighbor classification. IEEE Trans. Neural N. 21(12), 1984–1990 (2010)
26. Tuytelaars, T., Fritz, M., Saenko, K., Darrell, T.: The NBNN kernel. In: Proc. of the International Conference on Computer Vision, pp. 1824–1831. IEEE (2011)
27. Yen, C.W., Young, C.N., Nagurka, M.L.: A vector quantization method for nearest neighbor classifier design. Pattern Recog. Lett. 25(6), 725–731 (2004)
28. Zhang, J., Marszalek, M., Lazebnik, S., Schmid, C.: Local features and kernels for classification of texture and object categories: a comprehensive study. International Journal of Computer Vision 73, 213–238 (2007)

HOOSC128:
A More Robust Local Shape Descriptor

Edgar Roman-Rangel and Stephane Marchand-Maillet

CVMLab - University of Geneva, Switzerland
{edgar.romanrangel,stephane.marchand-maillet}@unige.ch

Abstract. This work introduces a new formulation of the Histogram-of-Orientations Shape-Context (HOOSC) descriptor [9], which has shorter dimensionality and higher degree of scale and rotation invariance with respect to previous formulations. We compare the performance of our proposed formulation in terms of dimensionality, computation time, robustness against scale and rotations transformations, retrieval precision and classification accuracy. Our results show that our approach outperforms previous formulations in all cases. We also propose the use of a normalized χ^2 test to compare the robustness of descriptors of different dimensionality against scale and rotations transformations.

Keywords: Binary images, local shape descriptor, content-based image retrieval, image classification.

1 Introduction

The Histogram-of-Orientations Shape-Context (HOOSC) is a local shape descriptor that is invariant to scale and rotation transformations, and that was proposed to deal with complex shapes that are rich in fine visual details [9]. Namely, the HOOSC descriptor was introduced to deal with binary images depicting syllabic instances of the ancient Maya writing system [9], and it has proven more effective than other shape descriptors like Shape Context [1] [7] and the Network of Adjacent Segments [4]; and than descriptors for gray-scale images than cannot handle properly binary images, e.g., SIFT [6] and HOG [2].

An improved version of HOOSC, that encodes only the most informative section around the location of interest, was proposed to improve retrieval performance [10]. Although this second version achieved better retrieval performance of Maya hieroglyphs, there is no guaranty that such a formulation remains optimal for generic shapes that depict object of daily use, e.g., Fig. 1.

In this work, we introduce a new formulation of the HOOSC descriptor that we call HOOSC128. Using a dataset of generic shapes [3], we compare our proposed formulation with the two previous versions of the HOOSC descriptor [9] [10] in terms of dimensionality, computation time, degradation after scale and rotation transformations, retrieval performance, and classification accuracy. Our results show that besides the resulting shorter vector, the proposed HOOSC128 formulation produces local descriptors of higher invariance to scale and rotation

J.F. Martínez-Trinidad et al. (Eds.): MCPR 2014, LNCS 8495, pp. 172–181, 2014.
© Springer International Publishing Switzerland 2014

Fig. 1. Some instances of the dataset of generic objects used in this work [3]

transformations, which in turn allow to achieve better retrieval and classification performance. Namely, the contributions of this work are:

1. A new formulation of the HOOSC descriptor which has shorter dimensionality and higher discriminative capabilities with respect to previous formulations. It is also more robust against scale and rotation transformations.
2. A thorough comparison of our proposed HOOSC128 definition with respect to two previous formulations. This comparison is both quantitative (dimensionality, computation time, robustness against scale and rotations transformations) and qualitative (retrieval and classification performance).
3. A normalized χ^2 test that we propose to compare the robustness of descriptors of different dimensionality after image transformations.

The rest of this paper is organized as follows. Section 2 explains the previous versions of the HOOSC descriptor, and it introduces our proposed HOOSC128 formulation. Section 3 describes the dataset and experimental protocol followed during our experiments. This section also introduces the normalized χ^2 test we used to compare descriptors of different dimensionality. Section 4 discusses our results. And section 5 presents our conclusions.

2   HOOSC Descriptor

The HOOSC method consists in the local description of a point of interest, which can be selected by a uniform random sampling of all the points in the shape contour [1]. Namely, this is a function of the local orientation of its neighbouring points, i.e., the orientation of the contour at the position of such points [9].

The original HOOSC formulation [9], which we refer to as HOOSC0, organizes the set of points around the point of interest by using the same log-polar grid that was first introduced as a support for the Shape Context descriptor [1]. This log-polar grid divides the local vicinity around the point of interest into 12 radial intervals uniformly spaced in steps of $\pi/6$ radians, and 5 distance intervals that are logarithmically spaced from $0.125T$ to $2T$, where the parameter T corresponds to the average pairwise distance between all pair of point selected for local description for a given shape. Therefore, the resulting grid contains 60 regions. Fig. 2a shows an example of this log-polar grid.

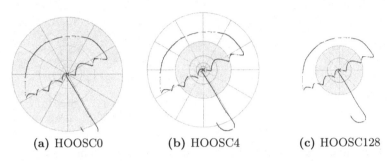

(a) HOOSC0   (b) HOOSC4   (c) HOOSC128

Fig. 2. Polar grids used by the different HOOSC formulations. The area in orange color correspond to the distance scope that is described by each formulation. HOOSC0 is to the original version of the descriptor [9]. HOOSC4 corresponds to an improved version [10], note that the most internal distance interval is in white color as it is not used for description. HOOSC128 is our proposed formulation, note that there are only 2 distance intervals and 8 radial intervals.

After organizing the neighbouring points into the log-polar grid, an 8-bin histogram is built for each of the 60 regions by integrating the local orientation of each of the points within such a region. Such an integration is done using a Gaussian kernel [9]. Finally, all the 60 8-bin histograms are stacked together to build the HOOSC0 descriptor, which therefore, consists in a 480-D vector.

A second formulation of the HOOSC descriptor was proposed to deal with very complex visual structures [10]. Following the naming convention used by Roman-Rangel et al., [10], we refer to this second formulation as HOOSC4. This formulation also relies on the same log-polar grid with the 12 radial intervals. However, instead of using all the 5 distance intervals, it only uses the intervals 2 to 4, which have shown to be the most informative for very complex structures, i.e., it removes the histograms with higher chance to be all zeros, thus increasing the discriminative potential of the descriptor. Fig 2b highlights the distance intervals used by the HOOSC4 formulation.

2.1 HOOSC128

We noticed that it is beneficial to merge the three most internal distance intervals of the log-polar grid, i.e., the intervals with outer boundaries at $0.125T$, $0.25T$ and $0.5T$. There are two reasons for this.

First, the most internal interval is very sparse as it often contains information only about the point of interest [10], as already pointed out. Second, the second and third distance intervals are very local and close to each other, that their respective histograms are often very similar. Based on our observations, we confirmed that the most external distance interval is often empty indeed [10]. Therefore, we propose to use only two distance intervals at $0.5T$ and T. Such wider distance intervals increase the scale invariance potential of the descriptor.

Also, we noticed that 12 radial interval is an excessive splitting of the local context, which harms the potential of the descriptor to be robust enough against rotation transformations. Thus, we propose to use only 8 radial intervals uniformly spaced at steps of $\pi/4$ radians.

The resulting descriptor is a 128-D vector which we call HOOSC128. Fig. 2c shows an example of the resulting polar grid. As shown in section 4, the HOOSC128 allows for better retrieval and classification performance.

Similar to the previous HOOSC formulations, we normalize the HOOSC128 independently per distance interval. Therefore, while HOOSC0 might sum up to 5 and HOOSC4 up to 3, the proposed HOOSC128 might sum up to 2.

3 Experiments

This section describes the dataset and the experimental protocol that we used to compare the following three HOOSC formulations:

- **HOOSC0:** corresponds to the original HOOSC descriptor [9] which uses the log-polar grid of 5 distance intervals and 12 radial intervals.
- **HOOSC4:** corresponds to the HOOSC descriptor that only uses the most informative section of the distance scope of the log-polar grid, i.e., the second, third, and fourth distance intervals [10], and 12 radial intervals.
- **HOOSC128:** is our proposed formulation described in section 2.1. This formulation divides the polar grid into 2 distance and 8 radial intervals.

3.1 Dataset

The dataset we used to compare the performance of the three HOOSC formulations consists in a collection of 20,000 manual sketches of generic objects [3]. This dataset has 250 visual classes, each of which contains 80 instances.

For experimental purposes, we organized the dataset into 4 disjoint folds of equal size. More precisely, we assigned randomly each of the 80 instances per class to one of the four folds, thus having 20 instances per class in each fold.

Note that the manual sketches in the dataset might have different sizes, however, all of them are centered inside a frame of 1111x1111 pixels. For efficient experimental performance, we resized all images to 256x256 pixels.

3.2 Statistical Validation

We started by comparing the dimensionality of the three HOOSC formulations, as well as the time they require to compute local descriptors.

After the initial comparison, we also compared their potential for scale and rotation invariance. To this end, we randomly selected 100 points from each class in the dataset, thus 25000 points. For each of these selected points, we computed its three versions of the HOOSC descriptor after applying either a scale or rotation transformation to its source image, as well as the corresponding re-localization of the point of interest in the transformed image. Namely, we used the logarithmic set $\{0.25x, 0.5x, 1x, 2x, 4x\}$ as scaling factors, and the set $\{0°, 30°, 60°, 90°, 120°, 150°, 180°\}$ for the rotation angles.

Note that the re-localization of a point of interest in the transformed images is a straightforward computation of the form,

$$x' = s \times x, \qquad y' = s \times y, \tag{1}$$

where x and y denote the coordinates of the point of interest in the source image, s is the scaling factor, and x' and y' correspond to the coordinates of the point in the scaled image. Likewise, the re-localization of the points of interest in the rotated images is obtained by,

$$x' = x \cos\theta - y \sin\theta, \qquad y' = x \sin\theta + y \cos\theta, \tag{2}$$

where θ indicates the angle of rotation.

After computing the HOOSC descriptors from the transformed images, we compared them with their corresponding descriptors computed from the original image. This comparison was done using the χ^2 test statistic, which statistically indicates the degree in which the observed frequency in each dimension of the HOOSC vector is preserved after the transformation. More precisely, we used the following normalized χ^2 metric as a measure of distance,

$$\chi^2\left(\mathbf{o}, \mathbf{t}\right) = \frac{1}{|\mathbf{o}|} \cdot \sum_{i=1}^{|\mathbf{o}|} \frac{\left(o_i - t_i\right)^2}{o_i + t_i}, \tag{3}$$

where, $\mathbf{o}$ and $\mathbf{t}$ denote two HOOSC vectors computed, at the same point of interest, from the original and the transformed images respectively, and $|\cdot|$ is the cardinality operator indicating the size of the vector. Note the use of the denominator $|\mathbf{o}|$ as a normalization parameter. This normalization is required since the simple summation would result in values of different order of magnitude for descriptors of different dimensionality, and therefore hinder their comparison.

3.3   Retrieval and Classification Performance

We also report the retrieval and classification performance achieved by each of the three HOOSC formulations. For this purpose, we represented each shape using the Bag-of-Visual-Words (BoW) approach [8] [12]. More precisely, we estimated visual vocabularies of 1000 visual words for each HOOSC formulation by using the k-means clustering algorithm [5]. Then, we quantized each local descriptor into one of the visual words in the corresponding vocabulary.

For the retrieval performance case, we report the mean average precision of the first 30 ranked elements (mAP@30), as well as the curves of the average precision versus the standard recall. For the classification performance case, we used the kNN classifier with majority voting, and we report the average classification accuracy as a function of the number of nearest neighbours.

In both cases, retrieval and classification performance evaluations, we relied on a cross-validation approach using the four folds of the data, as explained in section 3.1. We used the L1 norm to compare pairs of BoW representations.

4   Results

This section presents the results of our evaluations. First we compare the dimensionality and computation time of each HOOSC method, followed by a statistical analysis of their scale and rotation invariance capabilities. Then we present the retrieval and classification performance achieved by each method.

4.1   Dimensionality and Computation Time

Using each of the three HOOSC formulations, we computed the local descriptors for all 20000 shapes in the dataset and compared the average computation time.

As shown in Table 1, the dimensionality of the proposed HOOSC128 is considerably lower than the dimensionality of the other two formulations, which in turn results in faster computations, i.e., 37.5% and 16.7% of improvement with respect to the HOOSC0 and HOOSC4 respectively.

Table 1. Vector size and average time for the three HOOSC formulations

Formulation	HOOSC0	HOOSC4	HOOSC128
Dimensionality	480	288	128
Computation time (s)	0.08 ± 0.04	0.06 ± 0.03	0.05 ± 0.02

Table 2 shows the time required by the k-means algorithm [5] to cluster 100 points randomly selected from each class into 1000 clusters. As we can see, the time improves considerably as the dimensionality of the descriptor decreases.

Table 2. Time in seconds required by the k-means clustering algorithm and the three HOOSC formulations to cluster 25000 local descriptors into 1000 clusters

Formulation	HOOSC0	HOOSC4	HOOSC128
Time (s)	3,044.7	1,760.6	703.3

4.2   Scale and Rotation Invariance

As shown in Fig. 3a, all three HOOSC formulations incur in high levels of degradation when an image is scaled to 25% of its original size. This degradation is much lower for the scaling factors of 0.5, 2, and 4. Note that scaling factor of 1 corresponds to a simple copy of the source image, where no degradation happens.

The bars in Fig. 3a also show that the HOOSC0 formulation produces higher degradation rates. The reason for this is the last distance interval, which in this formulation varies a lot after the scale transformation. Although the HOOSC4 formulation varies much less than HOOSC0, it remains less stable than the

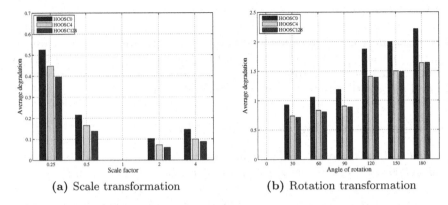

(a) Scale transformation   (b) Rotation transformation

Fig. 3. Average degradation after scale and rotation transformations for the three versions of the HOOSC descriptor. The degradation is measured by the χ^2 statistic for 25000 points randomly selected from binary images.

proposed HOOSC128 formulation, whose local descriptors are more consistent across scale transformations.

Similar to the degradation rates after scale transformations, we compare the degradation of the local descriptors after rotation transformations in Fig. 3b. In this case, both HOOSC4 and HOOSC128 are far more stable than the original HOOSC0, with HOOSC128 exhibiting a slight higher consistency in all cases.

4.3   Retrieval Performance

Besides the statistical comparison of the three HOOSC formulations, we also compared their performance in a retrieval scenario. Table 3 presents the mAP@30 obtained with the three variants of the HOOSC descriptor. As we can see, the proposed HOOSC128 achieves 1.8% and 3.8% of improvement in retrieval precision, in absolute terms, with respect to HOOSC0 and HOOSC4 respectively.

Table 3. Mean average precision of the 30 first retrieved elements by each of the three formulations of the HOOSC descriptor

Formulation	HOOSC0	HOOSC4	HOOSC128
mAP@30	0.267	0.247	0.285

Fig. 4 shows the average precision curves as a function of the standard recall rates. Note that in general, HOOSC4 performs lower than HOOSC0, and HOOSC128 improves the performance at all standard intervals.

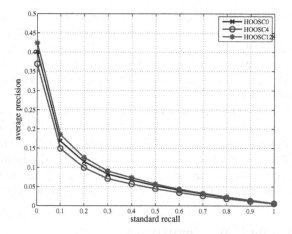

Fig. 4. Retrieval performance: average precision curves versus standard recall rates for the three formulations of the HOOSC descriptor

4.4   Classification Accuracy

Fig. 5 shows that the classification performance of three HOOSC formulation remains comparable with the retrieval results. More specifically, HOOSC4 performs the worst in this dataset, whereas HOOSC128 achieves the best classification performance.

In our results, the best performance was achieved using $k = 2$ nearest neighbours, which is different from the results reported by Eitz et al., [3], where the best performance for kNN with hard assignment is obtained with $k = 5$. However, note that we have two variations with respect to them: 1) they use SIFT

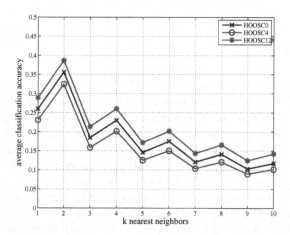

Fig. 5. Classification performance: average classification accuracy for the three formulations of the HOOSC descriptor using the kNN approach

descriptors [6] and a vocabulary of 500 visual words; and 2) they used full cross-validation instead of the 4-fold cross-validation that we implemented. Moreover, using all the elements in the dataset to train their kNN classifier, they obtained about 38% of classification accuracy with kNN and hard assignment (see Fig. 10 in Eitz et al., [3]), whereas we reached 38.67% with only 20 training elements in each fold, as shown in Fig. 5.

Furthermore, the HOOSC method seems to be a more suitable local descriptor for the binary shapes of the dataset than the well known SIFT descriptor [6], as in Eitz et al., [3], the classification accuracy obtained with 20 training elements is only about 27.5%. This observation is consistent with the intuition that the SIFT descriptor was designed to exploit the local details of intensity images [6], whereas the HOOSC descriptor was tailored to deal with binary images [9].

4.5 Evaluation on Maya Hieroglyphs

Finally we evaluated whether the proposed HOOSC128 outperforms HOOSC0 and HOOSC4 retrieving and classifying a set of shapes of the same nature as those for which they were proposed [9] [10]. To this end, we repeated the same experimental protocol used for the generic shapes on a dataset of 6240 Maya syllables equally distributed over 24 classes [11].

Table 4 shows that HOOSC128 also outperforms both HOOSC0 and HOOSC4 in retrieval performance.

Table 4. Mean average precision (mAP) achieved by the three HOOSC formulations on a dataset of Maya hieroglyphs

Formulation	HOOSC0	HOOSC4	HOOSC128
mAP	0.470	0.442	0.486

5 Conclusions

We proposed a new formulation of the HOOSC descriptor [9] called HOOSC128, which has smaller dimensionality with respect to previous formulations [9], [10].

We also proposed the use of a normalized χ^2 statistic to compare the capabilities of invariance against scale and rotations transformations of three formulations of the HOOSC descriptor that have different dimensionality.

Using a dataset of generic shapes, we also compared the performance of the three HOOSC formulations in the tasks of shape-based image retrieval and image classification. Our results show that the HOOSC128 formulation is more robust to scale and rotation transformations, and it achieves better retrieval and classifications performance than the previous formulations. Similar results were obtained during a retrieval experiment on a dataset of Maya hieroglyphs.

Acknowledgments. This research was supported by the Secretariat for Education and Research (SEK) under the grant C11.0043, supporting our participation in the COST ACTION MUMIA.

References

1. Belongie, S., Malik, J., Puzicha, J.: Shape Matching and Object Recognition Using Shape Contexts. IEEE Transactions on Pattern Analysis and Machine Intelligence 24(4), 509–522 (2002)
2. Dalal, N., Triggs, B.: Histograms of Oriented Gradients for Human Detection. In: IEEE Conference on Computer Vision and Pattern Recognition (2005)
3. Eitz, M., Hays, J., Alexa, M.: How Do Humans Sketch Objects? ACM Transactions on Graphics (TOG) – SIGGRAPH 2012 Conference Proc. 31(4), 44 (2012)
4. Ferrari, V., Fevrier, L., Jurie, F., Schmid, C.: Groups of Adjacent Contours for Object Detection. IEEE Transactions on Pattern Analysis and Machine Intelligence 30(1), 36–51 (2008)
5. Lloyd, S.: Least square quantization in PCM. IEEE Transactions on Information Theory 28(2), 129–137 (1982)
6. Lowe, D.: Distinctive Image Features from Scale-Invariant Keypoints. International Journal of Computer Vision 60(2), 91–110 (2004)
7. Mori, G., Belongie, S., Malik, J.: Efficient Shape Matching Using Shape Contexts. IEEE Transactions on Pattern Analysis and Machine Intelligence 27(11), 1832–1837 (2005)
8. Quelhas, P., Monay, F., Odobez, J.-M., Gatica-Perez, D., Tuytelaars, T.: A Thousand Words in a Scene. IEEE Transactions on Pattern Analysis and Machine Intelligence 29(9), 1575–1589 (2007)
9. Roman-Rangel, E., Pallan, C., Odobez, J.-M., Gatica-Perez, D.: Analyzing Ancient Maya Glyph Collections with Contextual Shape Descriptors. International Journal in Computer Vision, Special Issue in Cultural Heritage and Art Preservation 94(1), 101–117 (2011)
10. Roman-Rangel, E., Pallan, C., Odobez, J.-M., Gatica-Perez, D.: Searching the Past: An Improved Shape Descriptor to Retrieve Maya Hieroglyphs. In: ACM International Conference in Multimedia (2011)
11. Roman-Rangel, E., Marchand-Maillet, S.: Stopwords Detection in Bag-of-Visual-Words: The Case of Retrieving Maya Hieroglyphs. In: International Workshop on Multimedia for Cultural Heritage, The International Conference on Image Analysis and Processing (2013)
12. Sivic, J., Zisserman, A.: Video google: A text retrieval approach to object matching in videos. In: IEEE International Conference on Computer Vision (2003)

An Approach for Multi-pose Face Detection Exploring Invariance by Training

Eanes Torres Pereira, Herman Martins Gomes, and João Marques de Carvalho

Universidade Federal de Campina Grande
{eanes,hmg}@computacao.ufcg.edu.br, carvalho@dee.ufcg.edu.br

Abstract. In this paper, a rotation invariant approach for face detection is proposed. The approach consists of training specific Haar cascades for ranges of in-plane face orientations, varying from coarse to fine. As the Haar features are not robust enough to cope with high in-plane rotations over many different images, they are trained only until an accented decay in precision is evident. When that happens, the range of orientations is divided up into sub-ranges, and this procedure continues until a predefined rotation range is reached. The effectiveness of the approach is evaluated on a face detection problem considering two well-known data sets: CMU-MIT [1] and FDDB [2]. When tested using CMU-MIT dataset, the proposed approach achieved accuracies higher than the traditional methods such as the ones proposed by Viola and Jones [3] and Rowley et al.[1]. The proposed approach has also achieved a large area under the ROC curve and true positive rates that were higher than the rates of all the published methods tested over the FDDB dataset.

Keywords: face detection, orientation invariance by training, adaboost, haar features, tree of classifiers.

1   Introduction

The human face is a very important way of expressing emotions and the ability to recognise them is fundamental for interpersonal social interaction and for human-computer interaction [4]. Many approaches have been proposed for face detection [5–7, 3, 8, 9], among then those which presented higher accuracies use some variation of Adaboost and weak classifiers. Although the successful application of face detection in real life situations, pose variation still remains a challenge. The approach proposed in this paper is inspired by the JointBoost method [10–12] and aims to share features of different face poses to achieve pose invariant face detection.

The Rowley et al. [6] work contains one of the first successful classifier combination approaches for rotation invariant face detection. The kernel of that detector is composed of three neural networks. The first neural network is called router, which is designed the function to determine the rotation angle of the candidate window. The router network has three layers: the first with 400 neurons (corresponding to the quantity of pixels in the image with resolution

J.F. Martínez-Trinidad et al. (Eds.): MCPR 2014, LNCS 8495, pp. 182–191, 2014.
© Springer International Publishing Switzerland 2014

20 × 20 pixels), the hidden layer has 15 neurons, and the output layer has 36 neurons (corresponding to variations from 0° to 360° augmented by 10°).

The rotation angle is classified by the router network. The face candidate is rotated to an upright position, and is given as input to two other neural networks independently trained. The result of the two neural networks is combined by a logical *AND*. The candidate face is only classified as face if the two networks agree in classification. Rowley et al. [6] commented on the necessity of using bootstrapping to acquire representative samples of non-face images, and to explain how they used it. The images used for testing their method are available on-line, and nowadays are commonly used to evaluate face detection approaches. This set of images is known as CMU-MIT face database.

Although the approach proposed by Rowley et al. [6] used a simple combination of classifiers, it has the drawback that all classifiers need to process every candidate window. Viola and Jones [3] proposed a method to deal with that problem. Their method combines a fast and simple feature extractor (Haar-like features [13]) with a weak classifier combination method (AdaBoost [14]).

Among the appearance based object detection approaches, the one proposed by Viola and Jones [3, 8] has achieved greater popularity and more promising results in the area. Within their framework, there are contributions to classifier training as well as to the procedure of scrutinising the image searching for objects. There followed a great number of approaches, all of them further extending that method.

For example, Huang et al. [15] proposed the training of classifiers using Sparse Granular Features and Vector Boosting. Another variation of that method is the use of Width-First-Search (WFS) to traverse the search tree. A distinctive feature of the WFS approach is that it is possible to traverse more than one path through the tree at a time. If more than one leaf is achieved at the end of the traversal, than the leaf of higher degree of confidence is used for classification. Huang et al. [15] tested their detector by using the CMU-MIT images [1] and detected correctly, for the frontal face image set, more than 97% of the faces, with less than 100 false positives.

Another variation of the Viola and Jones framework was recently proposed by Vural et al. [16]. The major contribution of the authors is the use of rotated versions of Haar-like features with angles ranging from 0° to 180°. As the authors proposed a multi-view approach, they used a combination of trained cascades to achieve such aim. In the case of face detection, they used 6 different cascades (frontal, right, left, up, down, profile) combined by neural networks to correctly classify the faces. As the used features are more powerful, lower training time is needed for training the cascades, and less features are selected to create the cascade. They tested their detector on images and videos and obtained higher results than those implemented by the Viola and Jones approach available in the OpenCV library[1], which processed images of 4 mega-pixel in 15fps. A criticism to this experimental evaluation is that they did not use any well-known face image databases to evaluate their approach, such as CMU-MIT [1] or FDDB [2].

---

[1] http://opencv.willowgarage.com/wiki/

The AdaBoost term is an acronym for adaptive boosting. It was coined by Freund and Schapire [14] to name the process of adaptively weighting classifiers in combinations such that the weak classifiers receive more attention (high weights) than the strong ones. The weights are computed based on the classification rates of each corresponding classifier, those which obtain higher hit rates are assigned lower weights, and those that achieve lower rates are assigned higher weights. Many variations of AdaBoost were proposed after the publication of the first approach. The main difference among them is the method of assigning the weights based on the classifier accuracies. For instance, the Gentle AdaBoost uses an exponential function to relate classifications with weights, and it is described by Friedman et al. [17]. Friedman et al. [17] handle the AdaBoost algorithm using an additive model $F(x) = \sum_{m=1}^{M} c_m f_m(x)$, where c_m is constant that depends on the expectation over the training data. Each f_m is a separate function for each input variable. This leads to the interpretation of each feature as a weak classifier.

Within the above context, this paper presents a method for detecting faces at different in-plane orientations with any degree of rotation in image plane; with precision rates equal or higher than those obtained by other popular approaches such as those proposed by Rowley et al. [6] and Viola and Jones [8]. However, the proposed method uses less features and is trained faster than the methods proposed by Rowley et al. [6], Viola and Jones [8], and Huang et al.[15]. An approach that shares features among different poses was conceived. The proposed approach achieves in-plane invariance by training when using cascades of Haar-like features and Adaboost. The major objective of using invariance by training is to reduce the quantity of nodes in the classifier tree, and, consequently, this reduces the detection complexity.

2   Sharing Features for Multi-pose Face Detection

The method JointBoost [10–12] may be used to share features among multiple image classes. Considering different views of the same object as different classes, one may create a multi-pose classifier by employing this method. This will be explained here as a start point for the approach proposed in this paper.

Torralba et al. [12] argue that it is possible to demonstrate, subjectively (by means of visual inspection) as well as objectively (by evaluating the features extracted from images) that some characteristics of frontal faces are present on profile faces. In the same way, characteristics of non-rotated frontal faces are present in in-plane rotated frontal faces. This observation may be extended to other object categories, such as: cars, houses, and animals. From this reasoning, Torralba et al. [12] proposed a boosting approach for multi-class problem classification, the JointBoost.

In the JointBoost approach, at every cycle of weak classifier computation, the chosen feature would be that which has the lowest classification error for the highest number of different classes. Thus, one may assert that the feature is shared among different classes. The authors say that their experiments showed that classifiers jointly trained (using JointBoost) tend to select features that generalise well for various classes. Generally, those features are edges and blobs.

Haar-like features, such as those used by Viola and Jones [8], may also be used to generalise among multiple classes. However, such generalisation power is limited, i.e., it is not possible to obtain rotation invariance by training a classifier using only that type of features. In this paper, the term *rotation invariance by training* refers to training a Haar cascade, with GentleBoost, with rotating face images in-plane.

3   Proposed Approach

As a preliminary step of the present research, a number of experiments were performed in order to verify the possibility of training a rotation invariant face classifier simply by varying the training face rotations. Those experiments were to no avail. However, some important insights were drawn from those experiments. First, the classifier trained with Haar-like features could not generalise frontal faces in any in-plane rotation angle; however, until obtaining a number of training stages, the training converged well. As more stages are trained, the classification problem becomes more complex, and the available features cannot adequately generalise. Another idea inspired by those experiments is that classifiers obtained with invariance by training, but with a reduced set of stages, may be combined to yield a multi-pose classifier tree. Based on those observations, this section presents the proposed approach.

Figure 1 shows a simplified representation of a classifier tree obtained with invariance by training, and with reduced quantity of stages. This classifier tree may be used to detect frontal faces with any in-plane rotation. The tree root is a cascade with at most 5 stages, and it classifies frontal faces in any in-plane rotation. As the tree is binary, the orientation ranges are divided by two as the classification is propagated through the tree. The division by two allows more specific classifiers to be used in deeper tree levels. Besides, as in previous approaches, the false positives quantities go down exponentially at each tree level.

The circle on right left-hand side of the classifier tree illustrates the orientation pattern of faces. The pattern differs from the trigonometric circle, which establishes the angle of $0°$ corresponding to the angle of $270°$ presented in Figure 1. The difference between the patterns is simply an offset of $90°$ in such a way that the $0°$ corresponds to the upright face image.

Another important feature of the presented classifier tree is that each leaf actuates within a range of $20°$. Consequently, the classifiers in the leafs must be trained with face images that have a variation of $\pm10°$ in relation to the angle that labels the leaf. Besides, the neighbour leafs have an intersection of $10°$ in their angle coverage ranges. Thus, the central angle of a leaf corresponds to the *edge* angle of the neighbour leaf.

The arrangement of angle ranges of the leafs was designed to allow redundancy and reinforcement of the classification to possibly difficult angles, e.g. cases in

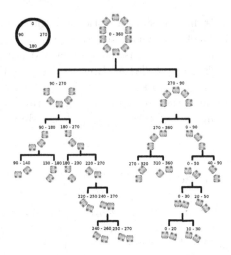

Fig. 1. Classifier tree for in-plane rotated frontal faces

which few training face samples have been used. The redundancy also allows that the candidate window be classified by more than one leaf. The leaf that will be used to classify such window will be the one that obtains the highest confidence level (which may be a threshold or a probability).

4   Experimental Evaluation

For training the cascades, 10,000 frontal face images and 10,000 profile face images were cropped from the following image databases: BioID [18], Caltech [19], CMU-PIE [20], YaleB [21] and Color FERET [22]. At each stage, 20,000 non-face image crops were used. The non-face images were selected from the author's personal images and from Naotoshi Seo web site on training Haar cascades[2]. In this section, two sets of experiments are described: experiments using the FDDB image database, and experiments using the CMU-MIT image database.

4.1   Detector Evaluation Using the FDDB Image Database

The FDDB image database (FDDB - Face Detection Data Base) [2] is a benchmark for evaluation of face detectors, without condition restrictions. That base has a companion protocol to evaluate the results obtained by the detectors applied on its images. The major motivation for the creation of the FDDB was the absence of coherent methods to compare face detectors. One image database traditionally used to evaluate face detectors is the CMU-MIT, which was used in its final version by Schneiderman and Kanade [23].

However, up to the creation of the FDDB, the image databases previously used to evaluate face detectors neither required, nor proposed an evaluation

---

[2] http://note.sonots.com/SciSoftware/haartraining.html

protocol. These bases were composed by a set of images accompanied by files containing the coordinates of the faces or some fiducial points. It must also be taken into account the fact that some face detectors are not available to the research community for evaluation. For example, one of the most popular face detectors, the detector proposed by Viola and Jones [8] has no available official implementation by the authors. A closer match of Viola and Jones' detector is implemented in OpenCV [24], which comes accompanied by some XML files with trained cascades for face detection. However, the results obtained by those detectors are inferior to the results published by Viola and Jones [8].

Apart from providing the images and the ground-truth, the FDDB provides the code that will be used to count the hits and errors. The measure used to count detection as a hit corresponds to the ratio between the area of intersection and the area of union of both the detected region and the labelled region [2]. The faces are annotated by using elliptical regions; however, the code performs the necessary conversions to compatible detection results that were marked as rectangles. The authors presented as features of their base: (1) the great quantity of images and faces: 2845 and 5171, respectively; (2) a great range of difficulties (occlusions, poses, low resolution, and faces with bad focus); (3) the specification of face regions using elliptical regions.

There are two ways to evaluate detectors using the FDDB: 10-fold cross-validation and training without restrictions. In the first case, the cumulative performance is reported as a mean curve of the 10 ROC curves (Receiver Operating Characteristic). In the second case, one is allowed to use images that are not part of the base to train the classifiers. However, in this case, the set is also divided into 10 parts, and the resulting ROC curve is obtained from the average of curves. The experimental mode was applied without restrictions in order to evaluate the proposed method. At the time this paper was written, all results presented on the FDDB site did use such experimentation mode.

Another peculiarity of the FDDB is that there are two evaluation metrics: the discrete metric and the continuous metric. The discrete metric counts as hit at every detection at which the ratio between the area of intersection and area of union with the ground-truth region is higher than 0.5. The continuous metric assigns a score to the detection equivalent to the ratio between areas of intersection and union.

On the result page of the FDDB's site[3] there are ROC curves for face detectors that had published papers and results without announced publications. The graphics of the ROC curves are separately presented as: one graphic pair (with continuous and discrete metrics, respectively) for the detectors whose methods were published, and a pair of graphics for the detectors whose approaches were not published. Among the detectors with published methods, those with higher results were proposed by Li et al. [25]. Other published results used for comparison are the results obtained by Jain and Miller [26], Subburaman and Marcel [27]. The OpenCV implementation represents the Viola and Jones approach [3].

---

[3] http://vis-www.cs.umass.edu/fddb/results.html

In Figures 2(a) and 2(b), detection results are presented for the two metrics. The curves labelled as *LiEtAl* refer to the results with the highest results found in the FDDB's site.

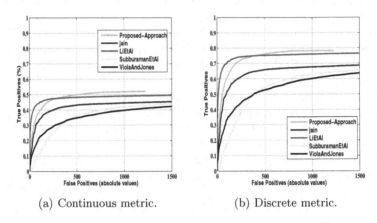

(a) Continuous metric.   (b) Discrete metric.

Fig. 2. Comparison of face detection results in the FDDB database

The results showed in Figures 2(a) and 2(b) were obtained by using the following methods: upright frontal detector trained via the proposed approach, the Jain and Miller detector [26] (which are the authors of FDDB), the Li et al. [25] detector, the Subburaman and Marcel [27] detector, and by the Viola and Jones detector represented by OpenCV implementation [24]. The small areas under the ROC curves are due to the fact that the base is composed by images of faces in different poses, and the detectors were trained only for frontal face detection with extreme in-plane rotations.

4.2   Detector Evaluation Using the CMU-MIT Image Database

To the best of our knowledge, the image database that has been largely used for rotation invariant face detector evaluation is the CMU-MIT [6]. The FDDB database has variations in-plane and out-of-plane, but does not present extreme variations (e.g., up-side down faces). Additionally, the CMU-MIT has been mostly used to compare results of diverse approaches. Figure 3 presents the results of face detection by using the rotated set of CMU-MIT images for four detectors: the proposed approach, the Jones and Viola's detector [28], the Rowley et al.'s detector [6], and the Huang et al.'s detector [15]. The curves which represent the results obtained by Jones and Viola [28] and Rowley et al. [6] were constructed from the tables of results reported in their corresponding papers.

The curve representing the results of Rowley et al. [6] has a sawtooth shape as it was obtained by the interpolation of just four points. The hit rate verification metric used in that approach is similar to the one mentioned by Lienhart

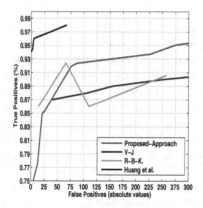

Fig. 3. Face detection results in the CMU-MIT rotated images (rotated set) database

et al. [29]. The results obtained by Huang et al. [15] are very high, with true positive rates higher than 90% without the occurrence of any false positive. A possible criticism to those results is related to its range of variation: Why did not the authors vary the parameters of testing sufficiently to show the results for quantities of false positives higher than 100? Another fact to be questioned is that Huang et al. [15] did not mention which metric was used to measure the hits, and they did not comment on the use of distances between the centers of the regions or on the use of the face areas.

In terms of complexity, the algorithms that use tree of classifiers may be compared by the quantity of stages. The detector created by Jones and Viola [28] is composed of two cascades: one to estimate rotation (with 11 stages), and another to distinguish between face and non-face (35 stages). Thus, according to this approach, a face candidate must pass through 46 stages of evaluation to be classified as face.

The face detector proposed by Huang et al. [15] has 234 nodes (each node corresponds to a weak classifier) and 18 stages. The classifier tree proposed in this paper has 192 nodes and 6 stages. It has 64 nodes for each view: frontal, left profile, and right profile. Thus, a candidate window should pass through less nodes, and less classification stages, when submitted to the detector proposed in this paper. Besides, the range of rotation angles used by the proposed detector are better fine-grained ($\pm 10°$) in relation to the range of Huang et al. [15]($\pm 15°$), that allows for much higher precision when estimating rotation angle.

Huang et al.[15] did not explain why they did not evaluate their detector using the CMU-MIT image test set without extreme rotations (Test Sets A, B, and C). Possibly, their detector would present inferior results, because it was trained with face images with resolution of 24×24 pixels, and it is known the mentioned image set has many images with lower resolution.

5   Conclusion

In this paper, a new approach for rotation invariant object detection is proposed. The major feature of the proposed approach is the rotation by training, in which sets of rotated images are presented in the classifier training stage and the features that best describe that set of rotated images are selected for usage as part of weak classifiers. The proposed approach demonstrates the viability of using weak and non-invariant features in order to obtain a robust and rotation invariant object detector. This is possible due to the fact that Haar-like features exhibit some degree of generalisation among multiple classes that may be exploited using classifier trees as it was explained in Section 2. Two well-known image databases were used for experimental evaluation: CMU-MIT, and FDDB. The proposed approach was evaluated in a face detection scenario and obtained better results than all the other published approaches evaluated on FDDB image database. The proposed approach obtained higher precisions than those of Rowley et al. [6] and Jones and Viola [28].

References

1. Rowley, H., Baluja, S., Kanade, T.: Neural network-basead face detection. IEEE Trans. Pattern Anal. Machine Intell. 20, 23–38 (1998)
2. Jain, V., Learned-Miller, E.: Fddb: A benchmark for face detection in unconstrained settings. Technical report, University of Massachusetts, Amherst (2010) (Relatório Técnico UM-CS-2010-009)
3. Viola, P., Jones, M.: Robust real-time object detection. In: Second Int. Workshop on Statistical and Computational Theories of Vision – Modeling, Learning, Computing, and Sampling, pp. 1–25 (2001)
4. Gong, S., Xiang, T.: Visual Analysis of Behaviour: From Pixels to Semantics. Springer (2011)
5. Sung, K.K., Poggio, T.: Example-based learning for view-based human face detection. IEEE Trans. Pattern Anal. Machine Intell. 20(1), 39–51 (1998)
6. Rowley, H., Baluja, S., Kanade, T.: Rotation invariant neural network-based face detection. In: Proc. of IEEE Conf. on Computer Vision and Pattern Recognition, pp. 38–44 (1998)
7. Schneiderman, H., Kanade, T.: A statistical model for 3d object detection applied to faces and cars. In: IEEE Conference on Computer Vision and Pattern Recognition, pp. 1–6 (2000)
8. Viola, P., Jones, M.J.: Robust real-time face detection. Int. J. of Comp. Vis. 57(2), 137–154 (2004)
9. Chen, H.Y., Huang, C.L., Fu, C.M.: Hybrid-boost learning for multi-pose face detection and facial expression recognition. In: IEEE International Conference on Multimedia and Expo., pp. 671–674 (2007)
10. Torralba, A., Murphy, K.P., Freeman, W.T.: Sharing features: efficient boosting procedures for multiclass object detection. In: Proc. of the IEEE Computer Society Conf. on Computer Vision and Pattern Recognition - CVPR, pp. 762–769 (2004)
11. Torralba, A., Murphy, K.P., Freeman, W.T.: Shared features for multiclass object detection. In: Ponce, J., Hebert, M., Schmid, C., Zisserman, A. (eds.) Toward Category-Level Object Recognition. LNCS, vol. 4170, pp. 345–361. Springer, Heidelberg (2006)

12. Torralba, A., Murphy, K.P., Freeman, W.T.: Sharing visual features for multiclass and multiview object detection. IEEE Trans. Pattern Anal. Machine Intell. 29(5), 854–869 (2007)
13. Papageorgiou, C.P., Oren, M., Poggio, T.: A general framework for object detection. In: Sixth Int. Conf. on Computer Vision, pp. 555–562 (1998)
14. Freund, Y., Schapire, R.E.: A short introduction to boosting. J. of Japanese Soc. for Artif. Intell. 5(14), 771–780 (1999)
15. Huang, C., Ai, H., Li, Y., Lao, S.: High-performance rotation invariant multiview face detection. IEEE Trans. Pattern Anal. Machine Intell. 29(4), 671–686 (2007)
16. Vural, S., Mae, Y., Uvet, H., Arai, T.: Multi-view fast object detection by using extended haar filters in uncontrolled environments. Patt. Recog. Lett. 33(2), 126–133 (2012)
17. Friedman, J., Hastie, T., Tibshirani, R.: Additive logistic regression: A statistical view of boosting. The Annals of Statistics 28(2), 337–407 (2000)
18. Jesorsky, O., Kirchberg, K.J., Frischholz, R.W.: Robust face detection using the hausdorff distance. In: Bigun, J., Smeraldi, F. (eds.) AVBPA 2001. LNCS, vol. 2091, p. 90. Springer, Heidelberg (2001)
19. Weber, M.: Frontal face dataset (2010), http://www.vision.caltech.edu/html-files/archive.html
20. Sim, T., Baker, S., Bsat, M.: The CMU pose, illumination, and expression database. IEEE Trans. Pattern Anal. Machine Intell. 25(12), 1615–1618 (2003)
21. Georghiades, A.S., Belhumeur, P.N., Kriegman, D.J.: From few to many: Illumination cone models for face recognition under variable lighting and pose. IEEE Trans. Pattern Anal. Machine Intell. 23(6), 643–660 (2001)
22. Philips, P.J., Moon, H.: The feret evaluation methodology for face-recognition algorithms. IEEE Trans. Pattern Anal. Machine Intell. 22(10), 1090–1104 (2000)
23. Schneiderman, H., Kanade, T.: A statistical method for 3d object detection applied to faces and cars. In: Proc. of the IEEE Computer Society Conf. on Computer Vision and Pattern Recognition, pp. 746–751 (2000)
24. Bradsky, G., Kaehler, A.: Learning OpenCV: Computer Vision with the OpenCV Library. O'Really (2008)
25. Li, J., Wang, T., Zhang, Y.: Face detection using surf cascade. In: IEEE International Conference on Computer Vision - ICCV, pp. 2183–2190 (2011)
26. Jain, V., Learned-Miller, E.: Online domain adaption of a pre-trained cascade of classifiers. In: IEEE Conference on Computer Vision and Pattern Recognition, pp. 577–584 (2011)
27. Venkatesh, B.S., Marcel, S.: Fast bounding box estimation based face detection. In: European Conf. on Computer Vision (ECCV) - Workshop on Face Detection, pp. 1–14 (2010)
28. Jones, M., Viola, P.: Fast multi-view face detection. Technical report, Mitsubishi Electric Research Laboratories, Technical Report TR2003-96 (2003)
29. Lienhart, R., Kuranov, A., Pisarevsky, V.: Empirical analysis of detection cascades of boosted classifiers for rapid object detection. Technical report, Micropocessor Research Lab and Intel Labs (2002)

Noise-Removal Markers to Improve PCA-Based Face Recognition

Santiago-Omar Caballero-Morales

Technological University of the Mixteca
Road to Acatlima, Km. 2.5, Huajuapan de Leon, Oaxaca, Mexico, 69000
scaballero@mixteco.utm.mx

Abstract. In this paper an approach based on insertion of "markers" is proposed to increase the performance of face recognition based on principal component analysis (PCA). The markers represent zero-valued pixels which are expected to remove information likely to affect classification (noisy pixels). The patterns of the markers was optimized with a genetic algorithm (GA) in contrast to other noise generation techniques. Experiments performed with a well known face database showed that the technique was able to achieve significant improvements on PCA particularly when data for training was small in comparison with the size of testing sets. This was also observed when the number of eigenfaces used for classification was small.

Keywords: face recognition, principal component analysis, genetic algorithms.

1 Introduction

Face recognition is one of the main problems studied in the field of pattern recognition. Achieving solutions for this problem has led to improvements in the development of technology for Human-Robot interaction, surveillance, automation, and interactive entertainment.

Among the most commonly used techniques for face recognition the following can be mentioned: Non-negative Matrix Factorization [2,14], Support Vector Machines (SVMs) and Principal Component Analysis (PCA) [3,5,9,11]. Performance under different conditions and test databases has been reported to be within the range of 95% [5] to 98% [3] for these techniques. Others as Artificial Neural Networks [6] and Hidden Markov Models (HMMs) [7] have been reported to achieve similar performance.

The work presented in this paper is aimed to provide a technique to improve the performance of PCA as a well known (and used) technique for face recognition. The proposed technique consists in the insertion of a set of "markers" in the form of zero-valued pixels to images to increase recognition. The type of distribution of markers required to achieve this goal without generating noise which would affect recognition is also studied by the present work.

J.F. Martínez-Trinidad et al. (Eds.): MCPR 2014, LNCS 8495, pp. 192–200, 2014.

The paper is organized as follows. The details of the proposed technique within the context of PCA are presented in Section 2. Then in Section 3 the experiments performed with this technique on a well known database are presented and the obtained results are discussed. Finally in Section 4 the conclusions and future work are presented.

2   Markers

In the literature some works have presented the insertion of elements (e.g., noise) to improve the performance of learning techniques. In [13] the addition of Gaussian noise was proposed to improve the performance of Artificial Neural Networks (ANNs) for problems with small and unbalanced data sets. It was found that noise addition was able to reduce the risk of overfitting by adding more differences to the existing input patterns [12,13].

In this work a different conception is considered and it is assumed that a pattern (in this case, an image) may already have elements (pixels) which may affect classification and should be removed. A "mark" which represents the removal of a "noisy" element (pixel) in an image by replacing it with a zero-valued pixel is proposed to improve the performance of a classification technique (in this case, PCA). This is different from considering additive or subtractive noise. Also, the distribution (positions) of these markers is considered to be specific for a particular input pattern, thus no assumption of Gaussian distribution is considered.

In practice, changing the value of an image's pixel to zero would be equivalent to add a mark to a person's face such as a mole. Such mark, in addition to other facial features, may support classification decisions. In Figure 1 the colored parametric-surfaces of an image from the *faces94* database [9,10] are presented. In Figure 1(a) the original image is presented while in Figure 1(b) the original image with a group of zero-valued pixels in the left side is presented. The zero-valued pixels are clearly differentiable from most of the other pixels in the image. Hence the zero level is considered to be reliable to effectively "mark" an image.

2.1   Integration of Markers

The process for PCA training and testing in this work is the standard scheme presented in [3,8,11]. In Figure 2 the overall process for the integration of the markers and evaluation of performance is presented. The markers are applied to each training image before the PCA process (leading to the markers being integrated into the estimation of the eigenfaces). These markers are also applied to each testing image before classification. Applying the markers is equivalent to the process of multiplying the vector representing the ith face Γ_i by a vector X of the same size with ones (1's) and zeros (0's). In this way, the entries with "1" in X preserve the associated pixel values in Γ_i, and the entries with "0" replace the associated pixel values in Γ_i. For illustration purposes the markers are presented as a matrix in Figure 2 where the black cells represent zeros (0's) and the white cells represent ones (1's).

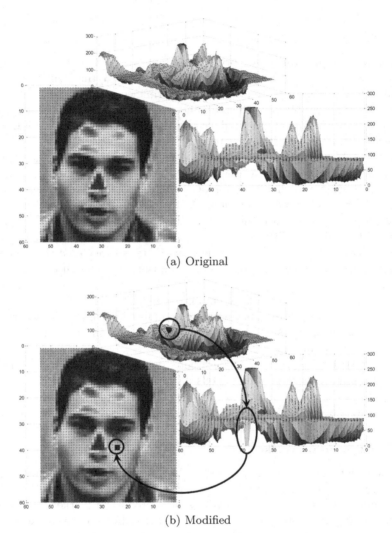

(a) Original

(b) Modified

Fig. 1. Effect of Replacing Pixels with Zero-Valued Markers

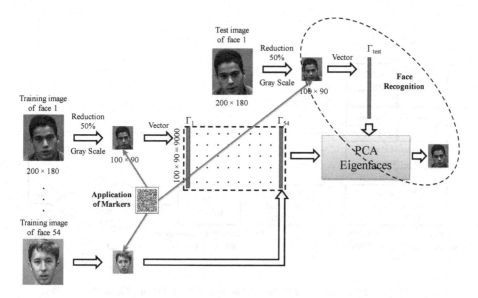

Fig. 2. Integration of Markers into the PCA Training and Testing Procedures

2.2   Estimation of Markers

The marker's distribution was estimated by means of a micro genetic algorithm (μGA) [1] where the chromosome consists of an X vector with "1" and "0" entries. The fitness value was measured as the PCA recognition performance obtained over a subset of test images considering the application of the X vector on these images and the training images. The use of a μGA was considered given the size of the chromosome (n columns $\times$ m rows) and also because it can converge quickly within a few iterations with a very small initial population, providing estimates as good as a conventional GA. The structure and parameters of the μGA are presented in Figure 3.

3   Experiments and Results

3.1   Face Database

For this work the *faces94* database was used [9,10]. This database consists of images from 153 individuals (20 females, 133 males) with a resolution of 180 by 200 pixels (portrait format). A total of 20 images from each individual are available in the database. These images have some minor variations between them as small changes in head turn, tilt and slant, position of face in image, and expressions.

For the experiments 54 individuals were randomly selected, and the set of images from each individual was separated into the following subsets:

- Images 1 to 4: for training scheme (TS) 1 (training with 4 images).
- Images 1 to 8: for training scheme (TS) 2 (training with 8 images).

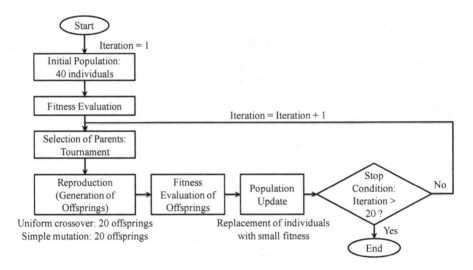

Fig. 3. Structure and Parameters of the Estimation Algorithm

- Images 9 to 12: for fitness evaluation of the GA.
- Images 13 to 20: for testing (recognition performance).

As presented two training schemes were considered. This was performed in order to evaluate the performance of the proposed technique with small and medium training data. Note that under the training scheme TS 2, both training and testing sets are equally sized. In contrast, under the training scheme TS 1 the testing set is twice the size of the training set.

Also the effect of the proposed technique on PCA performance was explored when the number of eigenfaces is varied. For this, the following numbers of eigenfaces were considered: 1, 4, 8, 12 and 16.

The results considering these conditions are presented and discussed in the following sections.

3.2   Convergence of the μGA

In Figure 4 the mean convergence plots of the μGA for the 54 individuals using 4 and 8 training images and different number of eigenfaces are presented.

Under both training schemes improvement in recognition is obtained with the use of the markers (PCA-Markers) when compared with the performance of the standard PCA (PCA-Original).

3.3   Distribution of Markers

In Table 1 the patterns (distribution) of the markers estimated with the μGA are presented for each experimental condition. Considering that each image consists of 100×90 pixels = 9000 pixels (after reduction), some markers consists of approximately 50% of the total number of pixels of an image.

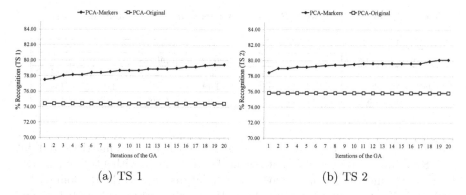

(a) TS 1   (b) TS 2

Fig. 4. Mean Convergence Plots of the μGA for Different Training Schemes and Number of Eigenfaces

Table 1. Distribution of Markers Estimated with the μGA

Train	Number of Eigenfaces				
	1	4	8	12	16
TS 1	2271 markers	4489 markers	2845 markers	2908 markers	4568 markers
TS 2	2819 markers	4430 markers	4491 markers	4540 markers	4489 markers

It is important to mention that no clear structures are presented in these patterns, and thus these may look like randomly generated patterns. To address this situation a comparison of the markers' distributions with randomly generated binary matrices was performed. Two random binary matrices, RndMat 1 and RndMat 2, were created for this purpose using a continuous uniform distribution.

If a marker's pattern Z is similar to a randomly generated matrix RndMat 1 (or RndMat 2), it is expected that the distance between Z and RndMat 1 (or RndMat 2) be similar to the distance between two randomly generated matrices (RndMat 1 and RndMat 2). In contrast, if Z is not similar to a randomly generated matrix, then the distance between Z and RndMat 1 (or RndMat 2) must be higher than the distance between two randomly generated matrices (RndMat 1 and RndMat 2). In Table 2 the normalized Earth Mover's Distances (EMD) between the random matrices and the markers distributions from Table 1 are presented.

Table 2. Distances between Randomly Generated Patterns and the Markers

Reference Pattern	Train	Comparison Patterns					
		Number of Eigenfaces					
		1	4	8	12	16	RndMat 2
RndMat 1	TS 1	3.14	1.00	2.49	2.25	1.00	1.00
	TS 2	2.38	0.99	1.02	0.96	0.96	1.00

Taking as reference the EMD distance between the random matrices RndMat 1 and RndMat 2, it is observed that the markers estimated with 4 training images (TS 1) and 4 and 16 eigenfaces have very similar distance to the random matrix RndMat 1. For the same training scheme the markers estimated with 1, 8, and 12 eigenfaces have a higher distance to the random matrix RndMat 1. From Table 1 it is observed that these markers have the lowest number of elements (2271, 2845, and 2908 respectively).

For the case with 8 training images (TS 2) the highest distance is obtained with one eigenface (2819 elements) while the similar distance to the random matrix RndMat 1 is obtained with the markers estimated for 4, 8, 12 and 16 eigenfaces (4430, 4491, 4540, and 4489 elements respectively). As the number of markers increases their distribution seems to resemble a random binary matrix. The highest distance from a random pattern (3.14) is obtained with the distribution with the lowest number of markers (2271). Thus, for initial evaluation of performance the pattern with the minimum number of markers was used.

3.4   PCA Performance

The performance of PCA with the selected pattern of markers (PCA-Markers) over the test set of 8 images is presented in Figures 5(a) and 5(b) for the training schemes TS 1 and TS 2. The numerical data associated to these figures is presented in Table 3.

While the mean gains observed in Figures 5(a) and 5(b) may look significant for small number of eigenfaces, when performing a technique of statistical analysis [4] it was found that some of these were not statistically significant. As presented in Table 3 for the case where PCA was trained with 4 images (TS 1), the improvement was statistically significant at the 0.10 level when one eigenface was used. On the other hand the improvement was marginally significant at the 0.15 level when 8 and 12 eigenfaces were used. When PCA was trained with 8 images (TS 2), the improvement was statistically significant at the 0.05, 0.10, and 0.15 levels when 4, 8 and 12 eigenfaces were used. Considering that the markers were those estimated with the PCA trained with 4 images (TS 1), statistically significant improvements were obtained in a PCA system trained with more data (TS 2).

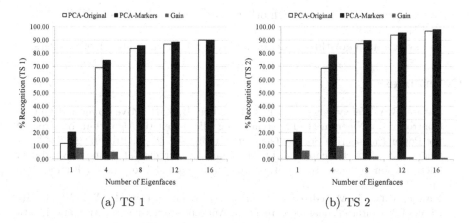

Fig. 5. Mean Recognition Performance on the Test Set (Histogram)

Table 3. Mean Recognition Performance on the Test Set (Numerical Data)

Train	Eigenfaces	PCA-Original	PCA-Markers	p-value	Conclusion
	1	11.81	20.37	0.0990	< 0.10
	4	68.98	74.54	0.2033	Not Significant
TS 1	8	83.33	85.65	0.1447	< 0.15
	12	86.81	88.43	0.1218	< 0.15
	16	89.81	90.05	0.8201	Not Significant
	1	13.89	20.14	0.2632	Not Significant
	4	68.75	78.70	0.0091	< 0.05
TS 2	8	87.50	89.58	0.0774	< 0.10
	12	93.98	95.37	0.1035	< 0.15
	16	96.99	97.92	0.2033	Not Significant

4 Future Work

In this paper an approach based on removal of (possibly) noisy pixels by the insertion of zero-valued pixels (markers) was presented. The approach was able to obtain statistically significant improvements on PCA for face recognition under different conditions of size of training data and number of eigenfaces. It is of particular attention that the test set was of equal size (and also larger) than the size of the training set.

Although these results may look encouraging it is very important to mention the exploratory nature of this work. Thus more extensive experiments must be performed to address the significance of these results. Among the ongoing and future work the following points are considered:

– to evaluate the performance of the technique with the complete *faces94* database and analyze the effect of all patterns of markers on the recognition process;

- to integrate the technique with other recognition techniques as NMF, ANNs, and HMMs;
- to develop an algorithm to define a threshold for the number of markers.

References

1. Bakare, G.A., Venayagagamoorthy, G.K., Aliyu, U.O.: Reactive Power and Voltage Control of the Nigerian Grid System Using Micro-Genetic Algorithm. In: Proc. of the Power Engineering Society General Meeting, vol. 2, pp. 1916–1922 (2005)
2. Chen, W.S., Pan, B., Fang, B., Li, M., Tang, J.: Incremental Nonnegative Matrix Factorization for Face Recognition. In: Mathematical Problems in Engineering, pp. 1–17 (2008)
3. Faruqe, M.O., Al Mehedi Hasan, M.: Face recognition using PCA and SVM. In: Proc. of 3rd International Conference on Anti-counterfeiting, Security, and Identification in Communication (ASID 2009), pp. 97–101 (2009)
4. Gillick, L., Cox, S.J.: Some statistical issues in the comparison of speech recognition algorithms. In: Proc. IEEE Conf. on Acoustics, Speech and Signal Processing (ICASSP 1989), vol. 1, pp. 532–535 (1989)
5. Heisele, B., Ho, P., Poggio, T.: Face recognition with support vector machines: Global versus component-based approach. In: Proc. of 8th IEEE International Conference on Computer Vision (ICCV 2001), vol. 2, pp. 688–694 (2001)
6. Islam, M.R., Toufiq, R., Sobhan, M.A.: Appearance and shape based face recognition using Backpropagation learning neural network algorithm with different lighting variations. Science Journal of Circuits, Systems and Signal Processing 2(4), 93–99 (2013)
7. Miar-Naimi, H., Davari, P.: A New Fast and Efficient HMM-Based Face Recognition System Using a 7-State HMM Along With SVD Coefficients. Iranian Journal of Electrical & Electronic Engineering 4(1), 46–57 (2008)
8. Moon, H., Phillips, P.J.: Computational and performance aspects of PCA-based face-recognition algorithms. Perception 30, 303–321 (2001)
9. Poon, B., Ashraful Amin, M., Yan, H.: Performance evaluation and comparison of PCA Based human face recognition methods for distorted images. International Journal of Machine Learning and Cybernetics 2, 245–259 (2011)
10. Spacek, L.: Collection of facial images: Faces94. In: Computer Vision Science and Research Projects, University of Essex, United Kingdom, http://cswww.essex.ac.uk/mv/allfaces/faces94.html
11. Turk, M., Pentland, A.: Eigenfaces for Recognition. Journal of Cognitive Neuroscience 3(1), 71–86 (1991)
12. Viegas da Silva, I.B., Adeodato, J.L.: An Approach for Learning from Small and Unbalanced Data Sets using Gaussian Noise during Artificial Neural Networks Training. In: Proc. of International Conference on Data Mining (DMIN 2010), pp. 23–30 (2010)
13. Viegas da Silva, I.B., Adeodato, J.L.: PCA and Gaussian Noise in MLP Neural Network Training Improve Generalization in Problems with Small and Unbalanced Data Sets. In: Proc. of International Joint Conference on Neural Networks (IJCNN 2011), pp. 2664–2669 (2011)
14. Xue, Y., Tong, C.S., Zhang, W.: Survey of Distance Measures for NMF-Based Face Recognition. In: Wang, Y., Cheung, Y.-M., Liu, H. (eds.) CIS 2006. LNCS (LNAI), vol. 4456, pp. 1039–1049. Springer, Heidelberg (2007)

Assembling Similar Tracking Approaches in Order to Strengthen Performance

Edgar Reyna-Ayala, Santiago E. Conant-Pablos, and Hugo Terashima-Marín

Tecnológico de Monterrey
Av. Eugenio Garza Sada 2051, Monterrey, N.L.
64849 Mexico
{a00800773,sconant,terashima}@itesm.mx

Abstract. In this paper we present a novel ensemble of two similar tracking approaches, which independently present good performance for different video sequences. We propose that by combining the response of these tracking approaches, we can strengthen their detecting capability and therefore increase the tracking performance of the ensemble. The Tracking-Learning-Detection (TLD) and the LocalTLD are the approaches we chose for building our ensemble. Our main motivation for assembling these two approaches is that both approaches focus on particular instances of an object and also manage different object representation, for instance, the TLD works reasonably well for planar rigid objects due to the global classifier it includes, meanwhile the LocalTLD focuses on invariant local features and is able to overcome the planar assumption. Combining these approaches, we are able to take advantage of their best qualities and overcome their biggest problems. For introducing our method, we first need to review the principal components of the two chosen approaches, and then we finally introduce the ensemble. The proposed ensemble is compared against results of the independent approaches using a data set of 10 video sequences, showing, in general, a significant improvement.

Keywords: Tracking, Semi-supervised Learning, Online Learning, Random Ferns, Template-based Classifier.

1 Introduction

The general case of tracking arbitrary objects in unconstrained environments is very challenging due to the existence of several factors that act as distractors such as changes in appearance, varying lighting conditions, cluttered background, the emergence of regions having appearance similar to the target. In some applications, the object to be tracked is known in advance and it is possible to incorporate specific prior knowledge. However, tracking arbitrary objects by simply specifying a single training example is a challenging open problem that deserves particular attention. In this scenario, the tracker must be able to model the object by generating and labeling image features and learning different appearances of the object. This basic formulation naturally leads to the semi-supervised learning approach.

J.F. Martínez-Trinidad et al. (Eds.): MCPR 2014, LNCS 8495, pp. 201–210, 2014.
© Springer International Publishing Switzerland 2014

Tracking by detection is a tracking technique that recent works [1], [2], [3] have shown it provides promising results. These methods train a discriminative classifier in an online fashion to separate the object from the background. These classifiers bootstrap themselves by using the current tracker state to extract positive and negative examples from the current frame.

The framework proposed in this investigation is built upon two approaches that have previously presented good results, and since both are structured in a similar fashion, they can be easily adapted for working together. The proposed ensemble is compared against results of the independent approaches using a data set of video sequences, showing, in general, a significant improvement. For introducing our method, we first review similar approaches in the state of the art, this is presented in Section 2, then we review the principal components and explain the ensemble in Section 3, in Section 4 we present the results obtained with the framework. Conclusions are finally given in Section 5.

2   Related Work

Most of the methods on the state of the art focus their efforts to solve the problem of tracking arbitrary objects in unconstrained environments by using different techniques like local feature matching, ensemble classifiers, keypoint classification, specialized filters, etc. A framework for adaptive visual object tracking based on structured output prediction is presented in [3]. By explicitly allowing the output space to express the needs of the tracker, they are able to avoid the need for an intermediate classification step. This method uses a kernelized structured output support vector machine (SVM), which is learned online to provide adaptive tracking. To allow for real-time application, they introduce a budgeting mechanism that prevents the unbounded growth in the number of support vectors, which would otherwise occur during tracking.

In [4] a tracking method based on the TLD system [5] is presented that exploits the context of the object of interest by characterizing it in two terms: Distractors and Supporters. Distractors are defined as regions that have similar appearance as the target and consistently co-occur. They keep track of these distractors to avoid drifting. Supporters are defined as local features around the target with consistent co-occurrence and motion correlation. Their main purpose is to make a stronger validation that the object is being tracked correctly.

The ALIEN algorithm [6] is based on local features for building the object model and a context model, which represents the object surrounding. Pernici et. al [6] propose a technique mainly motivated by Scale Invariant Features Transformation (SIFT features) [7] and by the underlying image formation process. It comprises multiple instances of local features combined with a global shape prior, expressed in terms of a 2D similarity transformation. This novel representation is exploited in a discriminative background/foreground online tracking (by detection) method, which performs feature selection and feature update. The resulting technique allows tracking to continue under severe visibility artifacts.

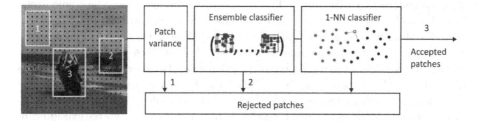

Fig. 1. Block diagram of the TLD detecting component, from [5]

3 Implementation

The framework proposed in this investigation is built upon two approaches that have previously presented good results when compared with the state of the art. The TLD [5] and the LocalTLD [8] are the approaches we chose for building our framework, since they are structured in a similar fashion, they can be easily adapted for working together. Our main motivation for assembling these two approaches is that both approaches focus on particular instances of an object and also manage different object representation, for instance, the TLD framework works reasonably well for planar rigid objects due to the global classifier it includes, meanwhile the LocalTLD framework focuses on invariant local features and is able to overcome the planar assumption. Therefore, we propose that by combining the responses of these two approaches, we can strengthen their detecting capabilities and hence increase the tracking performance of the ensemble. For introducing our method, we first need to review the principal components of the TLD and the LocalTLD, and then we finally introduce the ensemble.

3.1 Tracking-Learning-Detecting

The TLD system [5] retakes Viola-Jones cascade methodology [9] to design a global object detector. A new paradigm for learning from structured unlabeled data called P-N Learning is introduced, where the structure in the data is exploited by so called positive and negative structural constraints, which enforces certain labeling of the unlabeled set. The TLD system divides the process of tracking an unknown object into three basic tasks: tracking, learning and detecting. The tracking component and the detecting component represent different estimations of the object.

The Tracking Component. The tracking component estimates the motion of the object between two consecutives frames, and therefore can discover non-learned object appearances to generate training examples for the detecting component. This statement establishes the tracking component as the main component for triggering the learning process. The tracking component is based on Median-Flow tracker extended with failure detection [10].

The Detecting Component. The detecting component scans the whole frame in order to localize the object based on the object appearances previously observed and learned. Once the object is located, it corrects the tracking component response. For this component, Kalal et. al [5] retakes Viola-Jones cascade methodology [9] to design a global object detector. The cascade methodology is divided into three stages, as shown in Figure 1, a variance filter, an ensemble classifier and a template-based classifier. This methodology can be viewed as an object specific focus-of-attention mechanism, which provides statistical guarantees that discarded regions are unlikely to contain the object of interest [9].

The Learning Component. The learning component estimates the detecting component error and trains it to avoid making the same mistakes in the future. The learning component uses the methodology known as P-N learning [5]. The key idea of P-N learning is that two types of experts can identify the detector errors. The P-expert assumes that the object moves along a trajectory and extracts examples from such trajectory and the N-expert assumes that the object can occupy only a single location and extracts examples from the annular area of the trajectory, so they both depend on the validation of the trajectory given by the tracking component. Both experts may produce errors themselves; however, their independence enables mutual compensation of their errors.

3.2   LocalTLD

This approach is embedded into the Tracking-Learning-Detection (TLD) framework by performing a set of changes in the detection stage. In [8] the authors propose using invariant local features and a global appearance validation for assisting a robust object tracker initialized by a single example. The authors show how measuring the density of positive local features given by a binary classifier is a good signal of the objects presence, and in combination with a global appearance validation it yields a strong object detector.

The Tracking Component. LocalTLD also uses the Median-Flow tracker extended with failure detection, as in [10]. The original implementation initializes an uniform 10 x 10 keypoints grid within the last known bounding box and track those points. In the variant approach, a slightly modification is made on the points to track, by randomly select 100 keypoints given by the feature extraction stage since they are more likely to be stable for tracking purposes.

The Detecting Component. For this component the author uses three stages for the cascade methodology [9], as shown in Figure 2, an ensemble classifier for classifying the local features as belonging to the object or the background, then a feature density filter acting as the object specific focus-of-attention mechanism and finally, a template-based classifier similar to the one implemented in the TLD framework.

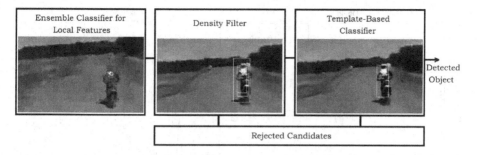

Fig. 2. Local features are extracted from the image and classified by an ensemble classifier as either belonging to the object (crosses) or the background. Then the feature density filter acts as an object specific focus-of-attention mechanism. Finally each candidate is passed through the global validation stage given by a template-based classifier.

The Learning Component. The learning component uses the methodology known as P-N learning [5], as in the TLD framework.

3.3   Assembling Approaches

After a careful analysis of the two approaches described before, we can conclude that in many cases there might be circumstances in which one approach is not suitable enough; in other words, none of the approaches can guarantee a competent performance for all kind of circumstances. We can observe in the behavior comparison of the two approaches (see Figure 3), that in certain circumstances the TLD outperforms the LocalTLD and in other distinct circumstances the LocalTLD outperforms the TLD.

By assembling these two similar approaches we provide the framework with new resources in such a way that when one detector is not able to detect the object, the second detector is most probably able to detect it, providing not only a valid response but also new information to update both detectors.

The Tracking Component. Since both approaches are based on the Median-Flow tracker [10], we implement it as well.

The Detecting Component. In this component, we implement both cascade detectors independently, as shown in Figure 4, each detector builds its own object model, has its own database of examples and computes its own posterior probabilities for the ensemble classifier. Although there are many ways to combine the response of various detectors, we keep them both working simultaneously and average their responses in order to retrieve a definitive response for the detecting stage.

For averaging the responses of the detectors, it is necessary to take into account two metrics, an overlapping measure with the tracking component response

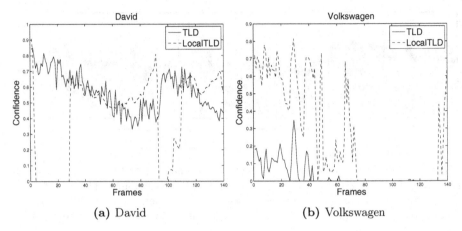

(a) David   (b) Volkswagen

Fig. 3. Comparison of performance between TLD and LocalTLD. In this graphs we can observe the average performance of both approaches in the same video sequences. We can observe how in the David sequence the TLD framework overcomes the LocalTLD, but in the Volkswagen sequence occurs the other way around.

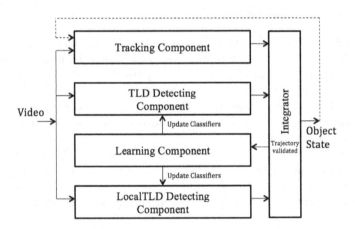

Fig. 4. Overview of the Ensemble analytical model

and a similarity measure computed as described in [5]. Then we proceed as follow, if both detectors have a high overlapping measure (above a predefined threshold), which means that both detectors agree with the location of the tracking component response, then we average the three responses. Moreover, if only one detector has a high overlapping measure, it means that the second detector does not agree with the location of the tracking component response. In this case, in order to determine which detector is correct, we have to compute the similarity of the response of each detector, and then the response with higher similarity is considered correct. If the selected response is also the one with high overlapping measure, then the response of the other detector is discarded and only average the selected response with the traking component response, otherwise the tracking component is reinitialized with the location of the selected response. Finally, if none of the detectors has a high overlapping measure, it means that no detector agrees with the location of the tracking component response, and we have to determine which response is correct similarly as described before. This methodology is effective for reinitializing the tracking component when it has lost the object and avoids introducing inappropriate information to the databases.

The Learning Component. The P-N learning method is implemented for the learning component of both detectors. As mentioned before, the validation of the trajectory given by the tracking component triggers the learning process. In order to validate the trajectory we need to compute the similarity of the tracking component response as in [5]. If the similarity is higher than a threshold then it is validated, otherwise it is not validated and the learning process is not executed. The learning process is an important process in the ensemble and its absence can lead to an inevitable loss of important information and in extreme cases the complete loss of the actual appearance of the object.

In the individual implementation of each detector, this dependency on the tracking component represents a problem, because there might be circumstances in which the detector is not competent enough, and therefore the similarity of the tracking component response will be mostly low, even though the trajectory is correct.

In our implementation, we propose to ease the restriction of the validation of the trajectory by exploiting the two detectors. We state that the validation of the trajectory by, at least, one of the detectors is reliable enough for triggering the learning process in both detectors. This modification causes that the databases of the detectors are no longer entirely independent, but also provokes that the detectors no longer lose valuable information in circumstances in which they cannot properly detect the object. The good performance in the longer video sequences, presented in Section 4, is in part because this partial independence between the detectors.

4 Experiments

For the experiments, we tested the proposed ensemble with the publicly available TLD data set, introduced in [5] and consisting of 10 video sequences. To compare our results against those of TLD and LocalTLD published in [8], we use metrics for precision, recall and F-measure. The sequences contain various objects in challenging conditions that include abrupt camera motion, motion blur, appearance change and partial or complete occlusions. Table 1 lists the properties of the sequences.

For the evaluation method, every box that has an overlapping percentage with the ground truth higher than 50% is considered as a valid prediction of the object location. The precision metric is computed as the number of valid predictions divided by the total number of predictions. The recall metric is computed as the

Table 1. TLD data set description, from [5]

Sequence	Frames	Mov. camera	Partial occ.	Complete occ.	Pose change	Illum. change	Scale change	Similar objects
1. David	761	yes	yes	no	yes	yes	yes	no
2. Jumping	313	yes	no	no	no	no	no	no
3. Pedestrian 1	140	yes	no	no	no	no	no	no
4. Pedestrian 2	338	yes	yes	yes	no	no	no	yes
5. Pedestrian 3	184	yes	yes	yes	no	no	no	yes
6. Car	945	yes	yes	yes	no	no	no	yes
7. Motocross	2665	yes	yes	yes	yes	yes	yes	yes
8. Volkswagen	8576	yes	yes	yes	yes	yes	yes	yes
9. Car Chase	9928	yes	yes	yes	yes	yes	yes	yes
10. Panda	3000	yes	yes	yes	yes	yes	yes	no

Table 2. Fixed Parameters

Parameter	Value
Minimum window size	15 pixels
Number of fern structures for TLD detector	10 structures
Number of fern structures for LocalTLD detector	10 structures
Size of every fern structure for TLD detector	13 comparisons
Size of every fern structure for LocalTLD detector	14 comparisons
Template-based classifier patch size	15 pixels
Maximum number of Template-based classifier examples	100 examples

number of valid predictions divided by the number of actual ocurrences of the object, given by the ground truth. Finally, the F-measure is the harmonic mean of the two measures described above.

4.1 Parameters

The classifiers have certain parameters that determine their accuracy and speed, such as the minimum window size, the number of fern structures, the size of the fern structures, and the patch size, among others. For each one of the approaches, in the original implementations, the authors fix these parameters according to the experiments described in [5], [8] and claim that the choice of the parameters is not critical. For the sake of consistency, we use the same parameter values. In Table 2 we show the fixed value for each parameter. The minimum window size is the minimum value that will be acceptable for any candidate bounding box dimensions. For the ensemble classifier there are two main parameters the number of fern structures that contain the ensemble and the size of every fern structure. For the template-based classifier there are two main parameters as well, the patch size of the examples in the database and the maximum number of examples that can be stored in the database at the time.

4.2 Results

In order to validate our hypothesis we compare the performance of the approaches with the publicly available TLD data set, consisting of 10 video sequences, and compare our measure of precision, recall and F-measure with the

Table 3. Tracking Performance Analisys

Sequence	Frames	TLD			LocalTLD			Ensemble		
		P	R	F	P	R	F	P	R	F
1. David	761	**1.00**	**1.00**	**1.00**	0.92	0.91	0.91	**1.00**	**1.00**	**1.00**
2. Jumping	313	**0.99**	**0.99**	**0.99**	0.66	0.55	0.6	0.92	0.83	0.87
3. Pedestrian 1	140	**1.00**	**1.00**	**1.00**	0.18	0.17	0.17	0.66	0.39	0.49
4. Pedestrian 2	338	0.89	0.92	0.91	**0.96**	**0.93**	**0.95**	0.74	0.86	0.79
5. Pedestrian 3	184	**0.99**	**1.00**	**0.99**	0.83	0.94	0.88	0.75	0.87	0.80
6. Car	945	0.92	0.97	0.94	0.95	0.97	**0.96**	0.94	**0.99**	**0.96**
7. Motocross	2665	0.67	0.58	0.62	0.70	**0.64**	**0.67**	**0.71**	**0.64**	**0.67**
8. Volkswagen	8576	0.54	0.4	0.45	**0.71**	0.88	**0.78**	0.65	**0.96**	**0.78**
9. Car Chase	9928	0.5	0.4	0.45	0.71	0.34	0.46	**0.69**	**0.45**	**0.55**
10. Panda	3000	0.32	0.34	0.33	0.35	0.21	0.26	**0.77**	**0.65**	**0.70**
Average	**26850**	0.56	0.47	0.5	0.68	0.58	0.6	**0.71**	**0.7**	**0.68**

results published in [8]. The results of our experiments are shown in Table 3. We can observe in bold font the higher measures for each video sequence; in average the ensemble outperforms the TLD and the LocalTLD in the tracking tasks. Also we can observe an improved performance in comparison to the results obtained by TLD and Local TLD in the longer video sequences (over 2000 frames), with this we can validate our initial assumption that by combining the two approaches, we can increase the tracking performance of the ensemble. The framework was tested at an average frame rate of 7 fps on a MacBook running OSX Mavericks with a 2.9GHz Intel Core I7.

It is important to point out that, on one hand the performance shown by the ensemble in very long video sequences overcomes the two approaches in which it is embedded, but on the other hand, in short video sequences the ensemble performance may slightly decrease, this is because the template-based classifiers are not entirely independent from each other, as explained in section 3.3. However further research about this point is considered as future work.

5 Conclusion

In this paper we address the problem of tracking an unknown object in long video sequences under complex interactions, such as changes in appearance, varying lighting conditions, cluttered background, etc. We introduce a novel ensemble of two similar tracking approaches, which each one of them presents good performance. We validate the assumption that by combining the responses of the two approaches, we can strengthen their detecting capabilities and therefore increase the tracking performanceof the ensemble. We chose the TLD and LocalTLD approaches among others because they are similarly structured and manage similar resources; also both approaches focus on particular instances of the object, manage different object representation and fit perfectly for the ensemble purposes.

We consider the parallel training of both detectors by one single validation of the trajectory as one of the principal characteristics of the ensemble, however the correlation between the classifiers is a characteristic that must be suppressed, further research about this subject is considered future work. Also as future work we are contemplating the possibility of adding another specialized detector to improve performance in circumstances in which none of the included approaches performs properly. Furthermore, it would be interesting to modify the scheme by which both detectors interact, for instance, introduce some intelligent method to determine which detector is most suitable for detecting according to the evolution of the video sequence and the circumstances in it.

Acknowledgment. This research effort was supported by the strategic project on Pattern Recognition and its application in Optimization and Medicine (grant PRY075) funded by Tecnolgico de Monterrey, and the National Council for Science and Technology (CONACyT).

References

1. Avidan, S.: Ensemble tracking. IEEE Transactions on Pattern Analysis and Machine Intelligence 29(2), 261–271 (2007)
2. Babenko, B., Yang, M.H., Belongie, S.: Visual tracking with online multiple instance learning. In: IEEE Conference on Computer Vision and Pattern Recognition, CVPR 2009, pp. 983–990 (2009)
3. Hare, S., Saffari, A., Torr, P.H.S.: Struck: Structured output tracking with kernels. In: 2011 IEEE International Conference on Computer Vision (ICCV), pp. 263–270 (2011)
4. Dinh, T.B., Vo, N., Medioni, G.: Context tracker: Exploring supporters and distracters in unconstrained environments. In: 2011 IEEE Conference on Computer Vision and Pattern Recognition (CVPR), pp. 1177–1184 (2011)
5. Kalal, Z., Mikolajczyk, K., Matas, J.: Tracking-learning-detection. IEEE Transactions on Pattern Analysis and Machine Intelligence 34(7), 1409–1422 (2012)
6. Pernici, F., Del Bimbo, A.: Object tracking by oversampling local features. IEEE Transactions on Pattern Analysis and Machine Intelligence (TPAMI) (in press, 2014)
7. Lowe, D.G.: Distinctive image feature from scale-invariant keypoints. International Journal of computer vision, 91–110 (Novemberl 2004)
8. Torres-Nogales, A., Conant-Pablos, S., Terashima-Marín, H.: Local features classification for adaptive tracking. Mexican International Conference on Artificial Intelligence (2012)
9. Viola, P., Jones, M.: Rapid object detection using a boosted cascade of simple features. In: Proceedings of the 2001 IEEE Computer Society Conference on Computer Vision and Pattern Recognition, CVPR 2001, vol. 1, pp. I-511 – I-518 (2001)
10. Kalal, Z., Mikolajczyk, K., Matas, J.: Forward-backward error: Automatic detection of tracking failures. In: 2010 20th International Conference on Pattern Recognition (ICPR), pp. 2756–2759 (August 2010)

Real-Time Classification of Lying Bodies
by HOG Descriptors

A. Beltrán-Herrera, E. Vázquez-Santacruz, and M. Gamboa-Zuñiga

CGSTIC, Center for Research and Advanced Studies of the National of Polytechnic
Institute of Mexico (Cinvestav-IPN), México D.F.
abeltran@computacion.cs.cinvestav.mx, {efvazquez,mgamboaz}@cinvestav.mx

Abstract. In this paper we show a methodology for bodies classification
in lying state using HOG descriptor and pressures sensors positioned in
a matrix form (14 x 32 sensors) on the surface where bodies lie down. it
will be done in real time. Due to current technology a limited number
of sensors is used, wich results in low resolution data array, that will
be used as image of 14 x 32 pixels. Our work considers the problem
of human posture classification with few information (sensors), applying
digital process to expand the original data of the sensors and so get more
significant data for the classification; however, this is done with low-cost
algorithms to ensure the real-time execution.

1 Introduction

Monitoring of leaning people is often used in a variety of hospital process as geri-
atrics, rehabilitation, orthopedics and even used in psichology and sleep studies [10]. Although patients monitoring is usually doctors and nurses activity, this
can be automated to have better control of the patients in any time [4] doing
human intervention only to rate different positions for which patient has passed,
the time spent in each posture and incurred transitions. This automatization
process is not new, as there are many attemps to recognize the position of a
body in a given surface [4,14,8,1,19], most of the systems for posture recognition
are based on the detection of the posture of patients on the bed, using presence
sensors, digital cameras, thermal cameras or mattress pressure sensors [9,4,16].
Digital and thermal cameras achieve high resolution. However, they are affected
by environment illumination, temperature conditions and occlusions. Mattress
pressure sensors are invariant to illumination and temperature conditions, all the
same these sensors have a limited resolution and accuracy. Commercial pressure
sensors are available with resolutions from 4 to 1024 sensor units, higher resolution are prohibitively expensive for many applications. Recent developments in
the fabrication of low cost pressure matrix sensors are base in organic devices.
In [17] a flexible 32×32 array of pressure sensors have been developed for skin
sensitivity with a density of 10 units per inch, it is based on organic field-effect
transistors. However, it is limited to small areas and are mostly used in applications such as tactile displays and mobile devices. In [13] pressure sensors based

J.F. Martínez-Trinidad et al. (Eds.): MCPR 2014, LNCS 8495, pp. 211–220, 2014.
© Springer International Publishing Switzerland 2014

on organic thin film transistors was developed and applied to wearable electron-ics, textiles and skin for robots. On the other hand, proposed pressure sensors using resistive devices have been tested at highly sensitivity and very short re-sponse times that can be inexpensively fabricated over large areas [12,15]. Thus, given the high cost in the fabrication of array pressure sensors, is neccesary a methodology that use the few data to solve the classification issue.

We choose four basic positions according to the famous study by professor Chris Idzikowski [10], who classified the most common sleeping positions in six classes, that is, *foetus, log, yearner, soldier, freefaller* and *starfish*. These positions can be grouped in four basic classes: *left lateral decubitus* position or foetus, *right lateral decubitus* position of which the log and yearner positions belong to this class, *supine* position of which the soldier and starfish belong to this class, and *prone* position or freefaller.

We use a flexible array pressure sensor with 448 units distributed in an area of 1860 × 886 mm. The pressure sensors are based on variable resistive sensors at 4096 pressure levels and normal resistance from 1 to 50 kiloOhm [18]. We construct a database with pression levels (scaled to 0-255 range) transformed by a normalization process and apply it the HOG algorithm [7], the database contain samples of four postures showed in Figure 1. With this database, we can construct a classification model using a *support vector machine* (SVM) classifier [3].

The organization of this article is as follows: in section 2 the HOG is intro-duced, in section 3 we describe the digital image processing for normalize and get an invariant image, in section 4 SVM classifier is given, in section 5 experiments for posture classification are shown and in section 6 the conclusions.

Table 1. Simulated basic posture positions

a) Left lateral decubitus (**class 1**) b) Right lateral decubitus (**class 2**)

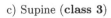

c) Supine (**class 3**)   d) Prone (**class 4**)

2   Image Descriptors

A descriptor is a representation of an image, it characterizes the most important features of interest. Descriptors are used in many applications such as image classification and recognition. For these tasks, the desired properties of an image descriptor are the invariance with respect to rotation, scaling, perspective and illumination,several descriptors exist as SIFT [11], SURF [2], DENSE-SIFT [20] and others, but given the features of our image (low quality and gray scale) and manly due their low computational cost, we decide to use the HOG descriptor, in experiments, HOG showed superior results at runtime compared to SIFT, Dense-SIFT and SURFT; commonly used in posture recognition works [6].

2.1   HOG Descriptor

HOG (*Histogram of Oriented Gradients*) descriptor is used in computer vision and image processing for object detection. This descriptor is based on the number of occurrences of the gradient directions in specific parts in an image. The main idea behind the HOG descriptor is that the local shape and appearance can be described as the distribution of gradient intensities. Based on that fact, an image is divided in several overlapping blocks, and for each block a histogram of gradient directions is computed. Thus, the HOG descriptor is the composition of all histograms for each block.

Figure 1 shows an example of a simulated pressure image and its gradient directions. The size of the HOG descriptor depends on the size of the blocks and on the number of bins in which the interval from 0 to 180 degrees is divided.

We use the HOG descriptor to characterize each pressure image. Therefore, for each pressure map, a vector of gradient directions is constructed. We consider that the histogram of gradient directions can be used for image classification,

Fig. 1. From left to right: simulated pressure map and image gradient directions

since that small changes in the pressure images are easily detected as changes in gradient directions.

3   Methodology for Posture Recognition

The proposed methodology takes the raw data of sensors and trasform it into HOG image, this representation as HOG image will be used as input in one SVM classificator, the final output is the classificator prediction about the position. Our system receives as input one array of 448 elements, with pression levels (0-4096 units of pression), each of wich represents one sensor in the surface where a person is lying down, these sensors are distributed in 32 rows and 14 columns. Figure 2 shows the main blocks of the proposed methodology for posture recognition. In the initial stage, the pressure distribution is obtained from the pressure sensor array, data obtained of the sensors is in range of 0 to 4096 levels of pression, where 0 is the maximun pression possible and 4096 is null pression. Then, in the second block we transform raw data taking three considerations, first, the pression applied by human body (considering weight between 40 to 150 Kg) is between 2500 to 4096 in the scale of pressures (see Figure 3), then we can cut the range only to human body requeriments and gain definition. Second consideration is an array scalation from 2500-4096 scale to 0-255 scale for process the array as gray scale image in the next block. The final consideration of the second block is applying a scale algorithm for images to obtain interpolated image of raw prresure data. In third stages, we use a feature extraction using HOG descriptor and applying it to the pressure distributions that are considered as gray scale images. In the stage delimited with broken line, we make the SVM model, the first three stages are repited several times with one human body in

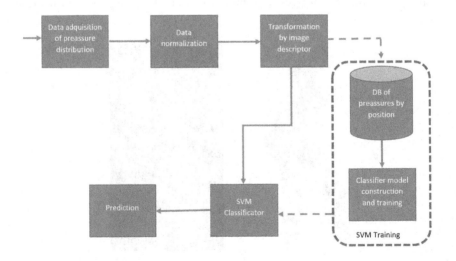

Fig. 2. Main blocks of methology for posture recognition

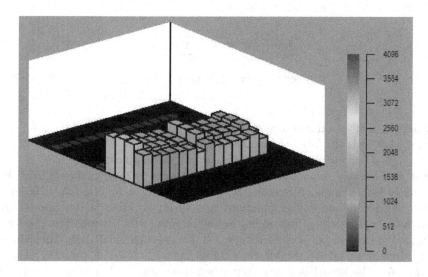

Fig. 3. Pression levels obtained of one person

different positions (We consider the positions described in Table I), and we make a data base with this, after we use this data base for make a SVM model, how we know the position in the wich was taken each measurement, we have a pression interpoled and classified data base, then we can construct a SVM model that predict the four positions of the Table I. When SVM model is ready, we can use it in order to monitor person movements, the fourth stage implies to take this SVM model and to use it as input the first three stages output, then the fifth stages have an accuratte prediction.

4   Classification

4.1   Support Vector Machines

Classification is a supervised learning technique which uses models (*classifiers*) from data to predict the category of previously unseen instances. Given a data set, it is split into training and testing subsets to develop a classifier. Each instance in the training set contains one *target value* (i.e., the class attribute or the label of the instance) and one or more *attributes* (i.e., the features or observed variables).

As a preprocessing step, data sets are cleaned and normalized. Cleaning usually involves deciding what to do with unknown values or with repeated instances. Normalization makes all values of attributes to be within a specific range, generally $[-1, 1]$ or $[0, 1]$.

Support Vector Machine (SVM) is one powerful classification method [5,3] that has been successfully applied in many applications. This classifier uses an optimal separating hyperplane to predict the label of instances. In order to compute the hyperplane, SVM require to solve the following optimization problem:

$$\min_{\mathbf{w},b,\xi} \frac{1}{2}\mathbf{w}^T\mathbf{w} + C\sum_{i=1}^{l}\xi_i \tag{1}$$

$$\text{subject to } y_i(\mathbf{w}^T\phi(\mathbf{x}_i) + b) \geq 1 - \xi_i,$$

$$\xi_i \geq 0.$$

where $\mathbf{x}_i \in \mathbb{R}^n$ is an instance of data set $(\mathbf{x}_i, y_i)$ with $i = 1, \ldots, l$.
$y_i \in \{1, -1\}$ is the label of instance $\mathbf{x}_i$.
$C > 0$ is a penalty parameter to allow some misclassification.

For non-linearly separable data sets, instances $\mathbf{x}_i$ are mapped from input space into a higher dimensional space by using a function ϕ, called the *kernel*. Two common kernel functions are *linear*, which is a function of the form $K(\mathbf{x}_i, \mathbf{x}_j) = \mathbf{x}_i^T\mathbf{x}_j$; and *radial basis function* (RBF), which has the form $K(\mathbf{x}_i, \mathbf{x}_j) = \exp(-\gamma\|\mathbf{x}_i - \mathbf{x}_j\|^2)$ with $\gamma > 0$. Kernels are usually non-linear functions, these must satisfy the Mercer's conditions.

Choosing the kernel is a key step when using an SVM. Linear kernels are preferred when the data are expected to be linearly separable, or when there is a strong evidence that the data can be easily discerned of their corresponding classes. Otherwise, a non-linear kernel, such as RBF function, is selected. Kernel's parameters are chosen using a grid search method. It consists in an exhaustive searching through a specified interval of values.

4.2 Cross-Validation

In order to evaluate the performance of a classifier, the *cross-validation* technique is commonly used. A classifier is build from training set, and then its accuracy is measured on testing set. The classification accuracy obtained from the testing set reflects the performance on unseen instances.

In v-fold cross-validation, the training set is divided into v subsets of equal size. Sequentially, one subset is tested using the classifier trained on the remaining $v - 1$ subsets. Thus, each instance of the whole training set is predicted once so the cross-validation accuracy is the percentage of data which are correctly classified.

5 Experiments

5.1 Pressure Maps Database

The pressure sensors array consists of two independently modules with a resolution of 16×14 units in an area of 930×886 mm. Each pressure sensor has a response between 0 to 25 kg/cm^2. We develop an interface to synchronize the two modules at a frequency of 100 measurements per second.

We construct four different pressure map data set for classification: Each data set consists of four classes, for every posture position (see table 1). For each class we generated 501 instances. We choose this number of instances according to study in [21]. Each data set has a number of 2004 instances and each data set in stored as individual data base, only after of apply the methodology described in section 3.

The data sets are described as follows:

1. *Data set interpolated to 640 x 640:*
2. *Data set interpolated to 320 x 320:*
3. *Data set interpolated to 100 x 100:*
4. *Data set in raw format (32 x 14):*

Figure 4 shows some examples of interpolated pressure maps. We normalize the range of values of each attribute vector, this was done in order to improve the performance of the classifier (see section 4). As we see in figure 4 the pressure maps obtained are more intuitive than the showed in figure 3.

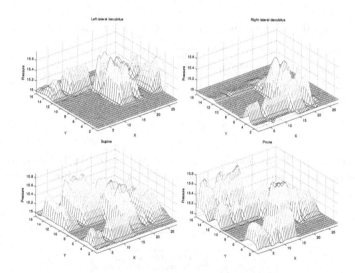

Fig. 4. Interpolated pressure maps corresponding to the four basic posture positions (see table 1) before of apply the proposed methodology

5.2   Posture Classification Using Pressure Maps

We use the LibLINEAR and LibSVM toolbox to perform the posture classification. The table 2 shows the results of the classification using the three databases with the proposed methodology. The classification results was obtained using 10-fold cross-validation. As can be seen the SVM with a linear kernel obtains good results using the raw and interpolated data. Using image descriptors, however, has a better performance with a RBF kernel. The advantage of using image descriptors is that the time to construct the model of the classifier is slower than using raw and interpolated data.

Table 2. Percentage of correctly classified instances

	Linear-SVM	RBF-SVM
640 × 640	51.05 %	54.10 %
320 × 320	96.21 %	98.57 %
100 × 100	98.54 %	99.01 %
32 × 14	84.32 %	85.89 %

We need not only the percentage of correctly clssified instances, for a real-time process we need to verify the computing time, logically the data sets with many elements will take longer time, but we need to found the balance between assetiveness and runtime. Table 3 shows the time that take each dataset for be processed by cross-validation in one computer with processor Intel pentium T4500 (2.3GHz).

Table 3. Percentage of correctly classified instances

	Time (seconds)
640 × 640	5412
320 × 320	977
100 × 100	72
32 × 14	17

Results in Table 3 are obtained of cross-validation algorithm that process 35,000 sensor arrays inputs, then in the table 4 we can show the number of sensor arrays what can be processed per second.

Table 4. Percentage of correctly classified instances

	Arrays per second
640 × 640	6
320 × 320	34
100 × 100	486
32 × 14	2058

Taking th results of tables 3 and 4, we can see that the better performance is obtained by 100 × 100 interpoled data set, that has 99.01% of assertiveness and can process 486 data arrays per second (although the hardware only give 100 per second).

6   Conclusions

This work presents a complete methodology which is useful to classificate the human bodies lying for real-time execution, the percentage of assertiveness is high, 99.01%, this ensuring correct monitoring in the majority of cases, also in the section of experiments, we show the correct size of interpolated arrays to get the best results, so that the system is able to process the 100 arrays per second that hardware is able to deliver.

References

1. Arcelus, A., Herry, C.L., Goubran, R.A., Knoefel, F., Sveistrup, H., Bilodeau, M.: Determination of sit-to-stand transfer duration using bed and floor pressure sequences. IEEE Trans. Biomed. Engineering 56(10), 2485–2492 (2009)
2. Bay, H., Ess, A., Tuytelaars, T., Van Gool, L.: Speeded-up robust features (surf). Comput. Vis. Image Underst. 110(3), 346–359 (2008)
3. Byun, H., Lee, S.-W.: A survey on pattern recognition applications of support vector machines. International Journal of Pattern Recognition and Artificial Intelligence 17(3), 459–486 (2003)
4. Chica, M., Campoy, P., Pérez, M.A., Rodríguez, T., Rodríguez, R., Valdemoros, Ó.: Corrigendum to "real-time recognition of patient intentions from sequences of pressure maps using artificial neural networks". Computers in Biology and Medicine 43(9), 1302 (2013)
5. Cortes, C., Vapnik, V.: Support-vector networks. Mach. Learn. 20(3), 273–297 (1995)
6. Dalal, N., Triggs, B.: Histograms of oriented gradients for human detection. In: IEEE Computer Society Conference on Computer Vision and Pattern Recognition, CVPR 2005, vol. 1, pp. 886–893 (2005)
7. Dalal, N., Triggs, B.: Histograms of oriented gradients for human detection. In: Proceedings of the 2005 IEEE Computer Society Conference on Computer Vision and Pattern Recognition (CVPR 2005), vol. 1, pp. 886–893. IEEE Computer Society, Washington, DC (2005)
8. De Vocht, J.W., Wilder, D.G., Bandstra, E.R., Spratt, K.F.: Biomechanical evaluation of four different mattresses. Applied Ergonomics 37(3), 297–304 (2006)
9. Grimm, R., Bauer, S., Sukkau, J., Hornegger, J., Greiner, G.: Markerless estimation of patient orientation, posture and pose using range and pressure imaging. Int. J. Computer Assisted Radiology and Surgery 7(6), 921–929 (2012)
10. Idzikowski, C.: Learn to Sleep Well. Watkins (2010)
11. Lowe, D.G.: Distinctive image features from scale-invariant keypoints. International Journal of Computer Vision 60(2), 91–110 (2004)
12. Mannsfeld, S.C.B., Tee, B.C.-K., Stoltenberg, R.M., Chen, C.V.H.-H., Barman, S., Muir, B.V.O., Sokolov, A.N., Reese, C., Bao, Z.: Highly sensitive flexible pressure sensors with microstructured rubber dielectric layers. Nature Materials 9(10), 859–864 (2010)
13. Manunza, I., Bonfiglio, A.: Pressure sensing using a completely flexible organic transistor. Biosensors and Bioelectronics 22(12), 2775–2779 (2007)
14. Nicol, K., Rusteberg, D.: Pressure distribution on mattresses. Journal of Biomechanics 26(12), 1479–1486 (1993)
15. Sekitani, T., Zschieschang, U., Klauk, H., Someya, T.: Flexible organic transistors and circuits with extreme bending stability. Nature Materials 9(12), 1015–1022 (2010)
16. Seo, K.-H., Choi, T.-Y., Oh, C.: Development of a robotic system for the bedridden. Mechatronics 21(1), 227–238 (2011)

17. Someya, T., Sekitani, T., Iba, S., Kato, Y., Kawaguchi, H., Sakurai, T.: A large-area, flexible pressure sensor matrix with organic field-effect transistors for artificial skin applications. Proceedings of the National Academy of Sciences of the United States of America 101(27), 9966–9970 (2004)
18. Sensing Tex Smart Textiles (2013), Webpage: http://www.sensingtex.com/
19. Townsend, D., Holtzman, M., Goubran, R., Frize, M., Knoefel, F.: Relative thresholding with under-mattress pressure sensors to detect central apnea. IEEE Transactions on Instrumentation and Measurement 60(10), 3281–3289 (2011)
20. Wang, J.-G., Li, J., Lee, C.Y., Yau, W.-Y.: Dense sift and gabor descriptors-based face representation with applications to gender recognition. In: ICARCV. IEEE (1860)
21. Hsu, C.W., Chang, C.C., Lin, C.J.: A practical guide to support vector classification (2010)

Wavelet Filter Adjusting for Image Lossless Compression Using Pattern Recognition

Oleksiy Pogrebnyak, Ignacio Hernández-Bautista, Oscar Camacho Nieto, and Pablo Manrique Ramírez

Instituto Politecnico Nacional, Centro de Investigacion en Computacion,
Ave. Miguel Othón De Mendizábal S/N, C.P. 07738, Mexico, D.F., Mexico
olek@pollux.cic.ipn.mx, ignaciohb@gmail.com,
{ocamacho,pmanriq}@cic.ipn.mx

Abstract. A method for image lossless compression using lifting scheme wavelet transform is presented. The proposed method adjusts wavelet filter coefficients analyzing signal spectral characteristics to obtain a higher compression ratio in comparison to the standard CDF(2,2) and CDF(4,4) filters. The proposal is based on spectral pattern recognition with 1-*NN* classifier. Spectral patterns of a small fixed length are formed for the entire image permitting thus the global optimization of the filter coefficients, equal for all decompositions. The proposed method was applied to a set of test images obtaining better results in entropy values in comparison to the standard wavelet lifting filters.

Keywords: image compression, lifting scheme, wavelets, pattern recognition.

1 Introduction

In the past two decades, the wavelet transform has become a popular, powerful tool for different image and signal processing applications such as noise cancellation, data compression, feature detection, etc. Nevertheless, a problem to choose or design the appropriate wavelet for a given application is still present. Different to many known orthogonal transforms, wavelet transform can use various basis functions and it is important that the chosen wavelet basis provides the best representation of the analyzed signal. For example, in signal detection applications, since the wavelet transform calculates the cross-correlation between the signal and wavelet, the wavelet matched to signal results in a greater peak in transformed domain. In signal compression applications the match results in better representation of the signal by wavelet, and therefore, in a better compression ratio.

The standard technique of finding orthonormal wavelet bases with compact support is Daubechies' classic technique [1], and in the case of biorthogonal wavelet bases the classical solution for univariate compactly supported wavelets of arbitrary high regularity is given by Cohen, Daubechies and Feauveau in [2]. Unfortunately, these techniques are not practical because they are complex and independent of the analyzed signal.

J.F. Martínez-Trinidad et al. (Eds.): MCPR 2014, LNCS 8495, pp. 221–230, 2014.
© Springer International Publishing Switzerland 2014

The first attempt at finding the optimal orthonormal wavelet basis for speech signals using parameterization was proposed by A.Tewfik *et al* in [3]. This method is limited to a finite number of scales and the optimization is performed in time domain in an iterative manner. Other existent design techniques mostly do not design the wavelet directly. Some techniques use a library of previously designed wavelets [4], some methods match the wavelet bases to the signal projecting the signal onto existing wavelet basis or transforming the wavelet basis [5].

Among the recent methods of wavelet matching those proposed by Chapa and Rao [6] and A.Gupta *et al.* [7] are the most notable. In [6], the authors adapt the generalized Meyer's wavelet minimizing the difference between wavelet and signal spectra, but their method is computationally expensive in phase matching and is designed for deterministic signal detection. In [7], the method of estimating of an analysis high pass wavelet filter is proposed for signals, which represent self-similar processes and their autocorrelation can be modeled analytically using the self-similarity index. Although authors state their method is simple, it requires in a self-similarity index a numerical search of a maximum likelihood estimator. Besides, the method yields filter banks without perfect restoration in general.

In this paper, we consider the application of wavelet transform for lossless image compression. For such uses, lifting scheme proposed by W.Sweldens [8] is a standard method for integer-to-integer transforms [9]. Lifting wavelet filters were obtained from known biorthogonal wavelet filters factoring the polyphase matrices [8], [10]. For lossless image compression, one step lifting filters CDF(2,2) and CDF(4,4) [9] are the most popular.

Various attempts of improving the performance of the lifting filters are known [11], [12], [13], [14], [15]. In common, the authors of these works try to optimize the lifting predictor minimizing the mean square prediction error at the output of the predictor in case of one step lifting, i.e., minimizing the energy of wavelet coefficients. With this, authors [11], [14], [15] obtain (sometimes, depending on the data) positive results if the combination with other improvements is used, but H. Thielemann [12] reported negative results for such least mean square optimization in comparison to CDF(2,2) performance. It is interesting to note, that the method of lifting predictor optimization presented in papers [14], [15] uses signal differences to compute the autocorrelation on them and not the standard calculation method.

An approach alternative to prediction error optimization was proposed in [16]. Analyzing the distribution of the wavelet coefficient distribution, the authors found that their distribution is well described by the generalized Gaussian distribution with the shape parameter close to 1 than to 2. As a result, they suggested the minimization of ℓ_1-norm instead of ℓ_2-norm, i.e., minimize the absolute value of error instead of error energy. Additionally, the update filter optimization by minimizing of ℓ_2-norm of the difference between the approximation signal and the decimated version of the output of the ideal low-pass filter was proposed. Unfortunately, the minimization of ℓ_1-norm is much more complex and requires sophisticated techniques, so convex analysis by proximity operators and an iterative algorithm were applied for the problem of the weighted ℓ_1-norm lifting prediction filter optimization. The case of lossy image compression was considered, and the obtained results show a slightly better performance than the standard 5/3 wavelet transform when the prediction filters were optimized separately. For other hand, the complexity of the proposed adaptive lifting algorithm is very high.

In this work, we introduce the method to improve the performance of the lifting predictor filters based on the use of the artificial intelligence techniques to design a model for wavelet filter automatic design for lossless image compression. To this end, we consider pattern classification algorithms, in particular, *k-NN*, to classify the image spectrum calculated in the discrete cosine transform domain. As a result, wavelet lifting filters coefficients are obtained not only for the lifting prediction but for the lifting update as well. The obtained wavelet lifting filters perform the wavelet transform more efficiently in terms of compression ratio comparing with the standard wavelet lifting filters CDF(2,2) and CDF(4,4).

The paper is organized as follows. In Section 2, the lifting scheme filters are described and generalized. Section 3 describes the proposed method to obtain the lifting filter coefficients using pattern recognition technique *k-NN*. Section 4 presents simulation results on lossless compression of different standard test grayscale images. Next, the conclusions are given in Section 5.

2 Lifting Scheme Generalization

The lifting scheme (or fast wavelet transform) is widely used in the wavelet based image analysis. Its main advantages are: the reduced number of calculations; less memory requirements; the possibility of the operation with integer numbers. The lifting scheme for integer-to-integer transform consists of the following basic operations: splitting, prediction and update [17].

Splitting is sometimes referred to as the lazy wavelet [8]. This operation splits the original signal $\{x\}$ into odd and even samples:

$$s_i = x_{2i}, \quad d_i = x_{2i+1}. \tag{1}$$

Prediction, or the dual lifting. This operation at the level k calculates the wavelet coefficients or the details $\{d^{(k)}\}$ as the error in predicting $\{d^{(k-1)}\}$ from $\{s^{(k-1)}\}$ [16]:

$$d_i^{(k)} = d_i^{(k-1)} + \left\lfloor \sum_{j=-\tilde{N}/2}^{\tilde{N}/2} p_j s_{i+j}^{(k-1)} \right\rfloor, \tag{2}$$

where $\{p_j\}$ are coefficients of the wavelet-based high-pass FIR filter and $\tilde{N}$ is the prediction filter order that corresponds to the number of vanishing moments. $\lfloor \theta \rfloor$ denotes a rounding operation; it truncates the real numbers without a bias: if $\theta \geq 0$, it maps $\theta + 0.5$ to the largest previous integer value; if $\theta < 0$, it maps $\theta - 0.5$ to the smallest following integer value.

Update, or the primal lifting. This operation combines $\{s^{(k-1)}\}$ and $\{d^{(k)}\}$, and consists of low-pass FIR filtering to obtain a coarse approximation of the original signal $\{x\}$ [17]:

$$s_i^{(k)} = s_i^{(k-1)} + \left\lfloor \sum_{j=-N/2}^{N/2} u_j d_{i+j}^{(k-1)} \right\rfloor, \qquad (3)$$

where $\{u_j\}$ are coefficients of the wavelet-based low-pass FIR filter and N is the prediction filter order.

The inverse transform is straightforward: first, the signs of FIR filter coefficients $\{u_j\}$ and $\{p_j\}$ are switched. Next, the inverse update followed by inverse prediction is calculated. Finally, the odd and even data samples are merged [17].

A different look at the lifting scheme first was done in [18], where the FIR filters that participate in the prediction and update operation are described in the domain of Z-transform. According to this approach, the transfer function of the prediction FIR filter can be formulated as follows [19]:

$$H_p(z) = 1 + p_0(z + z^{-1}) + \dots + p_{\frac{\tilde{N}}{2}-1}\left(z^{\tilde{N}-1} + z^{-\tilde{N}+1}\right). \qquad (4)$$

The $H_p(z)$ must have zero at $\omega = 0$, i.e., at $z = 1$. It can be easily found [18] that this condition is satisfied when

$$\sum_{i=0}^{\frac{\tilde{N}}{2}-1} p_i = -\frac{1}{2}. \qquad (5)$$

When the admissibility condition (5) is satisfied, $H_p(-1) = 2$ and $H_p(0) = 1$ that means the prediction filter has gain 2 at $\omega = \pi$ and unit gain at $\omega = \dfrac{\pi}{2}$.

Following this approach, the transfer function for update filter can be obtained. We prefer to formulate this transfer function in the terms of $H_p(z)$ [19]:

$$H_u(z) = 1 + H_p(z)\left\{u_0\left[(z) + (z^{-1})\right] \dots + u_{\frac{N}{2}-1}\left[(z^{N-1}) + (z^{-N+1})\right]\right\}. \qquad (6)$$

Note that Eq. (6) does not take into account the sub-sampling (1) and therefore corresponds to the case of so-called redundant transform [20]. However, the update filter $H_u(z)$ frequency response is the same as in the case of "normal" lifting using sub-sampling (1).

$H_u(z)$ should have a zero at $\omega = \pi$, i.e., at $z = -1$. It can be easily found [18] that this condition is satisfied when

$$\sum_{i=0}^{\frac{N}{2}-1} u_i = \frac{1}{4},$$ (7)

When the admissibility condition (7) is satisfied, $H_u(1)=1$ and the prediction filter has gain 1 at $\omega = 0$.

An elegant conversion of the formulas (5), (7) in the case of (4,4) lifting scheme was proposed in [18] to reduce the degree of freedom in the predictor and update coefficients. In our terms, the formulae for the wavelet filters coefficients are as follows:

$$p_0 = -\frac{128+a}{256}, \quad p_1 = \frac{a}{256},$$ (8)

$$u_0 = \frac{64+b}{256}, \quad u_1 = -\frac{b}{256},$$ (9)

where a and b are the parameters that control the DWT properties. It was shown, that for standard lifting filters CDF(2,2) with $p_0 = -0.5$, $p_1 = 0.0$, $u_0 = 0.25$, $u_1 = 0.0$, the values of a,b are $a=0$, $b=0$, and CDF(4,4) with $p_0 = -0.5625$, $p_1 = 0.0625$, $u_0 = 0.28125$, $u_1 = -0.03125$ has $a=16$, $b=8$. It can be concluded that changing the values of the coefficients a,b from 0 to 16, one can control the properties of the resulting wavelet lifting filters adjusting them to the signal spectral properties. This way, the filter characteristics are changed to achieve a higher image compression rate.

3   Proposed Method for Image Compression

The proposed method automatically obtains the wavelet filters coefficients from the image data, and can be described by the algorithm steps:

1. At the first step of the proposed algorithm the image power spectrum is calculated.

2. At the second step, the spectrum is analyzed using artificial intelligence methods to obtain the wavelet lifting filter coefficients.

3. Next, having the lifting filter coefficients, the fast wavelet transform is applied.

4. The transformed image has reduced entropy in wavelet coefficients and can be processed searching the non-zero coefficient trees [20, 21] and then coded by one of the existent entropy coders [22].

At the fourth step of the algorithm the proper image compression is performed, but in this paper we will concentrate on the steps 1-3.

The first step of the proposed algorithm is apply to the considered image $\mathbf{S}$ of size $M \times N$ the discrete cosine transform (DCT) [23] to obtain the mean power spectrum

$$S(i) = \frac{\alpha(i)}{MN} \left[\sum_{l=0}^{N-1} \sum_{q=0}^{M-1} s(l,q) \cos\left(\pi \frac{i(2q+1)}{2M} \right) \right]^2 \tag{10}$$

$$for \quad 0 \le i \le M-1.$$

where M is the number of rows and N is the number of columns of the processed image, $\alpha(i) = \begin{cases} 1, & 1 \le i \le M-1 \\ \frac{1}{\sqrt{2}}, & i = 0 \end{cases}$.

Subsequently, the resulting vector $\mathbf{x}$ is obtained interpolating the spectrum (10) to have a fixed length of 16 elements:

$$\mathbf{x} = F_{16}^{-1}\{F_M\{S(i)\}\}, \tag{11}$$

where $F_M\{\cdot\}$ denotes the direct Fourier transform of size M, and $F_{16}^{-1}\{\cdot\}$ is the inverse Fourier transform of size 16.

Thus, the image characteristic vector $\mathbf{x}$ of the reduced and fixed size is obtained. This vector can be considered as an input pattern. The set of coefficients a,b (8), (9) form the vector $\mathbf{y} = \{a,b\}$, which is the output pattern. Whilst the vector $\mathbf{x}$ is calculated using (10), (11), the vector $\mathbf{y}$ is found by exhaustive search varying the coefficients a,b to obtain those that minimize the transformed image entropy, or the data bitstream in the wavelet transform domain. The weighted entropy of the transformed image was proposed in [9] as a metrics to compare different image lossless compression algorithms. It can be formulated as:

$$H_q(\tilde{\mathbf{s}}) = -\frac{H(\tilde{\mathbf{s}}_a) + \sum_{q=1}^{Q}[H(\tilde{\mathbf{s}}_h) + H(\tilde{\mathbf{s}}_v) + H(\tilde{\mathbf{s}}_d)]}{MN}, \tag{12}$$

where $H(\tilde{\mathbf{s}}_a)$ is Shannon's entropy of the approximations $\tilde{\mathbf{s}}_a$, $H(\tilde{\mathbf{s}}_h), H(\tilde{\mathbf{s}}_v), H(\tilde{\mathbf{s}}_d)$ are entropies of the wavelet coefficients of each quadrant of q-th level of wavelet decomposition (horizontal $\tilde{\mathbf{s}}_h$, vertical $\tilde{\mathbf{s}}_v$ and diagonal $\tilde{\mathbf{s}}_d$ details), and Shannon's entropy in our terms can be calculated, as [22]

$$H(\tilde{\mathbf{s}}) = -\sum_{j=-n}^{n} p(\tilde{s}_j) \cdot \log_2 p(\tilde{s}_j), \tag{13}$$

where $\tilde{\mathbf{s}}$ is the transformed image, s_j is the wavelet coefficient having value j; $-n \le j \le n$ and n is the greatest value of the integer coefficients resulted from the wavelet lifting transform (1), (2), (3).

The patterns $\mathbf{x}, \mathbf{y}$ are associated with each image to form the fundamental set of patterns and perform the supervised learning and classification using 1-*NN* classifier.

We choose the *k-NN* technique because it is one of the most efficient and simple existed classification algorithms [24, 25].

With the characteristic vector **x** and the filter coefficients **y** the associative memory **M** is generated and learned. The learning stage in general form can be interpreted by the diagram:

$$x \Rightarrow \boxed{M} \Leftarrow y$$

Fig. 1. Block diagram of the learning stage

At this stage, the empirically obtained coefficients **y** are associated with the patterns **x** obtained with the proposed spectral model (10), (11). The diagram of the retrieval stage is shown below:

$$x \Rightarrow \boxed{M} \Rightarrow y$$

Fig. 2. Block diagram of the retrieval stage

At the retrieval stage, the patterns presented to the memory **M** are classified to obtain automatically the wavelet filter coefficients for their use in image compression.

4   Results

In this Section, the results obtained applying the proposed method are presented. The experiments were accomplished using the fundamental set of the standard gray scale test images [26, 27] of different size (2048x2560, 1524x1200, 1465x1999, 1024x1024, 512 x 512), some of them are shown in Fig. 3.

Fig. 3. Standard test images: Lenna, boats, F-16, man, baboon, sailboat, Elaine, couple, Tiffany, peppers, aerial, bike, cafe, tools, Zelda

For the classification, the associative memory **M** was generated using 1-*NN* classifier. The obtained classification results show that with this classifier all test images from the fundamental set were classified correctly.

The performance in image compression of the proposed method was compared to the performance of the standard wavelet lifting filters, CDF(2,2) and CDF(4,4). The quantitative results were calculated in terms of the entropies (12) of the transformed images. For the validation of the proposed method, the Leave-One-Out (LOO) [25] technique was employed for each image from the fundamental image set.

The obtained results are presented in Table. From this Table, one can conclude that the proposed method outperforms the standard wavelet lifting filters in compression ratio for all tested standard natural images.

Table 1. Results of compression of test images, obtained by the standard wavelet lifting filters CDF(2,2), CDF(4,4) and the proposed method, bits/pixel. The best results are marked with bold.

Image	CDF (2,2)	CDF (4,4)	Entropy obtained with optimal filters	Entropy obtained with LOO
aerial	5.27382	5.22282	**5.2218**	5.22509
aerial2	5.33433	5.30469	**5.30375**	5.30783
baboon	6.11119	6.08569	**6.08492**	6.08622
baloon	3.02992	3.01551	**3.01519**	3.01751
barb2	5.13575	5.08559	**4.96838**	4.96945
bike	4.81578	4.81534	**4.81405**	4.81733
board	3.8856	3.87838	**3.87676**	3.87741
boats	4.22419	4.18232	**4.18111**	4.1866
cafe	5.62476	5.6231	**5.61969**	5.6231
couple	4.89369	4.91841	**4.88488**	4.88529
Elaine	4.88923	4.8613	**4.86013**	4.86058
F-16	4.16842	4.13125	**4.13115**	4.13545
finger	5.49482	5.354	**5.3215**	5.33779
girl	4.07426	4.13125	**3.9699**	3.97926
gold	4.67736	4.6738	4.67202	**4.67175**
hotel	4.70622	4.69675	**4.69236**	4.69881
Lenna	4.33814	4.28893	**4.28734**	4.30198
man	4.73744	4.71113	**4.71089**	4.71466
peppers	4.60908	4.59882	**4.5944**	4.60044
sailboat	5.1793	5.14887	**5.14825**	5.15003
Tiffany	4.28675	4.27145	**4.27142**	4.27186
tools	5.64493	5.62856	**5.62782**	5.63006
txtur2	5.51308	5.50565	**5.50499**	5.50706
woman	4.75623	4.72292	**4.72139**	4.72376
Zelda	3.84339	3.83507	**3.80353**	3.80497
Mean	4.76991	4.74766	**4.73151**	4.73537

5   Conclusions

In this paper, we have proposed the method for wavelet lifting filter optimization based on the image spectral analysis in the DCT domain and on the use of artificial intelligence model, in particular, 1-*NN* classifier that demonstrated to be competitive versus other known models.

The designed algorithm was tested on different standard test images. The obtained lossless compression results were compared to the results obtained with the standard wavelet lifting filters CDF(2,2) and CDF(4,4). With the proposed method, a higher compression ratio in terms of entropy was obtained for all considered test images.

Though the presented results not reflected the real bitstreams of the compressed data, the optimization of the entropy resulted in less bitstream data. Nevertheless, the future work will be concerned with the implementation of some wavelet sub-band non zero data trees forming technique and entropy codec. As a future work, we consider also the implementation of the proposed method of optimization at each wavelet decomposition level expecting the better results in term of compression ratio.

Acknowledgments. This work was supported by Instituto Politecnico Nacional as a part of the research project SIP#20141215.

References

1. Daubechies, I.: Orthonormal bases of compactly supported wavelets. Commun. Pure Applied Math. 41, 909–996 (1988)
2. Cohen, A., Daubechies, I., Feauveau, J.C.: Biorthogonal bases of compactly supported wavelets. Commun. Pure Applied Math. XLV, 485–560 (1992)
3. Tewfik, A.H., Sinha, D., Jorgensen, P.: On the optimal choice of a wavelet for signal representation. IEEE Trans. Inform.Theory 38, 747–765 (1992)
4. Mallat, S.G., Zhang, Z.: Matching pursuit with time-frequency dictionaries. IEEE Trans. Signal Processing 41, 3397–3415 (1993)
5. Aldroubi, A., Unser, M.: Families of multiresolution and wavelet spaces with optimal properties. Numer. Func. Anal. 14(5/6), 417–446 (1993)
6. Chapa, J.O., Rao, R.M.: Algorithms for Designing Wavelets to Match a Specified Signal. IEEE Trans. Signal Processing 48(12), 3395–3406 (2000)
7. Gupta, A., Joshi, S.D., Prasad, S.: A New Approach for Estimation of Statistically Matched Wavelet. IEEE Trans. Signal Processing 53(5), 1778–1793 (2005)
8. Sweldens, W.: The lifting scheme: A new philosophy in biorthogonal wavelet constructions. In: Laine, A.F., Unser, M. (eds.) Wavelet Applications in Signal and Image Processing III. Proc. SPIE, vol. 2569, pp. 68–79 (1995)
9. Calderbank, A.R., Daubechies, I., Sweldens, W.: Boon-Lock Yeo.: Lossless image compression using integer to integer wavelet transforms. In: Proceedings of International Conference on Image Processing, ICIP 1997, October 26-29, pp. 596–599 (1997)
10. Daubechies, I., Sweldens, W.: Factoring Wavelet and Subband Transforms into Lifting Steps. Technical report, Bell Laboratories, Lucent Technologies (1996)

11. Boulgouris, N.V., Tzovaras, D., Strintzis, M.G.: Lossless image compression based on optimal prediction, adaptive lifting, and conditional arithmetic coding. IEEE Trans. Image Processing 10(1), 1–14 (2001)
12. Thielemann, H.: Adaptive construction of wavelets for image compression. Master's thesis, Martin-Luther-University Halle-Wittenberg, Institute of Computer Science, Germany (2001)
13. Thielemann, H.: Optimally matched wavelets. Ph.D thesis, Universität Bremen, Vorgelegt im Fachbereich 3 (Mathematik und Informatik), Germany (2005)
14. Li, H., Liu, G., Zhang, Z.: Optimization of Integer Wavelet Transforms Based on Difference Correlation Structures. IEEE Trans. Image Processing 14(11), 1831–1847 (2005)
15. Kitanovski, V., Kseneman, M., Gleich, D., Taskovski, D.: Adaptive Lifting Integer Wavelet Transform for Lossless Image Compression. In: Proc. of 15th International Conference on Systems, Signals and Image Processing IWSSIP 2008, pp. 105–108 (August 2008)
16. Kaaniche, M., Pesquet-Popesku, B., Benazza-Benyhahia, A., Resquet, J.-C.: Adaptive lifting scheme with sparse criteria for image coding. EURASIP Journal on Advances in Signal Processing 2012(1), 1–12 (2012)
17. Calderbank, A.R., Daubechies, I., Sweldens, W., Yeo, B.-L.: Wavelet Transforms That Map Integers to Integers. Applied and Computational Harmonic Analysis 5(3), 332–369 (1998)
18. Yoo, H., Jeong, J.: A Unified Framework for Wavelet Transform Based on The Lifting Scheme. In: Proc. of IEEE International Conference on Image Processing, ICIP 2001, Tessaloniki, Greece, October 7-10, pp. 793–795 (2001)
19. Pogrebnyak, O., Ramírez, P.M.: Adaptive wavelet transform for image compression applications. In: Tescher, A.G. (ed.) Applications of Digital Image Processing XXVI, Andrew G. Proc. SPIE, vol. 5203, pp. 623–630 (August 2003)
20. Shapiro, J.M.: Embedded Image Coding Using Zerotrees Of Wavelet Coefficients. IEEE Trans. Signal Processing 41(12), 3445–3462 (1993)
21. Said, A., Pearlman, W.A.: A new, fast and efficient image codec based on set partitioning in hierarchical trees. IEEE Transactions on Circuits and Systems for Video Technology 6, 243–250 (1996)
22. MacKay, D.J.C.: Information Theory, Inference, and Learning Algorithms. Cambridge University Press (2003)
23. Ahmed, N., Natarajan, T., Rao, K.R.: Discrete cosine transform. IEEE Transactions on Computers 23(1), 90–93 (1974)
24. Cover, T.M., Hart, P.E.: Nearest neighbor pattern classification. IEEE Transactions on Information Theory 13(1), 21–27 (1967)
25. Duda, R.O., Hart, P.E., Stork, D.G.: Pattern Classification, 2nd edn. John Wiley & Sons (1997)
26. http://sipi.usc.edu/database/database.php?volume=misc
27. http://ftp.csd.uwo.ca/pub/from_wu/images

Content-Based Image Retrieval with LIRe and SURF on a Smartphone-Based Product Image Database

Kai Chen[1] and Jean Hennebert[2]

[1] University of Fribourg, DIVA-DIUF, Bd. de Pérolles 90, 1700 Fribourg, Switzerland
`kai.chen@unifr.ch`
[2] University of Applied Sciences, HES-SO//FR, Bd. de Pérolles 80, 1705 Fribourg, Switzerland
`jean.hennebert@hefr.ch`

Abstract. We present the evaluation of a product identification task using the LIRe system and SURF (Speeded-Up Robust Features) for content-based image retrieval (CBIR). The evaluation is performed on the Fribourg Product Image Database (FPID) that contains more than 3'000 pictures of consumer products taken using mobile phone cameras in realistic conditions. Using the evaluation protocol proposed with FPID, we explore the performance of different preprocessing and feature extraction. We observe that by using SURF, we can improve significantly the performance on this task. Image resizing and Lucene indexing are used in order to speed up CBIR task with SURF. We also show the benefit of using simple preprocessing of the images such as a proportional cropping of the images. The experiments demonstrate the effectiveness of the proposed method for the product identification task.

Keywords: product identification, CBIR, smartphone-based image database, FPID, benchmarking.

1 Introduction

There is now a growing interest for mobile applications allowing a consumer to automatically identify a product and access information such as prices comparisons, allergens or ecological informations. For usability reasons, the use case involves that the user takes a picture of the product of interest, from which an identification procedure derives the most probable product label. We have build such a product identification mobile application, namely GreenT.

In our work, we focus on consumer product identification using camera phone devices. Different approaches have attempted to identify the product using a detection and recognition procedure of the bar code. While overall efficient, such approaches suffer from two drawbacks. First, some products do not have bar codes such as luxury products or products with small packaging. Second, many mobile phones do not present auto-focus capability resulting in a low-pass blurring effect when capturing a close shot of the bar code. Our approach is therefore to attempt recognizing the product from a product image using CBIR systems. As illustrated in Figure 1, such systems typically use a picture as query and find similar images from a reference database. Generally speaking, a CBIR system would proceed in five steps: image preprocessing, feature extraction, relevant images retrieval, post-processing, and closest product id identification.

J.F. Martínez-Trinidad et al. (Eds.): MCPR 2014, LNCS 8495, pp. 231–240, 2014.
© Springer International Publishing Switzerland 2014

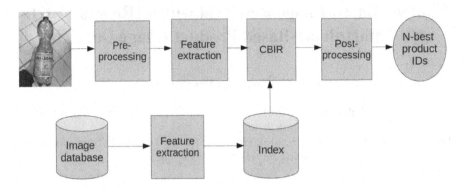

Fig. 1. General operations of a CBIR system using the FPID database

Many CBIR systems have been proposed and described in the literature, for example QBIC [4], GIFT [6], and FIRE [3]. In our work, we have chosen to use the open source java Lucene Image Retrieval (LIRe) library[1] [5]. Local feature SURF (Speeded-Up Robust Features) [1] is also employed for the product identification task. In this paper, we report on the evaluation of LIRe and SURF using the Fribourg Product Image Database (FPID) that has been released recently [2]. FPID is a smartphone-based image database. It contains more than 3'000 pictures of consumer products captured in supermarkets with various regular smart-phone cameras. Using the evaluation protocol proposed with FPID, we explore the performance of different preprocessing and feature extraction using LIRe and SURF. Compared with global feature methods, SURF takes more time. On the other hand, the size of image has a huge impact on the time taken for SURF approach. Therefore, image resizing and feature indexing approaches are used to speed up SURF in our system. The experimental results demonstrate the effectiveness of the proposed method for the product identification task.

This paper is organized as follows. We introduce the FPID smartphone-based image database and our CBIR protocol in Section 2. In Section 3 we present baseline CBIR performance as well as several improvements that we could obtain through the parameters of the feature extraction and preprocessing of the images. Section 4 presents conclusions and future works.

2   FPID and CBIR Evaluation Protocol

The evaluation of CBIR systems requires two elements. First, a database of reference images must be provided together with verified ground truth values for each images. Second, an evaluation protocol must be clearly defined, so that different teams can run their algorithms and compare their results.

For the work reported here, we used the "Fribourg Product Image Database" (FPID) [2]. This database has been recently released to the scientific community. Currently, FPID contains more than 3'000 pictures of retail products that can be found in

---

[1] http://www.semanticmetadata.net/lire/

Swiss and European supermarkets. The set of images covers about 350 products spread into 3 families: bottled water, coffee, and chocolate. Each product has at least one image in the database and the most popular products have about 30 images. The images have been captured using various mobile phones in different supermarkets without any control of the illumination. For identical products, the image features may therefore show a large variability. The ground truth information is the product label expressed as a character string, i.e., if two images have the same product label, then they are considered as relevant for a CBIR task. The product label is a character string uniquely identifying the product brand and model. The ground truth also includes the mobile phone brand/-model, the shop name and its location that allows for some advanced error analysis. Some images taken from FPID are illustrated on Figure 2.

(a) 169, Nokia n95, Manor Fribourg

(b) 497, Samsung g600, Coop Fribourg

(c) 1052, Sonyericson w880i, Migros Fribourg

(d) 1216, Sonyericsson w880i, Migros Fribourg

(e) 23, nokia n95, Migros Fribourg

(f) 2041, Nokia N78, Manor Fribourg

Fig. 2. Example images from FPID with the image id, the device name and location of the acquisition

In this paper, we follow strictly the evaluation protocols for product identification that are proposed with FPID [2]. These protocols are based on a subset S of 1200 images including 100 different products with 12 images per product. From the set S, disjoint sets T and Q for training and query are defined. The protocols are said to be *closed-set* as all query images belong to a product category that is represented in the training sets. In other words, the proposed protocols do not evaluate rejection performances of CBIR systems where a query image has zero corresponding relevant images.

As illustrated in Figure 3, different training sets T_k are defined, k representing the number of images per product in the set. All the training sets are balanced with, e.g., the training set T_4 containing exactly 4 images per products for a total of 400 images. Lists of images are provided on the web site of FPID[2] for $T_1, T_2, \ldots, T_{10}$. In a similar manner, a query set Q_2 including 200 images with 2 images per product is defined. Q_2 is of course disjoint to all the training sets T_n.

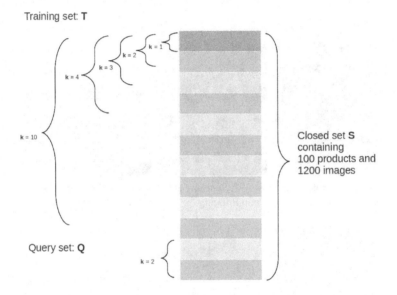

Fig. 3. FPID evaluation protocols

With FPID, it is proposed to report system performance using the recognition rate $RR_I(n)$ considering the n-best retrieved set of images. The rate $RR_I(n)$ is computed as the ratio of positive matches divided by the total number of queries. A match is considered positive when, for a given query image, there exists at least one relevant image in the retrieved n-best set of images. If there is no relevant image in the retrieved n-best set of images then this is a miss. Increasing the value of n in the n-best retrieved set of images will make the task easier. When n is equal to 1, the rate $RR_I(1)$ is actually equal to the *precision at 1* or $P@1$, frequently measured when benchmarking CBIR systems. For the experiments reported in this work, we used $n \in \{1, 2, 5, 10, 15, 20\}$. In a similar manner, we also measure the recognition rate $RR_P(n)$ which is the recognition rate considering the set of n-best retrieved product categories. In this case we retrieve, for

[2] http://diuf.unifr.ch/diva/FPID/

a given query image, the set of n-best images in which we keep only one representing image per product, the other one being discarded.

3 System Description and Results

Our CBIR system is based on the open-source library LIRe and SURF. The LIRe library offers different feature extraction possibilities that we have explored in this work. One of the difficulties of CBIR systems is indeed to select the most suitable feature extraction technique regarding the specificities of a given task. We have also explored the impact of the n value on the RR_I and RR_P performances as described in Section 2. We applied some meaningful preprocessing of the images and method of choosing most suitable feature that have lead to improvements over our baseline results. The SURF is a robust algorithm for local, similarity invariant representation and comparison. It outperformed all global features available in LIRe, but on the other hand it suffers the speed. We observed that the size of image has a direct impact on time taken. Image resizing and feature indexing approaches are taken to speed up the task. All our experiments are achieved in DALCO High Performance Linux Cluster with 64GB per Compute node in the University of Fribourg.

Global Features Comparison. Several global feature extraction are available in LIRe. Figure 4 shows the performances for the different features and the evolution of RR_I as a function of n in the set of n-best retrieved images. In LIRe, image is presented in feature vectors. For a given query image q, a training set T and feature f, we compute the distance $d_{q,i,f}$, such that $d_{q,i,f}$ is the Euclidean distance between feature vector of q and i^{th} images in T. Then we sort images in T by ascending order of this distance value. The first n images in T are considered as n-best relevant images to q.

As expected, the performances increase when n is getting bigger. We can also observe that the image feature "MPEG-7 edge histogram" gives the best performance. The second best feature is the "MPEG-7 color layout". Such results are actually meaningful if we consider that product packagings have purposely different shapes and colors that form their marketing identity. The texture features such as "Tamura"or "Gabor" seem to characterize less efficiently the products. Overall, the RR_I performances are not so much satisfying with, for example, 72% measured with $n = 10$ for "MPEG-7 edge histogram". We can also observe that the performances are very low when n tends to 1, which is a clear indication of the difficulty of the task with a probable explanation to find in the large variability of image characteristics.

Suitable Feature Selection. We observe that for different kind of products, same feature has different performance. In order to find the most suitable feature, for a given query image q and i^{th} images in T, the distance is re-defined as $d_{q,i} = \min_{f \in F} d_{q,i,f}$, where F is the feature set available in LIRe. After sorting the distances of ascending order, first n^{th} images are considered as the relevant images to q. The results shown in Figure 5a indicate us this method improve the performance slightly.

Products vs. Image Recognition. We show on Figure 5b the comparison of RR_I and RR_P rates for the test (T_{10}, Q_2) using "Combine global features" approach which is

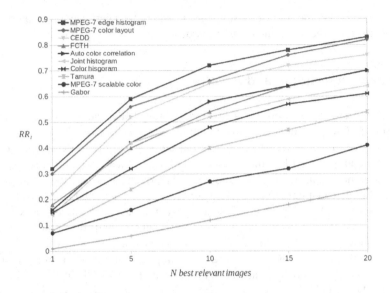

Fig. 4. RR_I evolution using (T_{10}, Q_2) for different features

described in previous section. As expected, RR_P rates are systematically higher as the task is easier. From the results we can observe an increase of 6% between $RR_I(20)$ and $RR_P(20)$. Similar results have been observed for all features.

Image Cropping. In our task, we can reasonably assume that most of the information to identify the products is located at the center of the image. The outer parts are, for most of the FPID images, showing the floor of the supermarket. We therefore attempted to remove these outer parts by implementing a proportional cropping. As illustrated in Figure 6a, we define the cropped area as a rectangle where the top left coordinate is defined by $x = (p \times width)/2$ and $y = (p \times height)/2$ where p is expressed as a percentage of width and height that is removed. The bottom right coordinate is computed in a similar manner. Figure 6b shows the evolution of $RR_P(10)$ as a function of p using our "Combine global feature" method. Interestingly, we see a significant gain of performance up to 86%, 85%, 85% recognition rate when 60%, 30%, 10% of the outer parts of the images are removed.

Local Features. SURF is a scale and rotation invariant detector and descriptor. The SURF algorithm contains three steps: (1) interest points detection. (2) building the descriptor associated with each interest points. (3) descriptor matching. The first two steps are rely on scale-pace representation, and on first and second order differential operators. All the three steps are speed-up by using integral image and box filters. For details of SURF, we refer to [1]. Table 1 gives the results on (T_{10}, Q_2) with cropping factor $p = 0.2$. The results indicate that SURF improve the performance drastically, e.g. $RR_P(3)$ increase from 52% to 94%.

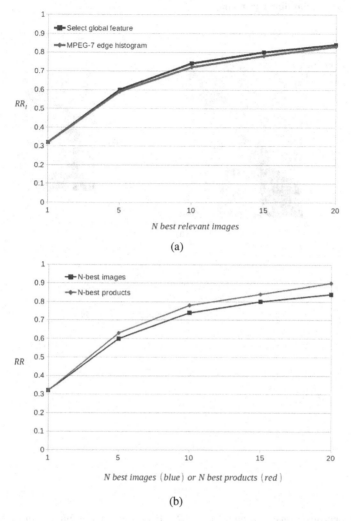

(a)

(b)

Fig. 5. 5a: RR_I evolution using (T_{10}, Q_2) for "combine global features" and "MPEG-7 edge histogram". 5b: $RR_I(10)$ and $RR_P(10)$ rates evolution for (T_{10}, Q_2) using as approach "combine global features"

However, compare to other global features methods, SURF suffers from the time of interest points extraction and matching. For a given query image and training set T_{10}, the average time used for global features is less than 2 seconds, on the other hand, by applying SURF method, it takes about 240 seconds. In order to reduce the time taken for SURF method, we proportionally reduce the image size. For a given image I, such that $width_{I'} = width_I \times w$, where $width_{I'}$ is the resized image width and w is the resizing factor. Figure 7a illustrates the impact of image size on the time taken. The impact of image size on performance is given in Figure 7b. We observe that reducing image

Proportional cropping

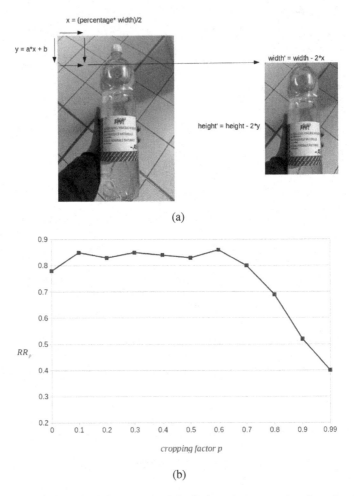

(a)

(b)

Fig. 6. 6a: Proportional image cropping. 6b: $RR_P(10)$ evolution as a function of p, the proportional cropping factor, for (T_{10}, Q_2) using "combine global features" approach.

size by choosing $w = 0.7$, we still have a high accuracy $RR_P(3) = 92\%$ compare to $RR_P(3) = 94\%$ with the original image size, but the time has been reduced from 240 seconds to 158 seconds. Inspired by LIRe, we use Apach Lucene[3] as feature indexing tool to speed-up SURF. For each image in T, we first extract the interest points with SURF, then these points are saved into a index by using Lucene. With this approach, we reduce the time from 158 to 80 seconds.

---

[3] http://lucene.apache.org/core/

Table 1. Comparison "combine global features" method with SURF

N-best products	1	2	3
Combine global features	0.32	0.43	0.52
SURF	0.72	0.90	0.94

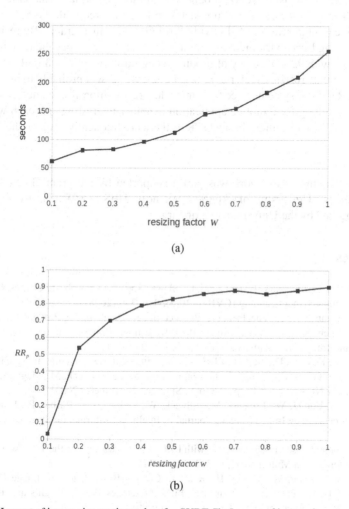

(a)

(b)

Fig. 7. 7a: Impact of image size on time taken for SURF. 7b: Impact of image size on performance for SURF.

4 Conclusion

We presented a product identification system based on CBIR. Experiments are made on LIRe (an open-source CBIR system part of Lucene) and SURF. The performances of the system have been evaluated using the protocols proposed with the FPID database. We have also found that the global features based on color layouts and edge histograms are the most performing one on our product identification task. Considering that product packagings have purposely different shapes and colors for marketing identity, such results are probably meaningful. Several improvements have been proposed over the baseline use of the LIRe system, including proportional image cropping and global features combination. By using SURF, product recognition performance increased to 94% (with $n = 3$ in the n-best retrieval products), to be compared with the 52% obtained using baseline configuration of LIRe with "MPEG-7 edge histogram". By resizing the images and using Lucene for indexing, for a given image, we reduce the time from 240 to 80 seconds, with 92% accuracy of product recognition (with $n = 3$ in the n-best retrieval products) by resizing factor $w = 0.7$. Future works will probably to increase the speed of SURF in our system, since for our product recognition system, nearly 1 minute per query is too long for a mobile application. Another interesting approach would be to combine CBIR with camera-based OCR as there are frequently texts on the labels of the products.

Acknowledgements. This work was partly supported by the grant Green-T RCSO ISNet from the University of Applied Sciences HES-SO//Wallis, by the HES-SO//Fribourg and by the University of Fribourg.

References

1. Bay, H., Ess, A., Tuytelaars, T., Van Gool, L.: SURF: Speeded Up Robust Features. Computer Vision and Image Understanding (CVIU) 110(3), 346–359 (2008)
2. Chen, K., Hennebert, J.: The Fribourg Product Image Database for Product Identification Tasks. In: Chen, K., Hennebert, J. (eds.) IEEE/IIAE International Conference on Intelligent Systems and Image Processing (ICISIP), pp. 162–169 (2013)
3. Deselaers, T., Keysers, D., Ney, H.: FIRE – flexible image retrieval engine: ImageCLEF 2004 evaluation. In: Peters, C., Clough, P., Gonzalo, J., Jones, G.J.F., Kluck, M., Magnini, B. (eds.) CLEF 2004. LNCS, vol. 3491, pp. 688–698. Springer, Heidelberg (2005)
4. Faloutsos, C., Equitz, W., Flickner, M., Niblack, W., Petkovic, D., Barber, R.: Efficient and Effective Querying by Image Content. Journal of Intelligent Information Systems 3, 231–262 (1994)
5. Lux, M.: Content based image retrieval with LIRe. In: Proceedings of the 19th ACM International Conference on Multimedia, pp. 735–738 (2011)
6. Squire, D.M., Müller, W., Müller, H., Raki, J.: Content-Based Query of Image Databases, Inspirations From Text Retrieval: Inverted Files, Frequency-Based Weights and Relevance Feedback. Pattern Recognition Letters, 143–149 (1999)

A New Retinal Recognition System Using a Logarithmic Spiral Sampling Grid

Fabiola M. Villalobos Castaldi[1], Edgardo M. Felipe-Riveron[2],
and Ernesto Suaste Gómez[1]

[1] Researches and Advanced Studies Center of the National Polytechnic Institute,
Av. Instituto Politécnico Nacional # 2508, La Laguna Ticoman, Gustavo A. Madero,
P.O. 07360, Mexico D.F., Mexico
{mvillalobos,esuaste}@cinvestav.mx
[2] Centro de Investigación en Computación, Instituto Politécnico Nacional, Av. Juan de Dios
Batiz and Miguel Othon de Mendizabal P.O. 07738., Mexico D.F., Mexico
edgardo@cic.cin.mx

Abstract. The retinal vascular network has many desirable characteristics as a basis for authentication, including uniqueness, stability, and permanence. In this paper, a new approach for retinal images features extraction and template coding is proposed. The use of the logarithmic spiral sampling grid in scanning and tracking the vascular network is the key to make this new approach simple, flexible and reliable. Experiments show that this approach can achieve the reduction of data dimensionality and of the required time to obtain the biometric code of the vascular network in a retinal image. The performed experiments demonstrated that the proposed verification system has an average accuracy of 95.0 – 98 %.

Keywords: Logarithmic spiral sampling grid, spiral scan and sampling, biometry, retinal images, time series representations.

1 Introduction

It has been proposed a number of authentication methods based on the retina. These methods have focused primarily on selecting the appropriate features to represent the retina (bifurcations, ending points, etc.). But the final representation of the features has never been studied carefully [2-16]. Biometric representation (*template*) is a machine readable and understandable form of a biometric trait. It influences the system's accuracy and the design of the rest of the system. The machine representation of a biometric is critical to the success of the matching algorithm. In a practical authentication system, the database can contain records of millions of people. Choosing an appropriate representation of the features in order to make the data base smaller in size, having a rapid response search and while retaining high accuracy in the verification, is a vital task.

A relatively high number of personal authentication methods based on the blood vessel network of the retina have been recently developed as biometric. These

J.F. Martínez-Trinidad et al. (Eds.): MCPR 2014, LNCS 8495, pp. 241–250, 2014.
© Springer International Publishing Switzerland 2014

methods are based on determining a given number of appropriate features that represent uniquely the retina.

From previous studies, the retina's features used for authentication can be classified into three main categories: structural, statistical and algebraic features. Some typical structural features include main lines (centerlines), branching points, crossing points, termination points, positions, angles, diameters, etc. [12], [33]. Some statistical features are the texture moments that were used in [2] and the random values that were used in [31]. Likewise, the algebraic features, such as band-tree based radial partition, the ring method, etc., were proposed in [26].

The general procedure of biometric systems for personal authentication based on the retinal vascular network comprises the following seven steps:

1. Acquisition of the eye fundus image.
2. Image enhancement (noise smoothing, contrast enhancement, size normalization)
3. Creation of the conditions for doing the next stage invariant to translation, rotation and scale at least in a narrow range. This step may include eventually the segmentation of the optic disc and the macula luteal.
4. Probably, the vascular network segmentation. Eventually, its skeletonization is also required.
5. Extraction of the structural characteristics to obtain a code which differentiate it.
6. Classification on the basis of the code previously found.
7. Authentication for recognizing/identifying the person.

Some algorithms do not segment the vascular network in order to save computational time (stage 4). In this paper we discuss mainly the novelty of the approach related to the steps 3, 4 and 5 and evaluation of the feature extraction method to be used for authentication of individuals (stages 6 and 7).

The main contribution of this paper is the implementation of a new biometric representation method based on coding blood vessel segments, through a new scanning and tracking algorithm by using a logarithmic spiral. Data obtained from the sampling of the vascular network constitute local features that are conformed in time series representations. The time series have been studied extensively in data mining, bioinformatics and pattern recognition in biometrics [1].

1.1   Logarithmic Spiral

The spiral is a curve that winds itself around a given point. While not being a circle, the radius will vary along the angle [20], [21]. The logarithmic spiral is that in which the radius grows exponentially with the rotation angle. The logarithmic relation between radius and angle leads to the name of logarithmic spiral. In this curve the distances where a radius from the origin meets the curve increases in geometric progression. In polar coordinates the logarithmic curve can be expressed matematically as (Eq. 1):

$$r = ae^{b\theta} \tag{1}$$

where r is the distance from the origin, θ is the angle from the horizontal x-axis, e is the base of natural logarithms, and a and b are arbitrary positive real constants. The constant a is the increasing rate of the spiral and its sign determines the rotation direction of the spiral (in this work a is known as the spiral roll). The logarithmic spiral is also known as the growth spiral, equiangular spiral, and spiral mirabilis. The logarithmic spiral is remarkable because of its unique self-similarity, that is, it is invariant after a similarity transform. After any scaling (uniformly increasing or decreasing the size) logarithmic spirals can be rotated and always match the original figure.

The retinal circulation of the normal human retinal vasculature is statistically self-similar, fractal and the Murray optimization principle is valid. Studies from several groups present strong evidence that the fractal dimension of the blood vessels in the normal human retina is approximately 1.7. This is the same fractal dimension found for a diffusion-limited growth process, which is consistent with the hypothesis that the development of human retinal vessels involves a diffusion process [34]. Fractal analysis provides a method for the quantitative study of changes in the retinal vascular network [33]. It has been suggested that fractal models are simple to encode genetically because the same branching mechanism is used repeatedly. All fractals have scale and rotational invariances, and any fractal formed from a process that has a non-zero rotational component will include logarithmic spiral forms [35].

1.2   Advantages of the Logarithmic Spiral Sampling Grid

In this work the scanning and tracking step is based on a sparse logarithmic spiral sampling grid, which has a log-polar geometry, meaning that the density of the sampling points decreases exponentially with the distance from the center. Such non-uniform sampling pattern, with frequency decreasing from the center to the periphery, shares the same geometric progression that the retinal vascular network has. This sampling grid offers the following advantages:

1. The data dimensionality is reduced because the retinal vascular network is represented by a sequence of only two real valued data [29].
2. Discontinuities caused by sampling the blood vessels are eliminated from the data [32]. This problem occurs when concentric flatted circles or other sampling methods are used [28].
3. Only data related to detected points of the vascular network along the spiral grid are encoded and not the entire region (blood vessels and background). The information of every point P extracted by the spiral is used as feature descriptors of the vascular network structure [31].
4. The vascular network travels and distributes across the retina in the same way as does the logarithmic spiral mapping grid. The most problematic area is located within the optical disc which is previously removed [39-41].
5. The most robust and stable structure of the vascular network is coded, that is, the vessel segments of the vascular network. Bifurcations and crossings of the venous and arterial networks are eliminated in order to avoid coding errors [22-26].

6.   It is not necessary to take into account whether a given vessel is a vein or an artery; only the midpoint of every vessel segment is used as the feature descriptor.
7.   The amount of coded information is increased because it is possible to extract more than one feature from the detected vessels along the spiral path [31].
8.   The size of the spiral grid is determined by the number of necessary points that ensures the subject's individuality [30]. The sampling is done in the thinned retinal blood vessels. This provides invariance to small changes in the scale.

2   The Recognition System

In our retinal recognition system, fundus images are analyzed with a logarithmic spiral sampling grid, and the geometrical characteristics of the retinal vascular network are coded using a time series approach. The retina images contained in the publicly available VARIA database were used to implement the recognition system and to assess its performance. The VARIA database is a set of retinal images used for authentication purposes. The database currently includes 233 images, from 139 different individuals. The number of images per subject is not constant. The images have been acquired with a TopCon non-mydriatic camera NW-100 model and are optic disc centered with a resolution of 768x584 pixels [38]. The detailed description of the system follows.

2.1   Logarithmic Spiral Sampling Grid

The recognition scheme proposed in this paper is based on a logarithmic spiral sampling grid which is positioned over the center of the optic disc. It travels throughout the retinal vascular network that surrounds the optic disc. For this, it is necessary to detect the optic disc and locate its center to be used as a reference point. The detection of the optic disc is carried out from the green plane of the color fundus image acquired in the RGB color space. This is because this plane presents more details and less noise with respect to the red and blue planes. Then a morphological opening and a morphological closing with a circular structuring element (disc) of 5 pixels diameter are performed to emphasize the areas of interest and to reduce the number of non-interesting ones. Once the optic disc is located it is hidden superimposing a black circular disc of a diameter 10% greater than the actual diameter of the optic disc.

2.2   Invariances of the Method

In order to couple the proposed scheme against eventual small rotation variations occurring during the image acquisition procedure, we use the macula center as another reference point, in order to link it with the optic disc center with a straight line (Fig. 1). To compensate the rotation variations, the image is then rotated accordingly so that the line is aligned with the horizontal axis. The methodology step by step for segmenting the optic disc and the macula, and to locate the centroid of both anatomic retina structures is beyond the scope of this paper [39-40]. The proposed method is also invariant to small translation variations since we always relate the sampling to the center of the optic disc. If the retinal vascular network suffers some translation during the acquisition process of the image, the logarithmic spiral sampling is always referred to the same reference coordinates.

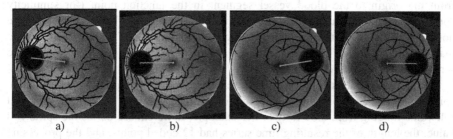

Fig. 1. Experimental results of the reinforcement of the proposed method against translation and rotation in some typical images. a) and c) not compensated images, b) and d) processed images.

2.3   Feature Extraction

Since it is not a particular goal of this paper to segment the vascular network, the feature extraction process starts from a binary image having the vascular network already segmented using the method previously proposed and published by the authors [36].

2.3.1 Morphological Thinning

Vessels in the vicinity of the optic disc could have different diameter size. To overcome this inconvenience, retinal vessel thinning (through a skeletonizing procedure) was implemented using a morphological operator that reduces the width of vessels to single-pixel width line segments, while preserving the extent and connectivity of the original shape. The thinned representation of the vascular network is processed easily in later stages savings either computing time and storage complexity [12]. The spiral grid is mapped along the thinned retinal network starting from the center of the masked optic disc towards the periphery of the vascular network. This step transforms the irregular retinal structure into sequential data. It is necessary to evaluate now the potential benefit of adapting the mapping grid to the dimensions of the image, instead of placing a mapping grid of constant size. Thus, an exhaustive analysis of the spiral mapping grid must be performed in order to select the most suitable size of the mapping grid for obtaining the most adequate biometric template congruence.

We configured the logarithmic spiral grid in several sizes employing different spiral roll values. The spiral roll value should not be so small because the resulting spiral grid will travel very gently, the number of wings will increase and then the length of the feature vector and the required computational time to analyze the retinal network will increase. Moreover, the spiral roll value should not be so large, because the resulting spiral grid travels so fast and the number of wings will be small and therefore, the length of the feature vector reduces and also the achieved data.

For each point that the spiral grid crosses with the thinned vascular network, two geometrical characteristics are encoded. For instance, we use as descriptor the radius from the origin to the blood vessel segment in the junction point (for simplicity "position"), and the angle that this blood vessel segment forms respect to the horizontal axis in that point (for simplicity "crossing angle"). For each feature mapped and coded, we created a sequence of real valued data; thus, we got two time series from each input retinal image.

We carried out the analysis in order to select the best mapping grid size varying the spiral roll value and computing the length of the resulting time series for each spiral roll value ranging from 0.01 to two. For example, if we choose 0.5 as the spiral roll value, the length of the resulting time series had 12 coded points, and the processing time to encode the retinal network was 0.8s. On the other hand, if we want to increase the time series length to 178, the spiral roll value must be 0.03 for which the system will require 3.9s. This let us to establish a range of allowed spiral roll values, without increasing the processing time while ensuring the efficiency of the recognition system based on the logarithmic spiral mapping grid. Based on the obtained results, we decided to select 0.2 as the most suitable spiral roll value that guarantees to encode an average of 50 points in a time of 1s; thus, the resulting time series length was 50 coded points. It means that the spiral grid was of a constant size for all the similar images contained in the database. Figure 2 shows both time series of a typical coded retinal image using a logarithmic spiral maping grid with a spiral grid value = 0.15942.

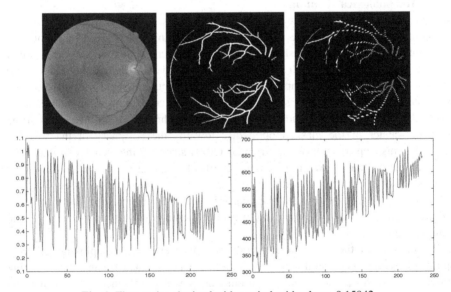

Fig. 2. Time series obtained with a spiral grid value = 0.15942

3   Experiments and Results

We use also a novel retinal recognition scheme to evaluate the discriminatory potential and the inter-individual differences based on the time series representation of the geometrical retinal network features, employing the logarithmic spiral as the sampling grid. In the recognition phase, we compare the presented biometric trait with the feature vector associated with the claimed ID stored previously in the database. Here, the user has to present his/her ID in order to retrieve the biometric feature template associated to his/her database. Then, the extracted feature vector from the input image (whose identity has to be recognized) is compared with the template retrieved from the database. The output of the comparison is an accept/reject decision. The recognition is positive if the distance between the claimed and the stored feature vector is less than a given threshold value. The metric used for the proposed recognition system is the Euclidean distance.

3.1   Evaluation of the Recognition System

The performance of the recognition phase depends on how good was created the biometric representation of the biometric feature and how good is the matching scheme. As it was mentioned previously, we coded the geometrical features of the retinal network and arranged them in a sequence of real valued data. We saved these time series as the feature vectors in the database along with the provided user ID. The distance measured is the matching score that cuantifies the response of the matching scheme. Based on the matching scores, and a predefined threshold value, it is possible to estimate the accuracy of the proposed logarithmic spiral sampling grid-based recognition system. The results of the accuracy of the proposed retinal recognition system are presented as follows: we considered each retinal fundus image in the database as one of a different user. We matched all retina feature vectors against each other. Based on the 233 images from 139 registered subjects in the VARIA database, the total amount of comparisons was $((233*232)/2) = 27028$. With this total number of comparisons it is now possible to compute the FAR (False Accepted Rate), the FRR (False Rejected Rate) and the thresholds. We carried out the evaluation of the recogniton system using separately each time series as the feature descriptor, i.e., the time series of the position and that of the crossing angle. It was concluded from the experimental results that we obtain lower error rates using as the feature vector the position time series; this result is consistent with that obtained by [27] concluding that the position of the blood vessel as a descriptor is the main contribution to retina template entropy. If the FAR and FRR rates for a series of threshold values are obtained, it is possible to plot these rates as a Receiver Operating Curve (ROC), where one axis displays FAR rates and the other displays FRR rates. Based on such a curve, it is possible to make tradeoff decisions regarding what FAR/FRR values that is desirable for a system. The graph is shown in Fig. 3. From this curve it is possible to observe that in a very small FAR we have large values of FRR for identification.

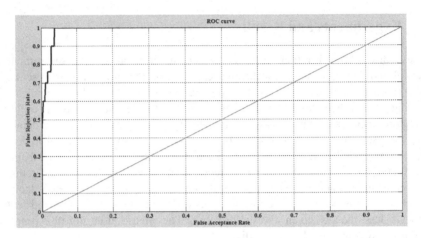

Fig. 3. Roc curve

4   Conclusion

A novel approach for the vascular network biometric coding based on a logarithmic spiral mapping grid was proposed. The main contribution of this proposal is the implementation of the logarithmic spiral mapping grid as the scan and tracking pattern method. This methodology share the fractal and geometrical characteristics that retinal network has; it is very flexible to implement since the spiral parameters, the geometrical retinal features and the size of the spiral sampling grid can be easily adjusted according to different system requirements; the time series representation makes it very convenient for the implementation of multi-biometrics using feature fusion, and the logarithmic spiral scan and sampling representation reduce the data dimensionality of the original retinal image to a real sequential data. Finally; the method reduces the computational time required for the template representation and the matching step. We obtained a maximal performance of the proposed system of 95 -98%, which is relatively high. The experimental results showed that the novel proposed retinal recognition system is an effective approach in biometric identification applications.

Acknowledgement. The authors of this paper would like to thank the COFAA, Postgraduate and Research Secretary, Centro de Investigación en Computación del Instituto Politécnico Nacional (IPN), CONACyT and Researchers National System (SNI), for their economic support to carry out this work.

References

1. Keogh, E., Chakrabarti, K., Pazzani, M., Mehrotra, S.: Locally Adaptive Dimensionality Reduction for Indexing Large Time Series Databases. In: Proceedings of ACM SIGMOD Conference on Management of Data, Santa Barbara, CA, May 21-24, pp. 151–162 (2001)

2. Jung, E., Hong, K.: Automatic Retinal Vasculature Structure Tracing and Vascular Landmark Extraction from Human Eye Image. In: Proceedings of the International Conference on Hybrid Information Technology. IEEE Computer Society (2006)
3. Hill, R.B.: Retina Identification, Portland, OR, USA (1992)
4. Hill, R.B.: Apparatus and method for identifying individuals through their retinal vasculature patterns. U.S. Patent No. 4109237 (1978)
5. Simon, C., Goldstein, I.: A new scientific method of identification. New York State. J. Medicine 35(18), 901–906 (1935)
6. Tower, P.: The fundus oculi in monozygotic twins: Report of six pairs of identical twins. Arch. Ophthalmol. 54, 225–239 (1955)
7. Marshall, J., Usher, D.: Method for generating a unique and consistent signal pattern for identification of an individual. U.S. Patent No. 6993161 (2006)
8. Derakhshani, R., Ross, A.: A Texture-Based Neural Network Classifier for Biometric Identification using Ocular Surface Vasculature. In: Appeared in Proc. of International Joint Conference on Neural Networks (IJCNN), Orlando, USA (2007)
9. Golden, B.L., Rollin, B.E., Switzer, J.R.V.: Apparatus and method for creating a record using biometric information. U.S. Patent No. 028343 (2004)
10. Ortega, M., Gonzalez, M.F.: Automatic system for personal authentication using the retinal vessel tree as biometric pattern, PhD. Thesis, Department of Computer Science of the Faculty of Informatics of the University of Coruña (2009), downloaded from: http://www.varpa.es/ (revised on June 10, 2012)
11. http://www.absoluteastronomy.com/topics/Retinal_scan (revised on June 10, 2012.)
12. Bevilacqua, V., Cambó, S., Cariello, L., Mastronardi, G.: Retinal Fundus Hybrid Analysis Based on Soft Computing Algorithms. Communications To Simai Congress 2 (2007) ISSN 1827-9015
13. Usher, D., Tosa, Y., Friedman, M.: Ocular Biometrics: Simultaneous Capture and Analysis of the Retina and Iris. Advances in Biometrics Sensors, Algorithms and Systems, 133–155 (2007)
14. Usher, D.B.: Image analysis for the screening of diabetic retinopathy, PhD thesis, University of London (2003)
15. Fukuta, K., Nakagawa, T., Yoshinori, H., Hatanaka, Y., Hara, T., Fujita, H.: Personal identification based on blood vessels of retinal fundus images (Proceedings Paper). In: Medical Imaging, Image Processing, Proceedings, vol. 6914 (2008)
16. Lee, S.S., Rajeswari, M., Ramachandram, D., Shaharuddin, B.: Screening of Diabetic Retinopathy - Automatic Segmentation of Optic Disc in Colour Fundus Images. In: Proc. 2nd International Conference on Distributed Frameworks for Multimedia Applications, pp. 1–7 (2006)
17. MacGillivray, T.J., Patton, N., Doubal, F.N., Graham, C., Wardlaw, J.M.: Fractal analysis of the retinal vascular network in fundus images. In: Proceedings of the 29th Annual International Conference of the IEEE EMBS, Cité Internationale, Lyon, France (2007)
18. Barry, R.: Fractal analysis of the vascular tree in the human retina, Masters. Annu. Rev. Biomed. Eng. 6, 427–452 (2004), doi:10.1146/annurev.bioeng.6.040803.140100
19. Taylor, R.P.: Chaos, Fractals, Nature: a New look at Jackson Pollock, Fractals Research, Eugene OR (200&)
20. http://mathworld.wolfram.com/LogarithmicSpiral.html (revised on September 20, 2012)
21. http://www.2dcurves.com/spiral/spirallo.html (revised on September 20, 2012)

22. Zana, F., Klein, J.C.: Robust Segmentation of Vessels from Retinal Angiography. In: International Conference on Digital Signal Processing, Santorini, Greece, pp. 1087–1091 (1977)

23. Zhoue, L., Rzeszotarski, M., Singerman, L., Cokreff, J.: The detection and quantification of retinopathy using digital angiograms. IEEE Transaction on Medical Imaging 13-4, 619-626 (1994)

24. Matsopoulos, G.K., Mouravliansky, N.A., Delibasis, K.K., Nikita, K.S.: Automatic retinal image registration Scheme using global optimization techniques. IEEE Trans. Information Technology in Biomedicine 3 (1999)

25. Wang, L., Bhalerao, A.: Model based segmentation for retinal fundus images. In: Bigun, J., Gustavsson, T. (eds.) SCIA 2003. LNCS, vol. 2749, pp. 422–429. Springer, Heidelberg (2003)

26. Farzin, H., Abrishami-Moghaddam, H., Moin, M.: A Novel Retinal Identification System. EURASIP Journal on Advances in Signal Processing, Article ID 280635, 10 pages (2008), doi:10.1155/2008/280635

27. Arakala, A., Culpepper, J.S., Jeffers, J., Turpin, A., Boztaş, S., Horadam, K.J., McKendrick, A.M.: Entropy of the Retina Template. In: Tistarelli, M., Nixon, M.S. (eds.) ICB 2009. LNCS, vol. 5558, pp. 1250–1259. Springer, Heidelberg (2009)

28. Fuhrmann, T., Hammerle-Uhl, J., Uhl, A.: Usefulness of Retina Codes in Biometrics. In: Wada, T., Huang, F., Lin, S. (eds.) PSIVT 2009. LNCS, vol. 5414, pp. 624–632. Springer, Heidelberg (2009), doi:10.1007/978-3-540-92957-4_54.

29. Che Azemin, M.Z., Kumar, D.K., Wu, H.R.: Shape Signature for Retinal Biometrics. In: 2009 Digital Image Computing: Techniques and Applications, DICTA 2009, pp. 382–386 (2009)

30. http://www.biometricnewsportal.com/retina_biometrics.asp

31. Chen, J., Moon, Y.-S., Wong, M.-F., Su, G.: Palmprint authentication using a symbolic representation of images. Image and Vision Computing 28, 343–351 (2010)

32. http://en.wikipedia.org/wiki/Connected_space#Path_connectedness

33. MacGillivray, T.J., Patton, N., Doubal, F.N., Graham, C., Wardlaw, J.M.: Fractal analysis of the retinal vascular network in fundus images. In: Proceedings of the 29th Annual International Conference of the IEEE EMBS, Cité Internationale, Lyon, France (2007)

34. Barry, R.: Fractal analysis of the vascular tree in the human retina, Masters. Annu. Rev. Biomed. Eng. 6, 427–452 (2004), doi:10.1146/annurev.bioeng.6.040803.140100.

35. Taylor, R.P.: Chaos, Fractals, Nature: a New look at Jackson Pollock, Fractals Research, Eugene OR (200&)

36. Villalobos, F.M., Felipe, E.F.: A Fast Efficient and Automated Method to Extract Vessels from Fundus Images. Journal of Visualization, J. Vis. 13, 263–270 (2010) ISSN: 1343-8875, doi:10.1007/s12650-010-0037-y

37. http://en.wikipedia.org/wiki/Macula_of_retina (last acceced, June 2013)

38. http://www.varpa.es/varia.html

39. Yu, H., Barriga, S., Agurto, C., Echegaray, S., Pattichis, M., Zamora, G., Bauman, W., Soliz, P.: Fast Localization of Optic Disc and Fovea in Retinal Images for Eye Disease Screening (2008), http://visionquest-bio.com/index.html

40. Youssif, A.A.A., Ghalwash, A.Z., Ghoneim, A.A.S.A.: Optic Disc Detection From Normalized Digital Fundus Images by Means of a Vessels' Direction Matched. IEEE Transactions on Medical Imaging 27(1), 11–19 (2008)

A Semi-supervised Puzzle-Based Method for Separating the Venous and Arterial Vascular Networks in Retinal Images

Edgardo M. Felipe-Riveron[1], Fabiola M. Villalobos Castaldi[2],
Ernesto Suaste Gómez[2], Marcos A. Leiva Vasconcellos[1],
and Cecilia Albortante Morato[3]

[1] Center for Computing Research, National Polytechnic Institute, Av. Juan de Dios Batiz and Miguel Othon de Mendizabal P.O. 07738,
Mexico D. F., Mexico
edgardo@cic.cin.mx, shadowalker25403@yahoo.com
[2] Researches and Advanced Studies Center of the National Polytechnic Institute,
Av. Instituto Politécnico Nacional # 2508, La Laguna Ticoman, Gustavo A. Madero,
P.O. 07360, Mexico D.F., Mexico
{mvillalobos,esuaste}@cinvestav.mx,
[3] University of Camagüey, Carretera Circunvalación Norte Km 51/2, Camagüey, Cuba
cecitog@yahoo.com.mx

Abstract. The focus of this work is to create a methodology to separate the entire vascular network into its independent veins and arteries networks in optical human fundus images. It has been developed following the logical procedure used by humans when they assemble a puzzle. In the development of the methodology we take into consideration physiological properties, topological properties of the tree structure and morphological properties of both networks, that is, they have only bifurcations, crosses and ending points, and also that crosses are produced always between venous and arterial branches. For arterial blood vessels we get a classification capability, based on the pixel counting, of 84.88% while for venous was 82.87%. This indicates that the methodology classified correctly as average 83.80% of the total blood vessels in the images.

Keywords: Retinal image analysis, retinal vascular network separation, puzzle-based method.

1 Introduction

The human retina is mainly conformed anatomically by the optic disc (OD), the macula luteal and the arterial and venous vascular networks. Arteries transport blood with high oxygen content to the organs and veins bring the oxygen-poor blood back to the heart-lung circulation. The separation of the retinal vascular network is a complex task. It can present some difficulties because frequently one of the networks obstructs the visibility of the other one, leading to a serious confusion between them. However, a good splitting of the vein and arterial networks allows the detection of some structural characteristics and functionalities that hides when the network is analyzed as a whole.

J.F. Martínez-Trinidad et al. (Eds.): MCPR 2014, LNCS 8495, pp. 251–260, 2014.

An important aspect to make a good vessel network splitting is to take into consideration the topology of the tree structure and the morphological properties of both networks. An ophthalmologist is able to track the venous and arterial networks, but when they have too many branches, it demands to track more than once each network in order to analyze the entire vessels.

The analysis of the vascular network by an ophthalmologist to make an accurate diagnosis will be easier and better if he/she have two images with the veins and arterial networks separated. The situation is the same, or maybe more justified, if our intention consists of analyze by a computer automatically the quality of the retinal venous and arterial networks. Undoubtedly, the analysis will be easier if both networks are completely independent. Some common analysis of the retinal vascular network could be related with the detection of stenosis, aneurysms, hemorrhages, thrombus, tortuosity, and many other conditions that could indicate that the vascular network is not healthy. It is taken into consideration for the development of the proposed methodology the important physiological property that arteries and veins never intersect between themselves neither creates loops, although a vein and an artery can concur forming an artery-vein joined trajectory.

The focus of this work is to create a methodology to separate the entire vascular network into its independent veins and arteries networks in human fundus images. The methodology has been developed following the logical procedure commonly used by humans when they assemble a puzzle.

2   Antecedents

There is a lot of works about blood vessel network segmentation in the literature. However, works related to the separation of vascular blood vessels networks in its venous and arterial branches has received a limited attention so far. Computerized analysis of retinal fundus images potentially reduce the workload of ophthalmologists and can improve in many ways the diagnostic efficiency, mainly when it is related to the quality of the patient's retinal vascular network [1-8, 13]. Its clinical status can say too much to physicians about the general status of the vascular network located in other zones in the human body. Besides this, particularly the retinal vascular network is affected with very dangerous results (blindness) with diabetes (diabetic retinopathy), high blood pressure (hypertensive retinopathy), and other common systemic diseases.

The automated classification of blood vessels in the retina as venous and arterials is still an open problem in image processing. In a fundus image veins and arteries differ visually in their shapes, thickness, color and texture. These differences can be easily appreciated in main vessels near to the optic disc, but varies strongly in vessels more far from the optic disk. That is one of the reasons that the separation of the vascular network of the retina cannot be done successfully under these bases.

3   The Proposed Method

The proposed methodology for splitting the retinal vascular network in their corresponding venous and arterial branches follows the steps indicated in the flow diagram shown in figure 1. In this paper are described only the last three steps (from step 4 to

6). This means that we start the procedure from images having the vascular network already segmented. For the interpretation of the references to color in this study, the reader is referred to the web version of the paper.

The algorithm is based on the analysis of adjacent cells appearing each time when the tracking through a given blood vessel is carried out. In this task is taken into account the situation occurring between the number of independent blood elements contained in each cell and the number of contacts that the branches of the vascular network makes with the sides of the corresponding cell. It is semi-supervised because at this stage of the work we have not solved yet the automatic initial classification in venous and arterial the cells bordering the optic disc. Currently this is done manually before running the program to separate the venous and arterial vascular networks, which is fully non-supervised (automatic). First of all, a rectangular (or square) regular grid is superimposed over the image before the beginning of the separation of the vascular network in its arterial and venous branches, regardless whether the image was rotated, translated or scaled. Therefore, it is not necessary to consider the amounts of translation, rotation or scaling. The separation of the networks will take place regardless of the conditions of the retina image to which the method is facing. Ten different images with well-segmented vascular network were more than enough to tune the separation algorithm and prove its effectiveness.

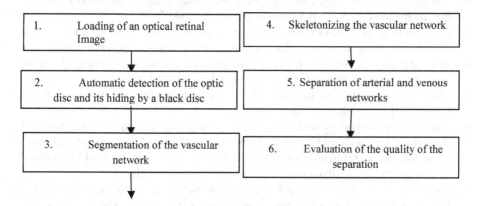

Fig. 1. Steps for separating the vascular networks of an optical retinal image

3.1   Retinal Image Databases

Since it is not a particular goal of our work to segment the vascular network, the system uses the corresponding segmented image from the DRIVE database, having the blood vessels visible at least until the second bifurcation. This means that the proposed methodology was developed and evaluated by using the set of 40 color fundus images of the training and test sets in the publicly available DRIVE database [9], [10].

We also worked with the images from the ARIA database [11]. Images with the segmented vascular network can also come from other systems using any algorithm or methodology reported in the literature for that task, if they provide good results and fulfill with the condition that branches of the network are clearly visible at least until the second bifurcation.

3.1.1 Physiological, Morphological and Morphometric Characteristics to Take into Consideration for the Separation of the Vascular Network

The main physiological, morphological and morphometric characteristics that distinguishes the vascular networks are:

- Both branches (venous and arterial) of the vascular network present a tree structure.
- The main topological characteristic of each type of network is the presence of bifurcations. Sometime could appear trifurcations which are transformed in two consecutive bifurcations.
- Arterial blood always enters the retina and venous blood leaves the retina.
- Through any of the branches of any vascular network the blood flows backward. Bifurcations cannot have an angle between branches greater than 90 degree.
- The main arterial branch is called central retinal artery and the main venous branch is called central retinal vein.
- Both branches dichotomize in nasal and temporal on each eye and then dichotomize again into upper and lower branches.
- In areas of the macula luteal are not appreciated either veins or arteries. Therefore, the fovea, located at the center of the macula, is avascular.
- The zone where the optic disc appears in the fundus image is the nasal zone. The macula luteal of each eye is located at the opposite side.
- Between two consecutive bifurcations, or between a bifurcation and a visible end of a vein or artery, appears correspondingly a single venous or arterial branch.
- In a normal retina, branches between two consecutive bifurcations always have the same thickness, i.e. the thickness of the branch is constant.
- The locations of venous or arterial bifurcations have not any relation with the locations of bifurcations of the other network.
- The primary, secondary and tertiary arterial and venous branches are the most interesting. In a primary branch occur the first bifurcations; in a secondary branch occur the second bifurcations and in a tertiary branch occur the third bifurcation. A bifurcation always divides a vessel into two thinner vessels.
- The branches of the arterial and venous networks at any level interbreed with a branch of another type. Crossings do not divide the branches. The crosses are always between venous and arterial branches. The crossing branches can be between arteries or veins of primary, secondary or tertiary level. The different branches of the arterial and venous networks may have crossings anywhere in the retina, except on the macular zone. The branches of the venous network normally travel below the arterial network.
- Both the veins and arteries in a normal network have tubular structure. We consider as circular the cross section of veins and arteries.

3.1.2 Mesh Creation

Since the separation in the venous and arterial networks was carried out by local analysis within cells in a square lattice superimposed over the original segmented image, the size of the square cell considered suitable for the study was 20 x 20 pixels. This size should ensure that the cells could contain a segment (or more than one) of a vein or of an artery, a branch of one kind or another, crosses between vessels of different types, or an ending point of either type [12]. This cell size constituted the "puzzle piece" of the proposed methodology.

With this size of 20 x 20 pixels the percent of cells that will not be analyzed is less than 1% in images with a previously hidden optic disc. The number of key cells with crosses between veins and arteries, and arterial or venous bifurcations or trifurcations remained with an acceptable frequency of occurrence of about 37%. The rest was occupied by single segments of veins or arteries, endpoints of one kind or another, or simply they were empty.

3.1.3 Methodology for the Separation of the Vascular Network

Although in this paper the separation process starts from a binary image with the vascular network already segmented, the complete methodology to separate the venous and arterial vascular networks covers the execution of the following procedures in the strict order indicated:

1. Detection of the optic disc.
2. Hiding of the optic disc with a black disc
3. Splitting the image of the segmented vascular network superimposing a grid (or mesh) of disjoint square cells of size 20 x 20 pixels.
4. Once the vessels around the optic disc have been manually classified as arterial or venous, explore the network starting from any of the previously identified cells surrounding the optic disc.
5. Determine every time the number of contacts of vessels inside the cell with its four edges and the number of connected components inside it.
6. With this information and the prior knowledge of the type of vessel(s) inside the current cell, and depending on the result of the analysis described in previous step 5, it is possible to determine if the type of network in the next cell in any direction (North, South, West or East) is a simple branch (venous or arterial); or a bifurcation (venous or arterial); or a cross between a venous and an arterial segments; or an ending point (arterial or venous); or simply an empty cell.
7. Based on the decision of the previous step 6, to store the necessary data to tabulate the group of related pixels to create later cell by cell the corresponding output images.

To determine the number of vessels contacts with the edges of the corresponding cell and the number of connected components within it, it is created the network skeleton of one pixel thick. The isolated pixels that do not make up a blood vessel are eliminated.

To keep control of results during the analysis of each cell, a State Matrix of m x n integer elements is created, where m is the number of cells of height and n is the number of cells of width of the segmented image. The values stored in the array (matrix) will indicate the status of the analysis of each cell according to their position in the image. This array will provide the necessary information for the separation algorithm to recognize the situation about all cells of the segmented vascular network being analyzed. Empty cells without any blood vessel inside it (zero in the matrix), obviously will be the last ones to be analyzed. A cell could be considered completely classified, when the analysis of it connection in all directions (N, S, W and E) has been completed.

The cells around (or near to) the optic disc whose vessels already have been classified correctly by the user, either as venous or as arterial, before to initiate the separation of the vessel sub-networks, are taken as the baseline. From these initial cells a tree structure will be created taking it as the root.

The tree indicates only the order in which the cells are analyzed sequentially according to the path of blood vessels inside it. In each cell to be analyzed, not only are taken into account the characteristics of the vessels contained therein, but also the information inside of the adjacent cells in all directions. The end of each one of the shafts is determined by cells containing endpoint which obviously no longer generate children.

As the tree is traversed, the characteristics or parameters from each cell are obtained to determine the structure and type(s) of vessels contained inside it. For this, it is necessary to determine previously the following features and data of each cell being analyzed:

- The number of contacts between the skeletonized vessels and the cell edges.
- The number of connected components inside the cell.
- Analyze each one of the connected components in the cell and with the aid of the skeleton determine if it is a bifurcation, trifurcation, crossing point, ending point, or simply a vessel segment.
- Measure the thickness of the each blood vessel touching the edges of the cell with coordinates (X, Y) being analyzed and store the data together with the coordinates (x, y) where any pixel of the skeletonized blood vessel contacts with the edge.

To carry out the entire process of classification of vessels contained in each cell, a decision tree must be generated with the necessary rules to be taken into account from the contents of each cell and those adjacent to it, in order to classify them as arterial or venous. These rules are the following:

- To differentiate a crossing point from a bifurcation.
- To detect the type of particular points of the segmented network.
- If there is a branch which by their nature or position cannot be classified when it outs the optic disc, simply it is classified as indefinite and the white color is assigned to it.
- Crosses are always between two branches of different type; the type of each vessel depends on the type of the vessel previously classified according to the direction that it comes from.

Based on the parameters setting described previously and the cells already labeled that are located around the cell under analysis, the task is to classify this cell in one of possible combinations depending on the number of contacts with their four edges and on the structure of blood vessels located within it. This procedure is repeated with each one of the cells included in the table of cells not classified yet and those cells which still remains as partially classified, until all cells of the segmented image are completely classified.

4   Experimental Results and Discussion

To evaluate the effectiveness of the module for separating the vascular networks, a total of 52 healthy fundus images were analyzed with respect to pathologies related to the blood vessels of the vascular network. From the 52 fundus images 26 proceed from the public DRIVE database [9] [10] and the other 26 images from the ARIA database [11].

Figures 2-12 show the resulting images after applying to an arbitrary image the proposed methodology to separate the venous and arterial networks. In Fig. 13 we can appreciate the vascular network manually separated in its venous and arterial branches. The metrics used to evaluate the quality of the separation of the vascular venous and arterial networks are the Recall, the Precision and the Coverage.

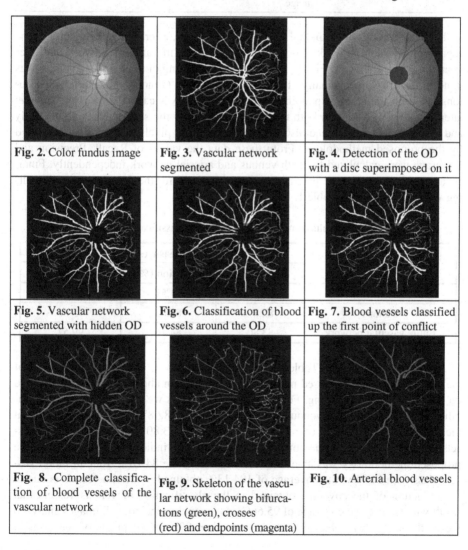

Fig. 2. Color fundus image

Fig. 3. Vascular network segmented

Fig. 4. Detection of the OD with a disc superimposed on it

Fig. 5. Vascular network segmented with hidden OD

Fig. 6. Classification of blood vessels around the OD

Fig. 7. Blood vessels classified up the first point of conflict

Fig. 8. Complete classification of blood vessels of the vascular network

Fig. 9. Skeleton of the vascular network showing bifurcations (green), crosses (red) and endpoints (magenta)

Fig. 10. Arterial blood vessels

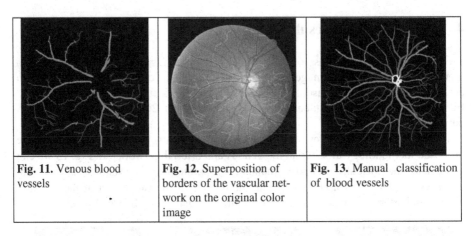

| **Fig. 11.** Venous blood vessels | **Fig. 12.** Superposition of borders of the vascular network on the original color image | **Fig. 13.** Manual classification of blood vessels |

The methodology was applied to the 52 test images, after which the quality of the separation of each network was analyzed, first from the arterial network and later from the venous network. Firstly, in each case, a counting of the number of pixels was done in the network manually classified of each type (venous and arterial) that belongs to each them, correspondingly; this parameter was called *total of the sample*; later counting was done in both resulting images after the separation, both correctly and incorrectly classified and also the number of those pixels that were not classified by the proposed methodology. From these data the values of Recall, Precision and Coverage were calculated for both venous and arterial network independently. Finally, average values of these parameters were calculated for the 52 test images. Resulting values are shown in Table 1.

Table 1. Results from the evaluation of the classification quality

Blood vessel type	Measures		
	Recall (%)	Precision (%)	Coverage (%)
Arterials	84.88	81.51	104.13
Venous	82.87	86.63	95.66
Entire vascular network	83.80	84.16	99.57

As it can be noted from Table 1, acceptable percent was obtained in the quality of the separation by the proposed methodology, all of them above of the 80% measured on the base of pixel counting. For arterial blood vessels we get a classification capability of 84.88% while for venous blood vessels was of 82.87%. This indicates us that the methodology classified correctly (as average) the 83.80% of the total blood vessels in the images. The value obtained for the Precision indicates that, as average, the proposed methodology was able to classify correctly the 84.16% from all blood vessels classified. Finally, the coverage of 104.13% obtained in arterial vessels is due to the reduction of the coverage obtained in the classification of venous vessels that result with an average coverage of 95.66%. As a conclusion, from all images analyzed the methodology was able to classify more than 99% of all pixels of the original networks. Likewise, Table 2 tabulates the average error in percent calculated comparing the images with both networks manually separated in the original image and images with the venous and arterial blood vessels separated by our methodology.

Table 2. Average error (in percent) obtained in vascular network classification

Blood vessel type	Average error (%)
Arterial	18.49
Venous	13.37
Entire vascular network	15.84

Another way to validate the quality of the separation of venous and arterial blood vessel networks is comparing the number of bifurcations and ending points, venous and arterials, as well as the crosses detected between the branches of both networks with the proposed methodology and those obtained from the composite image manually classified. As it can be noted the methodology was able to detect correctly, as average, 89.80% of crosses, 86.07% of bifurcations and 95.24% of ending points, resulting finally a global average detection of approximately 90%. Also, the methodology was evaluated with respect to the invariance to the affine transformations like translation, rotation and scale. These tests were carried out over 10 images from the test set of the DRIVE database, to which small variations were applied in each case. After the application of small variations to the affine transformations of translation, rotation and changes in scale, the results obtained do not vary appreciably with respect to those obtained in images without such transformations, inclusive the results are a little better probably because the test sample set is smaller than in all previous cases. Then, we can conclude that the proposed methodology is invariant to the affine transformations of translation, rotation and change in scale. This means that we can use the proposed procedure to separate the venous and arterial networks over different images of the same eye of the same person. In all cases the results will be similar.

5   Conclusions

In this paper it has been demonstrated that the retina vascular network can be separated in its venous and arterial branches following the logical rules used for assembling a puzzle. The procedure is based on the physiological properties of the human retina vascular networks and the morphological properties of a tree structure as well. For arterial blood vessels we get a classification capability, based on the pixel counting, of 84.88% while for venous blood vessels was of 82.87%. This indicates us that the methodology classified correctly (as average) the 83.80% of the total blood vessels in the images. The methodology was able to detect correctly, as average, 89.80% of crosses, 86.07% of bifurcations and 95.24% of ending points, resulting finally a global average detection of approximately 90%. The semi-supervised methodology was evaluated also with respect to the invariance to the affine transformations of translation, rotation and scale. These tests were carried out over 10 images from the test set of the DRIVE database, to which small variations were applied in each case. In the case of translation, for the entire vascular network a Recall of 87.69%, a Precision of 88.79%, Coverage of 98.76, and an error of 11.21% was obtained. In the case of the scale, corresponding values were 85.22%, 85.44%, 99.74% and 14.56%. Finally, for rotation they were, correspondingly, 85.45%, 86.49%, 98.80% and 13.51%. It is important to point out that the number of errors appears higher because those venous pixels located in cells where crosses were detected they were counted always as arterial ones. In the near future we will refine the error calculation when taking into consideration the venous pixels in all crosses detected.

References

1. Lei, T., Udupa, J.K., Saha, P.K., Odhner, D.: Artery-Vein separation via MRA- An image processing approach. IEEE Transactions on Medical Imaging 20(8), 689–703 (2001)
2. Rosa-Hernández, A., Olmedo-Maldonado, A., Hernández-Pérez, D., Felipe-Riverón, E.M., Sánchez-Garfias, F.A.: Separación y extracción de características de las redes vas-culares venosa y arterial en imágenes de retinas humanas.Tesis de licenciatura. IPN - Es-cuela Superior de Cómputo, México (2006)
3. Skands, U., Grunkin, M., Hansen, M.E.: Analysis of Fundus Images. United States Patent. US 6,996,260 B1 (2006)
4. Tek, H.: Method for artery-vein image separation in blood pool contrast agents. United States Patent. US2007/0249912A1 (2007)
5. Rothaus, K., Jiang, X., Rhiem, P.: Separation of the retinal vascular graph based upon structural knowledge. Image and Vision Computing (2008), doi:10.1016/j.mavis.2008.02.013
6. Niemeijer, M., van Ginneken, B., Abramoff, M.D.: Automatic classification of retinal vessels into arteries and veins. In: Medical Imaging 2009: Computer-Aided Diagnosis Proceedings of the SPIE, vol. 7620, pp. 7260IF–7260IF-8 (2009)
7. Tramontan, L., Ruggeri, A.: Computer estimation of the AVR parameter in diabetic retinopathy. In: WC 2009, IFMBE Proceedings 25/XI, pp. 141–144. Springer, Heidelberg (2009)
8. Muramatsu, C., Hatanaka, Y., Iwase, T., Hara, T., Fujita, H.: Automated selection of major arteries and veins for measurement of arteriolar-to-venular diameter ratio on retinal fundus images. Computerized Medical Imaging and Graphics 35, 472–480 (2011)
9. http://www.isi.uu.nl/Research/Datadase/DRIVE
10. Staal, J.J., Abramoff, M.D., Niemeijer, M., Viergever, M.A., van Ginneken, B.: Ridge based vessel segmentation in color images of the retina. IEEE Transactions on Medical Imaging 23, 501–509 (2004)
11. Farnell, D.: ARIA Online: Retinal Image Archive. St Paul's Eye Unit, Royal Liv-erpool University Hospital Trust, and Ophthalmology Clinical Sciences. University of Liverpool (2006), http://www.eyecharity.com/aria_online/
12. Villalobos-Castaldi, F.M., Felipe-Riverón, E.M., Albortante-Morato, C.: Segmenting Blood Vessels in Retinal Images Using an Entropic Thresh-olding Scheme. Advances in Computer Science and Engineering 42, 153–165 (2009) ISSN: 1870-4069
13. Martinez-Perez, M., Hughes, A., Stanton, A., Thom, S., Chapman, N., Bharath, A., Parker, K.: Retinal vascular tree morphology: A semi-automatic quantification. IEEE Transactions on Biomedical Engineering 49(8), 912–917 (2002)

Efficiency of DCT-Based Denoising Techniques Applied to Texture Images

Aleksey Rubel[1], Vladimir Lukin[1], and Oleksiy Pogrebnyak[2]

[1] National Aerospace University named by N.Y. Zhukovsky, Department of Receivers, Transmitters and Signal Processing, Chkalova St. 17, 61070, Kharkov, Ukraine
`edu.rubel@gmail.com, vladimlukin@yahoo.com`
[2] Instituto Politecnico Nacional, Centro de Investigacion en Computacion, Ave. Juan de Dios Batiz S/N, C.P. 07738, Mexico, D.F., Mexico
`olek@pollux.cic.ipn.mx`

Abstract. Textures or high-detailed structures contain information that can be exploited in pattern recognition and classification. If an acquired image is noisy, noise removal becomes an operation to improve image quality before further stages of processing. Among possible variants of denoising, we consider filters based on orthogonal transforms, in particular, on discrete cosine transform (DCT) known to be able to effectively remove additive white Gaussian noise (AWGN). Besides, we study a representative of nonlocal denoising techniques, namely, BM3D known as state-of-the-art technique based on DCT and similar patch search. We show that noise removal in texture images using the considered DCT-based techniques can distort fine texture details. To detect such situations and avoid texture degradation due to filtering, we propose to apply filtering efficiency prediction tests applicable to wide class of images. These tests are based on DCT coefficient statistic parameters and can be used for decision-making in relation to the use of the considered filters.

Keywords: denoising, filter, texture images, DCT, BM3D, AWGN, statistics, visual quality.

1 Introduction

Texture features of images or their fragments are widely exploited in numerous applications of pattern recognition [1], remote sensing [2], similarity search in large databases [3]. Often, in such applications noise is present in acquired (original) images. In fact, noise might be the most destructive factor for solving of all related practical problems. For this reason, the noisy data must be analyzed concerning decision-making in the followed processing [1-5]. Actually, for texture images the negative influence of noise might occur more apparently than for images with simpler structure. Fine texture details can be essentially disguised by the noise. Therefore, denoising becomes a desired stage in image processing chain. However, alongside with positive effect of noise removal, denoising can distort images in smaller or larger extent. Hence, it should be performed carefully, especially for texture images.

J.F. Martínez-Trinidad et al. (Eds.): MCPR 2014, LNCS 8495, pp. 261–270, 2014.

Rather efficient denoising techniques have been proposed recently [4-8]. First, filters based on orthogonal transforms have demonstrated good performance in additive white Gaussian noise (AWGN) removal [9]. One of such transforms widely used in image processing is the discrete cosine transform (DCT); certainly, wavelet transforms can be used as well [10]. The main reasons for applying DCT are clear. First, DCT has good compactness of signal energy or "sparseness". Second, fast DCT algorithms have been developed and implemented on general-purpose processors [11] and on FPGA architecture [12]. Third, DCT is performed in blocks and, due to this, is well adapted to local structure of any processed image [13].

The latter property of the standard DCT based denoising is useful. But all local approaches operate only on locally distributed spatial data, so-called "blocks" or "patches". This restricts potential efficiency of denoising images with distributed similar data. These types of data can be edges, textures or other singularities that exceed size of the used blocks. Recall that the commonly used block size in DCT-based denoising is 8x8 pixels [4, 7, 13].

Nonlocal approaches can perform processing of such image data more efficiently [5, 6, 8]. For these approaches, similar data (patches, blocks) are collected into arrays and processed together, e.g., using some weight function. Provided noise characteristics are known in advance, denoising procedure is a rather simple operation although essential efforts are spent of similar patch search. BM3D filter [8] which is currently state-of-the-art [13, 14] employs advantages of both nonlocal and transform domain approaches where DCT is used for data processing in 3D arrays of similar patches.

By excluding small amplitude spectrum components of transformed image data, noise removal is attained on one hand. On the other hand, this operation can delete or distort some image details. Nonlocal denoising approaches have advantages for images with rather large homogenous regions and sharp edges [13, 14]. Meanwhile, nonlocal filters might also run into difficulties for high-frequency data as texture or other complex structure images.

Thus, it could be nice to predict how denoising can affect an image at hand. The paper [14] presents a lot of useful data for preliminary analysis (including results for many standard test images). First, an approach to determining potential limit of filtering efficiency for images corrupted by AWGN is presented for nonlocal approach under condition of available noise-free image. The results show that noise removal in images with large homogenous regions is easy and there are possibilities to further improve filter performance for such images. Meanwhile, denoising of texture images as high-frequency data is hard. The best of existing filters have practically reached the potential limit for textural images (as, e.g., Baboon), especially for the case of intensive noise [14, 15]. Then, a natural question arises: "Is denoising really needed for a given image?" And this question most often arises just for texture images which are the main subject of our study.

Note that recently an attempt to predict denoising efficiency has been carried out in [16]. It has been shown that simple statistics of DCT coefficients is 8x8 blocks can serve for predicting a parameter characterizing filtering efficiency under condition that a dependence between them is established (approximated). The dependence obtained in [16] concerns the ratio of the output MSE and AWGN variance and this dependence is quite accurate for a set of the standard test images. However, this set did not contain many texture images. Therefore, it is worth paying special attention to texture images with the final goal of decision-making in denoising applying.

The structure of this paper is the following. In Section 2, two DCT-based denoising techniques are briefly discussed. Preliminaries of study (test images, noise characteristics, parameters of filters) are given in Section 3. Practical results of study are presented in Section 4.

2   DCT-Based Denoising

As mentioned above, local filters are usually quite simple procedures. Thereby, a used transform has to be a simple procedure, too. The algorithm that performs DCT as matrix multiplying, due to its linearity, is

$$\mathbf{B}_{trans} = \mathbf{T} \cdot \mathbf{B}_{spat} \cdot \mathbf{T}^{T}, \tag{1}$$

$$\mathbf{B}_{spat}^{filt} = \mathbf{T}^{T} \cdot \mathbf{B}_{trans}^{filt} \cdot \mathbf{T}, \tag{2}$$

where $\mathbf{B}_{spat}$ is a spatially represented block, $\mathbf{T}$ is a transform matrix, $\mathbf{B}_{trans}$ is a transformed block, $\mathbf{B}_{spat}^{filt}$ is a spatially represented filtered block, $\mathbf{B}_{trans}^{filt}$ is a filtered block in the transform domain. Such DCT implementation decreases computational burden and avoids iterative performing DCT in direct way for each block on image. Inverse transform (2) of filtered blocks $\mathbf{B}_{spat}^{filt}$ is carried out at once after denoising procedure. This approach can be used in parallel computations for filtering speed-up.

DCT-based denoising is a simple procedure. DCT filter processes data block-wise by hard thresholding in the following manner:

$$B_{out}(k,l) = \begin{cases} B_{in}(k,l) \leftarrow |B_{in}(k,l) > \beta \cdot \sigma| \\ 0 \leftarrow |B_{in}(k,l) \leq \beta \cdot \sigma| \end{cases} \tag{3}$$

where $B_{in}(k,l)$ and $B_{out}(k,l)$ are input and output blocks, respectively, of the image data transformed by DCT having indices $k,l = 0,...,7$, β is a thresholding parameter, σ denotes the standard deviation of the noise that is assumed zero mean AWGN with a priori known standard deviation.

Blocks are taken on whole image with overall overlapping [7, 13]. As it can be seen from (3), the spectrum components that do not exceed assigned pre-estimated threshold provided by noise standard deviation and β are excluded. After local denoising operation, the inverse DCT is performed. To get a final filtered value for a given pixel, the filtered values from all blocks that contain a given pixel are averaged. This essentially improves filtering performance compared to non-overlapping blocks.

Special attention is paid to setting β. In [18], it is shown that the optimal value of β is in the range 2...4. As it has been shown [7], the optimal β is equal to about 2.3...2.8 for a wide class of images. In particular, for texture images the optimal β values are about 2.3...2.5, but the gain of denoising efficiency is not significant compared to the standard choice. Thus, the DCT filter has a small computational cost and simple realization. BM3D filter [8] works in the same manner taking into account that denoising is simultaneously applied to the group of found similar blocks.

3   Simulation Preliminaries

In our studies, eight grayscale test images are used from the texture image database USC-SIPI Image Database [17]. These test images are shown in Fig. 1. As it is seen from Fig. 1, all images have different type and correlation degree of textures. The size of all test images is 512x512 pixels.

In simulations, AWGN with a required variance has been generated. Ten realizations of the noise have been considered for each test image and noise level. As denoising criterions, the output mean square error (MSE_{out}) and PSNR-HVSM [19] have been used. Recall that PSNR-HVS-M is the filtering efficiency criterion that takes into account features of human vision system to describe visual quality of original and processed images more adequately than standard metrics as MSE or PSNR.

Below we consider performance of two DCT-based filters described in Section 2. In addition to results obtained for these filters, two measures of denoising efficiency have been used. First, the approach for predicting potential efficiency of nonlocal filters proposed by P. Chatterjee and P. Milanfar [14] was exploited. This approach assumes that a noise-free image is available. Then, based on similarity search mechanism and nonlocal denoising principles, this approach allows obtaining potential output MSE for a given variance of AWGN. Thus, it is possible to theoretically predict (determine) what can be minimal output MSE and to compare the values obtained for the existing (analyzed) filters to the corresponding limit.

The second (practical) approach [16] is based on the following general idea. There is a known dependence of a parameter α characterizing filtering efficiency on a parameter γ able to characterize a noisy image. Then, estimating γ for the analyzed image, it becomes possible to determine α. Analyzing α, it becomes possible, in particular, to decide automatically is it worth to filter a given image or no.

As parameter γ, it is possible to exploit the probabilities $P_{2\sigma}$ or $P_{2.7\sigma}$, where the former is probability that absolute values of AC DCT coefficients in 8x8 blocks do not exceed 2σ and the latter is probability that these absolute values exceed 2.7σ. Note that these probabilities are dependent ($P_{2\sigma} + P_{2.7\sigma} < 1$) and for pure noise $P_{2\sigma} \approx 0.95$. The ratio MSE_{out}/σ^2 was used as the parameter α in [14]. In this paper, we also analyze improvement of PSNR-HVS-M (IPSNR-HVS-M, expressed in dB) calculated as difference of PSNR-HVS-M for denoised and original images.

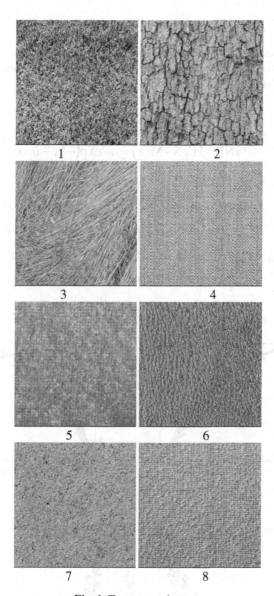

Fig. 1. Test texture images

4   Results

To study the filtering efficiency prediction, the DCT-based filter has been applied to a wide set of test images (32 test images including all images in Fig. 1) for three values of σ (5, 10, and 15). For each considered case, MSE_{out}/σ^2 or IPSNR-HVS-M have been presented as point at the corresponding scatter-plot where an argument is the corresponding $P_{2\sigma}$ or $P_{2.7\sigma}$ (see four scatter-plots in Fig. 2). We have obtained the prediction dependences using curve fitting. The fitted curves are presented in Fig. 2 by solid lines. The best obtained approximation functions for the analyzed denoising criterions are the following:

$$MSE_{out}/\sigma^2(x) = p_1 x^2 + p_2 x + p_3,\qquad(4)$$

$$IPSNR\text{-}HVS\text{-}M(x) = a \cdot \exp\!\left(-\left(x - b/b\right)^2\right),\qquad(5)$$

where x can either be $P_{2\sigma}$ or $P_{2.7\sigma}$. For approximation (4), we have obtained: $p_1 = -1.445$, $p_2 = 0.447$, $p_3 = 0.96$ for $P_{2\sigma}$ and $p_1 = -1.4$, $p_2 = 2.247$, $p_3 = 0.131$ for $P_{2.7\sigma}$. For the approximation (5): $a = -1.445$, $b = 0.447$, $c = 0.96$ for $P_{2\sigma}$ and $a = -1.4$, $b = 2.247$, $c = 0.131$ for $P_{2.7\sigma}$. The prediction can be carried out using any probability, $P_{2\sigma}$ or $P_{2.7\sigma}$. In further discussions, we exploit only $P_{2\sigma}$.

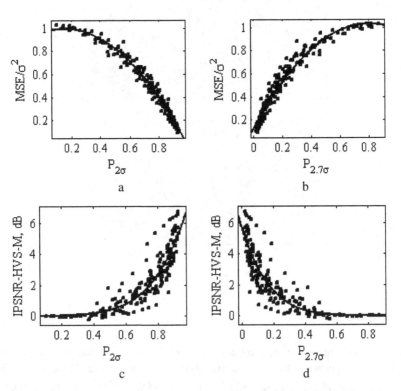

Fig. 2. Fitted curves in denoising results for $P_{2\sigma}$ (a, c) and $P_{2.7\sigma}$ (b, d) for the denoising criteria MSE_{out}/σ^2 and IPSNR-HVS-M

As it is seen, the fitted curves are close to almost all denoising results expressed by MSE_{out}/σ^2. For IPSNR-HVS-M criterion, the denoising results are more scattered. So, the curve fitting gives less precise approximation.

It is seen from Fig. 2 that if one has $P_{2\sigma} \leq 0.5$ (or $P_{2.7\sigma} > 0.5$), then filtering is not efficient, i.e. MSE_{out}/σ^2 is close to unity and/or IPSNR-HVS-M is small (about zero). Careful analysis for the considered test images (32 images in total) has shown that this mainly happens for textural images. Note that, in fact, $P_{2\sigma}$ and $P_{2.7\sigma}$ quite adequately characterize "complexity" of images subject to filtering. Our proposition is that it is not worth performing image filtering if $P_{2\sigma} \leq 0.5$ or $P_{2.7\sigma} > 0.5$.

Thus, a preliminary answer to the question "Are texture images a hard class for DCT-based denoising?" is affirmative. Then, the problem of more thorough analysis of denoising efficiency arises. Let us first express the denoising results in terms of the output MSE. Figs. 3-5 present the attained MSE_{out} for the DCT and BM3D filters, MSE_{out} predicted based on (8) under condition of known σ^2, and the lower bound MSE_{lb} for the Milanfar's approach. It is seen that for $\sigma = 5$ the obtained results are very close for all eight considered textures. Only for the 8-th test image the attained MSE_{out} is considerably smaller than σ^2, i.e. denoising is rather efficient for both considered techniques.

For a higher noise level ($\sigma = 10$ and $\sigma = 15$) the results are still close. There is almost no difference between MSE_{out} for both studied denoising techniques and MSE_{lb}. This means that it is difficult to expect improvement of filtering efficiency for non-local family of filters applied to processing grayscale textural images. There are some textural images (# 1 and 6), for which the noise practically cannot be removed even if its intensity is high.

The prediction analysis based on fitted curves shows that the prediction is quite accurate although it usually overestimates the filtering efficiency.

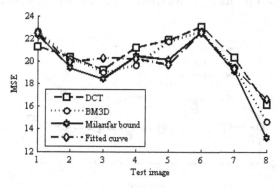

Fig. 3. Denoising results of test images expressed as output MSE for σ=5

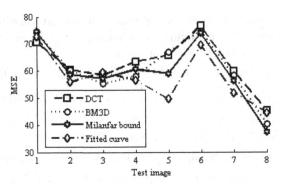

Fig. 4. Denoising results of test images expressed as output MSE for σ=10

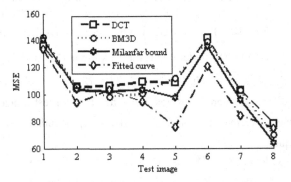

Fig. 5. Denoising results of test images expressed as output MSE for σ = 15

Similarly to Figs. 3-5, denoising results characterized by IPSNR-HVS-M are presented in Figs. 6-8. Milanfar test [14] does not allow estimating PSNR-HVS-M. Thus, Fig. 6-8 present three plots for each for σ. Predicted IPSNR-HVS-M occurs to be 1...2 dB larger than actual values provided by the DCT based and BM3D filters. This shows that it is desirable to improve prediction accuracy. Meanwhile, IPSNR-HVS-M almost never exceeds 1 dB for all considered textures and noise variance values.

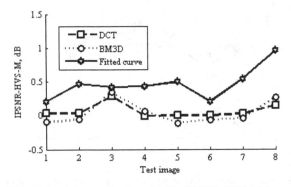

Fig. 6. Denoising results described by IPSNR-HVS-M for σ = 5

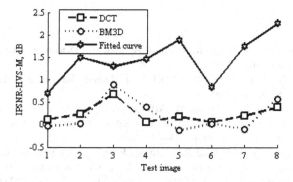

Fig. 7. Denoising results described by IPSNR-HVS-M for σ = 10

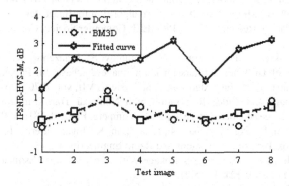

Fig. 8. Denoising results described by IPSNR-HVS-M for σ = 15

This means that filtering rarely provides essential improvement of visual quality. The obtained results also show that there is no necessity to apply time consuming BM3D filter for textural regions of images since much simpler DCT-based filter performs practically at the same level.

5   Conclusions

It is shown that efficient denoising is not provided by the considered DCT-based filters for texture images. Meanwhile, the used local DCT and nonlocal BM3D filters provide noise suppression efficiency close to values determined by the Milanfar's bound, i.e., to potential limit for non-local approach to filtering grayscale images. Visual quality of denoised images is also not considerably better than for the original ones even if noise is intensive.

This means that, probably, it is reasonable to avoid filtering texture images (or texture fragments of images). One step towards this can deal with using prediction of denoising efficiency discussed in this paper. At the same time, additional future work concerning filtering texture images, prediction of its efficiency and design of new approaches is obviously needed.

References

1. Haralick, R., Dori, D.: A Pattern Recognition Approach to Detection of Complex Edges. Pattern Recognition Letters 16(5), 517–529 (1995)
2. Schowengerdt, R.: Remote Sensing: Models and Methods for Image Processing, 560p. Academic Press (September 2006)
3. Cheikh, F., Cramariuc, B., Gabbouj, M.: MUVIS: A System for Content-Based Indexing and Retrieval in Large Image Databases. In: Proceedings Workshop on Very Low Bit Rate Coding, VLBV 1998, October 8-9, pp. 41–44 (1998)
4. Lukin, V., Tsymbal, O.: MM-band Radar Image Filtering with Texture Information Preservation. In: Proceedings of the Fourth International Kharkov Symposium "Physics and Engineering of Millimeter and Sub-Millimeter Waves", vol. 1, pp. 435–437 (June 2001)
5. Deledalle, C.-A., Denis, L., Tupin, F.: How to compare noisy patches? Patch similarity beyond Gaussian noise. International Journal of Computer Vision 99(1), 86–102 (2012)
6. Buades, A., Coll, A., Morel, J.M.: A non-local algorithm for image denoising. In: Computer Vision and Pattern Recognition (CVPR) IEEE Computer Society Conference, vol. 2, pp. 60–65 (2005)
7. Fevralev, D., Lukin, V., Ponomarenko, N., Abramov, S., Egiazarian, K., Astola, J.: Efficiency analysis of DCT-based filters for color image database. In: Proceedings of SPIE Conference Image Processing: Algorithms and Systems VII, vol. 7870, 12p. (2011)
8. Dabov, K.: Image and Video Restoration with Nonlocal Transform-Domain Filtering: Thesis for the degree of Doctor of Technology, Tampere, Finland, 181p. (2010)
9. Lukin, V., Oktem, R., Ponomarenko, N., Egiazarian, K.: Image filtering based on discrete cosine transform. Telecommunications and Radio Engineering 66(18), 1685–1701 (2007)
10. Sendur, L., Selesnick, I.: Bivariate Shrinkage With Local Variance Estimation. IEEE Signal Processing Letters 9(12), 4 (2002)
11. Zhou, X., Li, E., Chen, Y.-K.: Implementation of H.264 Decoder on General-Purpose Processors with Media Instructions. In: Proceeding of SPIE Conference on Image and Video Communications and Processing, vol. 5022 (2003)
12. Guo, B.-Z., Niu, L., Liu, Z.-M.: Implementation of 2-D DCT based on FPGA. In: International Conference on Image Processing and Pattern Recognition, vol. 7820, article id. 782004, p. 7 (2010)
13. Pogrebnyak, O., Lukin, V.: Wiener discrete cosine transform based image filtering. SPIE Journal of Electronic Imaging 21(4) (2012)
14. Chatterjee, P., Milanfar, P.: Is Denoising Dead? IEEE Trans. Image Processing 19(4), 895–911 (2010)
15. Lukin, V., Abramov, S., Ponomarenko, N., Egiazarian, K., Astola, J.: Image Filtering: Potential Efficiency and Current Problems. In: Proceedings of ICASSP, 4p. (2011)
16. Abramov, S., Krivenko, S., Roenko, A., Lukin, V., Djurovic, I., Chobanu, M.: Prediction of Filtering Efficiency for DCT-based Image Denoising. In: 2nd Mediterranean Conference on Embedded Computing (MECO), 4p. (2013)
17. http://sipi.usc.edu/database/database.php?volume=textures
18. Donoho, D.: Nonlinear wavelet methods for recovery of signals, densities, and spectra from indirect and noisy data. In: Proceedings Symposium Appl. Math., pp. 173–205 (1994)
19. Lukin, V., Ponomarenko, N., Egiazarian, K.: HVS-Metric-Based Performance Analysis Of Image Denoising Algorithms. In: Proceedings of EUVIP, pp. 156–161 (2011)

Thermal Image Processing for Breast Symmetry Detection Oriented to Automatic Breast Cancer Analysis

Mario I. Chacon-Murguia, Adrian J. Villalobos-Montiel,
and Jorge D. Calderon-Contreras

Visual Perception Applications on Robotics Lab, Chihuahua Institute of Technology, Mexico
mchacon,avillalobos{@itchihuahua.edu.mx}

Abstract. The present work presents a methodology to automatically detect the symmetry point of breast. In order to achieve this goal, the algorithm corrects thermal image tilt to find a breast symmetry axis, compute a modified symmetric index that can be used as a measure of image quality, breast cosmetic and pathologic issues, and a seed location for a former algorithm reported to automatically achieve breast cancer analysis. The methodology involves filtering, edge detection, windowing edge analysis and shape detection based on the Hough transform. Experimental results show that the proposed method is able to define the symmetry axis as precise as a person do, and correctly detected breast areas in 100% of the cases considered, allowing automatic breast analysis by a previous algorithm.

Keywords: breast segmentation, breast thermography, breast cancer.

1 Introduction

Breast thermography is a promising technique for the detection of breast cancer based on infrared technology [1]. A thermographic image shows the temperatures detected in the environment. In the case of breast thermography, temperatures of the different zones of the breast are shown. This allows us to detect areas where there might be a tumor due that in cancerous tissues there is an increased blood supply, and therefore an increased temperature of approximately 0.5 °C with respect to other tissues. Breast thermography also allows the detection of cancer through the study of asymmetry. If there is a large level of breast asymmetry, this may be due to the presence of a tumor that is being developed in one of the breasts, and is generating more breast mass. Different algorithms have been developed to segment and analyze areas of interest in order to detect possible tumors. But some of these are not automatic, and require the aid of a user to guide the program [2]. Other algorithms need the input images to be already segmented in order to process them correctly [3-5]. In some cases, thermal images are not taken properly so the systematic error increases, and the accuracy of the algorithm decreases [6]. An example of this is when the camera or the patient is inclined toward some direction when the image is taken. None of the reviewed algorithms that perform breast thermography analysis takes this into account, especially if it desired to design a mobile system. If this factor would not be considered, the asymmetry index and the internal segmentation of the breasts can be affected.

J.F. Martínez-Trinidad et al. (Eds.): MCPR 2014, LNCS 8495, pp. 271–280, 2014.
© Springer International Publishing Switzerland 2014

In 2007, a study was conducted at the Medical University of Vienna to define for the first time a breast symmetry index (BSI ©). The BSI can clearly differentiate between a good and a bad cosmetic appearance (BSI > 30%), and it is also used for clinical studies [7]. This paper presents the development of an algorithm that automatically locates the breast symmetry point. The algorithm provides important image data so that it can be used for the segmentation of the breasts, and help in the detection of tumors. These data are a level of symmetry between the breasts, and the symmetry axis defined by the angle to the x axis of the image, and its position in the x axis once the image inclination has been corrected. The degree of symmetry between the breasts is used to verify the proper functioning of the proposed algorithm, and it can also be used for detection of a possible tumor if this index is very low. Additionally, the algorithm provides the coordinates of a seed in the image that later can be used to perform internal breast segmentation and therefore determine risk areas.

In [2] a processing algorithm of thermal images that makes the segmentation and analysis of the breasts in order to evaluate the heat patterns in the breast tissue for diagnosis of breast cancer is described. The algorithm has a good performance achieving correct segmentations. However, this algorithm has the disadvantage that it requires an experienced person to indicate a seed, or select the coordinate of the midpoint between the breasts, according to his point of view. This point serves as a starting point for breast detection, so the results of the algorithm varied greatly if another coordinate was used. Therefore, the algorithm proposed in this article is oriented to locate the breast areas in the images, and then determine the coordinates of the seed so that the algorithm mentioned in [2] can work automatically.

The contributions of this paper are; a method to correct image tilt, a modified symmetric index that can be used as a measure of image quality, cosmetic and pathologic issues, and seed location for the algorithm reported in [2] to work automatically on breast cancer analysis. The organization of the paper is structured as follows. Section 2 explains the proposed method. Experimental results are presented in Section 3, and the conclusions are commented in section 4.

2   Development and Description of the Algorithm

The algorithm works with thermal images size of 120 x 160 pixels, $I(x,y)$. The images used for the design and test of the algorithm correspond to 12 woman, from whom 36 thermal images with a 0.1 °C resolution were acquired. The image acquisition protocol used and the information of the camera are described in [2]. Since the images were not taken under ideal conditions [6,8], some are clear and other blurred. There was a variety of breast sizes and positions. Based on the variety of images, five of these images that were considered as representative of the others, were chosen for the design stage of the algorithm. The first process performed by the algorithm is to copy the original image and paste it in the center of a blank image, $I_N(x,y)$, that has the dimensions of the original image plus 60 pixels on both dimensions. This process allows greater working space when detecting the symmetry axis, and it is very helpful for cases when the position of the person in the image is shifted to any direction compared to the ideal position where the breasts appear at the center of the thermographic image. Then, a Gaussian smoothing filter, is applied to the image in order to reduce the noise

$$G(x, y) = I_N(x, y) \Rightarrow I_S(x, y) \tag{1}$$

where
$$G(x, y) = \frac{1}{2\pi\sigma^2} e^{\frac{-(x^2+y^2)}{2\sigma^2}} \tag{2}$$

The σ used was 0.5, as this value preserves the desired extracted edges.

Once the image has been softened, an edge detector is applied. In order to choose the best edge detector, a study was conducted with different edge detector operators such as Sobel, Canny and Prewitt. Figure 1 shows an example of comparison of the edge operators. The Canny operator was selected with a threshold of 0.2 as this allows the detection of the desired breasts and bodies edges in most of the images.

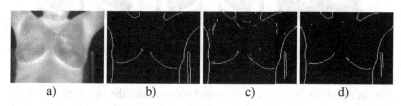

Fig. 1. Edge detection operators: a) Original Image, b) Canny with threshold = 0.2, c) Sobel with threshold = 0.04, d) Prewitt with threshold = 0.05

The next step is edge dilation in vertical, horizontal and diagonal directions, in order to enhance edges and to have an increased ability to detect symmetry. The dilation is achieved over each edge pixel $p_e(x,y)$

$$for\ each\ p_e(x,y)$$
$$N_8(p_e(x,y)) = 1. \tag{3}$$

After detecting the edges of the breasts, the image must be rotated. This is very important if it is desired to segment the breasts in two different regions. Otherwise, some pixels from one breast would be considered as pixels of the other breast and it can lead to different results when the internal analysis is performed. The rotation operator is defined by

$$x_2 = \cos(\theta)(x_1 - x_0) - \sin(\theta)(y_1 - y_0) + x_0 \tag{4}$$

$$y_2 = \sin(\theta)(x_1 - x_0) + \cos(\theta)(y_1 - y_0) + y_0 \tag{5}$$

where θ is the angle of rotation in a clockwise direction and (x_0,y_0) are the coordinates of the center of rotation [9]. The developed algorithm considers (x_0,y_0) as the center point of the image. It is important to note that if an image is rotated its dimensions change.

To carry out the angular correction and the symmetry analysis of the thermographic images, the algorithm looks in the image for those conditions in which an axis indicates a higher degree of symmetry. By reviewing the position of the breasts in the images used for the design of the algorithm, a common area in which it is very possible to find the breasts in any other similar image was delimited. This area was named the test area and it is defined as the region where y is in the range [30,151]. Two adjoining windows of size of 70 X 121 pixels, W_L and W_R, are defined inside the test area located in the left margin and at row 151. The specified parameters should be adapted in order for the algorithm to process images from other data bases. W_L and W_R are horizontal and continuously shifted and at each position, then W_R is horizontally reflected to compute a Boolean AND operation with W_L. The resulting image has pixels with a value of 1, only when W_L and the reflected W_R have both pixels of value 1 at the same pixel position. An example of this operation is shown in Figure 2.

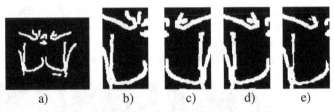

a)   b)   c)   d)   e)

Fig. 2. a) Edges image, b)W_L, c) W_R, d) W_R reflected, e) Result of the AND operation between W_L and W_R reflected

The symmetry index, *SI*, is then computed by counting the pixels that resulted with a value of 1 from this operator. *SI* is then used to obtain the symmetry axis, *SA*, as follows

$$SI_M = 0$$
for orientation -10° to 10° and increments of 1°
{ compute SI
    if SI > SI_M THEN SI_M = SI and SA = orientation
}

The algorithm detects the angle and windows shift position that defines a symmetry axis where there is the greatest symmetry between the breasts and surrounding areas. Since it doesn't exist a standardized way to measure symmetry, the count of 1s from the best condition was defined as the symmetry level of an image. Figure 3 shows an example in which the symmetry axis was found for a breast thermographic image. In this example, the symmetry axis is generated when the image is rotated 5° and at a position of 111 in the horizontal axis. The symmetry level in this image was determined to be 1151, which was basically determined by the information generated by the AND operation. Figure 4 shows the results displayed by the algorithm once an image has been processed. It displays the main steps to determine the symmetry axis, such as the best condition obtained after using the AND operator, and the symmetry axis over the borders image and over the original image.

Once the algorithm determines the degree of symmetry, it analyzes whether it is within an adequate range. For example, it is helpful to detect if the input image presents problems in its acquisition, or if there is great asymmetry between the breasts perhaps due to a malformation or a possible tumor. If the symmetry index is less than 700, the algorithm sends an error message related to image quality or a pathological issue. This threshold was selected because it was observed that good quality and non-pathologic images showed symmetry levels above this value.

Other important result of the proposed algorithm is that it also selects a coordinate in order to be used in [2] as the seed to perform automatic breast cancer analysis. Once the image angle has been corrected, the position of the axis will provide the *x*

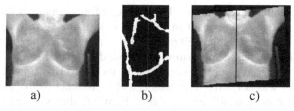

Fig. 3. Determination of symmetry axis: a) Original Image b) AND image generated with the greatest symmetry level conditions, c) Rotation of the image and positioning of the symmetry axis

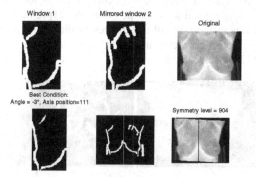

Fig. 4. Results displayed of the algorithm

component of the location of the seed. In order to find the *y* component, the Hough transform is used. Since breasts have similar shapes to circles, detecting circles from a breast thermography is helpful to locate the breasts in an image. The equation of a circle is given by

$$(x-x_r)^2 + (y-y_r)^2 = S^2 \qquad (6)$$

With this equation and the aid of the Hough transform, the algorithm locates 2 circles where the breasts are most likely positioned as shown in Figure 5. Because the formula of the circle has three parameters (x_r, y_r, S) [10], the Hough transform should be performed in a three dimensional space, where each pixel (x_i, y_j) is mapped to an accumulator H (x_r, y_r, S) in the Hough space. Each point that satisfies the Equation (6) will cause the accumulator increase one. The circles are defined by finding the accumulators with maximum values [11].

Fig. 5. Use of the Hough transform for detection of circles where the breasts might be located

One of the conditions given to the algorithm is that the radius of possible circles must be according to possible breast sizes and breast separation to avoid false detection and computational burden. The average of the y components of the circles' center is used as the y component of the seed only if the vertical distance between both origins is equal or less than 20 pixels. If this is not true, the y component of the circles closer to 110, the ideal position determined by inspection of the thermal images, will be considered as the y component for the seed. This situation indicates that one of the circles was not correctly detected, and an assumption that at least one of the circles detected belong to a breast is made. Figure 6 shows examples of the seeds selected for 3 different thermographic images. In Figures 6a and 6b, both breasts positions were detected correctly using the Hough transform. But in Figure 6c, only one breast was detected correctly. Therefore, the y component of the seed is based only on the circle that correctly detected a breast position. As explained in the next section, when the algorithm was tested with all the images available, in 100% of the cases the algorithm was able to detect correctly at least of one of the breasts, therefore the seed for the algorithm of [2] is correctly determined.

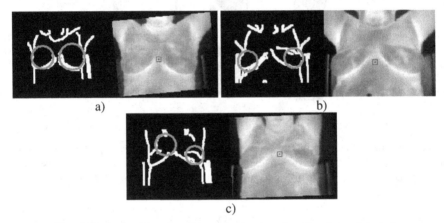

a)   b)

c)

Fig. 6. Examples of seed position selection based on the circles detected

3   Experimental Results

To evaluate the performance of the algorithm, it was tested with 36 different breast thermographies that were available. Some of these showed very poor quality. The performance of the algorithm about correctly determining the symmetry axis was first qualitatively evaluated for each of the processed images and classified as very good (VG), good (G) and bad (B). The criterion used was based on the location of the symmetry axis, and the body parts shown after the AND operator. VG performance involves correctly placing the symmetry axis and having few parts that do not belong to the breasts in the AND image. G performance involves correctly placing the symmetry axis, but having several parts in the AND image that don't belong to the breast areas. B performance involves a wrong location of the symmetry axis or many noise or additional parts shown in the AND image.

Of all the processed images, in 3 of them the algorithm was classified as B, in 12 images it was G and in the remaining 21, the performance was VG. At first glance, it was observed that the algorithm was doing an excellent job determining the position of the axis of symmetry. Table 1 contains some of the results provided by the algorithm and the performance evaluation for only 13 representative images due to space restrictions. As it can observed, the angle corrections ranged [-3°, 5°], so the algorithm considers about twice angle ranging which could be reduced to avoid unnecessary processing.

Table 1. Results of the algorithm for 13 representative images

Image	Correction Angle	Axis Position	Symmetry level	Performance
1	0	108	724	G
2	-3	110	1497	G
3	-3	111	1402	G
4	0	104	912	G
5	-4	119	911	VG
6	-3	112	704	VG
7	-2	112	1198	VG
8	0	104	2750	B
9	0	95	1531	VG
10	-3	111	904	VG
11	0	104	1333	VG
12	5	111	1151	VG
13	5	109	1252	VG

Reviewing the obtained positions of the axes of symmetry in the x axis, it was found that they were very different. Likewise, the symmetry level values obtained varied from 724 to 2750, and symmetry levels had an average of 1198 considering all the images. Figure 7 shows the positions of the detected symmetry axis for 2 images that were not used during the design of the algorithm. Although in both cases the symmetry axes were placed correctly, case (a) was considered G, and not VG as in case (b), because the breast curve did not appeared on its corresponding AND image. The border of the body was helpful in this case because it facilitated to find the symmetry of the whole image. If the body curves had been deleted, as presented previously as an option, then it would had been harder to find the symmetry axis. The corresponding AND images of the thermographies in Figure 7 are shown in Figure 8. In both cases, it can be observed that the chair in which patients were sitting is appearing in the AND images, and therefore, the algorithm is taking it into account for the symmetry detection, introducing the possibility of errors. The used images to develop and test the algorithm were provided by a third person. But for future uses, it is recommended to sit the patients in a bench instead of a chair, and control other similar conditions at the time of the acquisition to avoid this kind of problems.

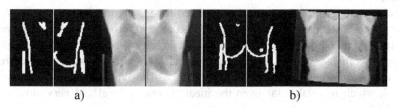

a)   b)

Fig. 7. Symmetry axes found with levels a) 912 and b) 755

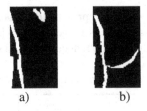

Fig. 8. AND images obtained from the thermographies from Figure 7

Figure 9 shows the case of an image not considered for the algorithm design and evaluation, but it is used to exemplify the importance of the symmetry average value. The algorithm performance was classified as B, this was due mainly because the image was taken under undesired conditions. The breast area temperature of the patient was not stabilized at the time of the image acquisition, so the image showed high variation on this area generating many edges which caused that the defined symmetry axis would not be on the desired position.

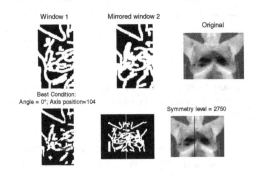

Fig. 9. Image in which the algorithm was classified as having a bad performance

This image resulted with a high symmetry level of 2750. Therefore, it can be noticed that a higher symmetry level does not necessarily mean that a better symmetry axis was detected. Better symmetry axis detection, as defined for this algorithm, is given when the symmetry level is closer to 1123, which is the average symmetry level obtained of images in which the program performance was VG. Having symmetry levels far away from this average may indicate, as in this example, the presence of low quality thermographic images to be processed by the algorithm. This situation also happened with the other images in which the algorithm performance was considered as B.

Another case using an image not considered for the algorithm design and evaluation to illustrate the robustness of the proposed algorithm is illustrated in Figure 10. This figure shows how a blurry image was correctly processed by the algorithm. Although this image was not taken properly, the symmetry axis was placed correctly due to the symmetry in the fuzziness of the image. The symmetry level of this image was 704, which is a value far from the ideal symmetry level and very close to the threshold that sends an error message to the user.

Fig. 10. Correct image processing of a blurry image

In order to evaluate the performance of the algorithm quantitatively, 10 people with no previous medical image analysis and interpretation training were provided with 5 digital breast thermographic images. They had to draw digitally on the images a thin red line in the axis of symmetry of the breasts according to their point of view. Their images were processed in order to calculate the angle specified by each person. The obtained angle values are in Table 2 to show how the values were spread out, and they were compared with those calculated by the algorithm, which are also shown in the table. The fields in yellow are those in which there was a difference equal or less than 1° with respect to the angles provided by the algorithm (shown in the blue fields). The table also considers the average of the values determined by the 10 people. The average of the 5 images resulted having a difference of 1° or below when compared with the angle values obtained by the algorithm. Therefore, it was concluded that the algorithm can detect the symmetry axes as well as a real person can do. Taking into account that the angle values obtained from the people varied greatly, the algorithm also has better precision than humans, and consequently can be trusted more than a person.

Table 2. Angles of rotation specified by the algorithm and 10 people

Image	Im1	Im2	Im3	Im4	Im5
Algorithm	-2	-3	5	0	0
Person 1	-6	-5	7	-2	-4
Person 2	-3	-3	3	0	-1
Person 3	-1	-2	1	0	0
Person 4	-4	-4	9	4	-2
Person 5	-4	-3	6	-1	-1
Person 6	0	0	6	4	2
Person 7	-3	-4	5	5	0
Person 8	-1	-8	6	-2	1
Person 9	-6	-5	13	-1	0
Person 10	-2	-3	4	-2	-1
Average of people	-3	-3.7	6	0.5	-0.6

The performance of the algorithm according to the seed selection was also evaluated. When the algorithm was tested with the 36 images available, in all of them, at least one of the breasts positions in each image was correctly defined by the Hough circles. In 61.1% of the images, the algorithm correctly placed the circles over the 2 different breasts. In 19.4% of the cases, the algorithm placed both circles over only one breast, and in the remaining 19.4% of the images, only one of the breasts was wrongly located in the image, while the other one was placed correctly. However, in this last case, the algorithm successfully used the correct circle to set the *y* component value of the seed. The selected seed coordinates of the 36 images were considered acceptable taking into account the criteria used in [2], allowing the algorithm in [2] correctly segment automatically the regions of interest and perform cancer diagnosis with the given seeds. The difference that exists in the calculation of the *y* component of the seed, between having correctly detected one or two circles over the breast area does not affect significantly the acceptance of a seed, but having two circles correctly detected doubles the possibility of setting correctly the *y* component of the seed coordinate.

4   Conclusions

It was possible the design of an algorithm that automatically process breast thermographic images in order to detect the symmetry axis and therefore, correct the rotation error and provide a level of symmetry. The developed algorithm was tested and had an excellent performance. It allowed successful process of images, even if they were of poor quality. Likewise, the algorithm provided in 100% of the images acceptable seed coordinates to aid another algorithm perform automatic internal breast segmentation.

Acknowledgements. The authors thanks to DGEST, for the support of this research.

References

1. Sharon, G.H., Budzar, A.U., Hoertobagyi, G.N.: Breast Cancer in Men. Annals of International Medicine 137(8), 678–687 (2002)
2. Calderon, J.D., Chacon, M.I.: Development of a breast tissue segmentation algorithm in thermal images for breast cancer detection. In: Proceedings of the National Congress on University and Health (2012)
3. Etehad Tavakol, M., Sadri, S., Ng, E.Y.K.: Application of K- and fuzzy c-means for color segmentation of thermal infrared breast images. Journal of Medical Systems 34(1), 35–42 (2010)
4. Boquete, L., Ortega, S., Miguel, J.M., Rodríguez, J.M., Blanco, R.: Automated detection of breast cancer in thermal infrared images, Based on independent component analysis. J. Medical Systems 36(1), 103–111 (2012)
5. Kapoor, P., Prasad, S.V.A.V., Patni, S.: Image Segmentation and Asymmetry Analysis of Breast Thermograms for Tumor Detection. International Journal of Computer Applications 50(9), 40–45 (2012)
6. Ammer, K., Ring, F.J.: Standard procedures for infrared imaging in medicine. In: Medical Infrared Imaging, pp. 32.1–32.14. CRC Press, Boca Raton (2012)
7. Fitzal, F., et al.: The use of a breast symmetry index for objective evaluation of breast cosmesis. In: The Breast, vol. 16, pp. 429–435. Elsevier, Edinburgh (2007)
8. Ng, E.Y.K.: A review of thermography as promising non-invasive detection modality for breast tumor. International Journal of Thermal Sciences 48(5), 849–859 (2009)
9. Ballard, D.H., Brown, C.M.: Computer Vision. Prentice Hall, Englewood Cliffs (1982)
10. Ballard, D.H.: Generalizing the Hough transform to detect arbitrary shapes. Pattern Recognition 13(2), 111–122 (1981)
11. Chen, B., Ma, Z.: Automated image segmentation and asymmetry analysis for breast using infrared images. In: International Workshop on Education Technology and Training (2008)

Relevance Feedback in Biometric Retrieval of Animal Photographs

Chelsea Finn[1], James Duyck[1], Andy Hutcheon[2], Pablo Vera[3],
Joaquin Salas[3], and Sai Ravela[1]

[1] Massachusetts Institute of Technology
[2] Department of Conservation, New Zealand
[3] Instituto Politecnico Nacional, Mexico

Abstract. The characterization of individual animal life history is crucial for conservation efforts. In this paper, Sloop, an operational pattern retrieval engine for animal identification, is extended by coupling crowdsourcing with image retrieval. The coupled system delivers scalable performance by using aggregated computational inference to effectively deliver precision and by using human feedback to efficiently improve recall. To the best of our knowledge, this is the first coupled human-machine animal biometrics system, and results on multiple species indicate that it is a promising approach for large-scale use.

1   Introduction

Tracking an individual animal's life history can substantially benefit conservation efforts [1]. Current strategies based on Capture-Mark-Recapture (CMR) are intrusive to varying degrees. Therefore, when an animal pattern is recognizable, a pattern recognition approach is beneficial. Contemporary systems [1–10] cannot automatically adjudicate identity without significant misjudgment. To deliver the high recall needed in most applications, Ravela *et al.* [8, 11] advance a pattern retrieval approach wherein images ranked by similarity of image features extracted from photographs of animals are subject to human judgment in cohort discovery, *i.e.*, finding the set of images with shared identity. Sloop [1, 8–10] is a system and framework for animal identification that is deployed operationally and delivers high performance. This paper explores the scalability achieved by incorporating dynamic feedback from human relevance judgments, including the role of crowds in providing large-scale relevance feedback. Relevance feedback has received some attention in image indexing but not animal biometrics, and the algorithms presented here follow from earlier work [11].

One of the earliest approaches for individual animal identification involved the use of 3D deformable patterns [2, 4, 12]. Generic feature methods promise extensibility and thus have become popular, including multi-scale differential feature histograms and multiscale-PCA [1]. For example, SIFT and variants have been used for marbled salamanders [9] and manta rays [13]. Shape contexts have been used in African penguins (*Spheniscus demersus*) [14]. Some deployed

J.F. Martínez-Trinidad et al. (Eds.): MCPR 2014, LNCS 8495, pp. 281–290, 2014.
© Springer International Publishing Switzerland 2014

systems include ECOCEAN [15], the recognition of chimpanzees and gorillas [16], and African Penguins (*Spheniscus demersus*) [14].

In contrast, Sloop contains a set of reusable tools that continue to be deployed for multiple new species. It contains implementations that are extensible to new applications. Sloop is in operational use for the Otago skink and grand skink [17] at the Department of Conservation in New Zealand. In this paper, we primarily explore the value of relevance feedback in the context of several recognition techniques available within Sloop. These include relevance feedback with SIFT on grand skinks, Otago skinks, and jewelled geckos, with hybrid context aggregating feature positions and feature densities on whale sharks, and with hierarchical deformable matching on marbled salamanders. The results obtained on these species are highly promising. Additionally, we propose hierarchical and aggregated matching methods that also appear to be promising as generic recognition methods that ultimately can reduce human effort while relevance feedback can improve system performance, thus producing an extensible, scalable system for biological users.

The remainder of this paper is organized as follows. In Section 2, the Sloop architecture is described. The application of the framework to different species is presented in Section 3, followed by a summary and conclusion.

2   The Sloop System Architecture and Process

Sloop is designed to bring three stakeholders together: biologists who provide data and use results for conservation efforts, the computer vision community that provides algorithms, and the "crowd" that provides data and relevance feedback for renumeration, entertainment, or citizen science.

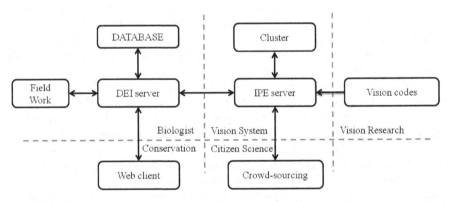

Fig. 1. The Sloop system is an interactive distributed image retrieval system with relevance feedback using crowdsourcing. It comprises of a Data Exchange and Interaction (DEI) server and an Image Processing Engine (IPE) that mediate the interaction between users, crowds, vision algorithms and computation.

Sloop comprises of a Data Exchange and Interaction (DEI) server that implements the user interface/database, and an Image Processing Engine (IPE) that provides tools for components of a work flow (see Figure 1). Typically, the inputs to Sloop include images and metadata, and the output is a table of identities associated with each image. A typical workflow includes interaction between the user and the system through stages of preprocessing, feature extraction, matching and relevance feedback. The stages of a workflow operate asynchronously and Sloop synchronizes the system (for example, closures for identities) during a "Nightly Build" process. The elements of a Sloop system's toolkit (version 3.0) include:

- Segmentation using mean-shift, SVM, and graph-cut methods.
- Illumination correction using global contrast correction techniques, and an interactive specularity removal algorithm [18] guided by the user (Figure 3).
- Rectification, including interactive spline methods (see Figure 2).
- Feature extraction in regions of interest (ROIs), including randomized representation of ROIs that perturb image position and scale to account for uncertainty of features and fiducials.
- Matching, including patch-based (Multi-scale PCA [1], Scale-Cascaded Alignment [9]), local feature-based (Histogram [11], SIFT [19] and affine invariant variations [8]), and hybrid shape context-based matching for point features. Additional features including HOG, SURF, and LBP and variants are also scheduled to be incorporated.
- Hierarchical matching, including coarse-scale matching with invariant features followed by deformable matching with Scale Cascaded Alignment (SCA).
- Aggregation, including rank and score aggregation.
- Relevance feedback, including metric modification and aggregation.
- Crowdsourcing, including Facebook and Mechanical Turk.

For any new species, the toolbox is typically used to develop workflows in a Sloop sandbox. A production Sloop is deployed after successful tests on the sandbox (see sloop.mit.edu for examples). For space limitations, and because several techniques are already published, here we will focus on two aspects. The first is the role of hybrid contexts in aggregated matching and the second is the role of relevance feedback in matching including hierarchical and aggregated matching.

2.1 Hybrid Context

The hybrid context algorithm uses Eulerian and Lagrangian shape contexts to match point sets. The method uses two iterations of correspondence and alignment. In the first iteration, one of two shape context approaches–Eulerian [20] or Lagrangian–is used to characterize and correspond the points, and in the end, the two approaches are aggregated using the most-successful matching. After one of the shape context methods is used to find a correspondence, the median distance is used to form an initial alignment. In the second iteration, points are matched

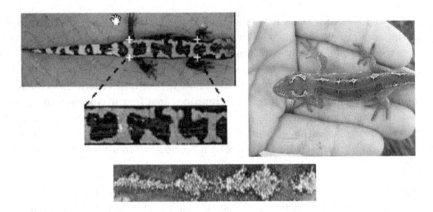

Fig. 2. Either segmented images or user marked key points are used to nonlinearly rectify images for feature extraction. Shown here are the rectified image of a marbled salamander (note distorted grid), a jewelled gecko with a spline for rectification, and the corresponding patches for both.

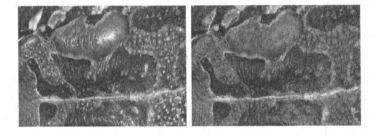

Fig. 3. Interactive example-based specularity removal

using a doubly-stochastic formulation [21] and realigned with an affine transform calculated through the RANSAC algorithm [22]. Aligned point sets are finally scored by considering the distribution of Euclidean distances between corresponding points. We note that neither context method, Eulerian or Lagrangian individually perform especially well, but when aggregated, the performance substantially improves, with even more gains achieved through relevance feedback. The results are presented in the next section.

2.2   Relevance Feedback

As the images are ranked, the user verifies by browsing the top few ranks (typically 20) and this information is used as feedback for subsequent rounds of matching to improve similarity matching, in two ways: a) the best score of the cohort group is used to re-rank the images and b) the population-based prior is replaced by a cohort-based posterior [11] estimate in a Bayesian sense. In the first approach, we estimate the probability $P(C = c_i|Q = q)$ to find the class c_i that matches the query q by maximum likelihood. Thus, as in [11, 23], for an ensemble of images $I_{1,c_i}I, \ldots, I_{e_i,c_i}$ belonging to class c_i and obtained through relevance feedback, the likelihood $P(Q = q|C = c_i) = \max_e P(Q = q|I = I_{e,c_i})$. In the second approach [11], feature vectors of the cohort are used to calculate new individual centered representations. The new bases are used for comparing a query to a cohort group, whilst returning the best match over the feature ensemble. In a Bayesian setting, $P(C = c_i|Q = q) \propto P(Q = q|C = c_i)P(C = c_i)$. This expression is evaluated comparing the query to each member in the relevance ensemble (likelihood) and by evaluating the probability of the ensemble member using the population statistics (prior).

Relevance feedback improves identification efficiency by incorporating information from all images that have been matched to a query image (see Figure 4). In particular, many image sets include left and right images that cannot be directly compared. Relevance feedback allows these images to be linked via intermediary left/right pairs that are matched to both lone images.

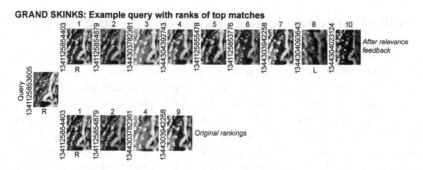

Fig. 4. Images matching a query withing the top 20 ranked matches, before and after relevance feedback. Relevance feedback is performed using matching images within the initial top 5 ranked matches. Numbers indicate the rankings, and L/R indicate a session where only one side of the animal was photographed.

Crowd sourcing can accelerate relevance feedback. Akin to ReCAPTCHA, in our approach, feedback is accepted when performance on control images (for which the results are known) is perfect. This self-normalization results in excellent candidate selection, a key issue if crowds are to be useful. On average, after a person performs well on 40 known-pairs (twenty tests) their recall is about 95%. The number of people passing this barrier is about a third of the total population (see Figure 5). While it is difficult to measure the accuracy of people who do not complete many tasks, the people who persist are overwhelmingly also very good at identification.

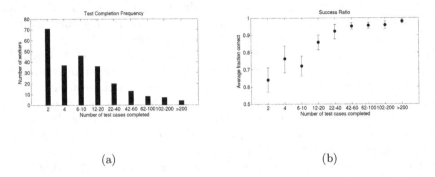

(a)   (b)

Fig. 5. Persistent test takers are somewhat infrequent (left). They are also the most skillful (right). The success rate is strongly correlated to the number of tests that a candidate undertakes, suggesting that persistent candidates are also the most skillful at identification.

3   Individual Identification Examples: Sloop Systems

Sloop algorithms are demonstrated on *Rhincodon typus* (whale shark, 35,000 photos/3,000 individuals), *Ambystoma opacum* (marbled salamander, 10,000 photos/2,000), *Naultinus gemmeus* (jewelled gecko, 10,000 photos/1,600 individuals), *Oligosoma otagense* (Otago skink, 8,900 photos/900 individuals), and *Oligosoma grande* (grand skink, 21,700 photos/2,500 individuals) (see Figure 6).

For whale sharks we use the spot patterning behind the gills of the whale shark on one or both sides [6]. Coordinates of the spots have been specified by users or extracted, and the identification algorithm matches pairs of coordinate sets rather than the images themselves. The scale-normalized spot distributions are compared using hybrid contexts. The Eulerian context is based on 16 overlapping bins at two ranges of distances. In the Lagrangian context, a spot's context consists of its five nearest neighboring point coordinates; subsequently, the top three highest matching contexts are used for alignment. After a final round of RANSAC-based affine alignment, the score of the aligned point sets is determined by the area between two CDF curves: the cumulative distribution of Euclidean distances between corresponding points and that of an ideal perfect match. Thus, lower scores indicate closer matches. The results of the two algorithms are aggregated by taking the minimum score. Relevance feedback is also applied to this method, with improved performance. To test our algorithm, we queried 147 images of 18 total individual whale sharks for which the cohorts were known against 5,200 or 9,300 photos from the database of left or right side photos respectively. The results of the individual, weak matching algorithms, compared to the aggregated version are shown in ROC curves (see Figure 7).

For marbled salamanders a hierarchical approach is used in which SIFT/MS-PCA is followed by SCA refinement. The performance, measured as the area

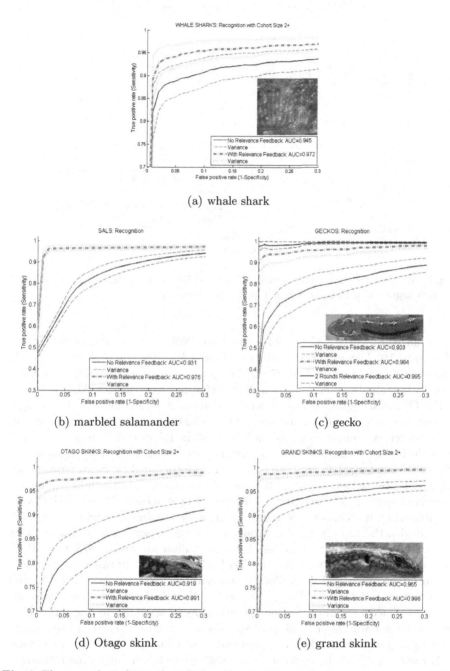

(a) whale shark

(b) marbled salamander

(c) gecko

(d) Otago skink

(e) grand skink

Fig. 6. These graphs indicate that the baseline performance is quite good and improves with coupled human-machine relevance feedback cycles. After relevance feedback was applied the ROC improvement is statistically significant and nonlinear.

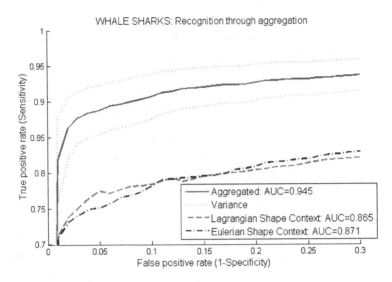

Fig. 7. ROC curves for whale shark of two weak matching algorithms, combined through aggregation to achieve much higher performance

under an ROC curve (AUC), improves from 90% with the use of SIFT/MS-PCA to 93.1% The addition of relevance feedback on the top 5 ranked retrievals results in an improvement to 97.8%. For jewelled geckos, a randomized SIFT with bidirectional matching is used. With relevance feedback the AUC is 99.5%.

For Otago and grand skinks a worker defines three patches on each image, between the nostril and eye, between the eye and ear, and between the ear and the shoulder. A capture may contain images of the left or right side of the animal or both, for up to six patches. The patches are normalized in orientation and scale. SIFT features [19] are then extracted from the patches. Next, corresponding patches on the same side of the animal are matched in the non-parametric Bayesian approach. The maximum score over the patch ensemble is used for ranking, removing the effects of low-scoring patches and features. Relevance feedback is done with the top ten results, producing excellent performance. On test sets of 1002 Otago and 1008 grand skinks, AUC values are above 90% with SIFT alone and above 99% after relevance feedback on the top 10 ranked retrievals.

The Otago and grand skink Sloop systems are in operational use at the Grand and Otago Skink Recovery Programme at the New Zealand Department of Conservation. Since a major protection operation has reversed the decline of the skink species, large datasets of skink photographs are produced yearly. These images need to be matched to identify individuals and to track population dynamics. This was formerly a labor intensive task, with up to half a million manual image comparisons taking place in 2011. In comparison, since Sloop presents ranked matches, matches are found in the top 100 comparisons (and most of these are in the top ten) 96% of the time for Otago skinks and 99% of the time for grand skinks. This reduces manual matching to 4% and 1%, respectively, of the labor that would otherwise be required.

Conclusion

The MIT Sloop system is an individual animal identification framework where hybrid systems utilize computer resources and human skills resulting in high performance recognition systems for large-scale conservation efforts. In this document, we described how this framework is applied and gives state-of-the-art results in five species.

Acknowledgment. The Sloop system and algorithms used for experiments here are developed by Ravela (version 2.0), revised by Yang and Ravela (version 2.5) and then by Duyck and Ravela (2.7-3.0) at the Earth Signals and Systems Group, MIT. This work is supported in part by AFOSR(FA9550-12-1-0313), NSF DBI-1146747, IPN-SIP 20140325, and MIT-Mexico Seed Fund (MISTI). Any opinion, findings, and conclusions in this material are those of the authors. We thank Jason Holmberg for whale shark data.

References

1. Gamble, L., Ravela, S., McGarigal, K.: Multi-scale Features for Identifying Individuals in Large Biological Databases: An Application of Pattern Recognition Technology to the Marbled Salamander *Ambystoma opacum*. Journal of Applied Ecology 45(1), 170–180 (2008)
2. Kelly, M.: Computer-Aided Photograph Matching in Studies using Individual Identification: An Example from Serengeti Cheetahs. Journal of Mammalogy 82, 440–449 (2001)
3. Araabi, B., Kehtarnavaz, N., McKinney, T., Hillman, G., Wursig, B.: A String Matching Computer-Assisted System for Dolphin Photoidentification. Annals of Biomedical Engineering 28, 1269–1279 (2000)
4. Hiby, L., Lovell, P.: A Note on an Automated System for Matching the Callosity Patterns on Aerial Photographs of Southern Right Whales. Journal of Cetacean Research and Management 2, 291–295 (2001)
5. Mizroch, S., Beard, J., Lynde, M.: Individual Recognition of Cetaceans: Use of Photo-Identification and Other Techniques to Estimate Population Parameters. In: Hammond, P., Mizroch, S., Donovan, G. (eds.) Computer Assisted Photo-Identification of Humpback Whales, Cambridge, UK. International Whaling Commission, vol. 12, pp. 63–70 (1990)
6. Arzoumanian, Z., Holmberg, J., Norman, B.: An Astronomical Pattern-matching Algorithm for Computer-Aided Identification of Whale Sharks *Rhincodon typus*. Journal of Applied Ecology 42(999-1011) (2005)
7. Kumar, N., Belhumeur, P.N., Biswas, A., Jacobs, D.W., Kress, W.J., Lopez, I.C., Soares, J.V.B.: Leafsnap: A Computer Vision System for Automatic Plant Species Identification. In: Fitzgibbon, A., Lazebnik, S., Perona, P., Sato, Y., Schmid, C. (eds.) ECCV 2012, Part II. LNCS, vol. 7573, pp. 502–516. Springer, Heidelberg (2012)

8. Ravela, S., Gamble, L.: On Recognizing Individual Salamanders. In: Asian Conference on Computer Vision, vol. 2, pp. 741–747 (2004)
9. Yang, C., Ravela, S.: Spectral Control of Viscous Alignment for Deformation Invariant Image Matching. In: International Conference on Computer Vision, vol. 1, pp. 1303–1310 (2009)
10. Ravela, S., Duyck, J., Finn, C.: Vision-Based Biometrics for Conservation. In: Carrasco-Ochoa, J.A., Martínez-Trinidad, J.F., Rodríguez, J.S., di Baja, G.S. (eds.) MCPR 2012. LNCS, vol. 7914, pp. 10–19. Springer, Heidelberg (2013)
11. Ravela, S.: On Multi-scale Differential Features and their Representations for Recognition and Retrieval. PhD thesis, University of Massachusetts at Amherst (2002)
12. Hiby, L., Lovell, P., Patil, N., Kumar, S., Gopalaswamy, A., Karanth, U.: A Tiger cannot Change its Stripes: Using a Three-dimensional Model to Match Images of Living Tigers and Tiger Skins. Biology Letters 5(3), 383–386 (2009)
13. Town, C., Marshall, A., Sethasathien, N.: Manta Matcher: Automated Photographic Identification of Manta Rays using Keypoint Features. Ecology and Evolution 3(7), 1902–1914 (2013)
14. Sherley, R., Burghardt, T., Barham, P., Campbell, N., Cuthill, I.: Spotting the Difference: Towards Fully-automated Population Monitoring of African Penguins *Spheniscus demersus*. Endangered Species Research 11(2), 101–111 (2010)
15. Holmberg, J., Norman, B., Arzoumanian, Z.: Estimating Population Size, Structure, and Residency Time for Whale Sharks *Rhincodon typus* through Collaborative Photo-Identification. Endangered Species Research 7, 39–53 (2009)
16. Loos, A., Ernst, A.: An Automated Chimpanzee Identification System using Face Detection and Recognition. EURASIP Journal on Image and Video Processing 12(1), 1–17 (2013)
17. Duyck, J., Finn, C., Hutcheon, A., Vera, P., Salas, J., Ravela, S.: Sloop: A Pattern Retrieval Engine for Individual Animal Identification. Pattern Recognition (2014)
18. Runge, J.: Reducing Spectral Reflections through Image Inpainting. Master's thesis, Massachusetts Institute of Technology (2009)
19. Lowe, D.: Distinctive Image Features from Scale-invariant Keypoints. International Journal of Computer Vision 60(2), 91–110 (2004)
20. Belongie, S., Malik, J., Puzicha, J.: Shape Matching and Object Recognition using Shape Contexts. IEEE Transactions on Pattern Analysis and Machine Intelligence 24(4), 509–522 (2002)
21. Rangarajan, A., Chui, H., Mjolsness, E., Pappu, S., Davachi, L., Goldman-Rakic, P., Duncan, J.: A Robust Point Matching Algorithm for Autoradiograph Alignment. Medical Image Analysis 1(4), 379–398 (1997)
22. Hartley, R., Zisserman, A.: Multiple View Geometry in Computer Vision, 2nd edn. Cambridge University Press (2004)
23. Ravela, S., Yang, C., Runge, J., Gamble, L., McGarigal, K., Chesser, M.: Visual Recapture for Movement Ecology at Interannual Timescales. In: Workshop on Visual Observation and Analysis of Animal and Insect Behavior (2008)

Using Song to Identify *Cassin's Vireo* Individuals. A Comparative Study of Pattern Recognition Algorithms

Julio G. Arriaga[1], Hector Sanchez[1], Richard Hedley[2],
Edgar E. Vallejo[1], and Charles E. Taylor[2]

[1] Computer Science Dept., Tecnológico de Monterrey, Campus Estado de México
Atizapán de Zaragoza, Estado de México, 52926, México
[2] Dept. of Ecology and Evolutionary Biology, University of California, Los Angeles
Los Angeles, CA, 90095-1606, USA

Abstract. In this paper, we present a comparative study on the application of pattern recognition algorithms to the identification of bird individuals from their song. A collection of experiments on the supervised classification of *Cassin's Vireo* individuals were conducted to identify the algorithm that produced the highest classification accuracy. Preliminary results indicated that Multinomial Naive Bayes produced excellent classification of bird individuals.

Keywords: Sensor networks, acoustic monitoring of birds, pattern recognition.

1 Introduction

Recent advances in sensor networks technologies hold the potential to transform research in ecology. In effect, the use of sensor networks in natural habitats for monitoring animal behavior and diversity is rapidly coming to be a vital tool in ecology studies [14].

The effective use of sensor networks in ecology relies crucially on the ability to identify relevant events from sensor data. Particularly, the accurate identification of individual animals from sensor data is a necessary condition for analyzing their behavior. Moreover, the identification task must be conducted efficiently given the tight energy constraints imposed by battery-operated sensor networks.

Our research is currently focused on the acoustic monitoring of different species of birds in several areas of the US and Mexico where they are abundant [2]. Our long term goal is to understand the structure and function of bird song. Particularly, the research described here aims at exploring the capabilities and limitations of different pattern recognition algorithms for the identification of *Cassin's Vireo* individuals from their song.

Toward that goal, we have designed a collection of datasets from song recordings representing different properties of the songs, then we applied different pattern recognition algorithms to identify the algorithm that produced the highest

J.F. Martínez-Trinidad et al. (Eds.): MCPR 2014, LNCS 8495, pp. 291–300, 2014.

classification accuracy. In the experiments reported here, Multinomial Naive Bayes produced the highest accuracy at the classification of bird individuals among the collection of algorithms used in this study.

2   Methods

The Cassin's Vireo (*Vireo cassinii*) is a small North American songbird which inhabits the area ranging from British Columbia through the western costal states of the U.S. During winter, the bird migrates, traveling from the Sonoran Desert to the south of Mexico. The CaVi is an excellent and persistent singer, with a repertoire of many different phrases strung together while singing.

2.1   Recordings

All recordings were performed on private land five kilometers north from the town of Volcano in Amador County, California between April 25 and June 8, 2013 by Richard Hedley. Recordings were performed opportunistically, beginning the recording when the researcher identified a bird singing and stopping when either the bird stopped for a significant amount of time or changed position becoming inaudible.

Recordings were subsequently segmented and tagged into phrase types -distinct bursts of song of less than a second long, identifiable by its stereotyped delivery- through visual inspection of their spectrograms using the Praat software [3]. Each phrase type was assigned a unique two letter code (aa, ab, ac, etc.) and added to a key file used for further phrase identification. Figure 1 shows spectrogram representations of a small subset of the phrase types. A total of 110 distinct phrase types were identified among the 7 different individuals in our study.

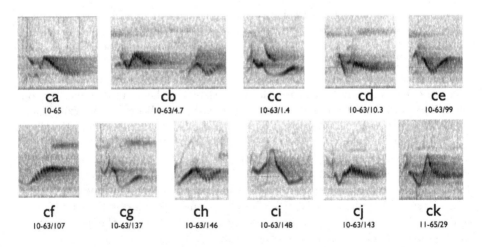

Fig. 1. Sample spectrogram

3   Individual Classification

All available samples were divided into two data sets: one certain and one uncertain. The certain data set contains samples with a high level of individual identity certainty as defined by the recordist: the recordist was able to verify the identity of the bird singing while performing the recording; the uncertain data set contains the remaining samples, those with a low level of identification certainty, determined by the recordist through careful consideration of territories and dates. The certain data set consists of 46 samples, while the uncertain one consists of only 9. For the purpose of this paper, the uncertain data set was not used.

Our approach for individual classification consisted of encoding each sample into a vector using different criteria, labeling it as the appropriate individual, and trying different supervised classification algorithms with 10-fold cross validation to measure their accuracy. Table 1 shows the classification algorithms tested. All algorithms were tested using the implementations found in the WEKA software package [10] with default parameters.

Table 1. Classification algorithms tested

Classifier	Description
Naive Bayes	Probabilistic classifier with strong independence assumptions based on Bayes' theorem. [11]
Multinomial Naive Bayes	Naive Bayes classifier using a multinomial model. [13]
SVM	Non-probabilistic linear or non-linear classifier. LIBSVM implementation. [6]
Multilayer Perceptron	Feedforward artificial neural network classifier learning through backpropagation. [16]
IBK	K-nearest neighbors classifier. [1]
K*	Instance-based classifier using an entropy-based distance function. [7]
Classification Via Regression	Classes are binarized and one regression model is built for each. [8]
PART	Generates a PART decision list by separate and conquer, building a partial C4.5 decision tree in each iteration and choosing the best leaf to be made into a rule. [9]
J48	Generates a pruned or unpruned C4.5 decision tree. [15]
LMT	Classifies by building classification trees with logistic regression functions at the leaves. [12]
Random Forest	Constructs a multitude of decision trees (in our case 10). [4]

Songs were encoded into vectors using different attributes, from acoustical properties of the song to more abstract representations of its structure.

3.1   Classification through Song Acoustic Features

Audio samples were split into smaller files consisting of exactly one phrase per file using the Praat software [3]. Using the Marsyas package [17], 124 audio features were extracted from each phrase and arranged into single vectors.[1]

$$\langle AF_0, AF_1, ..., AF_N, I \rangle . \tag{1}$$

Where AF_i represents an audio feature, and I stands for the individual identification.

Classification through acoustic features was conducted at two different levels: by song and by phrase type.

- Song level: All available vectors were arranged into a single data set.
- Phrase level: Vectors were divided according to their phrase type. The phrase *ch* was chosen for experimentation being the most used phrase type shared by all individuals; this way the largest amount of data possible was available for training and it was possible to asses its suitability for classifying all the individuals.

Results. Experimentation showed that applying a Principal Components filter [10] to the data set, reducing the vector's dimensionality by choosing enough eigenvectors to account for 95% of the variance in the original data, significantly improved the results. Both song and phrase approaches achieved poor results overall managing less than 70% accuracy, with the best results obtained by SVM and LMT for song and phrase respectively (see Figure 2). The main limitation of this approach is its high sensibility to noise in the recordings, as well as the great number of variables (recording equipment, terrain, proximity, weather conditions, etc.) resulting from field recordings.

3.2   Classification through Repertoire

Each sample song was encoded into a single vector.

$$\langle P_0, P_1, ..., P_N, I \rangle . \tag{2}$$

Where each P_i represents a different phrase type, and I stands for the individual identification.

Repertoire analysis was performed at two different levels: phrase usage and phrase frequency. For phrase usage, each P_n holds a binary value of 0 if phrase Ph_n is not used in the song and 1 otherwise. For phrase frequency, each P_n is given by Equation 3.

$$P_i = \frac{|Ph_i|}{|song|} . \tag{3}$$

Where $|Ph_i|$ is the number of occurrences of phrase Ph_i in the song, and $|song|$ is the length (number of phrases) of the song.

---

[1] For a complete list of the features extracted, check the Marsyas documentation (http://marsyas.info/documentation)

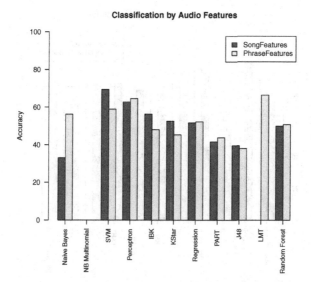

Fig. 2. Classification through song acoustic features. Comparison of results.

Results. Of the methods tested, the combination of the Multinomial Naive Bayes classifier with the binary repertoire vector produced the highest accuracy with 100% correctly classified instances. For the frequency repertoire vector, the multilayer perceptron proved the best match with a 95.65% accuracy (see Figure 3). Previous research suggests CaVis are capable of learning new phrase types from other individuals [5], changing their repertoires over time as a result of this learning process. Repertoire analysis seems sufficient to identify different individuals, however close interactions among neighboring individuals could potentially lead to near identical repertoires diminishing the accuracy of this method.

3.3   Classification through n-Gram Repertoire

Each song sample was encoded into a single vector.

$$\langle NG_0, NG_1, ..., NG_N, I \rangle. \tag{4}$$

Where I stands for the individual identification, and each NG_i represents a different n-gram. An n-gram is defined as a combination of n phrases occurring consecutively in a song.

N-Gram analysis was performed at two different levels: n-gram usage and n-gram frequency. For n-gram usage, each NG_n holds a binary value of 0 if n-gram Ph_n is not used in the song and 1 otherwise. In the case of n-gram frequency, each NG_i is given by Equation 5.

$$NG_i = \frac{|NG_i|}{|n - grams|}. \tag{5}$$

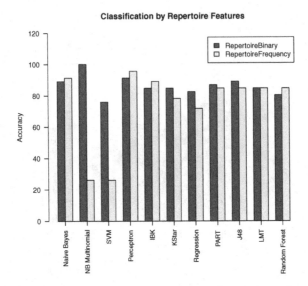

Fig. 3. Classification through repertoire. Comparison of results.

Where $|NG_i|$ is the number of occurrences of different n-gram NG_i in the song, and $|n - grams|$ is the number of n-grams in the song.

Results. N-gram analysis provides the benefit of retaining information about an individual's repertoire, while also encoding basic extra information about the song's structure. However, the amount of attributes required to represent it can grow exponentially when compared to just repertoire. For our experiments, we only considered bigrams (combinations of two phrases). As expected, the Multinomial Naive Bayes classifier achieved 100% accuracy (see Figure 4), however the dimensionality of the vector (1347 attributes) proved extremely large for certain algorithms like the multilayer perceptron.

We consider this approach not very useful considering the relatively little amount of extra information gained versus its huge impact on the representation's size.

3.4   Classification through Song Structure

Directed graphs were created from each sample song, with nodes representing different phrases and edges signifying adjacency between phrases in the song. Figure 5 shows a graph representation of a sample song. Songs were then encoded into vectors.

$$\langle GP_0, GP_1, ..., GP_N, I\rangle . \tag{6}$$

Where I stands for the individual identification, and each GP_i represents a graph derived property for each phrase type:

- Degree. The total number of edges to and from a node.
- Degree Centrality. The degree of a node, normalized by dividing by the maximum possible degree of the graph.
- Eccentricity. The maximum distance from one node to all other nodes.
- Clique number. The size of the largest maximal clique containing the node.

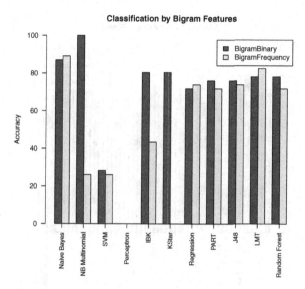

Fig. 4. Classification through bigram repertoire. Comparison of results.

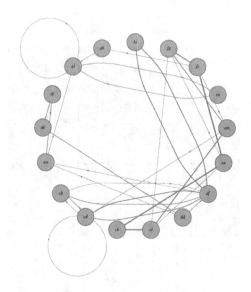

Fig. 5. Graph representation of sample song. Nodes denote distinct phrase types, edges denote adjacency between phrases in the sample song.

Results. Vectors derived from graph analysis have the benefit of containing repertoire information plus extra information about the song's structure without exploding in the size needed to encode them. Once again, the Multinomial Naive Bayes classifier achieved the best results, with 100% accuracy, for all our approaches except for graph centrality, for which the multilayer Perceptron proved to be the most effective (see Figure 6).

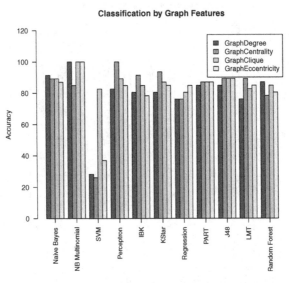

Fig. 6. Classification through song structure. Comparison of results.

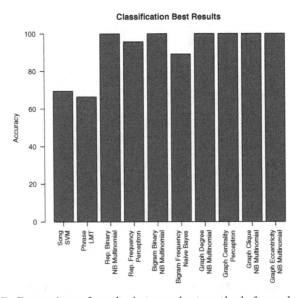

Fig. 7. Comparison of results between best methods for each approach

4   Discussion

In this study, we conducted a series of experiments on the classification of bird individuals from their song. We conducted a comparative study on the classification performance of different pattern recognition algorithms using a collection of dataset representing different properties of the bird song. See Figure 7 for a comparative view of the best results achieved per approach.

Preliminary experimental results indicated that Multinomial Naive Bayes outperformed the other pattern recognition algorithms employed in this study, including more sophisticated and highly regarded algorithms, such as SVMs.

Most notably, being a simple algorithm the generalization capabilities of Multinomial Naive Bayes proved to be highly accurate in contrast to the results produced by the other, more complex, methods. These impressive capabilities have been replicated by this method in other domains such as document classification, among others [18]. All in all, Multinomial Naive Bayes seems to be an excellent candidate algorithm for implementing real time recognition of bird individuals in sensor networks.

Similarly, the dataset encoding attributes extracted from the graph representation of the song allowed the highest accuracy in classification, suggesting that the organization of phrases in songs provides informative attributes that are useful to increase the accuracy of classification of *Cassin's Vireo* individuals.

Further experiments are required to assess the validity of the results reported here, including experiments on larger datasets and different species of birds. We expect that those experiments would contribute to increase the usefulness of sensor networks in ecology studies, generally.

Acknowledgments. This work was supported by the US National Science Foundation under Award Number 1125423 and by Consejo Nacional de Ciencia y Tecnología under Award Number I010/214/2012.

References

1. Aha, D.W., Kibler, D., Albert, M.K.: Instance-based learning algorithms. Machine Learning 6(1), 37–66 (1991)
2. Arriaga, J.G., Kossan, G., Cody, M.L., Vallejo, E.E., Taylor, C.E.: Acoustic sensor arrays for understanding bird communication. Identifying Cassins Vireos using SVMs and HMMs. In: 12th Europen Conference on Artificial Life (ECAL 2013), pp. 287–288. The MIT Press, Cambridge (2013)
3. Boersma, P., Weenink, D.: Praat: Doing Phonetics by Computer (Computer Program). Version 5.3.44., http://www.praat.org/ (retrieved April 7, 2013)
4. Breiman, L.: Random Forests. Machine Learning 45(1), 5–32 (2001)
5. Catchpole, C.K., Slater, P.J.B.: Bird Song. Biological Themes and Variations, 2nd edn. Cambridge University Press, New York (2008)
6. Chang, C., Lin, C.: LIBSVM - A Library for Support Vector Machines, Computer Program (2001), http://www.csie.ntu.edu.tw/~cjlin/libsvm/

7. Cleary, J.G., Trigg, L.E.: K*: An Instance-based Learner Using an Entropic Distance Measure. In: 12th International Conference on Machine Learning, pp. 108–114 (1995)
8. Frank, E., Wang, Y., Inglis, S., Holmes, G., Witten, I.H.: Using model trees for classification. Machine Learning 32(1), 63–76 (1998)
9. Frank, E., Witten, I.H.: Generating Accurate Rule Sets Without Global Optimization. In: Fifteenth International Conference on Machine Learning, pp. 144–151 (1998)
10. Hall, M., Frank, E., Holmes, G., Pfahringer, B., Reutemann, P., Witten, I.H.: The WEKA Data Mining Software: An Update. SIGKDD Explorations 11(1) (2009)
11. John, G.H., Langley, P.: Estimating Continuous Distributions in Bayesian Classifiers. In: Eleventh Conference on Uncertainty in Artificial Intelligence, San Mateo, pp. 338–345 (1995)
12. Landwehr, N., Hall, M., Frank, E.: Logistic Model Trees. Machine Learning 95(1&2), 161–205 (2005)
13. McCallum, A., Nigam, K.: A Comparison of Event Models for Naive Bayes Text Classification. In: AAAI 1998 Workshop on Learning for Text Categorization (1998)
14. Porter, J.H., Nagy, E., Kratz, T.K., et al.: New Eyes on the World: Advanced Sensors for Ecology. BioScience 59(5), 385–397 (2009)
15. Quinlan, R.: C4.5: Programs for Machine Learning. Morgan Kaufmann Publishers, San Mateo (1993)
16. Rumelhart, D.E., Hinton, G.E., Williams, R.J.: Learning Internal Representations by Error Propagation. In: Rumelhart, D.E., McClelland, J.L. and the PDP research group (eds.) Parallel Distributed Processing: Explorations in the Microstructure of Cognition, vol. 1, MIT Press (1986)
17. Tzanetakis, G.: MARSYAS: A Framework for Audio Analysis (Computer Program). Version 0.2., http://marsyas.info/download (retrieved January 8, 2013)
18. Witten, I.H., Eibe, F., Hall, M.A.: Data Mining. Practical Machine Learning Tools and Techniques, 3rd edn. Morgan Kaufmann, San Francisco (2011)

A New Method for Skeleton Pruning

Laura Alejandra Pinilla-Buitrago, José Fco. Martínez-Trinidad,
and J.A. Carrasco-Ochoa

Instituto Nacional de Astrofísica, Óptica y Electrónica
Departamento de Ciencias Computacionales
Luis Enrique Erro # 1, Puebla, México
{laurapin,fmartine,ariel}@inaoep.mx

Abstract. A Skeleton is a simplified and efficient descriptor for shapes, which is of great importance in computer graphics and vision. In this paper, we present a new method for computing skeletons from 2D binary shapes. The contour of each shape is represented by a set of dominant points, which are obtained by a nonparametric method. Then, a set of convex dominant points is used for building the skeleton. Finally, we iteratively remove some skeleton branches in order to get a clean skeleton representation. The proposed method is compared against other methods of the state of the art. The results show that the skeletons built by our method are more stable across a wider range of shapes than the skeletons obtained by other methods; and the shapes reconstructed from our skeletons are closer to the original shapes.

Keywords: skeleton, pruning, distance transform, binary shapes.

1 Introduction

Skeleton based representation has several advantages at reducing dimensionality and capturing geometrical and topological properties of shapes [1].

Many definitions of skeleton have been reported in the literature. One of the most accepted is the Medial Axis Transform (MAT) proposed by H. Blum. In MAT, a skeleton is a set of points, where each point is the center of a maximal disk inside object boundaries. The algorithms developed for skeleton extraction can be classified into five categories: direct simulation of grassfire model, analytical computation, iterative thinning with topology preserving, Voronoi diagram based, and distance transform based [2-3].

The representation of shapes by skeletons has shown being useful in tasks of object recognition and classification. However, in those cases where there are large deformations and intra-class variations of objects, boundary noise or small perturbations in the shapes, the skeleton obtained using conventional methods is usually accompanied with too many superfluous branches, and it affects the performance of object recognizers [3]. For this reason, some recently proposed algorithms for representation of shapes by skeletons include prunes of spurious branches.

J.F. Martínez-Trinidad et al. (Eds.): MCPR 2014, LNCS 8495, pp. 301–310, 2014.

In this work, we develop a new method based on the works proposed by Montero [4], Hesselink [5] and Prassad [6], in order to obtain a stable skeleton without unwanted branches.

This paper is organized as follows: In Section 2, we review the related work. In Section 3, we describe the proposed method. Section 4 shows experimental results of the proposed method compared with other state of the art methods. Finally, conclusions and future work are shown in Section 5.

2   Related Work

In the literature, there are many approaches for computing and pruning skeletons from binary shapes [2-4, 7-11]. During the process of skeletonization usually appear unwanted branches because of digital noise and deformation in the shapes; therefore pruning is an essential stage in skeletonization algorithms.

Several pruning methods into skeletonization algorithms have been proposed, which can be categorized in three main categories: assigning significance values to skeleton points and removing insignificant points according to a given threshold; preprocessing the shape's boundary (e.g., boundary smoothing, find knots or dominant points); and removing unwanted branches [7]. The methods of the first category could produce disconnected skeletons, breaking the skeleton into pieces or they cannot completely remove insignificant branches. The second kind of methods aims to remove unwanted boundary noise, but it could change the original shape and consequently shifting the skeleton and its topological properties. The methods in the last category prune the skeleton branch-by-branch taking into account local or global information, using significance measures of the skeleton branches [3-4, 7-10].

Until now, it does not already exist a non-parametric method or a method with parameters invariant for any shape that allows generating skeletons identical to hand-labeled shapes. However, in the literature, we can find some methods requiring less input parameters than others and sometimes the input values are independent for a wide range of shapes.

3   Proposed Method

The proposed method combines the non-parametric method for dominant point detection introduced in [6], with the skeleton construction and a modification of the pruning process presented in [4-5]. The proposed method is divided into three stages: piecewise curve segmentation, skeleton computation and skeleton pruning (Fig. 1).

In the first stage, we find the dominant points located in the shape with the method proposed in [6] (section 3.1). This is a non-parametric method which has as main advantage for our method that it does not need thresholds or input parameters. According to the literature, this method is considered as the only one non-parametric method for finding dominant points (see (a1) in Fig. 1). After, from the set of dominant points we obtain the convex points (see (a2) in Fig. 1), and unlike Montero and Lang in [4], we only use the set of convex dominant points to split piecewise curve split (see (a3) in Fig. 1).

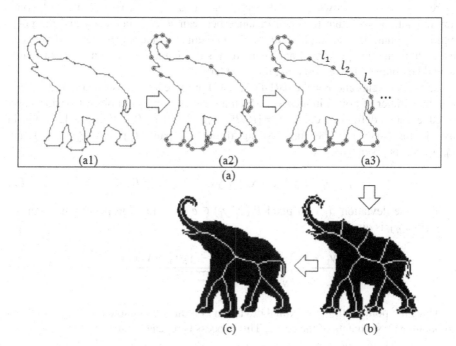

Fig. 1. (a) Curve segmentation by piecewise: (a1) Dominant point detection with a non-parametric method. (a2) Set of convex dominant points. (a3) Splitting of piecewise curve (b) Skeleton computation. (c) Skeleton pruning.

The piecewise curve is used to compute the skeleton by means of the integer medial axis (IMA) [4-5]. Our method produces a first approximation to the pruned skeleton (see (b) in Fig. 1) by selecting pixels as skeleton points. Skeleton construction by means of IMA considers a distance transform. The distance transform $D(x, y)$ is a function, which computes the distance from any point inside the shape to the closest point on the shape boundary.

In the last stage (see (c) in Fig. 1), we use a pruning criterion (Section 2.2) similar to the one proposed in [4] but we add additional conditions to ensure a more stable skeleton for a wide range of shapes using a single threshold. Moreover, in our experiments, several shapes belonging to different classes showed good results using the same threshold for the entire set of shapes, compared with the results obtained by other methods, which mostly need to specify parameter values for each shape.

3.1 Non-parametric Method for Dominant Point Detection

Since polygonal approximation allows representing a digital curve using less of points, some methods for building skeletons approximate the shape by polygons, either for removing noise as a previous step to the construction of the skeleton or for building the skeleton using the vertices of the polygons [4, 10].

Most of the methods for approximating shapes by obtaining dominant points require some of the following conditions: a) the number of vertices for the polygonal approximation, such that the error distance between shape´s boundary and the polygon is minimal; b) a threshold defining the maximum distance error allowed between the contour and the polygonal approximation, such that a minimum number of points would be obtained for representing the boundary.

Ramer, Douglas and Peucker (RDP) [12, 13] propose a recursive method for reducing the number of points in a curve, which are called dominant points. Consider a set of edge points defining a curve $e = \{P_1, P_2, ..., P_N\}$, where P_i is the ith edge point in the digital curve e. The line passing through a pair of points $P_a(x_a, y_a)$ and $P_b(x_b, y_b)$ is given by:

$$x(y_a - y_b) + y(x_b - x_a) + y_b x_a - y_a x_b = 0 \tag{1}$$

Then the deviation d_i of a pixel $P_i(x_i, y_i) \in e$ from the line passing through the pair $\{P_1, P_N\}$ is given by:

$$d_i = \frac{|x_i(y_1 - y_N) + y_i(x_N - x_1) + y_N x_1 - y_1 x_N|}{\sqrt{(x_N - x_1)^2 + (y_1 - y_N)^2}} \tag{2}$$

Thus, the point with the maximal deviation is found and denoted as P_{max}; it allows to obtain new segments of the curve. This process is repeated until:

$$\max(d_i) < d_{tol} \tag{3}$$

As we can see, this method requires a threshold d_{tol}. For making this method a non-parametric method, Prasad et al., in [6] consider the maximum deviation of the digital curve as an error function related to the quality of fitting, allowing the threshold to be automatically and adaptively obtained (see Fig. 2).

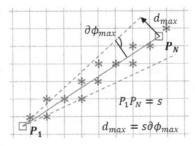

Fig. 2. The maxim deviation d_{max} of a line segment [6]

If a line segment in the continuous 2-dimensional space is digitized, the maximum difference between the angles made by the digital line segment and the continuous line segment with respect to the $x - axis$ is given by:

$$\delta\emptyset_{max} \approx \max\left(\tan^{-1}\left\{\frac{1}{s}(|\sin\emptyset \pm \cos\emptyset|)(1 - t_{max} + t_{max}^2)\right\}\right) \tag{4}$$

$$\emptyset = \tan^{-1}(m) \tag{5}$$

$$t_{max} = \left(\frac{1}{s}\right)(|\cos\emptyset| + |\sin\emptyset|) \tag{6}$$

$$d_{tol} = s\partial\emptyset_{max} \approx \max\left(s\tan^{-1}\left\{\frac{1}{s}(|\sin\emptyset \pm \cos\emptyset|)(1 - t_{max} + t_{max}^2)\right\}\right) \tag{7}$$

Where $\emptyset$ is the slope m of the continuous line segment P_1P_N and s is the P_1P_N distance.

3.2   Final Pruning

In our method, the two first stages allow us to obtain a skeleton with less unwanted branches in comparison to the skeleton obtained by conventional methods without pruning. Nevertheless, in order to obtain the desired final skeleton, some end branches need to be pruned.

Consider an end branch $\{b_p, ..., e_p\}$ with branch point b_p and an end point e_p, such that there are not any other branch point or end point except b_p and e_p, and let f be the distance transform computed for each point in order to obtain the IMA skeleton.

We propose to prune a branch $\{b_p, ..., e_p\}$ if the Euclidean distance between the distance transform and the branch point ($|f - b_p|_2$) with a scale factor s is greater than the sum of the Euclidean distances between each pair of consecutive points conforming the branch $\{b_p, ..., e_p\}$, i.e.:

$$\sum_{i=1}^{n-1} |p_i - p_{i+1}|_2 \leq s * |f - b_p|_2$$

$$\{b_p, ..., e_p\} = \{p_1, p_2, ..., p_n\} \text{ Where } p_1 = b_p \text{ and } p_n = e_p$$

This condition avoids pruning branches where the Euclidean distance $|e_p - b_p|_2$ is very close to the Euclidean distance between $|f - b_p|_2$, but the sum of Euclidean distances between every pair of consecutive points is much larger than $|e_p - b_p|_2$.

Additionally, when two or more end branches share the same junction point, we propose to delete just one end branch by iteration, eliminating only the shorter length branch. This condition, unlike the pruning proposed in [4], avoids losing structural information, as we will show in our experiments.

4   Experiments

For comparing the proposed method, we used the skeletonization algorithms proposed by Zhang and Suen [11], Bai et al. [10], and Montero and Lang [4] using Bezier Curve approximation.

In a first experiment, we show the stability of the proposed method using the same parameter value in comparison to the other methods, displaying the skeletons obtained for several shapes (Fig. 3).

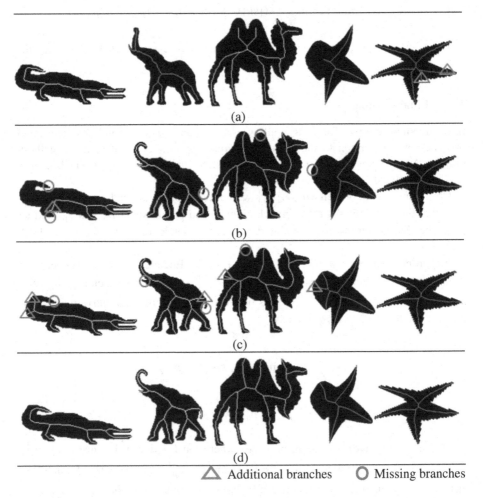

Fig. 3. Skeletons obtained with different methods: (a) Zhang and Suen [11]. (b) Bai et al. [10] for $N = 10$. (c) Montero and Lang [4] approximation to boundary by cubic Bezier curves with $d = 15$ and $s = 1.25$ (s is a minimum distance between the boundary and fitting curve). (d) Proposed method with $s = 1.27$.

In the experiments of the Fig. 3, we use the same input parameter value for all the shapes in each tested method. The threshold used for each method was obtained experimentally; we use the trial-and-error method for choosing the parameter value, which obtains the best visual results for whole data set. From our first experiment, we can see that the proposed method produces more consistent and stable skeletons, unlike the other two methods, where some skeletons have unwanted or missing branches.

In Fig. 4, we can see that our method generates good representations for several shapes using the same threshold value. Unlike the Bai et al. [10] where the parameter values are dependent on the specific shape. Furthermore, the Montero and Lang method, although produces lower number of errors respect to the results obtained with [10], requires two parameter values unlike our proposed method that needs just only one. Although the Zhang and Suen method [11] produces few unwanted branches, the thinning method does not ensure that the points of the skeleton are centers of maximal disk, which affects the reconstruction of the shape.

In a second experiment, we compare the speed of the methods using the same shape. Furthermore, we compute the quality of the skeleton obtained by a quantitative evaluation using the Baseski and Tari dataset (1000 shapes).

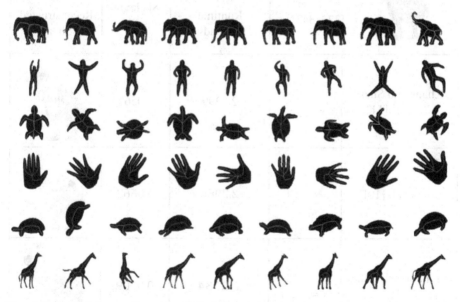

Fig. 4. Subset of shapes (Baseski and Tari dataset) and their respective skeletons with the proposed method with $s = 1.27$

One of the most common techniques for evaluating the quality of the skeletons obtained by algorithms for skeleton extraction is the reconstruction error ratio (RER). This measure evaluates the difference between the shape reconstructed through the skeleton and the original shape. The shape is reconstructed from the distance transform associated to each point of the skeleton. The RER is defined as:

$$RER(S, A) = \frac{|\text{Area}(A) - \text{Area}(R(S))|}{\text{Area}(A)} \tag{8}$$

Where S is a skeleton of the shape A and $R(S)$ is the shape reconstructed from S, $Area(.)$ denotes the area of a shape measured in pixels.

For comparing the quality of the obtained skeletons, in the table 1 we show the execution time and skeleton quality for an image chosen from the Baseski and Tari dataset. Where we can see that our method obtains better RER result and visually generates the best reconstructed shape, preserving the topology from the original shape.

Table 1. Comparison of the proposed method against the skeletons obtained by Zhang and Suen [11], Bai et al. [10] and Montero [4] methods in terms of the runtime and quality of the skeletons. The reconstructed shapes are red and the reconstruction errors are marked with black.

	[324x343]	Runtime (Seconds)	Skeleton quality (RER)	Reconstructed Shape
Zhang and Suen [11]	--	2.6399	0.0560	
Bai et al. [10]	N = 10	2.2068	0.0663	
Montero and Lang [4]	$d = 15$ $s = 1.25$	**1.2534**	0.0709	
Proposed method	$s = 1.27$	1.6842	**0.0281**	

In the table 2, we show the average for reconstruction error ratio and time execution for a whole dataset containing 1000 shapes (Baseski and Tari dataset), where we can see that our method obtains in average the best RER result.

The tests were carried out in a computer with the following characteristics: processor Intel core i5 at 2.30 GHz, 4 Gb of RAM, 64-bit Windows operating system. As it can be seen from tables 1 and 2, our method did not get the best runtime in comparison with the other methods, but it is very close to the best runtime obtained by Montero's method (the fastest).

Table 2. Average runtime and reconstruction error ratio of skeletons for the Baseski and Tari dataset over 1000 shapes

		Average execution time (Seconds)	Average skeletons quality (RER)
Zhang and Suen [11]	--	2.6488	0.0817
Bai et al. [10]	$N = 10$	2.5092	0.0392
Montero and Lang [4]	$s = 1.25$ $d = 15$	**0.8259**	0.0504
Proposed method	$s = 1.27$	1.1794	**0.0264**

5   Conclusions

In this work, we present a new method for computing skeletons from 2D binary shapes. The contour of each shape is represented by a set of dominant points, which are obtained by a nonparametric method. Then, a set of convex dominant points is used for building the skeleton. Finally, we introduce some new conditions in the pruning stage that allow iteratively removing some skeleton branches in order to get a clean skeleton representation.

From our experiments, we can see that in the proposed method the same threshold value works fine for several types of shapes; it is reflected in the fact that the skeleton's quality is clearly better in comparison to other methods widely used in the literature. Our experiments also show that our method allows representing shapes by simple and stable skeletons for a wider range of shapes than other methods.

As future work, we propose study the inclusion of the whole contour information for obtaining more consistent skeletons.

Acknowledgment. This work was partly supported by the National Council of Science and Technology of Mexico (CONACyT) through the project grants CB2008-106443 and CB2008-106366; and the scholarship grant 283120.

References

1. Bai, X., Latecki, L.J.: Path Similarity Skeleton Graph Matching. IEEE Transactions on Pattern Analysis and Machine Intelligence 30(7) (2008)

2. Duan, H., Wang, J., Liu, X., Liu, H.: A Skeleton Pruning Approach Using Contour Length as the Significance Measure. In: Third International Conference on Pervasive Computing and Applications, ICPCA, vol. 1, pp. 360–364, 6-8 (2008)
3. Shen, W., Bai, X., Hu, R., Wang, H., Latecki, J.L.: Skeleton growing and pruning with bending potential ratio. Pattern Recognition 44, 196–209 (2011)
4. Montero, A.S., Lang, J.: Skeleton pruning by contour approximation and the integer medial axis transform. Computers and Graphics 36, 477–487 (2012)
5. Hesselink, W.H., Roerdink, B.T.M.: Euclidean Skeleton of Digital Image and Volume Data in Linear Time by the Integer Medial Axis Transform. IEEE Transactions on Pattern Analysis and Machine Intelligence 30(12) (2008)
6. Prasad, D.K., Quek, C., Leung, M.K.H., Cho, S.: A novel framework for making dominant point detection methods non-parametric. Image and Vision Computing (Elsevier) 30(11), 843–859 (2012)
7. Liu, H., Wu, Z., Zhang, X., Hsu, D.F.: A skeleton pruning algorithm based on information fusion. Pattern Recognition Letters 34, 1138–1145 (2013)
8. Liu, H., Wu, Z., Hsu, S.F., Peterson, B.S., Xu, D.: On the generation and pruning of skeletons using generalized Voronoi diagrams. Pattern Recognition Letters 33, 2113–2119 (2012)
9. Duan, H., Wang, J., Liu, X., Liu, H.: A Skeleton Pruning Approach Using Contour Length as the Significance Measure. In: Third International Conference on Pervasive Computing and Applications, ICPCA 2008, vol. 1, pp. 360–364 (2008)
10. Bai, X., Latecki, J.L., Liu, W.: Skeleton pruning by contour partitioning with Discrete Curve Evolution. IEEE Transactions on Pattern Analysis and Machine Intelligence 29(3), 449–462 (2007)
11. Zhang, T.Y., Suen, C.Y.: A fast parallel algotithm for thinning digital patterns. ACM Commun. 27, 236–239 (1984)
12. Douglas, D.H., Peucker, T.K.: Algorithms for the Reduction of the Number of Points Required to Represent a Digitized Line or its Caricature. Cartographica: The International Journal for Geographic Information and Geovisualization, 112–122 (1973)
13. Ramer, U.: An iterative procedure for the polygonal approximation of plane curves. Computational Graphics Image Process, 244–256 (1972)

Deep Learning for Emotional Speech Recognition

Máximo E. Sánchez-Gutiérrez[1], E. Marcelo Albornoz[2],
Fabiola Martinez-Licona[1], H. Leonardo Rufiner[2], and John Goddard[1]

[1] Departamento de Ingeniería Eléctrica, Universidad Autónoma Metropolitana,
México
[2] Centro de Investigación SINC(i), Universidad Nacional del Litoral - CONICET,
Argentina
edmax86@gmail.com

Abstract. Emotional speech recognition is a multidisciplinary research
area that has received increasing attention over the last few years. The
present paper considers the application of restricted Boltzmann machines
(RBM) and deep belief networks (DBN) to the difficult task of automatic Spanish emotional speech recognition. The principal motivation
lies in the success reported in a growing body of work employing these
techniques as alternatives to traditional methods in speech processing
and speech recognition. Here a well-known Spanish emotional speech
database is used in order to extensively experiment with, and compare,
different combinations of parameters and classifiers. It is found that with
a suitable choice of parameters, RBM and DBN can achieve comparable
results to other classifiers.

Keywords: Emotional speech recognition, restricted Boltzmann machines, deep belief networks.

1 Introduction

The automatic recognition of emotions in human speech is part of the multidisciplinary research area of Human-Machine Communication, and has received
increasing attention over the last few years. One reason for this interest is the
growing number of applications which have benefitted from the research conducted in the field, like call centers, video games, and lie detection.

However, automatic emotional speech recognition involves many issues which
need to be carefully studied, such as: which emotions can we really identify,
what are the best features to use for the identification, and which classifiers give
the best performance. To illustrate these issues we can mention that although
it is common to consider the 'big six' emotions of joy, sadness, fear, disgust,
anger, and surprise, along with neutral, Douglas-Cowie, Cox et al. [1], proposed
a far greater list of 48 emotion categories; in the INTERSPEECH Challenges
from 2009 to 2012, the number of proposed features has increased from 384 to
6125 [2,3] without a final set being decided upon; finally, as Scherer [4] reports, a

J.F. Martínez-Trinidad et al. (Eds.): MCPR 2014, LNCS 8495, pp. 311–320, 2014.
© Springer International Publishing Switzerland 2014

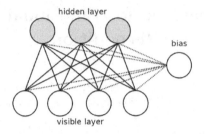

Fig. 1. Restricted Boltzmann Machine

wide range of classifiers, such as linear discriminant classifiers, k-nearest neighbor (KNN), Gaussian mixture model, support vector machines, decision tree algorithms (DT) and hidden Markov models have all been examined, and no definitive classifier has been chosen.

In this paper, we shall consider the application of RBM and DBN to the problem of classification of emotional speech recognition. The principal motivation lies in the success reported in a growing body of work employing these techniques as alternatives to traditional methods in speech processing and speech recognition [5,6].

Not much work has been conducted using RBM and DBN for the task of automatic emotional speech recognition. In [7], a Generalized Discriminant Analysis based on DBN showed significant improvement over support vector machines on nine databases. However, in [8], on the Likability Sub-Challenge classification task at INTERSPEECH 2012, it was found that the use of RBM helped in the task but that DBN did not. It seems that the parameters involved in training these algorithms are highly sensitive to small modifications, and that there is still work to be done in deciding how to use them for a particular task.

With this in mind, in the present paper we shall conduct an extensive experimentation with RBM and DBN in the context of a Spanish emotional speech database. The organization of the paper is as follows: in section 2 we briefly review the principal ideas of RBM and DBN, continuing in section 3 with information about the emotional speech database we use. In section 4 we describe the experiments we conducted and finally, in sections 5 and 6 discuss the results and end with some conclusions.

2 Deep Learning

2.1 Restricted Boltzmann Machines

An RBM is an artificial neural network with two layers, one layer formed with visible units, to receive the data, and the other with hidden units. There is also a bias unit. This architecture is shown in Figure 1. The hidden units are usually binary stochastic and the visible units are typically binary or stochastic gaussian. An RBM represents the joint distribution between a visible vector and a hidden random variable.

An RBM only has connections between the units in the two layers, and with the bias unit, but not between the units in the same layer. One reason for this is that efficient training algorithms have been developed (c.f. Hinton's Contrastive Divergence algorithm [9]) which allow the connection weights to be learned.

A given RBM defines an energy function for every configuration of visible and hidden state vectors, denoted v and h respectively. For binary state units, we define the energy function, $E(v, h)$ by:

$$E(v, h) = -a'v - b'h - h'Wv \tag{1}$$

where W is the symmetric matrix of the weights connecting the visible and hidden units, and a, b are bias vectors on the connections of bias unit to the visible and hidden layer, respectively.

The joint probability, $p(v, h)$, for the RBM mentioned above, assigns a probability to every configuration (v, h) of visible and hidden vectors using the energy function:

$$p(v, h) = \frac{\exp^{-E(v,h)}}{Z} \tag{2}$$

where Z, known as the partition function, is defined by:

$$Z = \sum_{v,h} \exp^{-E(v,h)} \tag{3}$$

The probability assigned by the network to a visible vector v is:

$$p(v) = \frac{1}{Z} \sum_{h} \exp^{-E(v,h)} \tag{4}$$

It turns out that the lack of connections in the same layer of an RBM contributes to the property that it's visible variables are conditionally independent, given the hidden variables, and vice versa. This means that we can write these conditional probabilities as:

$$p(v_j = 1|h) = \sigma(a_i + \sum_{j} h_j w_{i,j})$$

$$p(h_j = 1|v) = \sigma(b_j + \sum_{i} v_i w_{i,j}) \tag{5}$$

where:

$$\sigma(x) = \frac{1}{1 + \exp^{-x}} \tag{6}$$

is the sigmoid function.

The Contrastive Divergence (CD) algorithm is applied to find the parameters W, a, and b. The algorithm performs Gibbs sampling and is used inside a gradient descent procedure to compute weight update. A guide to training an RBM is given in [10].

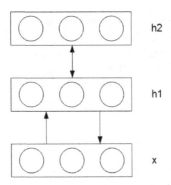

Fig. 2. Deep Belief Architecture. With x as the presentation layer and $h1$, $h2$ as hidden RBM layers.

When real-valued input data is used, the RBM is modified to have Gaussian visible units, and the energy function is altered to reflect this modification (c.f. [8]) as:

$$E(v, h) = \sum_i \frac{(v_i - a_i)^2}{2\sigma_i^2} - \sum_i \sum_j \frac{v_i}{\sigma_i^2} h_j w_{ij} - b'h \qquad (7)$$

With this modified energy function, the conditional probabilities are now given by:

$$p(h_j = 1|v) = \sigma\left(\sum_i \frac{v_i}{\sigma_i^2} w_{ij} + b_j\right)$$

$$p(v_i = v|h) = \mathcal{N}\left(v \Big| \sum_j h_j w_{ij} + a_i, \sigma_i^2\right) \qquad (8)$$

where: $\mathcal{N}(\cdot|\mu, \sigma^2)$ denotes the Gaussian probability density function with mean μ and variance σ^2.

2.2 Deep Belief Networks

As Bengio [11] states: *"there is theoretical evidence which suggests that in order to learn complicated functions that can represent high-level abstractions (e.g. in vision, language, and other AI-level tasks), one needs deep architectures."*

One type of deep architecture is the DBN. Their use has already given excellent results in certain speech representation and recognition problems (c.f. [5,6]).

A DBN consists in a number of stacked RBM, as shown in Figure 2. Hinton, Osindero and Teh [12] proposed an unsupervised greedy layer-wise training, in which each layer is trained, from the bottom upwards, as an RBM using the activations from the lower layer. This stacking method makes it possible to train many layers of hidden units efficiently, although with a large data set training may take a long time, and coding with GPU's has been a recent development.

When a DBN is used for classification purposes, there are essentially two modes we can use once it has been trained: either place a classifier above the top level and train the classifier in a supervised manner with the output from the RBM/DBN (we refer to this as 'mixed'), or, add another layer of outputs and apply back-propagation to the whole neural net.

3   The Emotional Speech Database

Most of the developed emotional speech databases are not available for public use. Thus, there are very few benchmark databases. Table 1 summarizes characteristics of some databases commonly used in speech emotion recognition.

Table 1. Characteristics of common emotional speech databases. Adapted from [13]

Corpus	Access	Language	Size	Emotions
LDC Emotional Prosody Speech and Transcripts	Commercially available	English	1050 utterances	Neutral, panic, anxiety, hot anger, cold anger, despair, sadness, elation, joy, interest, boredom, shame, pride, contempt
Berlin emotional database	Public and free	German	535 utterances	Anger, joy, sadness, fear, disgust, boredom, neutral
Danish emotional database	Public with license fee	Danish	260 utterances	Anger, joy, sadness, surprise, neutral
Natural	Private	Mandarin	388 utterances	Anger, neutral
ESMBS	Private	Mandarin	720 utterances	Anger, joy, sadness, disgust, fear, surprise
INTERFACE	Commercially available	English, Slovenian, Spanish, French	186, 190, 184, 175 utterances respectively	Anger, disgust, fear, joy, surprise, sadness, slow neutral, fast neutral

The variability between sentences, speech styles and even speakers, as well as the number of emotions considered, presents a challenge in emotional speech recognition. Here we shall minimize the number of variables involved by choosing a well-known Spanish emotional speech database [14], one female speaker, and take the emotions of joy, sadness, anger, fear, disgust and surprise along with neutral.

The database was created by the Center for Language and Speech Technologies and Applications (TALP) of the Polytechnic University of Catalonia (UPC) for the purpose of emotional speech research. The database was part of a larger project, INTERFACE, involving four languages, English, French, Slovene, and Spanish. In the case of Spanish, two professional actors, a man and a woman, were used to create the corpus. The speech corpus consisted of repeating 184 sentences with the big six emotions together with several neutral styles.

The 184 sentences include isolated words, sentences, which can also be in the affirmative and interrogative forms. The distribution is shown in Table 2.

Table 2. Spanish Corpus Contents

Identifier Corpus contents
001 - 100 Affirmative
101 - 134 Interrogative
135 - 150 Paragraphs
151 - 160 Digits
161 - 184 Isolated words

In a subjective test of the database with 16 non-professional listeners (UPC engineering students), it was found that over 80% of the sentences were correctly classified initially, and given a second choice, more than 90%. Each expression was correctly classified by at least half of the listeners.

It is interesting to note that errors were generally committed on the isolated words or short phrases, while all sentences and longer texts were classified correctly initially by all listeners. This subjective test is useful because we can compare it to the results obtained automatically by classifiers.

4 RBM and DBN Experiments

In this section we describe the details of the experiments performed in the paper. We first discuss the feature extraction stage, then we describe the configurations used in order to train and test the different classifiers.

We use audio files from the female Spanish speaker of the database. For every utterance within these groups (1,100 total), two kinds of characteristics were extracted: mel-frequency cepstral coefficients (MFCCs) and prosodic features. All the experiments were performed using a selected 70% of the patterns for training (770 patterns), 25% for testing (275 patterns) and 5% for validation purposes (55 patterns), all selected in a balanced manner. As usual, the training process continued until the generalization peak with respect to validation set was reached. In order to avoid a class biased data problem, each subset was sampled in a supervised manner to ensure that it was properly balanced.

The most popular feature representation currently used for speech recognition is MFCC [15]. It is based on a linear model of voice production together with a codification in a psychoacoustic scale.

Prosodic features have been used extensively for emotional speech recognition, such as energy, zero crossing rate and fundamental frequency, F_0, calculated for the speech signals considered [16]. In fact, many parameters can be extracted from the temporal evolution of prosodic features. Usually the minimum, mean, maximum and standard deviations over the whole utterance are used. This set of parameters has already been studied and some works have reported an important improvement in speech emotion discrimination [17].

In this work we have computed the average of the first 12 MFCC over the entire utterance, the average of F_0, the average of the zero crossing rate and the average of the energy, each one with their respective first derivative, all extracted using the OpenSMILE tool [18]. Hence, we represented each utterance with a 30-dimensional feature vector: $(1 + \Delta)(12\,\text{MFCCs} + \text{mean}\,F_0 + \text{mean}\,\text{ZCR} + \text{mean}\,\text{Energy})$.

For RBM and DBN experiments, we use the toolbox developed by Drausin Wulsin [19]. A large number of experiments were conducted in order to determine the best configurations and parameters for the RBM. These experiments consisted in different combinations of: varying the size of the batch (number of training vectors used in each pass of each epoch for the Contrastive Divergence algorithm), the learning rate, the number of hidden units, and the number of stacked RBM. All RBM had Gaussian units. DBN experiments were performed by adding one additional RBM layer to a previously trained DBN, and using the parameters shown in Table 3. The classification layer had seven output units, one for each class. The most probable class was considered as the unit with the highest activation level.

Table 3. Configuration parameters details for RBM/DBN training

Parameter	Values
Batch size	[6, 12, 18, 24, 30, 36, 42, 48, 54, 60]
Learning rate	[0.01, 0.001, 0.0001, 0.00001]
Hidden units	[28, 56, 84, 112, 140, 168]
Number of layers	[1, 2, 3, 4, ..., 13, 14, 15]

For the experiments performed with Support vector machines (SVM) we used the LIBSVM toolbox [20] and for the rest of the classifiers: K-nearest neighbors (KNN), Decision trees (DT) and Multilayer Perceptron (MLP), the Statistics and Neural Networks Toolboxes from Matlab were used [21]. The SVM was used with a radial kernel. For KNN three neighbors and the cosine distance measure were used. The DT was constructed using Gini's diversity index, and then pruned in order to obtain better generalization capabilities. The MLP was trained in a traditional way with one hidden layer and ten hidden units, all the activation functions were sigmoid except in the last layer where "tansig" functions were used. We also performed some "mixed" experiments where SVM, KNN, DT and MLP classifiers were fed the outputs of an RBM.

5   Results and Discussion

In this section we present the results of the previously described experiments. With DBN classifiers, some of the results for the different configurations presented in Table 3 are shown in Figure 3. The combination of parameters that yields the best result was: 112 hidden units, a batch size of 42 and a learning rate of 0.00001. With this configuration the DBN achieved an error rate of 18.37%.

In order to perform a second set of experiments with several stacked RBMs, we used the DBN with the best configuration. The results can be seen in the Figure 4. For the case of mixed classifiers, the outputs of RBMs can generally help the other classifiers to achieve better performance, as seen in Table 4. These results were obtained by feeding the classifier with the output of three trained RBMs as described above, as can be seen, the results obtained are better than those obtained with the other classifiers.

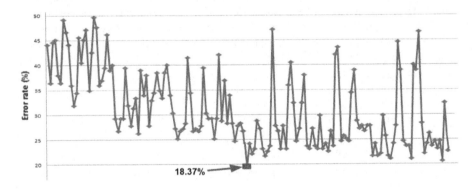

Fig. 3. Extract of some error rates of DBNs experiments for the different combinations of configurations seen in Table 3

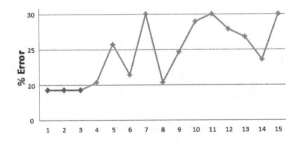

Fig. 4. Error rates against number of stacked RBMs. The best results were obtained with 1, 2 and 3 RBMs.

Table 4. Best performance obtained for the different classifiers

Classifier	Error rate (%)
DBN - RBM	**18.37**
K-nn	31.63
DBN - K-nn	24.49
DT	34.69
DBN - DT	23.47
MLP	40.82
DBN - MLP	20.41
SVM	25.43
DBN - SVM	18.97

It also can be seen that the best result was achieved with only one, two and three layers of RBMs and then it got worse. A possible explanation for this result is that with the aim of minimizing the number of variables, we are using a small subset of emotions and data; the more stacked RBMs, the more free parameters to train, requiring additional training data in order to properly estimate the parameters. Further work needs to be done so we can prove this affirmation.

6 Conclusions

In this work we considered the application of Restricted Boltzmann machines and Deep Belief Networks to the task of automatic Spanish emotional speech recognition. The results obtained are comparable, and in fact better than the results of other selected classifiers, when the parameters were correctly chosen. Future work includes extending these experiments to other languages in the database, and another using Mexican Spanish, that is being developed by us.

Acknowledgments. The authors wish to thank: *SEP* and *CONACyT* (Program SEP-CONACyT CB-2012-01, No.182432) and the *Universidad Autónoma Metropolitana* from México; *ANPCyT* and *Universidad Nacional de Litoral* (with PAE 37122, PACT 2011 #58, CAI+D 2011 #58-511) and *CONICET* from Argentina, for their support. We also want to thank ELRA for supplying the, Emotional speech synthesis database, catalogue reference: ELRA-S0329.

References

1. Douglas-Cowie, C.: Humaine d5f deliverable, obtainable from
   http://emotion-research.net/download/pilot-db/
2. Schuller, B., Steidl, S., Batliner, A.: The interspeech 2009 emotion challenge. In: 10th Annual Conference of the International, Speech Communication, Association INTERSPEECH 2009, pp. 312–315 (2009)

3. Schuller, B., Steidl, S., Batliner, A., Noth, E., Vinciarelli, A., Burkhardt, F., van Son, R., Weninger, F., Eyben, F., Bocklet, T., Mohammadi, G., Weiss, B.: The interspeech 2012 speaker trait challenge. In: Proc. INTERSPEECH (2012)
4. Scherer, K.R.: A blueprint for affective computing: a sourcebook. Oxford University Press, Oxford (2010)
5. Mohamed, A., Sainath, T., Dahl, G.E., Ramabhadran, B., Hinton, G., Picheny, M.: Deep belief networks using discriminative features for phone recognition. In: ICASSP 2011. ISCA, Portland (2012)
6. Hinton, G., Deng, L., Yu, D., Dahl, G., Mohamed, A., Jaitly, N., Senior, A.: Deep neural networks for acoustic modeling in speech recognition. IEEE Signal Processing Magazine (2012)
7. Stuhlsatz, A., Meyer, C., Eyben, F., Zielke, T., Meier, G., Schuller, B.: Deep neural networks for acoustic emotion recognition: Raising the benchmarks. In: Proc. Int. Conf. on Acoustics, Speech, and Signal Processing, ICASSP 2011, Prague, Czech Republic, pp. 5688–5691 (2011)
8. Bruckner, R., Schuller, B.: Likability classification - a not so deep neural network approach. In: Proceedings of INTERSPEECH 2012, 13th Annual Conference of the International Speech Communication Association (2012)
9. Hinton, G.E.: Training products of experts by minimizing contrastive divergence. Neural Computation 14, 1771–1800 (2002)
10. Hinton, G.E.: A practical guide to training restricted boltzmann machines. In: Montavon, G., Orr, G.B., Müller, K.-R. (eds.) Neural Networks: Tricks of the Trade, 2nd edn. LNCS, vol. 7700, pp. 599–619. Springer, Heidelberg (2012)
11. Bengio, Y.: Learning deep architectures for ai. Foundations and Trends in Machine Learning 2, 1–127 (2009)
12. Hinton, G.E., Osindero, S., Teh, Y.: A fast learning algorithm for deep belief nets. Neural Computation 18, 1527–1554 (2006)
13. El Ayadi, M., Kamel, M.S., Karray, F.: Survey on speech emotion recognition: Features, classification schemes, and databases. Pattern Recognition 44(3), 572–587 (2011)
14. Catalogue, E.: Emotional speech synthesis database, catalogue reference: Elras0329, http://catalog.elra.info
15. Rabiner, L., Juang, B.H.: Fundamentals of speech recognition. Prentice Hall PTR (1993)
16. Deller, J., Proakis, J., Hansen, J.: Discrete-time processing of speech signals. Prentice Hall PTR, Upper Saddle River (1993)
17. Albornoz, E., Milone, D., Rufiner, H.: Spoken emotion recognition using hierarchical classifiers. Computer Speech and Language 25, 556–570 (2011)
18. Eyben, F., Wollmer, M., Schuller, B.: Opensmile - the munich versatile and fast open-source audio feature extractor. In: Proc. ACM Multimedia (MM). ACM, Florence (2010)
19. Wulsin, D.: Dbn toolbox v1. Department of Bioengineering. University of Pennsylvania (2010), http://www.seas.upenn.edu/~wulsin/
20. Chang, C.C., Lin, C.J.: Libsvm: a library for support vector machines. ACM Transactions on Intelligent Systems and Technology (2011)
21. Guide, M.U.: Mathworks (2011), http://www.mathworks.com

Odor Plume Tracking Algorithm Inspired on Evolution*

B. Lorena Villarreal[1], Gustavo Olague[2], and J.L. Gordillo[1]

[1] Center for Robotics and Intelligent Systems, Tecnológico de Monterrey,
Monterrey, Nuevo León, México
[2] EvoVision Project, Computer Science Department, Applied Physics Division CICESE,
Ensenada, Baja California, México

Abstract. Smell sensors in mobile robotics for odor source localization are getting the attention for researches around the world. To solve the problem, it must be considered the environmental model and odor behavior, the perception system and the algorithm for tracking the odors plume. Current algorithms try to emulate the behavior of the animals known by its capability to follow odors. Nevertheless, the odor perception systems are still in its infancy and far to be compared with the biological smell sense. This is why, an algorithm that considers the perception system capabilities and drawbacks, the environmental model and the odor behavior is presented on this work. Besides, an artificial intelligent technique (Genetic Programming) is used as a platform to develop odor source localization algorithms. It is prepared for different environment conditions and perception systems. A comparison between this improved algorithm and a pair of basic techiques for odor source localization is presented in terms of repeatability.

Keywords: odor source localization, smell, genetic programming, sniffing robot.

1 Introduction

Smell sensors are being developed to distinguish all types of odors, intensities and concentrations. Odor source localization algorithms should be useful with any kind of odor sensors arrays and a good signal analysis that improve the measurement. The applications could be the detection of toxic gas leaks, the fire origin of a disaster, search and rescue operations, etc.

Smell sensors implemented on mobile robots started in 1984 with the use of chemical sensitive robots in the nuclear industry [1]. There are many algorithms used to support and increase the efficiency of odor source localization.These are most commonly classified by the terms of *chemotaxis* and *anemotaxis* depending on the environment and the capabilities of the odor sensors. Chemotaxis is used when the orientation and movement of the agent (mobile robot) is based on the chemical gradient of the environment [2]. On the other hand, anemotaxis, instead of following the gradient, considers the direction or current of a fluid [3,4] and the agent moves through it.

Some other algorithms for odor source localization that include predefined airflow models, different environment conditions, different types of odor sources and obstacle maps are described in [5,6,7,8].

* This research has been supported by CONACYT and Laboratorio de Robótica del área Noreste y Centro de México.

J.F. Martínez-Trinidad et al. (Eds.): MCPR 2014, LNCS 8495, pp. 321–330, 2014.
© Springer International Publishing Switzerland 2014

The principal disadvantage of this algorithms is the sensorial system itself. The chemical reactions change the sensor in a way that the recovery to its original state is slow [9]. In this research, genetic programming is used to evolve a solution considering the capabilities of the perception system, as well as its limitations. The work is based on the assumption that the direction from where an odor is coming can be obtained using the difference between a pair of nostrils as it was implemented on [10]. The results show that the algorithm obtained by this technique improves the achievement rate of common algorithms based on chemotaxis. It decreases the time to complete the task and increases repeatability.

This document is organized as follows. First, the complete definition of the problem is presented in section 2. In section 3 the theoretical analysis is shown. In section 4 is discussed the implementation and experimental set up. The preliminary results are shown in section 5. Finally, in section 6 the conclusions and future work are presented.

2   Problem Definition

There are three problems that need to be analyzed when solving the task of tracing odor sources with a robot: characterize the dynamic behavior of the atmosphere and odors; adequately perceive this environment so that the information can be useful for future analysis and the algorithm or technique to locate the odor source using this information.

Currently, techniques and nature-based algorithms emulate the behavior of some animals, such as casting, and sweeping spiral [11]. However, currently available sensors differ from the characteristics of the biological sensors that these animals have. This occurs basically because their brain does not only use this ability, but gathers information from all other sensors. This is the way in which the animals learned how to locate the odor. When a try of simulate this localization technique with a robot is done, the results are not the most optimal because the odor source is not located with high accuracy or requires a lot of task time to be reached.

However, if the 3 sub-problems are seen as one, considering the limitations of the sensors (desaturation time, concentration difference between sources, reaction time), features based on nature that must have at least, the mathematical model of it, a new technique with better results can be obtained by means of genetic programming. This task can be achieved regardless the information from other sensors such as anemometers.

In this research is presented the development of a genetic program (GP) that produces an odor tracking algorithm that integrates the simulation of a system device with the capability of directionality and the odor propagation model as the environmental conditions.

3   Theoretical Analysis

Different techniques for odor source localization can be used depending on the environment conditions and the perception system. Moreover, there are different configurations for the implementation of chemical sensors. The most commonly used into mobile robots are: directly exposed, continually exposed and cyclic exposed. The first one refers to the placement of the sensor without isolation. Monroy et al. are using a complete inverted sensor model [12] to obtain an estimation of the odor. The sensor is placed into the robot without isolation.

The second configuration is considered when airflow is induced directly to the sensors placed into an isolated chamber. In [13] are using a pair of chambers. An inlet pipe samples the surroundings by an airflow generated by a micro-pump emulating the inhalation stage of the ventilation process. Similar approaches [6,2,14] produce and direct airflow into an inlet through the sensors. When a constant odor source is present, as a gas leak, the sensors are being continually exposed to the odor no having time to recover its original state. In the other hand, cyclic exposed [15] refers to the use of a chamber with the capability of isolate the sensors from the environment for a certain time and prepare it for a new measurement.

Then, the development of algorithms for odor source localization must take in care the characterisitcs of both, environment and sensor model to achieve a better behavior. This way, the drawbacks of the physical implementation can de reduced. By genetic programming, these can be taken into consideration to produce an algorithm specific for the environment and perception system used. In this section, the environmental and sensor models in which the GP is based, will be explained.

3.1 Environmental Model

The propagation of odor molecules in the environment occurs in two different ways. When no airflows are present, the propagation is done by diffusion in a radial manner. On the other hand, when airflow is present, the propagation is done by advection in a laminar way.

In [16], diffusion is described as the process by which matter is transported from one part of a system to another due to molecular motions. Each molecule presents a random motion, and the set of random movements of all molecules results in the mix of the solute. The microscopic behavior however, is not what determines the odor trail. Instead, the random walk of molecules take place from a high concentration region to a low concentration region, depending on the concentration gradient, trying to homogenize the environment.

The general form for the diffusion equation is for a three-dimensional system is represented by

$$\frac{\partial C}{\partial t} = D\left(\frac{\partial^2 C}{\partial x^2} + \frac{\partial^2 C}{\partial y^2} + \frac{\partial^2 C}{\partial z^2}\right).$$

As a first approximation, in this research a constant diffusion source will be used as the environment condition.

3.2 Nose Model

The perception system considered for this work is based on [9,10], which implements a bio-inspired nose system with the capability of determine the direction from where an odor is coming. It is achieved by the use of a pair of notrils divided by a septum. In the inhalation process, the nose is able to concentrate the odor molecules near the sensorial system and at exhalation, the nose desaturates the sensors. This design complements the sensor model from [6,12] by including the cyclic behavior of a sensor placed into a chamber.

The model emulates the complete ventilation process, where different variables can be adjusted: the saturation level (R_{max}), the time constants of rise (τ_r), retaining the air (τ_a), and decay (τ_d), the time before the sensor started to respond (t_s), the time of the rising period (Δt_r), and the time of the sampling period (Δt_a).

In real applications, the smell process is cyclic, which means that the actual reading of the sensors depends on the last measurement. The model that represents this design into a continuous odorous environment is divided in two stages. For inhalation

$$r_i(t) = r_e(t-1) + (R_{max} - r_e(t-1))(1 - exp(-\tfrac{(t-t_s)}{\tau_r})),$$

and for exhalation

$$r_e(t) = \frac{r_e(t-1) - r_i(t)(exp(-\frac{(t-t_s-\Delta t_r-\Delta t_a)}{\tau_d})}{1 - exp(-\frac{(t-t_s-\Delta t_r-\Delta t_a)}{\tau_d})},$$

where $r_i(t)$ and $r_e(t)$ are the concentration values during inhalation and exhalation at the actual ventilation cycle. Consequently, $r_e(t-1)$ is the concentration value of the last cycle. So, after each cycle the initial reference is updated by

$$r_e(t-1) = r_e(t).$$

Based on this design with the presented behavior, the modeling and simulation of its physical properties can be used to obtain an algorithm developed to work specifically taking advantage of its features.

4   Implementation and Experimental Set-Up

Three algorithms of odor source localization are compared. The first is the one used by Rozas [17]. The second is going to be called for this purpose as " the basic algorithm". It was designed using ascend gradient method. The third is the one obtained by evolution. Them are going to be described in this section.

As the physical implementation requires a controlled environment for multiple characterization experiments and because the odor is extracted hardly from this environment to have exactly equal initial conditions, the experiments take a lot of time. Due this reason, a simulation environment was developed using NetLogo [18] to run any kind and quantity of experiments.

In the environmental model designed, the diffusion rate and the wind can be controlled varying the direction and the intensity or speed. The initial position, concentration and quantity of the sources can be also controlled. The sources can be spraying the odor at constant time intervals or can be always spreading it.

This environment simulates the diffusion through the air from a source as well as the interaction of the robot with the source considering the mathematical model described in section 3.2. The selected environment was a fixed odor source that diffuses through the air and a mobile robot capable of measuring the concentration difference at two emulated nostrils positioned $45°$ and $-45°$ respectively and 1 unit distance from the center of the robot. The three algorithms are represented as syntax trees, just as in genetic programming, using the same platform for all simulations.

4.1   Rozas Algorithm

The first robot implemented for odor source localization was presented by Rozas et al. [17] in 1991. The algorithm was design to follow odor gradients by taking spatial measurements at different times, thus, by chemotaxis. The algorithm used is shown in Fig. 1.

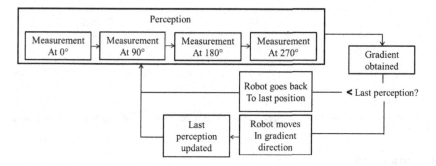

Fig. 1. Odor source localization algorithm implemented in [17] using chemotaxis

4.2   Basic Algorithm

It is a variation of the gradient descend method. The difference between two nostrils is used to detect the direction of the odor source and the step size of the robot, looking for the maximum concentration. The routine consists in two operating timed cycles: the aspiration process and the robot movement. In the aspiration process, each time the system inhales, the robot acquires odor concentration data through its sensors and saves it into the memory (Mem) of the adquisition system. In the other hand, the robot movement cylce starts by waiting certain time for measurement (t_m). Then, the average of the data accumulated by inhalation during this time lapse (t_i) is obtained. After that, it calculates its new direction and aligns with it. The direction of turn is limited by a maximum angle (θ_{max}). Finally, it moves s steps forward. A threshold (thr) is implemented to consider the uncertainty between nostrils when the source is near to the front face of the robot. In that case the robot moves $\frac{s}{k}$, where k is an experimental constant. The algorithm is shown in Fig. 2. This routine continues until the robot reaches a saturation value and is considered to have arrived, or exceeding a preset time limit. It is important to consider that the measurements used to obtain the direction are only those when the system is between inhaling and exhaling. The measurements at exhalation are ignored.

4.3   Genetic Programming

Based on the understanding of that the bio-inspired nose has limitations, it can be noticed that a basic algorithm as presented before may not be the best solution. However, knowing the mathematical model and operation of the system, by means of genetic programming an adequated localization algorithm was evolved taking into account these constraints.

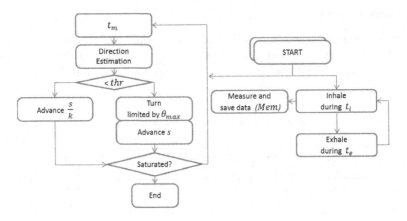

Fig. 2. Algorithm for reactive gradient ascend. The robot turns according to its measurement.

4.4 Parameters

NetLogo has an interface that communicates with Matlab and allows to exchange data between the two applications. The purpose of this integration is the use of genetic programming managed by this software whose experiments can be simulated by means of NetLogo. Matlab is responsible for the creation of the new generations based on the fitness while NetLogo runs the experiments an asigns the fitness on each candidate.

As in robotics, for this application the terminals are the actions of the robot [19,20]. The set of terminals for the GP was composed by:

- Move, Jump. Robot moves forward one or two steps respectively
- Measureminus. Robot average all measurements during last t_m
- Measurediff. Robot considers last measurement during last t_m
- MeasureTurn. Robot waits for sampling time and obtains a measurement, then it turns depending on the nostril's difference.
- Turnmeasured. Robot turns in the direction calculated.
- Turn90. Robot turns 90° to left or right depending on last measurement.
- Turn45. Robot turns 45° to left or right depending on last measurement.
- Turnrandom. Robot turns random in a range of −90° to 90°.
- Turnrandom45. Robot turns 45° in a random direction.
- HoldOn. Robots waits 1 time step.
- Goback. Robot turns 180° and moves forward one step.

The function set is composed by PROGN2, PROGN3 and IF(a,b). PROGN are the simplest nodes which are used for connecting parts of program together. It returns two or tree subtrees respectively in sequence. In the other hand, IF returns a when the treshold is reached and b otherwise.

The fitness function that evaluates each candidate is divided in 5 parameters:

- Distance reached (ΔD). At the end of the experiment, it evaluates how close or far the robot ends of the source relative to its initial position. Its range varies from −0.754 to 1, where 1 is better.

- Time Used (t_u). It is the time the robot takes to reach the source (t_{exp}) normalized by t_{max}, which is the time out of the experiment. Its range varies from 0 to 1, where 0 is better.
- Facing to Source (f_s). Considering that the robot's field of view (FoV) is at front, it refers to the percentage of times the robot's FoV is facing to the source. The FoV is considered 45°. Its range varies from -1 to 0, where 0 is better.
- Getting closer (N_c). It evaluates the percentage of movements when the robot was actually moving closer to the source. Its range varies from -1 to 0, where 0 is better.
- Arrived (ϵ_a). It is an additional 0.05 evaluation if the source has been reached.

Considering D_i as the inital distance from the robot to the source, D_f the final distance and D_{max} the maximum initial distance, these parameters can be obtained as:

$$\Delta D = \begin{cases} -0.75 & \text{if } \frac{(D_f - D_i)}{D_{max}} < -0.75 \\ \frac{(D_f - D_i)}{D_{max}} & \text{otherwise} \end{cases}, \quad \epsilon_a = \begin{cases} 0.05 & \text{if robot reaches the source} \\ 0 & \text{otherwise} \end{cases},$$

$$t_u = \frac{t_{exp}}{t_{max}}, \quad f_s = \frac{\text{headings}}{\text{time steps of experiment}}, \quad N_c = \frac{\text{times robot is moving closer}}{\text{time steps of experiment}}.$$

Finally, the fitness of each candidate (f_n) is the weighted sum of these parameters:

$$f_n = \Delta D \times 0.5 + (1 - t_u) \times 0.2 + f_s \times 0.25 + N_c \times 0.05 + \epsilon_a .$$

The weights of each parameter were calculated running 200 experiments of 10 different algorithms obtained by Genetic Programming. The results are presented in Table 1. The weights for each parameter were adjusted comparing the fitness versus: the quantity of experiments that at the end of the experiment reached the source, got closer to the source, or got lost (out of the experimental area). The trend lines for each comparison were adjusted trying to reach a r-squared bigger than 0.5 indicating a lineal tendency. Fig. 3 show the results using the weights mentioned before.

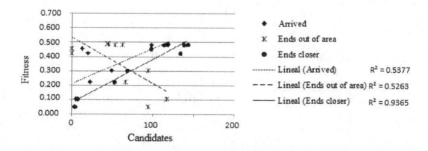

Fig. 3. Comparison between fitness and principal objectives of algorithm

Table 1. Comparison results of between 10 algorithms. 8 of them obtained by GP at different generations

	Ended Closer	Didn't Arrived	Ended Arrived	Ended Farther	Ended Out of area	Fitness (-135 to 150)	Normalized Fitness
a1	133	20	113	67	0	-13.51	0.426
a2	52	23	29	148	66	-70.62	0.226
a3	142	116	26	58	45	3.87	0.487
a4	113	98	15	87	62	2.12	0.481
a5	68	49	19	132	94	-48.5	0.304
a6	4	3	1	196	94	-120.02	0.053
a7	138	118	20	62	53	2.42	0.482
a8	97	13	84	84	0	-4.82	0.457
a9	137	119	18	63	44	5.08	0.492
a10	7	5	2	193	117	-105.12	0.105

5   Experimental Results

Using genetic programming, a better algorithm was obtained. The probabilities for crossover and mutation were 0.5 and 0.05 respectively. These were defined with this values because even when the objective is to look for new and different algorithms, it is trying not to lose important information at the same time. The roulette technique was used as the selection method. The number of candidates was 100 and the routine was evolved during 40 generations. The best algorithm obtained was a variation of gradient ascend, were instead of constant $k = 2$ was $k = 1$ and instead of save the measurements during t_m the algorithm waits until the inhalation cycle have finished. Fig. 4 represents the algorithm.

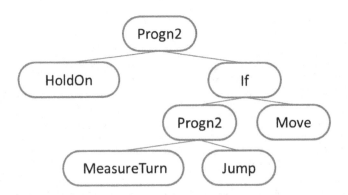

Fig. 4. Best so far algorithm at last generation. The robot waits for inhalation and then samples the odor. It turns and moves depending on this measurement.

Finally, the sintax trees compared were:

- Rozas. "progn2(evalcircle,if(goback,antmove))"
- Basic. "progn3(measureminus,HoldOn,if(progn3(turnmeasured,jump,move),move))"
- GP1. "progn2(HoldOn,if(progn2(MeasureTurn,jump),move))"

Table 2 show the results. It can be seen that in Rozas algorithm, around 60% of the experiments (candidates) finished closer to the source relative to its initial position. Nevertheless just 10% of the experiments reached the source. The impact of this algorithm is that none of the candidates ended out of the experimental area unlike Basic and GP1. However, around 30% ended farther. In the other hand, GP1 shows an important increment in fitness, basically because the candidates that reached the source represent almost 60% of the total amount and just as in Rozas, only 30% ended farther.

Table 2. Comparison results between three different algorithms

	Ended Closer	Arrived	Didn't Arrived	Ended Farther	Ended Out of area	Fitness (-135 to 150)	Normalized Fitness
Rozas	133	20	113	67	0	-13.51	0.426
Basic	56	25	31	144	46	-6.95	0.449
GP1	137	119	18	63	44	5.08	0.492

6 Conclusion and Future Work

A GP development was presented in this work for an odor plume tracking algorithm. Thanks to the obtained results, it can be said that, genetic programming is a powerful tool to develop odor source localization algorithms. A better solution was presented showing that the uncertainty of achievement was decreased.

Considering the capabilities of the perception system and the odor propagation model, the platform is prepared to run for several environments with different characteristics and perception systems. The next step is to find an algorithm in an environment where airflow is present, regardless the use of another kind of sensors. It must be compared with the common algorithms used in the literature. Then, the inclusion of obstacles and dynamic sources would be an interesting approach.

Acknowledgments. Specially thanks to CONACYT that has been supporting the research in conjunction with the Laboratorio de Robótica del área Noreste y Centro de México and to EvoVisión Team from CICESE that are providing the tools and expertise for this research.

References

1. Larcombe, M., Halsall, J.: Robotics in nuclear engineering: Computer-assisted teleoperation in hazardous environments with particular reference to radiation fields, vol. 9312. Graham & Trotman (1984)

2. Neumann, P.P., Hernandez Bennetts, V., Lilienthal, A.J., Bartholmai, M., Schiller, J.H.: Gas source localization with a micro-drone using bio-inspired and particle filter-based algorithms. Advanced Robotics 27(9), 725–738 (2013)
3. Kowadlo, G., Russell, R.A.: Robot odor localization: A taxonomy and survey. The International Journal of Robotics Research 27(8), 869–894 (2008)
4. Ishida, H., Tanaka, H., Taniguchi, H., Moriizumi, T.: Mobile robot navigation using vision and olfaction to search for a gas/odor source. Autonomous Robots 20(3), 231–238 (2006)
5. Cabrita, G., Sousa, P., Marques, L.: Odor guided exploration and plume tracking: Particle plume explorer. In: Proceedings of the 5th European Conference on Mobile Robots (ECMR 2011), pp. 183–188 (2011)
6. Lilienthal, A., Duckett, T.: A stereo electronic nose for a mobile inspection robot. In: Proceedings of the IEEE International Workshop on Robotic Sensing (ROSE 2003) (2003)
7. Loutfi, A., Coradeschi, S., Lilienthal, A., Gonzalez, J.: Gas distribution mapping of multiple odour sources using a mobile robot. Robotica 27, 311–319 (2009)
8. Ramirez, A., Lopez, A., Rodriguez, A., de Albornoz, A., De Pieri, E.: An infotaxis based odor navigation approach. In: Biosignals and Biorobotics Conference (BRC). ISSNIP, pp. 1–6 (2011)
9. Villarreal, B.L., Gordillo, J.L.: Perception model for the aspiration process of a biologically inspired sniffing robot. In: 2013 18th International Conference on Methods and Models in Automation and Robotics (MMAR), pp. 334–339 (August 2013)
10. Villarreal, B.L., Hassard, C., Gordillo, J.L.: Finding the direction of an odor source by using biologically inspired smell system. In: Pavón, J., Duque-Méndez, N.D., Fuentes-Fernández, R. (eds.) IBERAMIA 2012. LNCS, vol. 7637, pp. 551–560. Springer, Heidelberg (2012)
11. Vickers, N.J.: Mechanisms of animal navigation in odor plumes. The Biological Bulletin 198(2), 203–212 (2000)
12. Monroy, J.G., González-Jiménez, J., Blanco, J.L.: Overcoming the slow recovery of mox gas sensors through a system modeling approach. Sensors 12(10), 13664–13680 (2012)
13. Martinez, D., Rochel, O., Hugues, E.: A biomimetic robot for tracking specific odors in turbulent plumes. Autonomous Robots 20(3), 185–195 (2006)
14. Lochmatter, T., Raemy, X., Martinoli, A.: Odor source localization with mobile robots. Bulletin of the Swiss Society for Automatic Control 46, 11–14 (2007)
15. Villarreal, B.L., Gordillo, J.L.: Method and artificial olfactive system (metodo y sistema olfativo artificial). Mexico. Instituto Mexicano de la Propiedad Intelectual (IMPI). Patent pending Mx/a/2012/014 508 (2012)
16. Crank, J.: The mathematics of diffusion. Oxford Univerity Press (1976)
17. Rozas, R., Morales, J., Vega, D.: Artificial smell detection for robotic navigation. In: 5th International Conference on Advanced Robotics (ICAR). Robots in Unstructured Environments, vol. 2, pp. 1730–1733 (1991)
18. Wilensky, U.: Netlogo. Center for connected learning and computer-based modeling. Northwestern University, Evanston (1999), http://ccl.northwestern.edu/netlogo/
19. Paic-Antunovic, L., Jakobovic, D.: Evolution of automatic robot control with genetic programming. In: 2012 Proceedings of the 35th International Convention, MIPRO, pp. 817–822. IEEE (2012)
20. Lazarus, C., Hu, H.: Using genetic programming to evolve robot behaviours. In: Proceedings of the 3rd British Conference on Autonomous Mobile Robotics and Autonomous Systems, Manchester (2001)

Use of Lexico-Syntactic Patterns
for the Evaluation of Taxonomic Relations

Mireya Tovar[1,2], David Pinto[2], Azucena Montes[1,3], Gabriel González[1],
Darnes Vilariño[2], and Beatriz Beltrán[2]

[1] Centro Nacional de Investigación y Desarrollo Tecnológico (CENIDET), Mexico
[2] Faculty of Computer Science,
Benemérita Universidad Autónoma de Puebla, Mexico
[3] Engineering Institute,
Universidad Nacional Autónoma de Mexico
Puebla, México
{mtovar,amontes,gabriel}@cenidet.edu.mx,
{dpinto,darnes,bbeltran}@cs.buap.mx

Abstract. In this paper we present an approach for the evaluation of
taxonomic relations of restricted domain ontologies. We use the evidence found in corpora associated to the ontology domain for determining the validity of the taxonomic relations. Our approach employs
lexico-syntactic patterns for evaluating taxonomic relations in which the
concepts are totally different, and it uses a particular technique based
on subsumption for those relations in which one concept is completely
included in the other one. The integration of these two techniques has
allowed to automatically evaluate taxonomic relations for two ontologies
of restricted domain. The performance obtained was about 70% for one
ontology of the e-learning domain, whereas we obtained around 88% for
the ontology associated to the artificial intelligence domain.

Keywords: Lexico-syntactic patterns, Ontology evaluation, Taxonomic
relations.

1   Introduction

There is a huge amount of information that is uploaded every day to the World
Wide Web, thus arising the need for automatic tools able to understand the
meaning of such information. However, one of the central problems of constructing such tools is that this information remains unstructured nowadays, despite
the effort of different communities for give a semantic sense to the World Wide
Web. In fact, the Semantic Web research direction attempts to tackle this problem by incorporating semantic to the web data, so that it can be processed
directly or indirectly by machines in order to transform it into a data network
[18]. For this purpose, it has been proposed to use some knowledge structures
such as ontologies for giving semantic and some structure to unstructured data.
An ontology, from the computer science perspective, is "an explicit specification of a conceptualiation" [8]. An ontology typically includes classes, instances,

J.F. Martínez-Trinidad et al. (Eds.): MCPR 2014, LNCS 8495, pp. 331–340, 2014.

attributes, relations, constraints, rules, events and axioms. Even thought the ontologies may be structured with taxonomic and/or non-taxonomic relations, in this paper we focus the evaluation over the taxonomic relations, which normally are referred as relations of type "is-a" (hypernym/hyponymy or subsumption).

There are plenty of research works in literature that address the problem of automatic construction of ontologies. The major of those works evaluate the ontology created by using a gold standard, which in fact, it is supposed to be created by one expert. Using this approach, it is assumed that the expert has created the ontology in a correct way, but there is not a guaranty of such thing. Thus, we consider very important to investigate the manner of evaluate automatically the quality of these kind of resources, which are continuously been used in the framework of the semantic web.

Our approach attemps to find evidence of the relations to be evaluated in a reference corpus (associated to the same domain of the ontology), and therefore, we needed to analyze the different approaches reported in literature for automatic identification of ontology relations. A number of classification methods have been addressed for identifying relations between concepts or instances [4,5,16]. For instance, for identifying whether or not a given instance (a pair of words *flower:tulip*) belongs to a specific relation (class-inclusion) [21]. Other approaches identify the degree of semantic similarity between a set of word pairs in which it is known that belong to a certain semantic class (semantic relation) [10,20,19]. For the purpose of this paper, we focus our analysis on those techniques that identify taxonomic relations.

The remaining of this paper is structured as follows. Section 2 describes more into detail the lexico-syntactic patterns found in literature. In Section 3 we present the model proposed for addressing the problem aforementioned. Section 4 shows and discusses the results obtained by the presented approach. Finally, in Section 5 the findings and the future work are given.

2   Lexico-Syntactic Patterns

A seminal work in the task of automatic identification of hypernyms from raw texts is the one presented by Hearst [9]. She proposed six lexico-syntactic patterns, which actually are known as Hearst's patterns, that have been widely used in other works. In [1], for example, the authors obtain co-hyponyms by using the Hearst's patterns, but there are other approaches such as the following ones: [17,7,3,13]. Even though these patterns behave well on the above mentioned task, it is important to notice that they may be adjusted to work better in particular domains, which is our case.

There are other works proposing lexico-syntactic patterns, such as the one presented in [14], in which the authors focused on the romanian language. In [7], they propose a methodology that combine two techniques for the extraction of hyponymy, meronymy, co-hyponymy and near-synonymy in texts the Italian Wikipedia, i. e., lexico-syntactic patterns and statistical distributional systems. They use only five lexico-syntactic patterns, achieving good experimental results in this type of semantic relations. In [17], an automatic classifier for the hypernym and hyponym relation identification is built. It based in the use of dependency paths for some lexico-syntactic patterns.

In our case, we have collected 106 lexico-syntactic patterns, associated with the identification of taxonomic relations, from nine different sources [10,9,1,3,13,14,12,15,22]. Although we have found useful only 16 of these when we evaluated the two target ontologies, the rest of them may be useful for future investigations on ontology evaluation or automatic ontology learning tasks. Therefore, in Table 1, it can be seen all these lexico-syntactic patterns compiled.

Table 1. Database of lexico-syntactic patterns useful for detecting taxonomic relations

No.	Lexico-syntactic patterns
12	NP such as (NP,)* (or|and|the) NP
13	NP 's NP
15	such NP as (NP,)*
42	NP (is | are) NP
43	NP (is | are) (a | an) NP
46	NP such as (NP,)* (or|and) NP
50	NP (classify (in | into) | comprise | contain | compose (of)? | group (in | into) | divide (in | into) | fall (in | into) | belong (to)) NP
86	NP (and | or) (another | other) NP
92	NP (,)? such as (NP,)* (or|and|the)? NP
94	NP NP , is (a|an|the) NP
96	NP , (is | are) (NP,)* (or | and|the) NP
97	(NP,)* (or|and|the) (NP,)* (is | are) (a|an|the) NP
98	NP , including NP
104	NP as (NP,*) (or| and| the) NP
106	NP, for example, is (a|an|the) NP

3 Evaluation of Taxonomic Relations

The evaluation process proposed is based on finding evidence in a reference corpus using the "correctness" criterion [2]. We assume that there exist such a collection of documents associated to the ontology domain (reference corpus) from which it is possible to find evidence of the correctness of the taxonomic relations held by the ontology. This evidence is found throught the use of lexico-syntactic patterns.

The approach proposed the following three steps:

- Pre-processing stage: In this step, all data (ontology, reference corpus and lexico-syntactic patterns) receive a special treatment in order to have normalized information, representing them by their lemmas. For this purpose, we use the FreeLing PoS tagger[1]. An information retrieval system is used for

---

[1] http://nlp.lsi.upc.edu/freeling/

filtering those documents which contain information refering the two concepts of any of the relations extracted from the ontology to be evaluated[2].

- Discovering of taxonomic relations: For practical purposes, the lexico-syntactic patterns are transformed into regular expressions, which are used for discovering evidence of the ontology taxonomic relations in its reference corpus.

- Evaluation: Our system provide a score for evaluating the ontology by using the accuracy formulae: Accuracy(ontology) = $\frac{|S(R)|}{|R|}$, where $|S(R)|$ is the total number of relations from which our system considers that exist evidence in the reference corpus, and $|R|$ is the number of taxonomic relations in the ontology to be evaluated. This score, need to be evaluated in order to determine the quality of the approach presented. For this purpose, we compare the results obtained by our system with respect to those results obtained by human experts.

In order to evaluate the taxonomic relations in the ontology, we consider two different situations:

1. The two concepts of a given taxonomic relation are completely different. In this case, we propose to use our bank of lexico-syntactic patterns for finding evidence of relation validity in the reference corpus.
2. One of the two concepts (X) of a given taxonomic relation is part of the other concept (Y). In this case, we propose a subsumption technique [1], which basically searches evidence of the hyponym Y in the reference corpus.

Examples of these types of situations are given in the first three rows of Table 2. The last row of this Table shows an example of a semantic relation that exist in the ontology but the evidence in the reference corpus indicates that the relation is not taxonomic.

4   Experimental Results

In this section we present the datasets, so as the results obtained in the experiments. In order to have a better understanding of the particular lexico-syntactic patterns applied in the evaluation, in the first part of the results subsection, we show the frequency of their occurrence in the reference corpus.

4.1   Dataset

In Table 3 we present the number of concepts (C) and taxonomic relations (R) of the two ontologies evaluated in this paper. The following characteristics of their references corpus are also given: number of documents (D), number of tokens (T), vocabulary dimensionality (V), and the number of sentences filtered (O)

---

[2] We used Jena for extracting the taxonomic relations from the ontology (http://jena.apache.org/)

Table 2. Examples of taxonomic relations in the artificial intelligence domain

Num.	Concept$_1$	Concept$_2$	Sentence
1	human natural language	language	Natural language processing (NLP) is a field of computer science and linguistics concerned with the interactions between computers and human natural languages.
2	problems of ai	problem	The central problems of AI include such traits as reasoning, knowledge, planning, learning, communication, perception and the ability to move and manipulate objects.
3	knowledge representation	tree	Other knowledge representations are trees, graphs and hypergraphs, by means of which the connections among fundamental concepts and derivative concepts can be shown.
4	kr	data structure	Reminder a KR is not a data structure.

Table 3. Datasets

Domain	Ontology		Reference corpus			
	C	R	D	T	V	O
AI	276	205	8	10,805	2,180	464
SCORM	1,461	1,038	36	32,644	2,154	1,632

by the information retrieval system (S). As can be seen, the two domains used in the experiments are: Artificial Intelligence (AI), and the standard e-Learning SCORM ($SCORM$)[3] [23].

As we mentioned before, we requested human experts to evaluate the validity of the ontology taxonomic relations, according to different sentences obtained from the reference corpus. This manual evaluation was used to determine the performance of our approach. The results obtained are shown in the following subsection.

4.2   Results

In Table 4 we show the frequency of occurrence of the lexico-syntactic patterns that found evidence of taxonomic relations in the reference corpora. They are sorted according to their frequence in descending order.

In order to evaluate the stability of occurrence frequency of the bank of patterns given in Table 4, we used the Kendall tau correlation coefficient [11] that determines the degree in which the two lists matches, according to the descending order established.

The Kendall tau coefficient (τ) is calculated as $\tau = \frac{2P}{(k(k-1))/2} - 1$, where k is the number of items, and P is the number of concordant pairs obtained as

---

[3] The two ontologies together with their reference corpus can be downloaded from http://azouaq.athabascau.ca/goldstandards.htm

Table 4. Results of lexico-syntactic patterns

No.	Lexico-syntactic pattern p	$fr(p, AI)$	$fr(p, SCORM)$
96	NP , is (NP,)* (or | and|the) NP	7	55
43	NP (is | are) (a | an) NP	5	24
92	NP (,)? such as (NP,)* (or|and|the)? NP	7	13
97	(NP,)* (or|and|the) (NP,)* is (a|an|the) NP	4	12
46	NP such as (NP,)* (or|and) NP	4	7
42	NP (is | are) NP	2	6
12	NP such as (NP,)* (or|and|the) NP	1	4
94	NP NP , is (a|an|the) NP	3	2
15	such NP as (NP,)*	0	1
50	NP (classify (in | into) | comprise | contain | compose (of)? | group (in | into) | divide (in | into) | fall (in | into) | belong (to)) NP	0	1
86	NP (and | or) (another | other) NP	0	1
98	NP , including NP	1	1
104	NP as (NP,*) (or| and| the) NP	0	1
13	NP 's NP	1	0
106	NP, for example, is (a|an|the) NP	1	0

the sum, over all the items, of those items ranked after the given item by both rankings.

The Kendall tau coefficient value lies between -1 and 1, and high values imply a high agreement between the two rankings. Therefore, if the agreement (disagreement) between the two rankings is perfect, then the coefficient will have the value of 1 (-1). In case of obtaining the value 0, then it is said that the rankings are completely independent.

By ordering the lexico-syntactic patterns in descending order, we obtain a Kendall tau equal to 0.733, which means that exist a high agreement in the order obtained in the two reference corpus. This means that there exist a consistency in the application of these patterns, independently of being applied in different domains. This fact is true, at least for the two ontologies used in the experiments.

Table 5 show the result obtained by the approach when the AI ontology is evaluated using the accuracy criterion. The three last columns indicate the quality of the system prediction according to three human experts (E_1, E_2 and E_3). We consider that the quality obtained (91%, 82% and 86%) is a good result, however, we need to investigate the reason because we were not able to detect the remaining percentage of taxonomic relations. In general, our approach assigns an accuracy of 0.87% to the quality of the AI ontology.

Table 5. Accuracy of the AI ontology, and quality of the system prediction

Accuracy	Quality(E_1)	Quality(E_2)	Quality(E_3)
0.87	0.91	0.82	0.86

Table 6 shows the result obtained by the approach when the SCORM ontology is evaluated using the accuracy criterion. Again, the last columns indicate the quality of the system prediction according to three human experts (E_1, E_2 and E_3). According to the human experts, the accuracy result we obtained for the SCORM ontology (0.59) is less reliable than the one we obtained for the AI ontology. The experts assigned a quality value less than 80%. Despite this result, we assume that our system is capable of give a valuable accuracy that provides a clue for the quality of the target ontology.

Table 6. Accuracy of the SCORM ontology, and quality of the system prediction

Accuracy	Quality(E_1)	Quality(E_2)	Quality(E_3)
0.59	0.78	0.69	0.72

In order to validate the results obtained by the approach presented here, we have evaluated the agreement between each human expert evaluation (also named raters) and the system result, by using the Cohen's Kappa coefficient [6]. This measure is calculated as shown in Eq.(1); $Pr(a)$ is the relative observed agreement among one rater and the system result, and $Pr(e)$ is the hypothetical probability of chance agreement, using the observed data to calculate the probabilities of each result randomly saying each category. If the rater and the system are in complete agreement then $\kappa = 1$. If there is no agreement between them other than what would be expected by chance (as defined by $Pr(e)$), $\kappa = 0$.

$$\kappa = \frac{Pr(a) - Pr(e)}{1 - Pr(e)} \quad (1)$$

The results obtained by the Cohen's kappa statistical measure are shown in Table 7.

Table 7. Agreement between experts and system results

ontology	Cohen's kappa		
	E_1	E_2	E_3
AI	0.51	0.18	0.09
SCORM	0.54	0.23	0.36

The interpretation of the results obtained by the Cohen's kappa coefficient follows. Two human experts show light agreement ($0.01 \leq \kappa \leq 0.20$), whereas one expert show moderate agreement ($0.41 \leq \kappa \leq 0.60$) for the AI ontology. In the case of the SCORM ontology, again the expert E_1 obtained a moderate agreement, whereas the other two human experts showed fair agreement with $0.21 \leq \kappa \leq 0.40$.

The results presented above were obtained with samples of the taxonomic relations because of the great effort needed for manually evaluate their validity.

For the AI ontology we used 205 relations, whereas the SCORM ontology was evaluated only with 169 relations. Actually, we only provide samples of the reference corpora to the human experts for validating the taxonomic relation, which may bias the overall result. Therefore, in order to have a complete evaluation of the two ontologies, we have calculated the accuracy for both ontologies, but in this case considering all the sentences associated to the relations to be evaluated. Table 8 shows the number of taxonomic relation evaluated ($TaxRel$), the number of taxonomic relations found by the system ($TaxRelFound$), and the accuracy assigned to each ontology ($Accuracy$).

Table 8. Accuracy given to the two ontologies

Ontology	TaxRel	TaxRelFound	Accuracy
AI	205	181	88.29%
SCORM	1038	731	70.42%

As can be seen, the system obtain a slightly better accuracy for the AI ontology. This result is obtained because, in this case, the system have a greater number of sentences associated to each relation, therefore, having more oportunity to find evidence of the validity of the taxonomic relation. The SCORM ontology accuracy obtained was significantly better because, in this case we have evaluated a greater number of relations (1038) compared with those used in the sample evaluation (169). Besides this fact, in this last experiment, we have used a greater number of sentences which improves the oportunity of finding evidence in the reference corpus.

5   Conclusions

Evaluating the quality of ontologies is a very challenging topic that need to be addressed by the computational linguistic community. In this paper we have presented an approach based on lexico-syntactic patterns and reference corpora that allows to determine the accuracy of taxonomic relation of a given ontology of restricted domain. The experiments show that there exist a high agreement in the frequency of occurrence for the patterns used in the evaluation process, independently of the ontology domain. The approach assigned an accuracy of 88.29% for the AI ontology and 70.42% for the SCORM ontology, which reflects in some way the quality of the ontology. These results should be read in terms of the quality of our system, that was evaluated by two experts obtaining an average of 80% of reliability. As future work, we plan to evaluate the reliability of the system considering a greater number of relations. Besides that, we would like to use other ontologies for the evaluation process.

References

1. Bhatt, B., Bhattacharyya, P.: Domain specific ontology extractor for indian languages. In: Proceedings of the 10th Workshop on Asian Language Resources, pp. 75–84. The COLING 2012 Organizing Committee, Mumbai (December 2012), http://www.aclweb.org/anthology/W12-5209

2. Cantador, I., Fernández, M., Castells, P.: A collaborative recommendation framework for ontology evaluation and reuse. In: Actas de International Workshop on Recommender Systems, en la 17th European Conference on Artificial Intelligence (ECAI 2006), Riva del Garda, Italia, pp. 67–71 (2006)

3. de Cea, G.A., de Mon, I.A., Montiel-Ponsoda, E.: From linguistic patterns to ontology structures. In: 8th International Conference on Terminology and Artificial Intelligence (2009)

4. Celli, F.: Unitn: Part-of-speech counting in relation extraction. In: Proceedings of the 5th International Workshop on Semantic Evaluation, SemEval 2010, pp. 198–201. Association for Computational Linguistics, Stroudsburg (2010), http://dl.acm.org/citation.cfm?id=1859664.1859707

5. Chen, Y., Lan, M., Su, J., Zhou, Z.M., Xu, Y.: Ecnu: Effective semantic relations classification without complicated features or multiple external corpora. In: Proceedings of the 5th International Workshop on Semantic Evaluation, SemEval 2010, pp. 226–229. Association for Computational Linguistics, Stroudsburg (2010), http://dl.acm.org/citation.cfm?id=1859664.1859714

6. Cohen, J.: A coefficient of agreement for nominal scales. Educational and Psychological Measurement 20(1), 37–46 (1960), http://epm.sagepub.com/cgi/content/refs/20/1/37

7. Giovannetti, E., Marchi, S., Montemagni, S.: Combining statistical techniques and lexico-syntactic patterns for semantic relations extraction from text. In: Gangemi, A., Keizer, J., Presutti, V., Stoermer, H. (eds.) SWAP. CEUR Workshop Proceedings, vol. 426, CEUR-WS.org (2008)

8. Gruber, T.R.: Towards Principles for the Design of Ontologies Used for Knowledge Sharing. In: Guarino, N., Poli, R. (eds.) Formal Ontology in Conceptual Analysis and Knowledge Representation. Kluwer Academic Publishers, Deventer (1993)

9. Hearst, M.A.: Automatic acquisition of hyponyms from large text corpora. In: Proceedings of the 14th International Conference on Computational Linguistics, pp. 539–545 (1992)

10. Jurgens, D., Mohammad, S., Turney, P., Holyoak, K.: Semeval-2012 task 2: Measuring degrees of relational similarity. In: *SEM 2012: The First Joint Conference on Lexical and Computational Semantics – vol. 1: Proceedings of the Main Conference and the Shared Task, and vol. 2: Proceedings of the Sixth International Workshop on Semantic Evaluation (SemEval 2012), June 7-8, pp. 356–364. Association for Computational Linguistics, Montréal (2012), http://www.aclweb.org/anthology/S12-1047

11. Kendall, M.G.: A new measure of rank correlation. Biometrika 30(1/2), 81–93 (1938)

12. Klaussner, C., Zhekova, D.: Lexico-syntactic patterns for automatic ontology building. In: Temnikova, I., Nikolova, I., Konstantinova, N. (eds.) RANLP Student Research Workshop, pp. 109–114. RANLP 2011 Organising Committee (2011)

13. Maynard, D., Funk, A., Peters, W.: Sprat: a tool for automatic semantic pattern-based ontology population. In: International Conference for Digital Libraries and the Semantic Web (2009)

14. Mititelu, V.B.: Hyponymy patterns in romanian. Memoirs of the Scientific Sections of the Romanian Academy, vol. XXXIV, pp. 31–40 (2011)
15. Montiel-Ponsoda, E., Aguado de Cea, G.: Using natural language patterns for the development of ontologies. In: Researching Specialized Languages, pp. 332–345 (2008)
16. Negri, M., Kouylekov, M.: Fbk_nk: A wordnetbased system for multiway classification of semantic relations. In: Proceedings of the 5th International Workshop on Semantic Evaluation, SemEval 2010, pp. 202–205. Association for Computational Linguistics, Stroudsburg (2010),
    http://dl.acm.org/citation.cfm?id=1859664.1859708
17. Snow, R., Jurafsky, D., Ng, A.Y.: Learning syntactic patterns for automatic hypernym discovery. In: NIPS (2004)
18. Solís, S.: La Web Semántica. Lulu Enterprises Incorporated (2007)
19. Tovar, M., Pinto, D., Montes, A., Vilariño, D.: Determining the degree of semantic similarity using prototype vectors. In: Carrasco-Ochoa, J.A., Martínez-Trinidad, J.F., Rodríguez, J.S., di Baja, G.S. (eds.) MCPR 2012. LNCS, vol. 7914, pp. 364–373. Springer, Heidelberg (2013)
20. Tovar, M., Reyes, J.A., Montes, A., Vilariño, D., Pinto, D., León, S.: Buap: A first approximation to relational similarity measuring. In: Proceedings of the 6th International Workshop on Semantic Evaluation (SemEval 2012), June 7-8, pp. 502–505. Association for Computational Linguistics, Montréal (2012),
    http://www.aclweb.org/anthology/S12-1071
21. Turney, P.D.: Similarity of semantic relations. Computational Linguistics 32, 379–416 (2006)
22. Volkova, S., Caragea, D., Hsu, W., Drouhard, J., Fowles, L.: Boosting biomedical entity extraction by using syntactic patterns for semantic relation discovery. In: 2010 IEEE/WIC/ACM International Conference on Web Intelligence and Intelligent Agent Technology (WI-IAT), vol. 1, pp. 272–278 (2010)
23. Zouaq, A., Gasevic, D., Hatala, M.: Linguistic patterns for information extraction in ontocmaps. In: Blomqvist, E., Gangemi, A., Hammar, K., del Carmen Suárez-Figueroa, M. (eds.) WOP. CEUR Workshop Proceedings, vol. 929, CEUR-WS.org (2012)

Applying Mathematical Morphology
for the Classification of Iberian Ceramics
from the Upper Valley of Guadalquivir River

M. Lucena[1], A.L. Martínez-Carrillo[2], J.M. Fuertes[1], F. Carrascosa[1], and A. Ruiz[2]

[1] Department of Computer Science, University of Jaen, Spain
mlucena@ujaen.es
[2] Research University Institute for Iberian Archaeology, University of Jaen, Spain
caai@ujaen.es

Abstract. Although the potential of morphometrics for the study of archaeological artefacts is recognized, quantitative evaluation of the concordance between such methods and traditional typology and the potential of these techniques as supported methodologies in the archaeological analysis is a pending task. We present a new method to characterize and classify wheel-made pottery by its profile, using Mathematical Morphology. Each piece is represented as a vector, obtained by sampling the so called morphological curves *(erosion, dilation, opening and closing)*, and Euclidean Distance is used as a similarity measure. The proposed technique has been studied using a sample of 1133 complete ceramic vessels from the Iberian archaeological sites from the upper valley of Guadalquivir River (Andalusia, Spain), showing that it is compatible with the existing corpus, established by experts.

Keywords: Ceramic Profiles, Typologies, Shape Matching, Mathematical Morphology.

1 Introduction and Related Work

The study and analysis of archaeological ceramics constitutes one of the most frequent activities of the archaeological work, which consists habitually of classifying the thousands of ceramic fragments gathered in the interventions and selecting those that contribute to deduce forms, functions and chronology [1].

The different criteria used in the elaboration of classifications do not contribute to homogenize the analysis of the pottery shapes, since the election of criteria depends on each researcher and moment [2]. In this sense, Shepard saw three phases in the election of criteria: the study of whole vessels as culture-objects; the study of sherds as dating evidence for stratigraphic sequences; the study of pottery technology as a way of relating more closely to the potter, but she did not try to put dates to them.

Chronologically, the most used criteria have been artistically, typological, functional, technological, statistical, and contextual. Finally we can see developing interest in integrating ceramics into a wide analysis of finds assemblages. This must be the next step in ceramic studies: having integrated the various aspects of ceramics studies in the contextual phase (1960 and after), we must now begin to integrate ceramic studies into the wider field of general finds assemblages.

J.F. Martínez-Trinidad et al. (Eds.): MCPR 2014, LNCS 8495, pp. 341–350, 2014.

Morphology-based classification systems (do not confuse with Mathematical Morphology, the theory in which our method is based) emphasize the attributes of the shape of a vessel. Starting from the early works of Shennan and Wilcock [3], many systems have been developed to classify vessels from the shape of its profile [4]. Some methods try to find parametric representations of the shapes [5], mainly for archiving purposes, and measurement of different volumetric features, such as height, width, diameter or volume [6]. Other methods are designed to allow the automatic comparison between profiles. In [7], a measure based on the overlap maximization between two profiles is defined, although the authors recognize that it is not well suited for vessels because of the elongated shapes of the profiles. Other works rely on local features, such as context descriptors [8], to characterize profile shapes [9], along with a multivariate analysis to compare and group profiles into clusters of similar vessels. Other authors [10, 11] propose a profile representation based on a continuous, sub–pixel approximation of the profile shape, and calculate its radius, tangent and curvature along the contour. Similarity is then computed using a weighted Euclidean Distance.

This paper presents a novel method for encoding morphological data of wheel-made pottery profiles, in order to be later recovered and compared, providing us with a tool to help the archaeologist to find in a profile database the most similar classes to a given shape. Each profile, defined as the cross section of the vessel in the direction of the rotational axis of symmetry (see Figure 1), is characterized by means of several morphological curves [12, 13] extracted from its shape, a method that has been used successfully in other shape recognition related problems [14, 15].

The Iberian pottery (S.VI B.C. − I A.C.) from the upper valley of Guadalquivir River (Spain) has been chosen for this purpose, because is a well documented region with many excavated sites [16–18]. The selected ceramic material for the morphological analysis comes from different archaeological settlements located in the provinces from Jaén, Granada and Córdoba. Most of the ceramic vessels have been documented in the province of Jaén, since they pertain to Iberian period.

This paper is organized as follows: Section 2 is devoted to explain the corpus of pottery, provided by experts, on which our experiments are based. Section 3 explains the fundamentals on morphological analysis, and how it is used in our method. Section 4 shows in detail how the profiles are characterized and classified. Experimental results and conclusions are shown in Sections 5 and 6.

2   The Corpus of Ceramics and the Traditional Classification

The selected ceramic material comes from different archaeological settlements located in the East area of Andalusia, specifically the provinces from Jaén, Granada and Cordoba. Most of the ceramic vessels have been documented in the province of Jaén, since them pertaining to Iberian period (S.VI B.C. − I A.C.). In this area has been one expanded tradition with respect to the study of ceramic typologies of the Iberian period, emphasizing the works of Pereira [19] for the Iberian painted ceramics of the valley of Guadalquivir.

The combination of different archaeological sites, with different chronologies makes the accomplishment of a diachronic and synchronous study possible, allowing to contrast materials of different archaeological sites with different chronologies.

In total, we have a database of 1133 vessel profiles, corresponding to Iberian pottery, found in 16 archaeological sites belonging to the upper valley of Guadalquivir River (Spain).

Our classification is based on morphometric criteria supervised by an expert. Several formal parts of a ceramic vessel have been differentiated (lip, neck, body, base and handles) to facilitate both the comparison between vessels. Classes are defined taking into account the presence or absence of parts, and the ratio between their sizes.

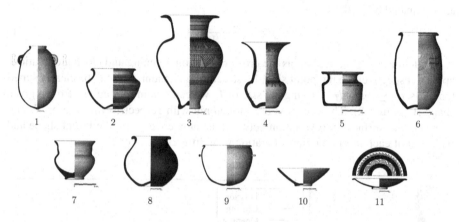

Fig. 1. Example profiles of each of the eleven classes

Following this classification criterion we have defined 11 classes (representative profiles are shown in Figure 1). The first nine correspond to *closed forms*, while the latter two correspond to *open forms*:

1. Shapes in which the body predominates over the other parts of the vessel. The shape of the body is oval.
2. Shapes in which the body has form of *conic bifrustum*. The joints of the different body parts are discontinuous.
3. Shapes with developed, parallel walls neck, and body globular body.
4. Shapes with developed, divergent walls neck, and globular body. This shape is also named *chardon vessel*.
5. Shapes with cylinder body. Also known as *kalathos*.
6. Lengthened shapes.
7. Shapes with profile in form of *S*.
8. Shapes with globular body. The joints of the different body parts are continuous.
9. Shapes with globular body and a largely developed rim.
10. Shapes with semi-spherical body.
11. Shapes with semi-spherical body and reversed rim.

3   Morphological Filtering

Mathematical Morphology [12] is based in set theory, and provides us with a powerful approach to numerous image processing problems [13]. A morphological description of a binary image is the set of 2D vectors representing the coordinates of all the foreground (black in our case) pixels. One shape within an image can be represented as a random set A, where the probability that a point x belongs to the A is $p = P(x \in A)$.

Given a set W of points representing the entire image, the above probability can be approximated by [20]:

$$\overline{p} = \frac{\text{area}(A \cap W)}{\text{area}(W)} \tag{1}$$

We define e_T, d_T, o_T and c_T as the erosion, dilation, opening and closing operations applied respectively to the point set A by structuring element T. It can be clearly stated that $e_T \leq o_T \leq c_T \leq d_T$. Varying the size of T, we can obtain four curves from a given shape A (Figure 2). These curves are monotonic with respect to the size of T, and represent the surface ratio variation between the area covered by the initial shape and the result of each morphological operation with different sizes of T.

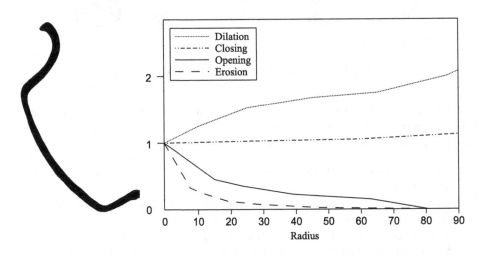

Fig. 2. Erosion, Dilation, Opening and Closing characteristic curves of a profile of the database, using an isotropic (circular) structuring element, normalized by the area of the profile

We will use the curves we have just defined, computed with different structuring elements, to obtain a characteristic vector for each profile in our database, starting from a binary image representing the shape of the corresponding vessel. We will describe in detail the full process in the following section.

4   Profile Characterization

To obtain a characteristic vector for each profile, we will follow a three stage process: a pre-processing step, where we split the profile into several parts; a morphological step, where the four characteristic curves are computed with several structuring elements for each part; and finally the characteristic vector computation itself.

4.1   Pre-processing

In order to be processed, we start by splitting each profile it into several parts and compute the characteristic curves from each of them. We will define d as the length of the line segment joining the upper point of the profile rim **u** with the lowest point of the base **v** (Figure 3). We also denote **p** as the lowest profile point located at the rotation axis. Three sub-profiles are then defined:

- *Rim*: Points whose distance to **u** is lower than $d/3$.
- *Base*: Points whose distance to **p** is lower than the distance between **v** and **p**.
- *Body*: The rest of the points.

If the horizontal distance between **v** and **p** is lower than their vertical distance, we consider that the *base* sub-profile is empty.

Our *base* and *body* parts correspond respectively to the *base* and *body* parts defined by the experts, while our *rim* part corresponds approximately to the union of *lip*, *neck*, and eventually the *handle*, if present. In the experimental section, we show results with characteristic curves for *rim*, and *body* parts, as these are the ones that are used by experts to assign a class to a given profile.

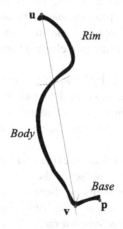

Fig. 3. Segmentation of a profile into *rim*, *body* and *base* parts

4.2 Morphological Curves

In order to capture features with different orientation, we will use several anisotropic structuring elements. Specifically, a centred, variable length line with a 1-pixel constant width, with two parameters: an orientation angle, and the length of the line itself.

To align the points where the characteristic curves will be sampled, we have used the following strategy: first, we obtain the minimal length l for the structuring element that completely eliminates the shape by erosion, and then sample the erosion, dilation, opening and closing curves with a set of lengths obtained by multiplying l by several fixed coefficients. This procedure makes our technique scale invariant. Finally, once computed, each curve is normalized by the area of the initial profile so that it gives us a value of 1.

4.3 Characteristic Vector

After segmenting the initial profile into sub-profiles, the four morphological curves are computed and sampled from each sub-profile and anisotropic structuring element, giving us a series of coefficients that we assemble into a single vector. With two sub-profiles, N angles for the structuring element, and four curves sampled in Q points we obtain for each profile a vector of $2 \times N \times 4 \times Q$ components.

In our experiments, we have used $N = 16$ different orientations for the structuring element. Also, the set of coefficients that multiply the minimal length l previously defined is $\{0.15, 0.2, 0.3, 05, 0.75, 1\}$, so $Q = 6$. Therefore, we have a vector of length 768 for each profile.

5 Experiments

Our database has 1133 profiles, grouped into 11 classes, ranging from 10 to 373 elements each. Profiles are represented as white background PNG binary images, ranging from 0.5 to 2 megapixels in size, proportional to the actual size of the corresponding vessel. However, the size of the images is not relevant, as long as they have enough resolution, as the lengths of the structuring elements are scaled independently for each one.

In all of our experiments, similarity between two profiles has been computed as the Euclidean Distance between their associated vectors. Firstly, we will show the first 10 nearest neighbours of some sample profiles, along with the measured similarity for each one (Figures 4 to 6). As can be seen, the recovered profiles correspond with the typologies defined by the experts.

We have also carried out a classification experiment, using a leave-one-out cross validation strategy. For a given profile, we select the class that appears more times among the M nearest neighbours. Results with one, three and five neighbours are shown in Table 1. We have compared our results with the ones obtained by the method proposed in [11], obtaining clearly better recognition rates. We can also see that increasing the number of neighbours does not improve classification rates.

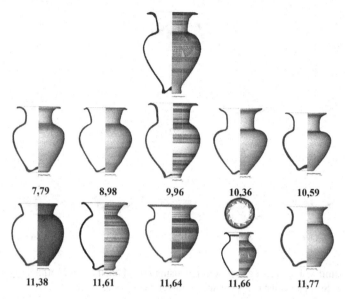

Fig. 4. Most similar shapes to a given example, using our Mathematical Morphology based similarity distance. Similarity distances are shown under each piece.

Fig. 5. Most similar shapes to a given example, using our Mathematical Morphology based similarity distance. Similarity distances are shown under each piece.

Table 1. Classification rates obtained by our method and the one proposed by Karasik *et al.* [11] and previously propounded by Saragusti *et al.* [10], with 1, 3 and 5 neighbours.

Neighbours (M)	Morphological Vector	Karasik *et al.* [11]
1	**85.70%**	76.88%
3	84.20%	74.93%
5	84.47%	74.23%

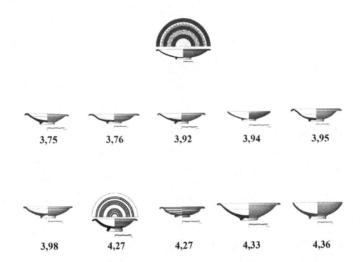

Fig. 6. Most similar shapes to a given example, using our Mathematical Morphology based similarity distance. Similarity distances are shown under each piece.

Figure 7 show the normalized confusion matrix with one neighbour. Each row contains all the profiles of a single class, while each column contains all the profiles that our method assigns to the corresponding class.

We can note that our method classifies wrongly many class 2 (biconical trunk) and class 9 (globular with large rim) profiles as class 8 (globular), but not conversely. This is possibly due to the small size of classes 2 (47 samples) and 9 (22 samples) versus class 8 (293 samples), together with the fact that these three classes are morphologically very similar.

Rim - Body

	1	2	3	4	5	6	7	8	9	10	11
1	83.33	0	0	0	0	3.33	0	13.33	0	0	0
2	0	42.55	0	0	0	0	4.26	53.19	0	0	0
3	0	2.67	72.00	4.00	0	1.33	2.67	16.00	0	0	0
4	0	0	0	80.00	0	0	10.00	10.00	0	0	0
5	0	0	0	0	100.00	0	0	0	0	0	0
6	0	0	1.92	0	3.85	78.85	0	13.46	1.92	0	0
7	0	0	0	0	0	2.00	86.00	4.00	2.00	6.00	0
8	1.37	3.41	2.39	0	0	1.37	0.34	89.42	1.37	0.35	0
9	0	0	0	0	0	9.09	0	40.91	45.45	4.55	0
10	0	0.54	0.27	0	0	0	0	0	0.27	94.37	4.29
11	0	0	0	0	0	0	0	0	0.80	19.20	80.00

Fig. 7. Normalized confusion matrix resulting of the application of our method to the database, using the *rim* and *body* sub-profiles

6 Conclusions

The above-mentioned investigations demonstrate that in the field of archaeological investigation of pottery the collaboration between archaeologist and computer scientists permits the development of useful applications for the classification of archaeological ceramics.

We have proposed a new method to classify vessel profiles, based on well known mathematical operators, that captures most of their morphometric features, allowing us to identify the most similar profiles in a database. Through this methodology for measuring the similarity between ceramic profiles it is possible the search of parallels in a particular region, that in this case is the upper valley of Guadalquivir River (Spain), showing the concordance between morphometrics and traditional typology.

Our vector characterization captures the morphological features of the profiles. The results are clearly better than the ones obtained by other, state of the art methods. Although, unlike others, our representation does not allow to reconstruct the profile shape, the graphical data that we use as input is compact enough to be stored together with the vector itself.

As a future work, it would be interesting to include the *base* part of the profiles into the characteristic vector, and compare the results to know if it gives some improvement. Other interesting work would be the use of our method to obtain an automatic clustering of the database, and compare the resulting classes to the ones defined by the experts. The proposed technique can also be used with other similar profile databases, in order to better test its applicability.

Acknowledgement. This work has been supported by the Excellent Projects Program of CICE (regional government), the European Union ERDF funds under research projects P07-TIC-02773, the *Computer Graphics and Geomatics* Research Group (TIC-144) of the University of Jaén, and the Andalusian Economics, Innovation, Science and Employment Council under project TIC-7278.

References

1. Orton, C., Tyers, P., Vince, A.: Pottery in Archaeology. Cambridge University Press (1993)
2. Shepard, A.: Ceramics for the archaeologist. Carnegie Institution of Washington (1956)
3. Shennan, S., Wilcock, J.: Shape and style variation in central german bell beakers. Science and Archaeology 15, 17–31 (1975)
4. Rice, P.M.: Pottery Analysis. University of Chicago Press, Chicago (1987)
5. Nautiyal, V., Kaushik, V.D., Pathak, V.K., Dhande, S., Nautiyal, S., Naithani, M., Juyal, S., Gupta, R.K., Vasisth, A.K., Verna, K.K., Singh, A.: Geometric modeling of indian archaeological pottery: A preliminary study. In: Clark, J., Hagemeister, E. (eds.) Exploring New Frontiers in Human Heritage, CAA 2006, Fargo, United States. Computer Applications and Quantitative Methods in Archaeology (2006)
6. Kampel, M., Sablatnig, R.: An automated pottery archival and reconstruction system. Journal of Visualization and Computer Animation 14(3), 111–120 (2003)
7. Mom, V.: Where did i see you before. holistic method to compare and find archaeological artifacts. In: Decker, R., Lenz, H. (eds.) Advances in Data Analysis. Proceedings of the 30th Annual Conference of the Gesellschaft fr Klassifikation. Springer, Berlin (2006)

8. Belongie, S., Malik, J., Puzicha, J.: Shape matching and object recognition using shape contexts. IEEE Transactions on Pattern Analysis and Machine Intelligence 24(4), 509–522 (2002)

9. Maaten, L., Lange, G., Boon, P.: Visualization and automatic typology construction of pottery profiles. In: Frischer, B. (ed.) Making history interactive: computer applications and quantitative methods in archaeology (CAA). BAR International Series, vol. 2079, Archaeopress, Oxford (2009)

10. Saragusti, I., Karasik, A., Sharon, I., Smilansky, U.: Quantitative analysis of shape attributes based on contours and section profiles in artifact analysis. Journal of Archaeological Science 32(6), 841–853 (2005)

11. Karasik, A., Smilansky, U.: Computerized morphological classification of ceramics. Journal of Archaeological Science 38(10), 2644–2657 (2011)

12. Matheron, G.: Random Sets and Integral Geometry. Wiley (1975)

13. Haralick, R., Sternberg, S., Zhuang, X.: Image analysis using mathematical morphology. IEEE Transactions on Pattern Analysis and Machine Intelligence 9(4), 532–550 (1987)

14. Fuertes, J., Lucena, M., Pérez de la Blanca, N., Fdez-Valdivia, J.: Combining morphological filters and deformable models to desing a 2d shape based retrieval system. In: 12th Scandinavian Conference on Image Analysis (SCIA 2001), Bergen (Norway), vol. 1, pp. 646–653 (June 2001)

15. Fuertes, J., Lucena, M., Pérez de la Blanca, N., Ruiz, N.: Objects matching combining color and shape. In: 4th EURASIP Conference focused on Video/Image Processing and Multimedia Communications, vol. 1, pp. 201–208 (2003)

16. Chapa, T., Pereira, J., Madrigal, A., Mayoral, V.: La Necrópolis ibérica de Castellones de Ceal (Hinojares, Jaén). Consejería de Cultura. Junta de Andalucía (1997)

17. Ruiz Rodríguez, A., Molinos, M., López, J., Crespo, J., Choclán, C., Hornos, F.: El horizonte ibérico antiguo del Cerro de la Coronilla (Cazalilla, Jaén). Cortes A y F. Cuadernos de Prehistoria de la Universidad de Granada (8), 251–295 (1983)

18. Ruiz Rodríguez, A., Hornos Mata, F., Choclán, C., Cruz Garrido, J.: La necrópolis ibérica Finca Gil de Olid (Puente del Obispo-Baeza). Cuadernos de Prehistoria de la Universidad de Granada (9), 195–234 (1984)

19. Pereira Sieso, J.: La cerámica ibérica de la cuenca del Guadalquivir. Trabajos de Prehistoria 46, 149–159 (1989)

20. Serra, J.: Image Analysis and Mathematical Morphology. Academic Press, Inc., Orlando (1983)

Radiological Pain Predictors in Knee Osteoarthritis, a Four Feature Selection Comparison: Data from the OAI

Jorge I. Galván-Tejada, José M. Celaya-Padilla, Carlos E. Galván-Tejada, Victor Treviño, and José G. Tamez-Peña

Tecnológico de Monterrey, Monterrey, Nuevo León, México
Bioinformatics
Escuela de Medicina
{gatejo,ericgalvan}@uaz.edu.mx,
{a00811434,vtrevino,jose.tamezpena}@itesm.mx

Abstract. In medical science, the image based biomarkers are a recent tool for disease diagnostic and prognostic, the different medical imaging techniques brings a big amount of useful data for analysis and interpretation. The osteoarthritis (OA) is a very common and disabling disease in the industrialized world, pain is the most important and disabling symptom in knee OA, having a preventive treatment is one of the most important tasks in the OA studies. In this work a bioinformatic tool is used to obtain pain prediction models, using genetic algorithms with different feature selection functions multivariate prediction models were obtain and compared based on the medical requirements to investigate radiological features that precede the onset of knee pain, and to identify a radiological-based multivariate prognostic model of knee pain.

1   Introduction

Osteoarthritis (OA) is a chronic and complex disease that reduces the quality of life of millions of adults around the world, affecting 1 in every 10 adults over 60 years in the United States [1]. Knee joint pain is the most common and incapacitating symptom [2, 3]. Lifestyle and age of the general population are factors of an increment in the knee OA cases [4-7]. OA remains still poorly understood [8], for a better study and understanding of pain etiology, the Osteoarthritis Initiative (OAI) has been recollecting thousands of clinical data (features) in OA patients; all these features bring important information about the stages of the pain, and other subject characteristics.

Medical imaging is a very important and effective tool to diagnose OA, it is also the most common first hand patient information, using different radiological techniques such as Magnetic resonance imaging (MRI) or X-ray imaging it is possible to obtain a good approach of the OA stage. Differences and advantages of X-ray or MRI techniques have been studied [9-14], it is important to take into account that in emerging countries the first approach to diagnose knee OA is

J.F. Martínez-Trinidad et al. (Eds.): MCPR 2014, LNCS 8495, pp. 351–360, 2014.

X-ray imaging, in early stages of OA the use of MRI images in an exploratory stage is not allowed by the monetary cost to the public health systems. This is an important reason to develop a robust prognostic method based on a very extended imaging tool, the X-ray imaging technology. The Osteoarthritis Research Society International (OARSI) assessment scale of knee OA [15, 16], have been adopted as a standard in many health systems and OA studies around the world. Measured by these scales, Joint Space Width (JSW) is commonly associated with OA stages [17, 18], this measurements helps to see the density of the cartilage and the loss of it.

In case of OA, there is no effective treatment other than knee replacement in advanced stages, the pain prediction is important to develop an effective treatment to prevent the disease to reach disabling stages. It is a challenge to correlate the features extracted from x-ray imaging and OA symptoms as has been presented in other works [19-22]. An exploratory computational analysis of medical data can contribute to get a better understanding in some diseases, prevent some disorders associated with early stages, and in some risk subjects can contribute to the improvement of health systems around the world, computational statistics and Bioinformatics tools can be a powerful way to find some unexpected connections between some subjects characteristics and the symptoms of a certain disease, the objective of bioinformatics was to explore the human genome, but have shown to be effective in the association of subjects characteristics and symptoms in other diseases [24-27].

Using GALGO[23] an R package based on genetic algorithms bioinformatics tool, five different classification methods; logistic regression; linear discriminant; nearest centroid; KNN, were used to obtain a pain prediction model, with all the clinical and radiological information available in the OAI databases, a yearly observed case/control group of subjects was used to predict the pain development based on X-ray assessed features.

The objective of this work is to determine if using different classification methods in bioinformatics tools we can have a better correlation between the features obtained from the knee radiological features and the future pain symptom.

2   Methods

2.1   Study Design

In this work, a case/control group was defined from OAI databases was selected based on the right knee radiological assessments, only subjects with no radiological or clinical missing data were included in this study, 163 (93) subjects (females). The criteria inclusion for all subjects was; not presenting pain as a symptom; not presenting a symptomatic status; and taking no pain medication at the baseline visit; all control and case should accomplish the inclusion criteria, the selection process is presented in Figure 1. Of all these subjects, having pain as a chronic symptom at some timepoint after their baseline and up to their 60 month visit were considered cases. The rest, the ones with no pain and no pain medicated from their baseline until their 60 month visit, were considered controls. The demographic information is shown in Table 1. Looking for a pain prediction model, the one year before pain incidence radiological assessments were used as predictive variables (T-1).

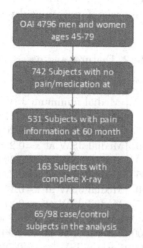

Fig. 1. Subject Selection Process

Table 1. Demographic characteristics of study participants

SD	Case	Control	All
Subjects (Females)	65 (38)	98 (55)	163 (93)
Average height (SD) [m]	1.69 (.09)	1.68 (.1)	1.68 (.09)
Average BMI (SD)	27.05(4.3)	26.27 (4)	26.58 (4.1)
Average age (SD)	62.69 (9.6)	61.80 (10.1)	62.15 (9.9)
Age range	46 - 78	45 - 79	45 - 79

Datasets used in this work were: Central Assessment of Longitudinal Knee X-rays for Quantitative JSW ver. 1.6, from which quantitative data were obtained, and Right knee symptom status, from which the predicted variable, chronic pain, was obtained. This information was pre analyzed by a radiologist group associated to the OAI using the OARSI quantitative grading scale [28, 29][30-32].

2.2 Statistical Analysis

For statistical analysis, seventeen quantitative features were measured in right knee radiographs, the description of the features is shown in table 2. Since men are generally taller, all image features from the quantitative datasets went through a height and gender adjustment using a linear regression [33]:

$$JSWadj = JSW - b0 - (Height * b1) - (Gender * b2) \qquad (1)$$

Where JSWadj represents the adjusted measurement, JSW is the original measurement, and b0, b1 and b2 are the coefficients obtained from the linear regression. The values assigned to the Gender variable were 0 for males and 1 for females. The data collected was Z normalized using the rank-based inverse normal transform.

Table 2. Features and description

Feature ID	Description
MCMJSW	Medial minimum JSW [mm]
JSW175	Medial JSW at x=0.175 [mm]
JSW200	Medial JSW at x=0.200 [mm]
JSW250	Medial JSW at x=0.250 [mm]
JSW300	Medial JSW at x=0.300 [mm]
JSW225	Medial JSW at x=0.225 [mm]
JSW150	Medial JSW at x=0.150 [mm]
JSW275	Medial JSW at x=0.275 [mm]
LJSW850	Lateral JSW at x=0.850 [mm]
LJSW900	Lateral JSW at x=0.900 [mm]
LJSW700	Lateral JSW at x=0.700 [mm]
LJSW825	Lateral JSW at x=0.825 [mm]
LJSW750	Lateral JSW at x=0.750 [mm]
LJSW875	Lateral JSW at x=0.875 [mm]
LJSW725	Lateral JSW at x=0.725 [mm]
LJSW800	Lateral JSW at x=0.800 [mm]
LJSW775	Lateral JSW at x=0.775 [mm]

After data transformation and normalization, four multivariate searches were then performed, using the T-1. For all searches, the 60 month visit right knee pain information was used as the outcome variable. These searches were performed using Galgo. The algorithm was set to return 1000 predictive models, with 5 features each. Each one of these models evolved throughout 600 generations, replicating, recombining and mutating from a set of models with random features, optimizing for its accuracy, obtained using a 3-k fold cross validation with a 2/3-1/3 train-test proportion. Using the same seed to train and test, four classification strategies were used (Logistic regression, linear discriminant, KNN and nearest centroid), one on each model, for all searches the best prediction model was refined using the same strategy: Features were then ranked according to their frequency in the 1000 models, and using such rank, a Forward Selection strategy was carried out, prompting a new predictive model. Finally, the size of this model was shrunk by using a Robust Gene Backward Feature Elimination algorithm, in which features were removed if their contribution to the accuracy of the model, measured using the same cross-validation strategy. For all four predictive models the Area Under Receiver Operating Characteristics (AUROC) was calculated to obtain the specificity vs sensitivity value. A univariate correlation with the outcome of the data was performed to test the correlation of each feature with the outcome of pain prediction. All statistical analysis was done using R software [34].

3   Results

The obtained results:

- For logistic regression as cost function the best performing model was a four feature model, obtained an AUCROC of 0.6612, the curve is shown in figure 2a.
- For Linear Discriminant, the best performing predictive model was a two feature model, obtained an AUCROC of 0.5845, the curve is shown in figure 2b.
- For Knn, the best performing model was a two feature model, obtained an AUCROC of 0.5232, the curve is presented in figure 3a.
- For Nearest centroid experiment, the best performing model was a five feature model, obtained an AUCROC of 0.6216, the curve is presented in figure 3b.

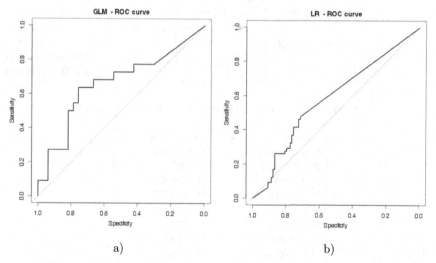

a)   b)

Fig. 2. ROC Curves a)Logistic Regression b)Linear Discriminant

In table 3, the description of the predictive models and its features is presented. In the univariate experiment, as expected the correlation was minimal, due the high variability of the data, nevertheless, the top 10 rank correlated features is presented in table 4 as the absolute correlated value of the feature.

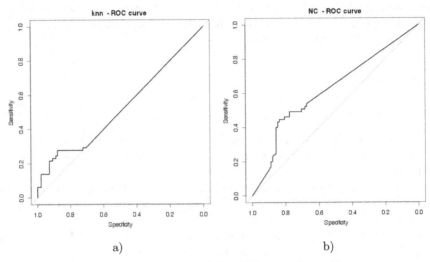

Fig. 3. ROC Curves a)Knn b)Nearest Centroid

Table 3. Predictive models description

Classifier	Logistic regression	linear discriminant	Knn	Nearest Centroid
Features	AV06JSW300, AV06JSW150, AV06LJSW750	AV06JSW275 AV06LJSW750	V06JSW300 V06LJSW775	AV06JSW300 AV06LJSW750 AV06LJSW875 AV06LJSW775 AV06LJSW800

Table 4. Top ten features correlated to the Outcome

Feature	Correlation to Outcome
AV06LJSW875	0.2088991
AV06JSW275	0.2067434
AV06JSW300	0.1998420
AV06LJSW800	0.1829875
AV06LJSW825	0.1827017
AV06LJSW900	0.1820316
AV06LJSW850	0.1819792
AV06LJSW775	0.1666364
AV06JSW250	0.1645778
AV06JSW200	0.1531015

4   Conclusions

Based on the experiment results, the logistic regression and nearest centroid models showed a better performance in sensitivity and specificity, is important to say, this models are a tool to find symptoms as a risk factors to develop knee pain, this way, the features in the predictive models are features associated with advanced stages in the disease, if some early changes in this measures can be predictive a year before of the pain appearance it could be helpful for preventing treatment development.

Due to its nature, pain is complicated to measure; nevertheless, the data appears to have a good performance in pain prediction. Some early radiological features can be associated with OA symptoms; it is possible to achieve future pain prediction with multivariate models based on X-ray features. The association of future pain with X-ray features can be used to develop a prevention strategy for chronic pain. The public health systems can be beneficial with the use of a radiological Biomarker.

In other hand, the computational analysis of data sets can be very helpful to develop image based biomarkers, due to its nature, this analysis can manage a big datasets and perform millions of operations to correlate some subject factors with disease symptoms and this way have a better and faster diagnosis.

The present study shows a close relation between the X-ray based models obtained in the multivariate regression and the development of clinical pain associated with the disease, which strongly suggest the feasibility of a Bio-Marker based in those features, this Bio-Marker can be used to aid the radiologist in the process of diagnose the patient or a second opinion, this represent a great area of impact specially in developing countries, in which access to the high level health care system is very restricted.

Acknowledgements. This work was partially supported by the Consejo Nacional de Ciencia y Tecnologa (CONACYT), by Grant 16864 Ciencia Bsica from CONACYT, and by Catdra de Bioinformtica (CAT220) from Tecnolgico de Monterrey. . J. I. G.T. and C. E. G. T. thanks to PROMEP for partially support his doctoral studies. "The OAI is a public-private partnership comprised of five contracts (N01-AR-2-2258; N01-AR-2-2259; N01-AR-2-2260; N01-AR-2-2261; N01-AR-2-2262) funded by the National Institutes of Health, a branch of the Department of Health and Human Services, and conducted by the OAI Study Investigators. Private funding partners include Merck Research Laboratories; Novartis Pharmaceuticals Corporation, GlaxoSmithKline; and Pfizer, Inc. Private sector funding for the OAI is managed by the Foundation for the National Institutes of Health. This manuscript was prepared using an OAI public use data set and does not necessarily reflect the opinions or views of the OAI investigators, the NIH, or the private funding partners."

References

1. White, D.K., TudorLocke, C., Felson, D.T., Gross, K.D., Niu, J., Nevitt, M., Lewis, C.E., Torner, J., Neogi, T.: Do radiographic disease and pain account for why people with or at high risk of knee osteoarthritis do not meet physical activity guidelines? Arthritis & Rheumatism 65, 139–147 (2013)

2. Neogi, T.: The epidemiology and impact of pain in osteoarthritis. Osteoarthritis Cartilage 21, 1145–1153 (2013)
3. Agaliotis, M., Fransen, M., Bridgett, L., Nairn, L., Votrubec, M., Jan, S., Heard, R., Mackey, M.: Risk factors associated with reduced work productivity among people with chronic knee pain. Osteoarthritis Cartilage 21, 1160–1169 (2013)
4. Neogi, T., Bowes, M.A., Niu, J., De Souza, K.M., Vincent, G.R., Goggins, J., Zhang, Y., Felson, D.T.: Magnetic resonance imaging-based three-dimensional bone shape of the knee predicts onset of knee osteoarthritis: data from the osteoarthritis initiative. Arthritis Rheum. 65, 2048–2058 (2013)
5. Colbert, C.J., Almagor, O., Chmiel, J.S., Song, J., Dunlop, D., Hayes, K.W., Sharma, L.: Excess body weight and four-year function outcomes: comparison of African Americans and whites in a prospective study of osteoarthritis. Arthritis Care Res. (Hoboken) 65, 5–14 (2013)
6. Riddle, D.L., Stratford, P.W.: Body weight changes and corresponding changes in pain and function in persons with symptomatic knee osteoarthritis: a cohort study. Arthritis Care Res. (Hoboken) 65, 15–22 (2013)
7. Tanamas, S.K., Wluka, A.E., Davies-Tuck, M., Wang, Y., Strauss, B.J., Proietto, J., Dixon, J.B., Jones, G., Forbes, A., Cicuttini, F.M.: Association of weight gain with incident knee pain, stiffness, and functional difficulties: a longitudinal study. Arthritis Care Res. (Hoboken) 65, 34–43 (2013)
8. Abhishek, A., Doherty, M.: Mechanisms of the placebo response in pain in osteoarthritis. Osteoarthritis Cartilage 21, 1229–1235 (2013)
9. Guermazi, A., Niu, J., Hayashi, D., Roemer, F.W., Englund, M., Neogi, T., Aliabadi, P., McLennan, C.E., Felson, D.T.: Prevalence of abnormalities in knees detected by MRI in adults without knee osteoarthritis: population based observational study (Framingham Osteoarthritis Study). BMJ 345, e5339 (2012)
10. Wirth, W., Duryea, J., Hellio Le Graverand, M.-P., John, M.R., Nevitt, M., Buck, R., Eckstein, F.: Direct Comparison of Fixed Flexion Radiography and MRI in Knee Osteoarthritis: Responsiveness Data from the Osteoarthritis Initiative. Osteoarthritis and Cartilage (2012)
11. Cotofana, S., Wyman, B.T., Benichou, O., Dreher, D., Nevitt, M., Gardiner, J., Wirth, W., Hitzl, W., Kwoh, C.K., Eckstein, F., Frobell, R.B., Group, O.I.: Relationship between knee pain and the presence, location, size and phenotype of femorotibial denuded areas of subchondral bone as visualized by MRI. Osteoarthritis Cartilage 21, 1214–1222 (2013)
12. Baert, I.A., Staes, F., Truijen, S., Mahmoudian, A., Noppe, N., Vanderschueren, G., Luyten, F.P., Verschueren, S.M.: Weak associations between structural changes on MRI and symptoms, function and muscle strength in relation to knee osteoarthritis. Knee Surg Sports Traumatol Arthrosc (2013)
13. Neogi, T., Felson, D., Niu, J., Nevitt, M., Lewis, C.E., Aliabadi, P., Sack, B., Torner, J., Bradley, L., Zhang, Y.: Association between radiographic features of knee osteoarthritis and pain: results from two cohort studies. BMJ 339, b2844 (2009)
14. Haugen, I.K., Slatkowsky-Christensen, B., Boyesen, P., van der Heijde, D., Kvien, T.K.: Cross-sectional and longitudinal associations between radiographic features and measures of pain and physical function in hand osteoarthritis. Osteoarthritis Cartilage 21, 1191–1198 (2013)
15. Kellgren, J., Lawrence, J.: Radiological assessment of osteo-arthrosis. Annals of the Rheumatic Diseases 16, 494 (1957)
16. Altman, R.D., Gold, G.: Atlas of individual radiographic features in osteoarthritis. Osteoarthritis and Cartilage 56, A1–A56 (2007) (revised)

17. Bloecker, K., Guermazi, A., Wirth, W., Benichou, O., Kwoh, C.K., Hunter, D.J., Englund, M., Resch, H., Eckstein, F., Investigators, O.: Tibial coverage, meniscus position, size and damage in knees discordant for joint space narrowing - data from the Osteoarthritis Initiative. Osteoarthritis Cartilage 21, 419–427 (2013)
18. Attur, M., Krasnokutsky-Samuels, S., Samuels, J., Abramson, S.B.: Prognostic biomarkers in osteoarthritis. Curr. Opin. Rheumatol. 25, 136–144 (2013)
19. Kinds, M.B., Marijnissen, A.C., Bijlsma, J.W., Boers, M., Lafeber, F.P., Welsing, P.M.: Quantitative radiographic features of early knee osteoarthritis: development over 5 years and relationship with symptoms in the CHECK cohort. J. Rheumatol. 40, 58–65 (2013)
20. Glass, N.A., Torner, J.C., Frey Law, L.A., Wang, K., Yang, T., Nevitt, M.C., Felson, D.T., Lewis, C.E., Segal, N.A.: The relationship between quadriceps muscle weakness and worsening of knee pain in the MOST cohort: a 5-year longitudinal study. Osteoarthritis Cartilage 21, 1154–1159 (2013)
21. Shimura, Y., Kurosawa, H., Sugawara, Y., Tsuchiya, M., Sawa, M., Kaneko, H., Futami, I., Liu, L., Sadatsuki, R., Hada, S., Iwase, Y., Kaneko, K., Ishijima, M.: The factors associated with pain severity in patients with knee osteoarthritis vary according to the radiographic disease severity: a cross-sectional study. Osteoarthritis Cartilage 21, 1179–1184 (2013)
22. Hochman, J.R., Davis, A.M., Elkayam, J., Gagliese, L., Hawker, G.A.: Neuropathic pain symptoms on the modified painDETECT correlate with signs of central sensitization in knee osteoarthritis. Osteoarthritis Cartilage 21, 1236–1242 (2013)
23. Trevino, V., Falciani, F.: GALGO: an R package for multivariate variable selection using genetic algorithms. Bioinformatics 22, 1154–1156 (2006)
24. Galván-Tejada, J., Martinez-Torteya, A., Totterman, S., Farber, J., Treviño, V., Tamez-Pena, J.: A wide association study of predictors of future knee pain: data from the osteoarthritis initiative. Osteoarthritis and Cartilage 20, S85 (2012)
25. Martinez-Torteya, A., Galván-Tejada, J., Totterman, S., Farber, J., Treviño, V., Tamez-Pena, J.: Can T2 relaxation be used to predict koos other symptoms?-data from the osteoarthritis initiative. Osteoarthritis and Cartilage 20, S208–S209 (2012)
26. Martinez-Torteya, A., Treviño-Alvarado, V.M., Tamez-Peña, J.G.: Improved multimodal biomarkers for Alzheimer's disease and mild cognitive impairment diagnosis: data from ADNI. In: SPIE Medical Imaging, pp. 86700S-86700S-86709. International Society for Optics and Photonics (Year)
27. Torteya, A.M., Tamez Peña, J.G., Treviño Alvarado, V.M.: Multivariate predictors of clinically relevant cognitive decay: A wide association study using available data from ADNI. Alzheimer's & Dementia: The Journal of the Alzheimer's Association 8, P285–P286 (2012)
28. Neumann, G., Hunter, D., Nevitt, M., Chibnik, L., Kwoh, K., Chen, H., Harris, T., Satterfield, S., Duryea, J.: Location specific radiographic joint space width for osteoarthritis progression. Osteoarthritis and Cartilage 17, 761–765 (2009)
29. Duryea, J., Li, J., Peterfy, C., Gordon, C., Genant, H.: Trainable rule-based algorithm for the measurement of joint space width in digital radiographic images of the knee. Medical Physics 27, 580 (2000)
30. Kellgren, J., Lawrence, J.: Atlas of standard radiographs: the epidemiology of chronic rheumatism, vol. 2. Blackwell, Oxford (1963)
31. Felson, D.T., Nevitt, M.C., Yang, M., Clancy, M., Niu, J., Torner, J.C., Lewis, C.E., Aliabadi, P., Sack, B., McCulloch, C.: A new approach yields high rates of radiographic progression in knee osteoarthritis. The Journal of Rheumatology 35, 2047–2054 (2008)

32. Hing, C.B., Harris, M.A., Ejindu, V., Sofat, N.: The Application of Imaging in Osteoarthritis
33. Suri, P., Hunter, D.J., Rainville, J., Guermazi, A., Katz, J.N.: Presence and extent of severe facet joint osteoarthritis are associated with back pain in older adults. Osteoarthritis Cartilage 21, 1199–1206 (2013)
34. http://www.r-project.org/

Speech Based Shopping Assistance for the Blind

J. Farzana[1], Aslam Muhammad[1], A.M. Martinez-Enriquez[2],
Z.S. Afraz[1], and W. Talha[1]

[1] University of Engineering and Technology, Lahore, Pakistan
farzanajbn@yahoo.com, maslam@uet.edu.pk
[2] Department of Computer Science, CINVESTAV-IPN, D.F. Mexico
ammartin@cinvestav.mx

Abstract. Vision loss is one of ultimate obstacle in the lives of blind that prevent them to perform tasks on their own and self-reliantly. The blind are trusting on others for the selection of trendy and eye-catching accessories because self –buying effort lead them in such collection that is mismatch with their personalities and society style. That is why they are bound to depend upon on their family for shopping assistance, who often may not afford quality time due to busy routine. The thought of dependency rises lack of self-confidence in blinds, absorbs their ability to negotiate, decision making power, and social activities. Via uninterrupted speech communication, our proposed talking accessories selector assistant for the blind provides quick decision support in picking the routinely wearable accessories like dress, shoes, cosmetics, according to the society drifts and events. The foremost determination of this assistance is to make the blind liberated and more assertive.

Keywords: Speech processing, image processing, knowledge based system, wearable item selection, visual impairment.

1   Introduction

According to the surveys of world Health Organization (WHO), the number of blind persons is round about 40 - 45 million. The 135 million people have low vision and approximately 314 million have some kind of visual impairment [1].The ratio of blind persons is greater in developing countries rather than industrial countries approximately 1% and 0.4% respectively [2,3]. Visual impairment can be characterized as partially or complete loss of vision, these two main categories influence the requirement of the user interfaces [4].

In general, loss of vision is a major hurdle in daily living; people have to face a series of problems in how to read, write, access information, way findings, moving liberally in fluctuating environments, selecting daily wearable items, interaction with people and surroundings. That is why everyone has his/her own set of rules and standards regarding perception. Regrettably, sometimes the way of dressing is used to signify the personality. Dressing is essential to be properly either for going to a job interview or to attend a social event, i.e., dressing provides control to represent someone as an individual in the society. Then, how can they meet such a critical criteria to represent themselves according to the standard of this society? Although the blind

J.F. Martínez-Trinidad et al. (Eds.): MCPR 2014, LNCS 8495, pp. 361–370, 2014.

persons have ability to locate day-to-day commodities by using their self-arranging methods, they cannot differentiate among products in case of colors, fashion, and new trends. That is why blind people are cautious to attend the formal functions because of the dearth of deciding on wearable items. This scarcity makes them realize their reliance on the others that results in loss of social activities and they enclosed themselves in their rooms. These emerging issues point out the need of wearable item selector assistance for the blind.

We propose a Talking Accessories Selector Assistant for the Blind (TASA-Blind) system. Our approach is based on the knowledge based systems, includes speech processing technology to provide direct communication facility and image processing heuristics to encourage the blind to express needs willingly and buy items that are well-matched to the personality at all events. Our desktop application with dual interface (speech and keyboard selection mode) is built to deploy in shopping environment where it assists customers (visually impaired and blind) as well as salesman too in understanding the needs of blinds.

Section 2 introduces the background and literature review about the speech based interface systems .Section 3 illustrates the system design and provides implementation detail of actual real system in order to validate our proposal. Finally, Section 4 summarizes our contributions and offers possible future research and expansions.

2   Related Work

Electronic Program Guide (EPG) is a multimodal media center interface, designed for sighted, visually impaired and blind persons. Thus, extended features like proper use of color contrast, zooming focus, typography, GUI coupled with speech output and haptic feedback really make the interface more useful than traditional EPG views [5]. *Framework for Blind user interface development* is useful for children in educational purposes [6].The *framework* comprises a set of user design guidelines, the programming library, and an interface development toolkit. Interface combining speech and pattern recognition enables user friendly admittance to computer [7]. After selecting one color from the color picker module, users can place it anywhere, and then shift module used to control the computer via speech commands. The *SICE framework* [8] can be used for design and development of speech based Web supporting applications. SICE provides flexibility without requiring telephony. *TrailBlazer* [9] is a CoScripter that interfaces with JAWS screen reader and facilitate users to share macro's database. The interface allows the blind to read the pseudo natural language description of each action in the macro. *Skipping and Hybrid techniques* are used in real time to process the detection of skin tone [10].Instead of testing each pixel, this technique skips predetermined number of pixels. The heuristic considers that the nearest color pixels of the skin are also skin pixels, particularly in Web mature images. *A clustering unsupervised technique* [11] is used for sorting skin color. *Step Wise Linear Discriminant Analysis* (SWLDA) technique performs forward and backward processes for image feature extraction in fast and efficient way [12]. The prominent features are selected from the feature space based on partial F-test value, and then categorize them into classes on the basis of regression values. Skin extraction using *HSV color space* extracts skin region from a given image. Firstly, the system converts image to hue, saturation, and lightness (HSV) color space and then detects which pixels' H component lie in the range of 6 to 38[13]. *Facial and head boundary* extraction [14] is a technique of double thresholding to trace the outer (head) and inner (face) boundary in a given image having a frontal face. The input image is first smoothed using a median filter and the edges are detected using Wechsler and Kidode's method for edge detection [15].

Consequently, existing interface based applications have revolutionized the life of the blind, however selection of personal accessories remains an unresolved problem.

3 Talking Accessories Selector Assistant for the Blind: TASA-Blind

TASA-Blind is an interface based shopping system that plays the role of assistant by making assessment about wearable accessories.

a. Model Schema of TASA-Blind

The principal physical devices, responsible for user interaction with TASA-Blind are: a web cam, a microphone, a gait detector, a laser range finder device and a work station. In order to get personal information, the general architecture includes: the knowledge based system (KBS), image feature extraction process (IFE), categories description module (CDM), the speech processing module (SPM), and the graphic user interface (GUI) (see Fig. 1).

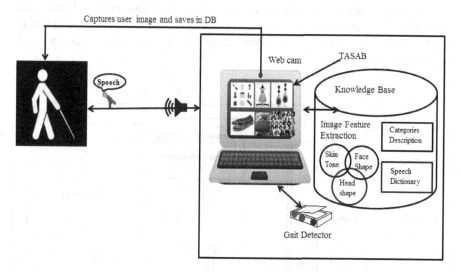

Fig. 1. Schema of the TASA-Blind system

In addition, our infrastructure includes a trial room particularly designed for the blind. All physical components of speech based assistance are equipped into the trial room, where the blind can responsively interact with the whole system in loneliness. The user's snapshot is captured, and forwarded to the IFE module (see Fig. 2). Based on voice instruction, GUI explains the way in which users can benefit of the whole infrastructure (see Fig. 2).

b. System Architecture

The information collector system extracts facial features and précises skin tone by using sampling mechanism [16]. A gait detector sensor determines the foot size and the walking style of the user [17]. This device contains pressure sensors, placed on solid surface. In order to determine user's foot size, user has to walk over the platform with bare footed. Once the user starts walking, the pressure sensors of the gait detector measure the whole user's pressure foot of different positions, the size, and flat foot, among other useful information. To measure the precise height of a person, a laser range finder is affixed in the ceiling of trail room that emits laser beam on the beneath standing person and measures height accurately [18]. Speaker and microphone are resources for the interaction between the system and the user. During all the process, users are guiding with precise verbal instructions regarding the use of the whole infrastructure. System inquires about personal information, sort of category and function, favorite item stuff, price range, etc.

1. Perception Vector (PV)

Information from sensors (image, data) and user's voice are received by PV that behaves like an interactive intermediate module with other component of TASA-Blind. PV is made up of two components: 1. Momentary storage I/O buffers for Input perception: voice, image, sensory input and output. Buffer stores input data from location sensors and from user, preserving Output data from convertor selector respectively. 2. English speech synthesizer system converts text to speech with artificial human voice [19]. Speech synthesizer has its own catalogue that is used for the storage of text description, speech dictionary. The system recognizes the user's vocabulary using the building grammar.

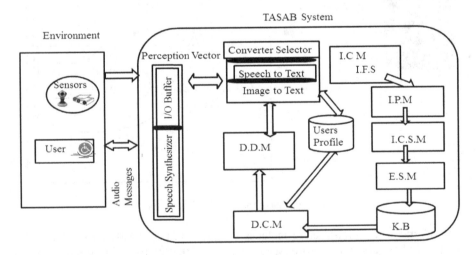

Fig. 2. Architecture of the TASA-Blind system

2. Convertor Selection Module (CSM)

Convertor selector Module (CSM) receives acuity input from PV that is being present in the I/O buffers. CSM performs a list of tasks after getting the input. The foremost task is to save a copy of user's captured image into IDB repository, then check the input format that can be either an image or speech. According to the input format, CSM directs data converting: text2speech or image2text.Existing models and algorithms are used for the conversion: Hamming Trace Transform (HTT) method for image2text, for extracting user's facial features [19]. The HTT method is blend of different concepts like Trace transform and Fourier transform, for detecting facial feature from the target image. In order to measure the skin tone, the sampling mechanism [16] is practiced, while for object detection machine learning approach is used. Machine learning methodology further uses AdaBoost algorithm. Speech convertor contains Single Point of Contact (SPOC) text to speech system [20] based on Hidden Markov models (HMM) for the speech recognition process. Speech convertor welcomes user's voice messages.

3. Information Collector Module (ICM)

ICM extracts personal information like gender, height, weight, waist, skin color tone, favorite color, flat footed, foot size, high sole, and event nature from the facts. ICM sends collected information (images and voice messages) to the item category selector module (ICSM). ICSM further handovers data to ICM.

4. Image Processing Module (IPM)

Based on different image processing techniques various features are extracted like skin tone, eye color, and face feature (lips, eyes) shape detection (see Fig.3). Image is converted into gray scale for building a histogram. Skin tone is checked to Von Luschan Chromatic scale [21]. Red Green Blue values of these types are determined and stored for future reference. Image is converted into HSV color space [22], [13]. The skin segments use predefined ranges of Hue, Cb, and Cr components of image. The ranges defined for these components are: Hue: 0.01 to 0.1, Cb: 140 to 195, and Cr: 140 to 165. The most frequently occurring Red Green and Blue components of skin region are determined for selecting the corresponding skin tone. Applying accessories, different facial points are extracted using image processing toolkit. Facial features are extracted based on Viola Jones's algorithm [23].

5. Items and Category Selector Module (ICSM)

ICSM manages different categories of wearable items according with the nature of events like causal (sport), or formal (wedding, party, and convocation), climate (cold, warm, etc.) size (small, medium, large, extra-large), height, gender, and body structure. Wearable items like dress, shoes, jewelry, bags, hairstyles, cosmetics, make up get ups and glasses are also selected. ICSM selects the wearable items category on the basis of event nature and personal information. ICSM accedes the knowledge base (KB) that retains record of wearable items according with color, size, and events. The queries are directed to the inference engine that consults KB and displays the list of inquiring items.

The inference engine consults inference rules for retrieving the commodities. Each rule is started with 'Startrule', describing the item category for which the rule is relevant. The end of the rule is indicated with 'Endrule'. For instance:

Startrule "Wedding dress suggestion"
  If user(Trial) = X
     user (X) = "customer"
     gender(X) = "female"
     selectedItem (X) = Y
     requestedItem(Y) = "dress"
     skinTone (X) = fair
     height (X) = 42
     eventCategory (Y) = "wedding"
     color (Y) = deep red
     requestStuff (Y) =crinkle chiffon
     requestStyle(Y)= Lehenga
     priceRange =50000 /*Local currency */
  Then
    Display(Item(Y) style(Y) ← LehengaListsDeepRedcolor)
    Suggest(X) ← Display (newlyFashionedList(dress, color)
Endrule

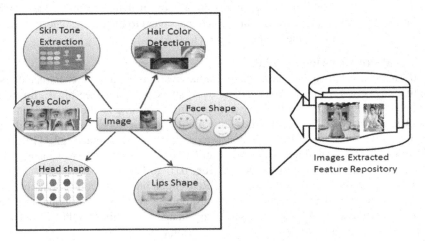

Fig. 3. Image Processing and Feature Extraction Module

The inference rule determines to display all related items that match with the required characteristics and in addition suggests others according with the user's features (see Fig. 4). Analogous rules are used for the suggestion of shoes, glasses, hairstyles commodities. There are other rules to suggest dresses for male with variety of different colors, price range event category: Party or Casual.

In addition, some questions can be enquired about the category of jewelry:

Earring: E category. A rule stores further facts about color, material shape of the earrings in the last price range. This rule is used to display rounded shape earrings with green stones. Similar rules are used to suggest for round shape face also.

Bracelets: B, Necklace: N, Rings: R, Watches: WW

Knowledge base is populated by storing similar rules for other commodities of female and male bags according to color, price range, category (HandClutch HC, HandBag   HB ,Gents Wallets GW, ..).

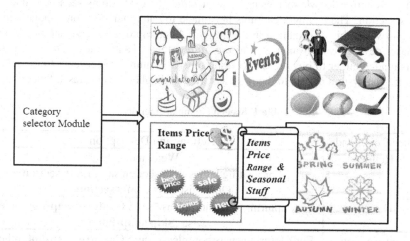

Fig. 4. Category Selector Module

6. Decision Module

DM receives a list of selected wearable items from KB. This list is built according to the precise information that ICMS provides to the knowledge base. When no precise match exists according to the user's requirements, the inference engine takes advantage of the reasoning ability delivers same item within same price range size but with different contrasts. After acquiring the image DM checks item by item on users snapshot forwards those snapshots to the decision dispatcher module (DDM).

7. Decision Dispatcher Module

Before displaying any result to the user, DDM has to perform two main tasks: **1.** DDM saves all the images that he received from the DCM into the local decision support system database. By means of the Hamming Distance Algorithm (HDA), DSS makes comparisons among different images, selects one of them that well-matched with the appearance of the user [17]. All images are sending to the convertor selector that converts the image description into text directs to PV. PV hover text information to the speech synthesizer that notifies user by describing verbal explanation about all images. **2.** DDM directs the selected items number bar code to the counter system, so that they can pack accessories for the user, prepare payment receipt for the user.

TASA-Blind is developed within Dot Net platform. For speech assistance, SAPI 5.4 and MS Speech DLL are used for the voice support TTS to STT conversion. AForge.NET DLL is used for capturing image.

Preliminary Evaluation. The speech grammar defined for the system works only with the expected words. Table 1 provides the standard user voice commands. Thus, the users know the vocabulary in order that they can properly interact with the system.

Let's consider a shopping mall, where Tania is a blind girl who wants to purchase a dress for a wedding event. When Tania enters into the trial room, TASA-Blind welcomes her, asking if she wants to interact with the Speech based interface: Please, select *Speech based* item section otherwise select *Manual selection*. She selects the former. System asks whether wants to visit *ladies* or *gents* items section, Tania says *ladies* section. Then camera captures her image to catch her skin tone, facial appearance, forwards this information to the system. After capturing image and height from the laser device, system navigates to the *ladies* items. Tania selects *Dress,* and then she is guided either to buy dress according to event nature or according to the seasonal stuff. The system moves to the next section that displays Event Based Selection.

Table 1. Speech Grammar Interface

Voice Commands	Actions and Description
Hello?	Welcome! For visiting ladies item section say : **Lady section** Otherwise say: **Gents section.**
Lady section	For capturing snapshot, please say : **Capture snapshot**, otherwise :**Skip snapshot**
Gents section	For capturing snapshot, please say : **Capture snapshot**, otherwise :**Skip snapshot**
Capture snapshot	Thank you, your picture has been already captured Now, Select desiring items, saying : **Dress, Shoes, Bags,** . . .
Skip snapshot	Ok! your snapshot will not be captured. You can select desiring items, saying : **Dress, Shoes, Bags, . . .**
Dress	When you want to choose dress according to events, say : **Event** , otherwise say : **Seasonal stuff**
Event	Now, select the event type, saying : **Wedding, Party, Sport . . .**
Wedding	For Mehndi dresses say : **Mehndi Wedding** In South Asia, Mehndi is a cultural social event before wedding day. For wedding day function say : **Wedding day**
Mehndi Wedding	Mehndi dresses are displayed and description item manufacturing material style is announced. Do you want to visit other items or **Close the session**?
Seasonal Stuff	If you are interested in season stuff, say it : **Summer, Winter, ,.**
Close	Gladly and cordially to receive you!

Now, the system asks her the kind of event. Tania Says: wedding. *As wedding is included within the set of events (wedding, sports, party, formal or casual event, . .),* the system asks her about any particular activity in wedding. Figure 5 shows the retrieved result of yellow Mehndi dresses from accessories stored in KB. All dresses taken out from KB are forwarded to DCA that acquires Tania's image from the user data base, putting on all dresses to the Tania's image according to the acquired height that helps to suggest best size and fitting for Tania. Snapshots of Tania are transferred to the decision support system (DSS) of DDA that explains each dress appearance in terms of new trends like heavy embroidery with quelott, light ribbons work with trouser, stone work frock with pajamas by means of speech synthesizer. DSS also makes comparisons between all images, and informs Tania that the dress with light stone work is looking more beautiful than other dresses. Finally, Tania selects a slightly embroidered dress with long shirt trouser for a Social function. DDA order placement module sends the nominated dress bar code to the counter system places order for the dress. System inquires Tania if she would like to buy another item. Tania says : No so system thanks Tania for using TASA-Blind, and asks her to make payment at the counter. In this way, our system provides the impressive shopping assistance to its users.

Fig. 5. Yellow Mehndi Dress for Tania suggested by TASA-Blind

4   Conclusion and Future Work

TASA-Blind is an attempt for social integration. It helps blind to share ideas frankly, to shop individually, raise social activities and pay attention towards their look and personality. C Dot.Net platform is used for the development of TASA-Blind that supports both speech recognition and synthesis. Rules based on Predicate logic are used for the extraction of desiring wearable items from the base of rules. Additionally, a decision support system based on Hamming distance algorithm for making comparisons between user's suitable get ups. Speech synthesizer notifies users by describing verbal explanation about images, so user can easily make decision according to his/her own choice. As a future work, we will extend the vocabulary in order that visually impaired can talk freely instead using limited words.

References

1. Jacquet, C., Bellik, Y., Bourda, Y.: Electronic locomotion aids for the blind: Towards more assistive systems. Intelligent Paradigms for Assistive and Preventive Healthcare 19, 133–163 (2006)
2. Visual impairment and blindness-Fact Sheet (282), http://www.who.int/mediacentre/factsheets/fs282/en/ (visited on February 2012)
3. Blindness and Low Vision, Fact Sheet (2013), https://nfb.org/fact-sheet-blindness-and-low-vision (accessed March 19, 2013)
4. Slavík, P., Němec, V., Sporka, A.J.: Speech based user interface for users with special needs. In: Matoušek, V., Mautner, P., Pavelka, T. (eds.) TSD 2005. LNCS (LNAI), vol. 3658, pp. 45–55. Springer, Heidelberg (2005)
5. MarkkuTurunen, H., Soronen, S., Pakarinen, H.J., et al.: Accessible multimodal media center application for blind and partially sighted people. CIE 8(3), 16 (2010)
6. Alonso, F., Fuertes, J.L., Gonzalez, A.L., Martinez, L.: User-interface modelling for blind users 5105, 789–796 (2008)
7. Jian, Y., Jin, J.: An interactive interface between human and computer based on pattern and speech recognition. In: ICSAI, pp. 505–509. IEEE (2012)
8. Verma, P., Singh, R., Kumar Singh, A.: SICE: An enhanced framework for design and development of speech interfaces on client environment. IJCA 28(3), 1–8 (2011)
9. Bigham, J.P., Lau, T., Nichols, J.: Trailblazer: enabling blind users to blaze trails through the web, Sanibel Island, Florida, USA, pp. 177–186. ACM (February 2009)
10. Mahmoud, T.M.: A new fast skin color detection technique. World Academy of Science, Engineering and Technology 43, 501–505 (2008)
11. Sangho Yoon, M., Harville, H.: Baker, and N.Bhatii. Automatic skin pixel selection and skin color classification. In: Image Processing, pp. 941–944. IEEE (2006)
12. Siddiqi, M.H., Farooq, F., Lee, S.: A robust feature extraction method for human facial expressions recognition systems. In: IVC 2012, NZ, pp. 464–468. ACM (2012)
13. Oliveira, V.A., Conci, A.: Skin detection using hsv color space. In: Pedrini, H., Marques de Carvalho, J. (eds.) Workshops of Sibgrapi, pp. 1–2 (2009)
14. Shih, F.Y., Chuang, C.-F.: Automatic extraction of head and face boundaries and facial features. Information Science 158, 117–130 (2004)
15. Wechsler, H., Kidode, M.: A new edge detection technique and its implementation. Systems, Man and Cybernetics and Transaction on IEEE 7(12), 827–836 (1977)
16. Lee, J.S., Kuo, Y.M., Chung, P.C.: The adult image identification based on online sampling, pp. 2566–2571. IEEE (July 2006)
17. Aasim, K., Muhammad, A., Martinez-Enriquez, A.M.: Intelligent Implicit Interface for Wearable Items Suggestion. In: An, A., Lingras, P., Petty, S., Huang, R. (eds.) AMT 2010. LNCS (LNAI), vol. 6335, pp. 26–33. Springer, Heidelberg (2010)
18. Human Height Measuring, http://www.acuitylaser.com/products/category/human-height-measuring (visited on March 2013)
19. Fooprateepsiri, R., Kurutach, W., et al.: A fast and accurate face authentication method using hamming-trace transform combination. IETE Technical Review 27(5), 365 (2010)
20. BalaMurugan, M.T., Balaji, M., Venkataramani, B.: Spoc-based speechtotext conversion. National Institute of Technology, Trichy (2006)
21. Terrillon, J.-C., Akamatsu, S.: Comparative performance of different chrominance spaces for color segmentation and detectionof human faces in complex scene images. Vision Interface 99, 1821 (1999)
22. Patil, Y.M., Patil, M.M.: Robust skin colour detectionand tracking algorithm. IJERT 1(8), 1–6 (2012)
23. Paul, S.K., Uddin, M.S., Bouakaz, S.: Extractionof facial feature points using cumulative histogram. IJCSI 9 (2012)

Rotor Unbalance Detection in Electrical Induction Motors Using Orbital Analysis

José Juan Carbajal-Hernández[*], Luis P. Sánchez-Fernández,
Sergio Suárez-Guerra, and Ignacio Hernández-Bautista

Center of Computer Research – National Polytechnic Institute, Av. Juan de Dios Bátiz s/n,
Nueva Industrial Vallejo, Gustavo A. Madero, México D.F., C.P. 07738, México
{jcarbajalh,lsanchez,ssuarez}@cic.ipn.mx

Abstract. Deterioration in mechanical parts of a motor causes faults that generate vibrations. Those vibrations can be related with a different type of motor fault. In this work, we propose a new computational model for identifying rotor unbalance problems in electrical induction motors. Measured vibrations are preprocessed in order to create orbits which represent characteristic patterns. Those patterns are used in a recognition process using an artificial neural network. Experimental results using vibration signals extracted from real situations show a good performance and effectiveness of the proposed model, providing a new way for recognizing unbalance problems in induction motors.

Keywords: induction motor, fault, unbalance, rotor, orbit.

1 Introduction

Electrical induction motor is the most common engine used worldwide in industry. The normal usage of the engine generates deterioration in its physical parts over time, representing a problem when mechanical faults appear as a natural consequence. Induction motor fault detection is an important research field that uses different techniques for analyzing behaviors of the different conditions of the engine such as motor acoustic [1], electrical behaviors [2], orbital electromagnetic analysis [3] or motor vibrations [4]. In the literature, several technics for identifying some types of motor faults have been proposed using different mathematical theories such as spectral analyses, wavelet analysis, time warping, time frequency analysis, Wigner-Ville distribution, etc. [5–9]. On the other hand, artificial intelligence has been proposed as an alternative way for recognizing some specific motor faults using technics such as artificial neural networks, Bayesian networks, support vector machine and fuzzy logic [10–15]. Thus, the importance of detecting and preventing motor faults before they appear is a challenge clearly recognized and some works are currently focused in this problem.

---

[*] Corresponding author.

J.F. Martínez-Trinidad et al. (Eds.): MCPR 2014, LNCS 8495, pp. 371–379, 2014.
© Springer International Publishing Switzerland 2014

Motor vibrations are generated by the normal operation of the engine; however, when some faults appear, those vibrations increase significantly their levels and can generate some characteristic vibrations that can be studied. The most common induction motor fault presented is the rotor unbalance, and it is represented by an increment in vibration amplitudes. In this sense, we hypothesized that unbalance motor fault can be modeled using orbital analysis, where the amplitude of measured vibrations surely will modified a characteristic orbit; this behavior is used for recognizing the motor fault using a defined classifier. Although some works has been focused on using several learning models for motor fault recognizing, our main contribution is based on the pattern building, designing a new way for representing a motor fault. Hence, the core of this work is based on the feature extraction of vibration signals for building orbital patterns.

This work proposes a new computational model for identifying rotor unbalance faults in induction motors in three stages. First, some preprocessing steps are used in order to clean and prepare measured signals. Then, orbital patterns are generated indicating some features of a normal or a rotor unbalance operation. Finally, an artificial neural network is used for classifying those patterns with the mentioned problem.

2   Rotor Unbalance Fault

Failures in electrical induction motors can be classified in two types: mechanical or electrical fault. Those failures may occur frequently in the three main motor components: rotor, stator and bearings [10, 16–18]. In this work, we are mainly interested on studying the unbalance rotor fault due to it is most commonly presented fault. Therefore, rotor unbalance can be defined as the unequal mass distribution on the motor rotation center and in most of the cases; it is the main cause of vibration problems in induction motors (Fig. 1a). Unbalance occurs at a 1×rpm frequency of the selected rotary member and the main harmonic presents amplitudes higher than normal [17]. Rotor unbalance can be classified as static or coupled unbalance (Fig. 1).

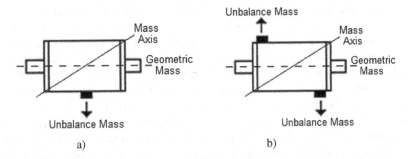

Fig. 1. Rotor unbalance representations: a) static unbalance and b) couple unbalance

3   Signal Acquisition

Mechanical motor faults can be detected if vibrations are monitored and measured continuously. A piezoelectric accelerometer sensor is used for measuring vibrations in the motor chassis. This device employs the piezoelectric effect of certain materials to measure dynamic changes in mechanical variables (e.g., acceleration, vibration, and mechanical shock). A piezoelectric accelerometer converts vibrations into an electrical signal which can be measured using an analog to digital converter [19]. As each motor have a different rotation speed, standards as ISO 10816 (1995) [20] and VDI 2056 (1964) [21] have established sampling frequency rates for motor measuring. According to them, the sampling frequency established was 50 kHz, being large enough to obtain a good quality signal over tested induction motors.

Orbital analysis are made using two signals plotted in a (x, y) axis. Those signals are measured using two piezoelectric accelerometers placed orthogonally in the motor chassis. Fig. 2 shows the correctly accelerometers position.

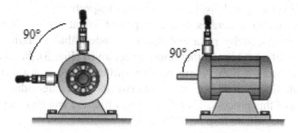

Fig. 2. Accelerometer placement at 90° over the engine

Vibration signals obtained from induction motors contains several harmonics that can be considered as spurious information. In order to avoid those harmonics a previous signal treatment is needed in order to obtain good quality orbits. The following section explains this important process.

4   Orbital Pattern Building

In the literature, some works have focused their efforts on studying the induction motor behaviors using the orbital analysis across mechanical vibrations and electromagnetic forces [22, 3]. Generally, motor unbalance analyses has been made using spectral technics such as Fourier analysis. In this section, we propose an alternative way for transforming vibration input signals into characteristic patterns without using any type of spectral analysis (frequency domain). One advantage of the proposed model is that all processing steps are made in time domain, since no frequency transformations are needed. According to this, orbital analyses are used to create shapes using the time stamp of measured signals that remarks particular behaviors of an unbalance rotor problem.

Preprocessing

In order to create an orbital pattern, some preprocessing steps are required in order to have a good quality orbit. First, each signal is preprocessed separately in order to preserve their particular features. An accelerometer measures signals in acceleration units. Fault orbits are plotted using different signal factors such as vibration amplitudes and distance between phases; hence, it is important to convert the current signal domain (acceleration) into a displacement domain; this unit conversion is computed by integrating the acceleration signal in time domain using the following definition [19]:

$$v(t) = \int_0^t a(t)dt + v_0 \tag{1}$$

$$d(t) = \int_0^t v(t)dt + d_0 \tag{2}$$

where $a(t)$, $v(t)$ and $d(t)$ are the acceleration, velocity and displacement signals; v_o and d_o are the initial velocity and displacement values respectively.

An induction motor generates several types of vibrations, but we are interested only in those produced by rotor unbalances. Undesirable vibrations considerably distort the shape of an orbit and they must be removed (Fig. 3). In this sense, signals must be filtered using a Butterworth passband filter. There is not a specific rule for using a digital filter; however, the Butterworth filter algorithm simplifies the implementation of this process. Therefore, signal filtering can be computed according to the following magnitude response [23, 24]:

$$|H(\omega)|^2 = \frac{1}{1 + \left(\dfrac{c - \cos \omega}{\Omega_0 \sin \omega}\right)^{2N}} \tag{3}$$

where $\omega = 2\pi f/f_s$, f_s is the sampling frequency, $\Omega_0 = \tan(\omega_0/2)$ and c can be expressed as follows:

$$c = \frac{\sin(\omega_{pa} + \omega_{pb})}{\sin \omega_{pa} + \sin \omega_{pb}} \tag{4}$$

where $\omega_{pa} = 2\pi f_{pa}/f_s$, $\omega_{pb} = 2\pi f_{pb}/f_s$ and $[f_{pa}, f_{pb}]$ is the passband.

In this work, we used a bandpass frequency of 10 Hz, this value provided a good quality in the orbit shape, removing undesirable harmonics.

Vibration signals generate continuously orbits with the same symmetry. However, for practical purposes, only one orbit is needed for detecting an unbalance in the rotor. In this sense, orbit isolation is made determining the Euclidian distance between the starting and ending points according with a low tolerance (*T*) according with the following equation [23]:

$$d = \sqrt{(x_2 - x_1)^2 + (y_2 - y_1)^2} \tag{5}$$

where d is the distance between points, and (x, y) are the orbit points coordinates respectively. There is not a specific rule for establishing the tolerance value. In this case, we used the median between point distances as follows:

$$T = \frac{1}{n} \sum_{i=1}^{n} d_i \tag{6}$$

Where n is the number of distances used. Finally, the extracted orbit is normalized into a [0, 1] range using the following expression:

$$s_{1,2}(n) = \frac{d_{1,2}(n)}{max\{|d_1(n)|, |d_2(n)|\}}, \quad \forall n = 0, 1, 2, ..., N-1 \tag{7}$$

where N is the number of points in the signal.

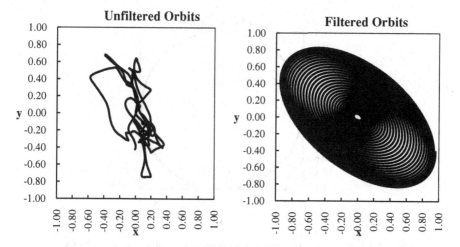

Fig. 3. Differences between filtered and unfiltered orbits, where the spurious harmonics has been removed

Finally, rotor unbalance problems can be directly seen in the shape of the orbit, where a perfect circular shape represents a good condition motor and elliptical shapes correspond to unbalanced rotor fault. Fig. 4 shows these concepts.

Pattern Building

According with the orbital signal analysis, orbit shapes where used for creating motor fault patterns. However, resulting signal orbits are not practical to be used in a neural network due to they have different lengths. In order to have uniform patterns, all orbits signals were resampled for having 100 points of length, where each one is a bidimensional pattern (x, y). A training database with 324 patterns was created to be used in the learning phase of the ANN. Orbit shapes of this database were measured from different induction motors, which had 314 unbalance patterns and 10 patterns from good condition motors.

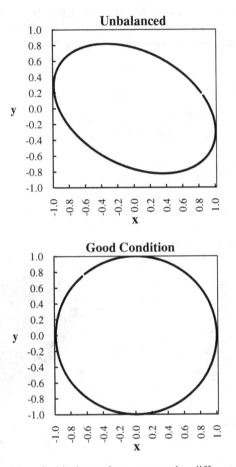

Fig. 4. Examples of orbit shapes that correspond to different motor faults

5   Pattern Recognition and Experimental Results

There are several technics for pattern recognition that can be used for orbits shape identification [1–11]. In this work, Artificial Neural Networks (ANN) are used as classifiers, because they have proved being a very effective learning model with high rates of effectiveness. The ANN architecture that better fitted to the problem context was of [200 – 150 – 2]. In this case, the inputs were fixed at 200 neurons, where the first half is for x-axis and the other half for y-axis. 1000 epochs where used for training the ANN having a MSE of 1×10^{-10}. The hidden layer was initialized between 2 and 200 neurons sequentially, where 150 neurons was the configuration with better results. It was used three sets to evaluate the performance of the ANN (dividing the training database for different purposes on the training process); one inside set for the training algorithm (484 partners from the available data to train), one validation set (97 patterns from the available data) and one final testing set to evaluate the final performance of the algorithm (64 partners from the available data), with correlation coefficients (r) of 0.998, 0.989 and 0.995 respectively. The training process used by the ANN learning was the Levenberg-Marquardt algorithm.

Additionally, an experimental database was built and used for validating the performance of the proposed system as part of a recovering process. This database was built using different kind of motors and with different levels of unbalance. It is important to remark that this database was compounded by different motor measurements than those used in the database of the learning process. In this case, the size of the database was of 645 motor fault patterns as follows: 635 rotor unbalance patterns and 10 patterns of good condition motors.

The neural network was created using the training database and was tested with the experimental database with patterns of different unbalance and intensities. In the evaluation were extracted signals from real motors with history of failure. Table 1 shows the results of the recovering process using the proposed database. A second experiment was using the experimental database contaminated with Gaussian noise and a SNR of 10, having interesting results and where a low percentage of patterns were misclassified.

Table 1. Orbital pattern recognition results with the original experimental database and the Gaussian noise contaminated database

Experimental database	Number of Patterns	Recalled patterns	ANN	
			Efficiency	Error
Original patterns	645	642	99.53%	0.47%
Patterns contaminated with Gaussian noise	645	597	92.55%	7.45%

6   Discussion and Conclusions

In this work, we propose a new computational model for detecting rotor unbalance problems in electrical induction motors. This model was implemented using the orbital analysis for creating pattern shapes that have characteristic features of the fault. Although several methodologies for detecting mechanical faults in induction motor have been developed, the proposed model represents a feasible and alternative way for motor misalignment fault detection. In this model, some preprocessing steps implemented before the ANN classification phase are needed for extracting the main features of signal patterns. One advantage of this work is that no spectral analyses were made, having low computational burden rates against conventional models. As an unbalance distorts considerably an orbit, a characteristic shape is built and it can be perfectly identified by a classifier such as an ANNs, reducing the complexity of the modeling step. It is important to remark that this paper provides a preliminary study of unbalance identification in induction motors using orbital pattern analysis, and future works are needed such as detection of more type of failures or model effectiveness increasing. Anyhow, this model can be used as an important tool for preliminaries motor analysis, when the good functioning of the machine is essential in critical time production.

References

1. Gaylard, A., Meyer, A., Landy, C.: Acoustic evaluation of faults in electrical machines. In: Electrical Machines and Drives, Conference Publication, vol. 412, pp. 147–150 (1995)
2. Yahya, L., Saleem, T., Hasan, B.: The application of Neural Network to Electrical Motor's Sound Recognition System. Journal of Engineering and Applied Sciences 7(2), 191–193 (2012)
3. Ha, K., Hong, J., Kim, G., Chang, K., Lee, J.: Orbital analysis of rotor due to electromagnetic force for switched reluctance motor. IEEE Transactions on Magnetics 36(4), 1407–1411 (2000)
4. Iorgulescu, M., Beloiu, R., Cazacu, D.: Vibration monitoring for electrical equipment faults detection using fast fourier transform. In: Proceedings of the 1st International Conference on Manufacturing Engineering, Quality and Production Systems, vol. 1, pp. 34–38 (2009)
5. Kim, K., Parlos, A.: Induction motor fault diagnosis based on neuropredictors and wavelet signal processing. IEEE/ASME Transactions on Mechatronics 7(2), 201–219 (2002)
6. Climente, V., Antonino, J., Riera, M., Puche, R., Escobar, L.: Application of the Wigner–Ville distribution for the detection of rotor asymmetries and eccentricity through high-order harmonics. Electric Power Systems Research 91, 28–36 (2012)
7. Liu, D., Zhao, Y., Yang, B., Sun, J.: A new motor fault detection method using multiple window S-method time-frequency analysis. In: International Conference on Systems and Informatics, pp. 2563–2566 (2012)
8. Yang, D.: Induction motor bearing fault diagnosis using Hilbert-based bispectral analysis. In: International Symposium on Computer, Consumer and Control, IS3C, Taichung, Taiwan (2012)
9. Zhen, D., Wang, T., Gu, F., Ball, A.: Fault diagnosis of motor drives using stator current signal analysis based on dynamic time warping. Mechanical Systems and Signal Processing 34(1-2), 191–202 (2013)
10. Chow, M.: Methodologies of using neural network and fuzzy logic technologies for motor incipient fault detection. WorldScientific, Singapore (1997)
11. Banerjee, T., Das, S.: Multi-sensor data fusion using support vector machine for motor fault detection. Information Sciences 217, 96–107 (2012)
12. Gardel, P., Morinigo, D., Duque, O., Pérez, M., Garcia.: Neural network broken bar detection using time domain and current spectrum data. In: Proceedings of the 20th International Conference on Electrical Machines, No. 6350234, pp. 2492–2497 (2012)
13. Liang, B., Iwnicki, S., Zhao, Y.: Application of power spectrum, cepstrum, higher order spectrum and neural network analyses for induction motor fault diagnosis. Mechanical Systems and Signal Processing 39(1-2), 342–360 (2013)
14. Sun, C., Duan, Z., Yang, Y., Wang, M., Hu, L.: The motor fault diagnosis based on neural network and the theory of D-S evidence. Advanced Materials Research 683, 881–884 (2013)
15. Zidani, F., Benbouzid, M., Diallo, D., Naït, M.: Induction Motor Stator Faults Diagnosis by a Current Concordia Pattern-Based Fuzzy Decision System. IEEE Transactions on Energy Conversion 18(4), 469–475 (2003)

16. Palomino, E., Sánchez, A., Cabrera, J., Sexto, L.: Preliminary Diagnosis of Rotational Machinery. In: Experiences in the Implementation of a Predictive Maintenance Program and Certification of Human Resources in a Cuban Cement Industry. Advances in Vibration Control and Diagnostics, pp. 177–184. Polimetrica International Scientific Publisher (2006)

17. Arun, K., Mohanty, A.: Model based fault diagnosis of a rotor–bearing system for misalignment and unbalance under steady-state condition. Journal of Sound and Vibration 327(3-5), 604–622 (2009)

18. Chen, F., Jhe, S., Min, P., Wen, T.: Study of start-up vibration response for oil whirl, oil whip and dry whip. Mechanical Systems and Signal Processing, Elsevier 25(8), 3102–3115 (2011)

19. Han, S.: Retrieving the time history of displacement from measured acceleration signal. Journal of Mechanical Science and Technology 17(2), 197–206 (2003)

20. ISO 10816. Mechanical vibration: evaluation of machine vibration by measurements on non-rotating parts (1995)

21. VDI 2056. Standards of evaluation for mechanical vibrations of machines, Germany (1964)

22. Dongfeng, S., Lianfsheng, O., Ming, B.: Instantaneous purified orbit: a new tool for analysis of nonstationary vibration of rotor system. International Journal of Rotating Machinery 7(2), 105–115 (2001)

23. Proakis, J., Manolakis, D.: Tratamiento digital de señales, 4a edn. Pearson Education, vol. 1. España (2007)

24. Orfanadis, S.: Introduction to Signal Processing. Prentice Hall (2009)

Remote Identification of Housing Buildings with High-Resolution Remote Sensing*

José Luis Silván-Cárdenas[1], Juan Andrés Almazán-González[1], and Stéphane A. Couturier[2]

[1] Centro de Investigación en Geografía y Geomática "Ing. Jorge L. Tamayo"
A.C. Contoy 137, Lomas de Padierna, Tlalpan, Mexico D.F. 14240
jlsilvan@centrogeo.org.mx
http://www.centrogeo.org.mx
[2] Laboratorio de Análisis Geoespacial, Instituto de Geografía, UNAM
Cto. de la Investigación Científica s/n, CU, Coyoacán, México D.F. 04510
andres@igg.unam.mx
http://www.igeograf.unam.mx/sigg/

Abstract. Identifying housing buildings from afar is required for many urban planning and management tasks, including population estimations, risk assessment, transportation route design, market area delineation and many decision making processes. High-resolution remote sensing provides a cost-effective method for characterizing buildings and, ultimately, determining its most likely use. In this study we combined high-resolution multispectral images and LiDAR point clouds to compute building characteristics at the parcel level. Tax parcels were then classified in one of four classes (three residential classes and one non-residential class) using three classification methods: Maximum likelihood classification (MLC), Suport Vector Machines (SVM) with linear kernel and SVM with non-linear kernel. The accuracy assessment from a random sample showed that the maximum MLC was the most accurate method followed by SVM with linear kernel. The best classification method was then applied to the whole study area and the residential class was used to mask-out non-residential buildings from a building footprint layer.

Keywords: Remote sensing, LiDAR, housing units, land use classification.

1 Introduction

Mapping housing units in urban environments is needed for a number of urban planning process as well as for scientific studies such as population estimation, risk analysis and evacuation routes design. Identifying housing units from remote sensing involves building detection and land use classification with at least two classes, one for residential and one for non-residential land uses.

* This research was funded by the National Council of Science and Technology (CONACYT) project "Small-area population estimation by means of remote sensing" Grant 187593.

J.F. Martínez-Trinidad et al. (Eds.): MCPR 2014, LNCS 8495, pp. 380–390, 2014.

The land use classification problem has been addressed through observable land cover characteristics from remote sensing products, such as spectral reflectance, texture, impervious surface and surface temperature, as well as from existing geographic information layers, including zone maps, population density and road maps, among others [1]. A wealth number of decision rules have been also developed and applied to land use/land cover classification problems, among which the maximum likelihood decision rule stands as the most common one. In the last two decades, statistical learning theory has provided non-parametric decision rules for solving complex classification problems. These techniques include artificial neural networks (ANN), decision trees (DT) and support vector machines (SVM). In general, non-parametric methods tend to outperform the maximum likelihood classification (MLC) method with varying degree of performance depending on specific configurations, with SVM being less sensitive to the increase in data dimensionality and presence of correlation [2–4].

Despite this, observations are not conclusive because most comparative studies have applied decision rules on pixels (pixel-based classification) rather than on segments extracted from the image (object-based classification), or on preestablished administrative boundaries (field-based classification). While pixel-based classification methods tend to be more efficient as they can operate exclusively with data in raster format, some researchers have also noted that classification results are noisy and less accurate than when classifying groups of pixels altogether, specially when using high-resolution data [5]. Furthermore, in urban environments, tax parcels are owner's land demarcations and, therefore, they has been claimed as the natural land use unit [6, 7].

This article describes mayor processing steps of a methodology for identifying housing units by integrating LiDAR altimetry data, multispectral satellite images and cadastral layers from a GIS. Since the building detection problem has been the focus of a related study [8] this article focus on evaluation of the land use classifications component of the whole process. The rest of the paper is organized as follows. Section 2 presents the fundamentals of Support Vector Machines (SVM), which is one of the methods tested in the study. Then, in Section 3 the overall processing flow for extracting housing units is described. In Section 4 the accuracy assessment results for the land use classification are presented and its impact in the whole process are discussed. Major conclusions drawn from the study are presented in Section 5.

2 Background

The theory of support vector machines (SVMs) formulates linear discriminants for solving binary classification problems where classes may overlap in the feature space [9]. The linear version of the problem consists in finding the maximum margin hyperplane that separates samples from two given classes. Mathematically, this is formulated as follows.

Given a training set of n exemplar pairs $(x_1, y_1), (x_2, y_2), \ldots, (x_n, y_n)$ of feature vectors $x_i \in \mathbb{R}^d$ and class labels $y_i \in \{1, -1\}$, find the hyperplane

$x_i^T\omega + \theta = 0$ that creates the biggest margin between the training points for the two classes. This problem is equivalent to the following optimization problem:

$$\min \frac{1}{2}||\omega||^2 + c\sum \varepsilon_i \quad \text{subject to} \quad y_i(x_i^T\omega + \theta) \geq 1 - \varepsilon_i, \varepsilon_i \geq 0, \forall i \quad (1)$$

where ε_i are slack variables that account for the overlapping of classes and c expresses the cost of accepting discrimination errors. This cost is infinity in the separable case.

The optimization problem above is quadratic with linear constraints. This convex problem is typically solved with Lagrange multipliers, which also results convenient because the solution depends on scalar products of certain feature vectors, called *support vectors*. Moreover, this allows for construction of nonlinear boundaries through the use of kernels that represent the scalar product in a transformed vector space. Most popular kernel functions include a polynomial of a given degree, the sigmoid function and the radial basis function (RBF). The latter, which was used in this study, is expressed as

$$K(x, x') = e^{-\gamma||x-x'||^2} \quad (2)$$

The extensions of SVMs to solve multi-class problems include methods that consider all classes at once and those that use multiple binary SVMs, whose outputs are combined through common strategies such as "one-against-all", "one-against-one," and directed acyclic graphs (DAG). Since solving multiclass SVM in one step implies a much larger optimization problem, experiments have shown that the "one-against-one" and DAG methods are more suitable for practical use than the other methods [10].

3   Materials and Methods

This section describes the major processing steps and datasets used in the study. The overall workflow is outlined in Fig. 1 and a 3-d view of some of the data sets generated are shown in Fig. 3.

3.1   Data Used

The study area is located in the historical and cultural center of Mexico City, and corresponds to one of the borough of the Federal district, Cuatémoc. Being the oldest part of the city, it hosts historical buildings as well as modern skyscrapers, government buildings, market and commercial centers, and residential buildings, most of which are multifamily type. With a total area of 32.44 km² and a population of over half million people as of 2010, it represents the highest population density of the city (16,000 peoples/km²).

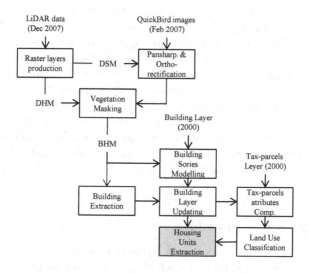

Fig. 1. Work flow for housing units identification

LiDAR Data and Derived Products. In November and December of 2007, the ALS50-II LiDAR system was flown over the Mexico valley covering the entire Federal District and the area of Chalco in the State of Mexico. The system delivered 3-d coordinates of locations where the laser hit the Earth's surface. Along with the 3-d coordinates, the system recorded the return intensity and the return number (for up to four returns per pulse) attached to each point. The average point density was 0.433 points/m^2 with average point distance of 3.0 m and a vertical accuracy of 7.3 cm (RMSz).

The data was provided in LAS format by the National Institute of Geography, Statistics and Informatics (INEGI) and then rasterized in tiles of 1 km by 1 km to form digital surface models (DSM) of 1 meter resolution (blocks of 1000-by-1000 pixels). A mosaic DSM of 7-by-8 km was also built to cover the entire study area. Each DSM tile was also normalised by removing the terrain variation using the ground filtering method described in [11], thus resulting in a digital height model (DHM) of the same resolution and coverage as the DSM (7-by-8 km).

Multispectral Imagery. A QuickBird bundle image with multispectral (at 2.4 m spatial resolution) and panchromatic (at 0.6 m spatial resolution) bands acquired on February 2007 was used in this study. The four multispectral bands were fused with the panchromatic band using the Gram-Schmidt pan-sharpening method [12] resulting in four multispectral bands of 1 m resolution. The spatially enhanced image was then orthorectified using the rational polynomial coefficients provided by the image vendor. This method required the DSM and a set of on-screen ground control points.

Cadastral Layers. Cadastral data with a time reference of year 2000 was acquired through the Ministry of Urban Development and Housing (SEDUVI). The data was acquired in DXF format, so that layers were extracted and coverted to ESRI's shapefile format. Two shapefiles were built for the entire administrative limits of Cuauhtémoc, one for tax parcels boundaries and one for building boundaries. Both layers underwent an extensive editing process to correct numerous errors, some of which were generated during the conversion process.

In addition to the geometry information, two annotation layers available in the original DXF files were also extracted, namely the number of stories and the land use key. The number of stories layer was included as field of the building geodatabase, whereas the land use key was included as field of the tax parcel geodatabase.

3.2   Building Stories Modelling

The number of stories of a building is strongly related to the buildings height. Building height was computed for each building footprint using a LiDAR-derived product. Although the DHM represents the building height for every square meter, it also contained some other information that can lead to erroneous estimation of building height, particularly the high vegetation hanging over the building roofs.

In order to eliminate vegetation height from the DHM, a vegetation mask was generated with the QuickBird image. This was accomplished by simply thresholding the normalized difference vegetation index (NDVI), so that a new raster surface, termed the building height model (BHM), was generated by setting height values in the DHM to zero for detected vegetation pixels. The building height was then calculated as the median value of BHM pixels within the building polygon. The median height was preferred over the mean as it is more robust to outliers due to above-roof installations such as antennas and water tanks.

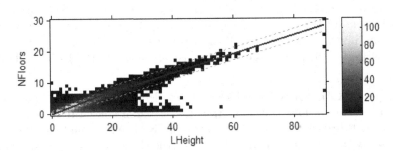

Fig. 2. Piece-wise linear model (blue line) fitted to the NFloors-LHeight scatterplot (ramp color image). The discontinuous green lines show a tolerance error of ± 2 floors for buildings higher than 15 meters and of ± 1 for lower buildings.

The scatter-plot of building height (LHeight in Fig. 2) against number of building stories (NFloors) was examined and a piece-wise linear model was visually adjusted. The model is expressed as:

$$N = \begin{cases} [H/2.8] & \text{for } H < 15 \\ [H/3.3] & \text{for } H \geq 15 \end{cases} \tag{3}$$

where N and H represent the number of building stories and the corresponding building height, respectively.

3.3 Building Extraction

A method for extracting building footprints was also implemented based on a previously developed method for tree-crown segmentation [13]. Two major differences were implemented in the new method.

First, instead of taking the original DHM as input, the gradient of the BHM was used as input. The rationale of this method is that the variations in building roofs height naturally creates edges between building roofs. This is not necessarily true when a number of attached buildings have the same height. Nonetheless, the tax parcel polygons can be used to further split those segments that covered more than one tax parcel.

Second, once potential building segments were extracted, segments with a median height lower than a minimum height (2.0 m) were eliminated from the segmentation image. Also, segments with an area lower than a minimum area (e.g., 16m^2) were merged to the largest neighbouring segment.

The segments so computed are used to select those buildings that required updating. So far the updating has been carried out manually, while automated methods are being developed. At this point, the height of all buildings was also updated by applying the piece-wise linear model of Eq. 3. In order to account for errors in building height estimations, the updating took place only if the estimated number of stories differed from the original value beyond one 1 floor for buildings lowers than 15 meters and of 2 floors for higher buildings. This criterion is based on the observation that taller buildings are less unlikely to change by a few levels.

3.4 Land Use Classification

A number of tax-parcel attributes fields were derived at the parcel level by aggregating building features at parcel level. These fields included the maximum number of building stories, the total built-up area, the number of buildings in the parcel, percent of built-up area, the total area of the parcel, and the habitable space. The latter is a volumetric measure of the potentially habitable space of buildings within a parcel and is defined as:

$$S_i = \sum_j A_{i,j} N_{i,j} \tag{4}$$

where $A_{i,j}$ and $N_{i,j}$ are the area and number of stories of the i-th building in parcel j.

Three supervised classification methods were tested. The first classification method is the well known maximum likelihood classification (MLC) method, which is a parametric method that depends on second order statistics of Gaussian probability distribution functions (PDF) [14]. It is the optimal solution to a classification problem when the PDF of classes is multivariate Gaussian. The second and third methods corresponded to SVM with linear and with nonlinear kernels, respectively.

Both the linear and nonlinear formulations were implemented in MATLAB based on previously published codes [15]. However, since SVM has been designed for solving binary classification problems, a majority voting of the One-Against-One approach was also implemented as suggested by [10]. According this approach, one SVM is developed for each pair of classes, whereas the classification result from each SVM is treated as a 'vote' to one of the classes. Then, the class assigned to each input feature vector is based on the majority of votes. When ties result, the SVM involving the tied classes has a quality vote that is used to solve the tie. If tie cannot be solved even with the quality vote, then the feature is tagged as unclassified.

4   Results

Despite the detailed classification system that was available through the land use classification key, a simplified classification system was used in this study as provided in Table 1. This classification system obeyed the objective of examining the potential of supervised classification methods to discriminate residential land uses from a reduced number of parcel and building characteristics, namely the total area of the parcel, the maximum number of stories, the built-up area, the number of buildings in the parcel, percent of built-up area, and the habitable space.

Table 1. Land use classification system used in the study

Level 1	Level 2 Description
	R0 No buildings
Residential	R1 Buildings with 1 or 2 stories
	R2 Buildings with 3 or more stories
Non Residential	NR Commercial, Industrial and all other

A random sample was selected for training and testing purpose from the entire set of tax parcels. In order to ensure the representativeness of the various residential and non-residential land uses a two-stages strategy was implemented. In the first stage a mesh of cells of 9 hectares (300 by 300 m) was overlaid on the study area. The cells were ranked according to a diversity index, which accounted for the number of distinct land uses present within the cell. The first 20 cells with the highest diversity index were used to narrow down the potential tax parcels that were going to be used. In the second selection stage, a stratified random selection was applied, according to which 100 tax parcels were selected for the classes R1, R2 and NR described in Table 1. Whilst there were only 30 tax parcels of the class R0 in the entire study area, all of which were included in the sample. Finally, the sample was randomly split in two sets with half-half proportion except for R0, in which all 30 samples were included in both sets.

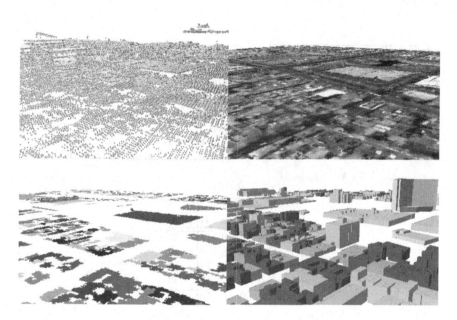

Fig. 3. 3-d view of major products derived from the study: classified LiDAR point cloud (upper left), false calor composite of QuickBird image wrapped on the DTM (upper right), Segments extracted from the BHM (lower left) and extruded polyhedral representation of MLC-classified buildings (lower right). Residential buildings are in yellow (R1) and red (R2), whereas non-residential are shown in light blue.

The three classification methods were trained using one of these sets (training set), whereas classification accuracy was assessed using the other set (testing set). The confusion matrices are shown in tables Table 2. Results indicated that MLC was the most accurate classification method followed by the linear SVM and non-linear SVM with an overall accuracy of 73.3%, 63.3% and 60.5%, respectively. The linear SVM presented a couple of tie conflicts that could not be resolved with the quality vote criterion. Nonetheless, even if these conflicts were solved in one or another sense, the accuracy of the classifier remained under that of MLC. When looking the per-class user and producer accuracies, MLC showed consistently the best performance for all classes whereas all methods showed the best performance for the class R0 (User Accuracy ranging from 70% to 90%)

and the worst performance for the class NR (User Accuracy ranging from 40% to 57%). This result suggests that while class R0 can accurately be represented by a Gaussian PDF, the other classes were not properly represented by this PDF. Furthermore, the relative low performance of SVM methods may have been affected by the voting strategy, the relatively small sample size, the overfilling of training sample.

Table 2. Confusion matrices for each classification method tested (a) MLC, (b) Linear SVM (c) Non-linear SVM

(a)

Class	Reference R0	R1	R2	NR	Total
R0	30	0	0	3	33
R1	0	44	1	9	54
R2	0	2	37	17	56
NR	0	4	12	21	37
Total	30	50	50	50	180

(b)

Class	Reference R0	R1	R2	NR	Total
R0	30	0	0	3	38
R1	0	39	1	9	52
R2	0	0	37	17	40
NR	0	7	12	21	48
Unclassified	0	2	0	0	2
Total	30	50	50	50	180

(c)

Class	Reference R0	R1	R2	NR	Total
R0	30	2	0	11	43
R1	0	37	8	9	54
R2	0	6	25	13	44
NR	0	5	17	17	39
Total	30	50	50	50	180

The classification accuracy reflects the accuracy of correctly identifying housing buildings assuming buildings have been accurately extracted. This assumption is nearly true in our case, as an existing building layer was manually updated. If a fully automated updating method is to be implemented, then the building extraction method can further lower the overall identification accuracy. In a previous study [8] we have evaluated some building detection methods which can extract buildings with average detection rate of around 85% and with average commission errors of around 20%. With this figures, one may identify residential buildings with an accuracy as high as 60% which is only a moderate accuracy.

5   Conclusions

A method for identifying residential buildings based on remote sensing and GIS layers was outlined. The two major components of the method include building extraction, characterization and updating through LiDAR and multispectral imagery. The second part involved per-field land use classification of buildings. The accuracy assessment based on a stratified random sample showed that the MLC showed the highest accuracy over SVMs. This seems to contradict prior studies where SVM outperformed MLC [2–4]. However, it should be noted that those studies have performed the classification and its accuracy assessment at the pixel-level, while this study was based on tax parcels. Moreover, that the number tax parcel features have been kept relatively low (6 features) maybe the reason why MLC still performed well. Further investigation is needed to determine if SVM with a higher number of attributes, such as vegetation attributes, can lead to better performance than that achieved by low-dimensional MLC.

References

1. Lu, D., Weng, Q.: Use of impervious surface in urban land-use classification. Remote Sensing of Environment 102(1), 146–160 (2006)
2. Dixon, B., Candade, N.: Multispectral landuse classification using neural networks and support vector machines: one or the other, or both? International Journal of Remote Sensing 29(4), 1185–1206 (2008)
3. Guan, H., Li, J., Chapman, M.A., Zhong, L., Ren, Q.: Support vector machine for urban land-use classification using lidar point clouds and aerial imagery. In: International Symposium on LiDAR and RADAR Mapping: Technologies and Applications, Nanjing, China, pp. 26–29 (May 2011)
4. Srivastava, P.K., Han, D., Rico-Ramirez, M.A., Bray, M., Islam, T.: Selection of classification techniques for land use/land cover change investigation. Advances in Space Research 50(9), 1250–1265 (2012)
5. Myint, S.W., Gober, P., Brazel, A., Grossman-Clarke, S., Weng, Q.: Per-pixel vs. object-based classification of urban land cover extraction using high spatial resolution imagery. Remote Sensing of Environment 115(5), 1145–1161 (2011)
6. Bauer, T., Steinnocher, K.: Per-parcel land use classification in urban areas applying a rule-based technique. GeoBIT/GIS 6, 24–27 (2001)
7. Wu, S., Silván-Cárdenas, J., Wang, L.: Per-field urban land use classification based on tax parcel boundaries. International Journal of Remote Sensing 28(12), 2777–2801 (2007)
8. Silván-Cárdenas, J.L., Wang, L.: Extraction of buildings footprint from liDAR altimetry data with the hermite transform. In: Martínez-Trinidad, J.F., Carrasco-Ochoa, J.A., Ben-Youssef Brants, C., Hancock, E.R. (eds.) MCPR 2011. LNCS, vol. 6718, pp. 314–321. Springer, Heidelberg (2011)
9. Hastie, T., Tibshirani, R., Friedman, J.: 12 Support Vector Machines and Flexible Discriminants. In: The Elements of Statistical Learning, 2nd edn. Springer Series in Statistics, pp. 417–458. Springer (2009)
10. Hsu, C.W., Lin, C.J.: A comparison of methods for multiclass support vector machines. IEEE Transactions on Neural Networks 13(2), 415–425 (2002)
11. Silván-Cárdenas, J.L.: A multiscale erosion operator for discriminating ground points in lidar point clouds. In: Carrasco-Ochoa, J.A., Martínez-Trinidad, J.F., Rodríguez, J.S., di Baja, G.S. (eds.) MCPR 2012. LNCS, vol. 7914, pp. 213–223. Springer, Heidelberg (2013)
12. Laben, C.A., Brower, B.V.: Process for enhancing the spatial resolution of multispectral imagery using pan-sharpening (2000)

13. Silván-Cárdenas, J.L.: A segmentation method for tree crown detection and modelling from liDAR measurements. In: Carrasco-Ochoa, J.A., Martínez-Trinidad, J.F., Olvera López, J.A., Boyer, K.L. (eds.) MCPR 2012. LNCS, vol. 7329, pp. 65–74. Springer, Heidelberg (2012)
14. Richards, J.A.: 8-Supervised Classification Techniques. In: Remote Sensing Digital Image Analysis: An Introduction, 5th edn., pp. 247–318. Springer (2003)
15. Mangasarian, O., Musicant, D.: Lagrangian support vector machines. Journal of Machine Learning Research 1, 161–177 (2001)

Author Index